For Rodney Walt[...]
(Clan Carmichael — Great
grandson of D. M. T.
Carmichael).

Best Wishes
Howell Hughes

A Judge in the Senate

A JUDGE IN THE SENATE

Howell Heflin's Career of Politics and Principle

JOHN HAYMAN

WITH CLARA RUTH HAYMAN

To Rodney — a great Carmichael and cousin — with best wishes,

Clara Ruth

2001

NewSouth Books

Montgomery

NewSouth Books
P.O. Box 1588
Montgomery, AL 36102

Copyright © 2001 by Clara Ruth Hayman
All rights reserved under International and Pan-American Copyright Conventions. Published in the United States by NewSouth Books, a division of NewSouth, Inc., Montgomery, Alabama.

Library of Congress Cataloging-in-Publication Data

Hayman, John, 1929-1999
A Judge in the Senate: Howell Heflin's career of politics and principle / John Hayman; with Clara Ruth Hayman
    p. cm.
Includes index.
ISBN 1-58838-026-2
1. Heflin, Howell. 2. Legislators—United States—Biography. 3. United States. Congress. Senate—Biography. I. Hayman, Clara Ruth, 1947-
II. Title

E840.8.H435 H39 2001
328.73'092--dc21
[B]
2001045223

Design by Randall Williams
Printed in the United States of America
by Phoenix Color Corporation

TO OUR SIBLINGS
POD, NANA, BARBARA

CONTENTS

Foreword / 9
Preface / 12
1 Between Sharks and Barracudas / 17
2 People of the Old South / 22
3 The Minister's Son / 33
4 School Days / 45
5 Birmingham-Southern College / 58
6 The Marines / 67
7 Learning Law / 91
8 Debut of a Country Lawyer / 101
9 Success and Recognition / 119
10 Prelude to Office / 138
11 Judicial Reform Begins / 152
12 The Judicial Article / 172
13 Implementation and National Attention / 187
14 Defeating Wallace in the 1978 Senate Race / 203
15 Starting Fast with Ethics and the Judiciary / 215
16 Friend of the Farmer / 238
17 Champion of Equal Rights / 260
18. Into a Second Term / 280
19 Strong for Space, Defense, and Research / 299
20 Iran-Contra, Bork, and the Spotlight / 321
21 Bane of Environmentalists / 345
22 Senior Senator / 362
23 His Finest Hour / 385
24 At the End, a Man Respected / 408
25 Candidate of the Alfalfa Club / 421
26 The Qualities of An Effective Senator / 423
27 Views of the Presidents / 436
28 An Affirmation of America / 445
Appendix / 456
Notes / 462
Index / 470

Foreword

by Bob Dole

I HAVE HAD the privilege to know and to work with many fine people over the years. Few have been so dedicated in their work and so committed to their cause as Howell Heflin. This book admirably tells the story of Howell Heflin, who had both the courage to defend his country in battle and to break out of the "Old South" mode of thinking in order to defend all citizens in his roles as an attorney, a judge, and as a U.S. Senator. John Hayman's deft reflection on Howell's life and decisions, which were made in the face of unpopular sentiment, provides the reader an insight into this folksy but complex man.

One cannot think about this country without thinking of the stories of families. Some families are more colorful, more distinguished, or have made greater contributions than others. One such family has been that of Howell Heflin. From the beginning, when the Heflin family immigrated to the United States, its sons made special efforts to help their fellow man in public and private service—particularly in the areas of medicine, ministry and politics. But not all of the Heflin family are remembered with honor. Howell's uncle, J. Thomas "Cotton Tom" Heflin, is now remembered as a racist, bigot, and an embarrassment. Few remember that he was a reflection of the times and the people he represented.

During Howell Heflin's early life, the Jim Crow laws were in full force. The Ku Klux Klan was actively spewing out its venom. Blacks and whites could not eat in the same restaurants, drink out of the same water fountains, use the same restroom facilities, nor sit beside each other on the bus. Though many whites were haters and abusers of the black race, there were also many whites who were not. Though they did not approve of the conditions, they just accepted the *status quo*. Local, state and national leaders also followed this same pattern and made little effort to change the system.

Howell's growing up in the rural South did not provide him with an objective perspective on the racial matter. He, too, accepted the system without question. However, his world began to change when he went to college and was exposed to differing viewpoints and a variety of people, though his college years were in a segregated institution. Further progression occurred when he served in the Marine Corps during World War II and had the opportunity to see the world beyond his rural, Southern roots. This exposure reshaped his thinking, so by the time he was discharged from the military and entered law school, Howell knew that change had to occur nationwide. He was determined to be a positive part of this change.

The modern civil rights movement, beginning in 1954 with *Brown v. Board of Education,* and exploding in 1955 when Rosa Parks refused to give up her bus seat to a white person in Montgomery, Alabama, actively continued until 1965 when the Voting Rights Act was passed. Other major conflicts of the civil rights movement occurred in Alabama from the bus boycotts, murders of civil rights workers, to the bombing of a church and the subsequent murder of four young girls. The list is long.

Howell never let himself become a part of this white supremacy movement. As a country lawyer in northwest Alabama, he defended blacks in cases that other white attorneys refused to handle. He remained loyal to the national Democratic party. As a candidate for political office, Howell openly presented his position to the black community and solicited their votes, while many other white candidates wanted the black vote but refused to be identified with the black community. As Alabama's Chief Justice, Howell made sure that all people were treated fairly within the court system and received quick and sure justice.

My first encounter with Howell Heflin was when he became a member of the U.S. Senate in 1978. At that time, there were still some "Old South" senators. In his low-key, humorous, story-telling way, Howell influenced these other members of Congress into a more open-minded, progressive mode of thought. He defused many volatile situations, and helped others to see that the future of this country rested on the fulfillment of "all men are created equal."

In his role as a member of the ethics commission and the judiciary committee, Howell gave great testimony to his understanding of the law. Those who came before him had no doubt that they would receive a fair hearing. His work on the agricultural committee educated his fellow senators and saved family farms.

Howell's involvement with the space program was exemplary. It is important to note that the space program is one of the preeminent contributors to current medical and technological breakthroughs.

It is difficult to move beyond the teachings and indoctrinations of one's childhood. It takes a special effort to step from one world to another. In my opinion, Howell Heflin took that step. He is loyal to the South and to Alabama. However, he realized that things were not perfect; he realized that the practices of the past were no longer relevant to the present nor to the future. He never crossed over into the liberal realm, but he helped move the South and the nation to a greater acceptance of diversity. He represented the transition from the old to the new, the old South to the New South, Jim Crow to equal rights.

Howell drew upon his past, his religious background and beliefs, his exposure to a variety of experiences and people, and the opportunity to see life from many angles. He and I worked closely together during our Congressional tenure. We both worked diligently to do our part in strengthening this country and move it forward.

Howell Heflin could be counted on to look at situations carefully and objectively. He did not make quick decisions. He did not always reflect the views of the people he represented, but he did reflect the moral and ethical views of his conscience. He was willing to take political risks. He was fair with others, and worked in a bipartisan way without rancor. He is a compassionate and understanding man. He has a broad sympathy for the human condition and took the responsibility of his job seriously. He is a man of vision, integrity, a statesman, and a modest man. It is my pleasure to call Howell Heflin my friend.

Preface

By Clara Ruth Hayman

THIS BOOK TELLS the life story and chronicles the multi-faceted career of Howell Thomas Heflin. It is a combination of oral history and extensive research. It explores Heflin's early years growing up as the son of a Methodist minister, his college days, distinguished military record, law practice, and his journey into politics both as chief justice of Alabama and as U.S. Senator.

Heflin is an Alabama treasure who contributed significantly to both the state and nation, often working behind the scenes and keeping a low profile. He retired as a much-respected man and politician.

Heflin's story serves as an example for us all, demonstrating that one can be successful in a variety of fields during various stages of one's life, that hard work and perseverance can pay off, and that bipartisan politics is both possible and desirable. His story reflects an oft-forgotten principle that one can be a politician while simultaneously exemplifying integrity, humor, a sense of purpose, commitment, right and wrong.

I never expected to be the person writing this preface. In 1996, John Hayman—my husband, the author—was seeking endorsements for his book *Bitter Harvest: Richmond Flowers and the Civil Rights Revolution*. Because Heflin had played a role in getting Flowers a presidential pardon, John contacted Heflin about an endorsement. Heflin read the manuscript, wrote an endorsement, and enclosed a note stating that he liked John's writing style.

John continued with his writing projects. Then, in 1997, Heflin retired from the Senate, and John contacted him about writing his biography. John wanted the Senator's participation in the project. Several months later, the Senator called and asked could he come by our house for a meeting. Thinking positively, we agreed. However, there was no commitment from the Senator.

A couple of months passed and the Senator phoned again. Could we please join him and Elizabeth Ann, his wife, for lunch? Delighted at the invitation, we were certain that this time there would be an agreement. Again we left with no commitment, and with John and I shaking our heads in wonder.

Another couple of months passed and another phone call, "John, could you and Clara Ruth have lunch with Elizabeth Ann and myself?" Again, we agreed, but perhaps with less enthusiasm.

We arrived at the restaurant at the appointed time. As we were eating, John asked the Senator if he had made a decision. Heflin's response was, "Write me a proposal." John replied, "We've written proposals, sent materials and talked. It's time to fish or cut bait." The Senator reared back, broke into a big grin, gave his famous guffaw, stuck out his hand and said, "You've got a deal." John looked at Elizabeth Ann and me and verified that we were trustworthy witnesses to the fact.

Work began immediately. Heflin had donated the majority of his papers and memorabilia to the University of Alabama Law Library in Tuscaloosa, and we were given access to the files. John and I spent months reading and researching these files.

Interspersed with the research were numerous hours of personal interviewing with the Senator notating his thoughts, memories, and personal anecdotes. He made available his papers, speeches, articles, and correspondence as well as photographs.

While in the process of completing the second draft of the book, my husband unexpectedly died. Since I had been intimately involved in all aspects of the book, I decided to continue with the project.

It has been a test of fortitude for me to get this book in print, and it has been both a painful and a cathartic experience. As a result, this book is a loving tribute to my husband, the Senator, and Elizabeth Ann.

I certainly did not complete this book alone. There are so many knowledgeable and capable people who have my gratitude, including those persons not mentioned here.

Above all, I remember John for his enthusiasm and hard work in sorting through the vast array of information and putting it in a readable and usable format. I would like to thank Senator and Elizabeth Ann Heflin for their time, patience and sharing.

A special thanks goes to Paul Pruitt, director, University of Alabama Law Library, who so graciously and knowledgeably came to my aid in helping locate materials, answering questions, making suggestions and critiquing the manuscript. His assistant, David Durham, also has my deep gratitude for all his help, legwork, and reading of the manuscript.

Dr. David Orr and Dr. Barry Clemson were invaluable in their critique of the manuscript. Both are published authors and lent their critical eye to the content and style of the book.

Others that made their own contributions were Lucille Howard, John's high school English teacher; Mike House and Steve Raby, former Heflin chiefs of staff; Bert Haltom, Joe Ware, Charles Carmichael, Charles Rosser, and Conrad Fowler, who gave their personal insights into Howell's life and works; and Don Heflin, who contributed geneological information.

Especially to my family and friends who wiped my tears, held my hand, and encouraged me, I will be forever indebted.

Last but certainly not least, my thanks goes to Randall Williams and Suzanne La Rosa for their faith in and their willingness to work with me and to publish this book. They are not only my publishers but my friends.

A Judge in the Senate

A Note on the Formatting

This book is based partly on extensive recorded interviews with Senator Heflin. Passages where he is quoted at length without narrative interruptions by the authors are displayed in indented bold type.

I

Between Sharks and Barracudas

On the floor of the U.S. Senate, heated debate pitted old-time conservatives against progressives and liberals. Senator Carol Moseley-Braun, an African American, was at the podium. As she spoke — "The Senator from Alabama has a question he would like to put. I yield for that purpose . . ." — all eyes turned toward the formidable man making his way forward. His demeanor was serious. He knew that what he was about to do, what he must do, could affect his political future. He also knew that he was turning away from his ancestral roots. But his religious background, his social conscience, and his commitment to represent all Alabama citizens took precedent.

He paused, looked at his colleagues, and began, "Mr. President. I rise with a conflict that is deeply rooted in many aspects of controversy . . ." Thus, Howell Heflin presented an impromptu speech reflecting serious thought and deep convictions. The speech was instrumental in the Senate's defeat of an extension to the United Daughters of the Confederacy's special patent for their insignia that included the first national flag of the Confederacy.

On another occasion, this time over the issue of abortion, tempers flared. Fingers were pointed. Personal and religious convictions were injected and ears and minds seemed closed to other arguments. Into this tense moment came Heflin's drawl, "Weellll, as a former fetus myself . . ." Laughter broke the tension, and debate resumed.

These two incidents from his Senate career provide a mini portrait of Howell Heflin, a man of strong convictions and principles who weighed the issues and was not afraid to take a stand.

ALABAMA is a state of surprises and contradictions. The landscape itself attests to this — from the forested hills of north Alabama, through the rich, dark soil of the Black Belt, and meandering on down to the flat, sandy soil of the Wiregrass and the white sands of the Gulf beaches. By the closing decades of the twentieth century, the state was home to world-renowned medical research facilities, high tech auto factories, the Marshall Space Center, and diverse, prosperous agribusiness. On the other hand, the state still endured pockets of unrelenting rural poverty; shockingly high rates of infant mortality, teenage pregnancy, and incarceration; and simultaneously high divorce rates on the one hand and on the other overwhelming poll responses of belief in Bible-based "family values."

Alabama's historical politics are no less contradictory. In 1901, Alabama enacted a rigidly segregationist state constitution that disenfranchised its black citizens and many of its poor whites. It concentrated political and economic power in the hands of the powerful interests. In the view of most historians, the 1901 Constitution continues to shackle the state a century later.

However, in the 1930s and 1940s, the political atmosphere changed. Alabama's congressional delegation included such progressives as John Sparkman and Lister Hill. They sponsored and supported advances in public health, education, and other reforms. Constitutional rights champion Hugo Black, an Alabamian, sat on the U.S. Supreme Court. His brother-in-law Clifford Durr was a high official in FDR's New Deal. Twice in the decade after World War II, voters chose "Big Jim" Folsom, a populist and a racial moderate, as governor.

Even though the Great Depression, the New Deal, and World War II brought progressives and reformers to the forefront of Alabama politics, their grip did not hold. Resistance to the Civil Rights Movement, beginning with reaction to the *Brown* school desegregation ruling in 1954, rapidly tilted Alabama back to the politics of white supremacy. Alabama became defined by the firehoses and snarling dogs of Bull Connor and by George Wallace's banty rooster defiance of the federal courts.

WITHIN THIS CONTEXT looms another Alabama surprise and contradiction, Howell T. Heflin, the nephew of the infamous J. Thomas "Cotton Tom" Heflin. Unlike his uncle, Howell did his best to undo the effects of segregation and racial discrimination. The contrast between uncle and nephew was sharply in focus many times during Howell Heflin's career.

On the surface Howell Heflin seemed an unlikely revolutionary. In his prime, he stood six feet, four inches tall and weighed 250 pounds . . . or more. He once observed that candidates for the Roman Senate wore only a toga when campaigning, prompting this response from a well-known Alabama newspaper columnist: "Visualize if you can Howell Heflin, our 275-pound U.S. Senator, campaigning in a toga. He would look like a white buffalo."[1] A staff member wrote of the former chief justice of Alabama: "His judicial robe could best be made by Omar the Tentmaker."[2] These physical traits, his drawl, his lumbering gait, and his frequent use of Southern humor sometimes made Heflin an easy target of comedians and editorial cartoonists who compared him to Foghorn Leghorn. Those who worked with Heflin knew better. His fairness, knowledge, persistence, and ability to muster bipartisan support made him one of the most effective senators of his time. He used his appearance and manner to his own advantage. He may not seem the type to be an international media star, but he was described as just that by London's Independent Television News. Saturday Night Live's Chris Farley lampooned Heflin, caricaturing the senator's role in the nationally televised Senate hearings on the confirmation of Supreme Court nominee Clarence Thomas during the early 1990s. Columnist Robert Novak even wrote that a Heflin decision triggered "Black Monday," the 1987 stock market crash.

Howell Heflin rose from small-town Alabama to become a Washington insider. His career began as a "country lawyer" in northwest Alabama, where he established himself as one of the state's best legal minds and advocates, and an opponent of the Ku Klux Klan. He developed a reputation as a reformer in the legal profession and judicial systems while serving as president of the Alabama State Bar Association.

Throwing his hat into the political arena for chief justice of Alabama, he defeated former Governor John Patterson, a segregationist. During his six-year tenure on the Supreme Court, he led a successful movement to reform Alabama's antiquated court system and to adopt modern rules of practice and procedure in all elements of the law. This system continues to be heralded as a national model.

As a U.S. senator, Heflin had a front row seat in U.S. political and judicial history through four decades, which were marked by unusual events such as the dissolution of the Soviet Union, reunification of Germany, fundamentalists revolution in Iran, Camp David Accords and the beginning of the Peace Process, and the Persian Gulf War. He figured prominently in some of the Senate's most dramatic events in the 1980s and 1990s including:

- The Iran-Contra hearings,
- The Clarence Thomas hearings,
- The debate on the Strategic Defense Initiative,
- The building of the international space station, and
- The continuing battle for civil rights and racial justice.

As a member of the Senate Judiciary Committee, he was in the middle of the controversial and bitterly fought Supreme Court nomination of Robert Bork. As the raucous debate progressed, other members of the committee were declaring themselves. With the known votes counted, it appeared that Heflin would cast the deciding vote. Reporters followed him around Washington, trying to determine which way he leaned. His answer to their queries characterized the agony he sometimes faced in listening to his own conscience at the same time he represented a conservative constituency. He remarked, "We're walking on the gangplank whatever we do; there are barracudas on one side and sharks on the other."[3]

He was between barracudas and sharks many times in his Senate career. He was conservative on financial and judicial issues, but in the emotionally charged area of civil rights, and on social programs generally, he was liberal. His Senate leadership seated black federal judges in Alabama; he unfailingly fought for civil rights legislation; and he voted against Bork, the darling of the conservatives.

These decisions drew criticism at home. An influential small-town editor wrote, "Heflin's vote has left him in the political doghouse among his conservative constituents . . . who wanted 'their' senator to finally make a responsible decision. This summer Heflin embarrassed Alabamians by his derogatory demeanor and condemnatory attitude when Lt. Colonel Oliver North went before the special congressional committee on national television for questioning."[4]

Howell Heflin won many fights, but he also lost some. He was hated in some quarters and regularly vilified by some of the leading newspapers of his state. But he was loved and respected by the great majority of Alabamians, and as Andrew Jackson believed and demonstrated, the people are sovereign.[5]

William Stewart, chairman of the Political Science department at the University of Alabama, called him the most outstanding Alabama Senator of the twentieth century[6] — placing him above John Bankhead, Lister Hill, John Sparkman, and Heflin's uncle, "Cotton Tom" Heflin.

Howell Heflin retired from the U.S. Senate in January 1997. He was greatly respected by his Senate colleagues. Senator Paul Wellstone of Minnesota said, in a tribute after Heflin had announced his retirement, "He is the alternative to cynicism. He is hope. And he is honor."[7]

2

People of the Old South

Howell Thomas Heflin was born June 19, 1921. He came from people who had been in America many generations. Some were pioneers, many were involved in forming and fighting for the Confederacy, and all who followed were steeped in the traditions and myths of the Old South.

There is some evidence that Heflin's ancestors came from Normandy and crossed the Channel to the British Isles with William of Orange in 1688. Some family genealogists say the Heflins originally came from Ireland, while others say Germany. It is a matter of record that some Heflins came to America from Scotland, and some came from England.[1]

The Heflin family in Alabama traces its line to *Joab* Heflin who lived in England in the first half of the eighteenth century. According to the best available records, Joab's son, *James*, was born in England about 1750. He came to America as a young man, before the Revolutionary War, and settled in Virginia. About 1770 William, James, John, and Charles Heflin moved from Virginia to a land grant they held in Granville County, North Carolina. James later moved to Hancock County, Georgia, where he died in 1801.

James was the father of *Wyatt Homer* Heflin, Howell's great-grandfather. Wyatt was born in Orange County, North Carolina, in 1789 and married Sarah A. Stell in Hancock County, Georgia. Sarah's great-great-grandfather had migrated from England to North Carolina in the early 1700s.

TO ALABAMA. Wyatt, the first Heflin to live in Alabama, was an Indian trader and a lawyer. Records show that he moved in 1829 to Louina, a village in eastern Alabama's Randolph County, and built a house there. That area of Alabama still had a large number of Indians, even though the Battle of Horseshoe Bend in 1814 rendered the native Creeks virtually powerless. Louina was said to be named for an old Indian woman.

Randolph County was created by the legislature on December 18, 1833, from the last Creek cession. A reporter wrote, "It was practically a wilderness for a few bold adventurous spirits who had either squatted or settled within its bounds. Wadley, Roanoke, and Louina were the chief trading points, and Louina was for a considerable period larger than both of them. It is hard to realize that less than 100 years ago, things in the section were so primitive. To help you visualize, keep in mind that the first courthouse built in Randolph County was without doors or shutters. There were no seats for the judge and jury."[2]

In Georgia, Wyatt had shown an early inclination for public service and achievement and was elected to the Georgia legislature. After moving to Alabama, he represented Randolph County in the legislature for three terms, in 1841, 1843, and 1845. He was sheriff of Randolph County several times.[3]

Wyatt's four sons were Judge John T. Heflin, Robert S. Heflin, Dr. *Wilson L.* Heflin, and Dr. Watson Heflin, who died in 1842. John T. made his reputation as a lawyer and circuit judge. He served in the state senate two years and was a member of the Alabama Constitution Convention of 1875. Robert S., also a lawyer, served as both a representative and a senator in the state legislature. He was probate judge after the Civil War and later served in Congress.

Dr. Wilson L. Heflin, Howell's grandfather, lived in Randolph County into the twentieth century. He received his medical degree at the University of Georgia Augusta Medical College in 1858, then set up practice in Louina. Wilson practiced in and around Louina and Roanoke, making rounds with a horse and buggy.

Wilson moved in 1892 to Roanoke, now the county seat of Randolph County. He had eight sons and three daughters, two of whom died in infancy. One son, John T. Heflin, served as mayor of Roanoke and as probate judge of Randolph County. Robert L. was a farmer in Roanoke. Harrington P. settled in Birmingham and became a circuit court judge. Wyatt and Howell T. were physicians, and Walter was a Methodist minister. J. Thomas Heflin practiced law in LaFayette and served in the United States Congress for twenty-four years, beginning in 1904. These were Howell Heflin's uncles. Howell's Aunt LaVicie married Haden Reid.

THE FAMILY GAINS PROMINENCE. The Heflins were a prominent Alabama family at the beginning of the twentieth century. An article on Wilson's eightieth birthday celebration calls him "one of Alabama's distinguished citizens" and refers to the "famous family." A writer a few years later said he visited the site of Louina because it "turned out so many sons who had made names for themselves in a bigger world."[4]

Thirteen descendants of Wyatt and Sarah Stell Heflin became doctors, beginning with their sons, Watson and Wilson. Dr. Wilson L. Heflin was Howell's grandfather. Two of Wilson's sons — Dr. Wyatt Heflin, a pioneer in surgery, and Dr. Howell Heflin, the uncle for whom the Senator is named — moved to Birmingham when it was a very young city. About 1890 the two brothers founded the Heflin Hospital on a site in downtown Birmingham near where Hillman Hospital would later be built and where University Hospital, part of the University of Alabama in Birmingham, is now located.

Howell thinks the medical inclination in his family can be traced to his great-grandmother, Sarah Stell Heflin, who was listed in the census as a midwife and a herbalist. She assisted his grandfather Wilson in his medical practice. Two of their daughters married doctors.

Another branch of the Heflin family went into law and politics. Howell explains about two John T.s who were lawyers. "One was a brother of Wilson Heflin, my grandfather. He helped establish a law firm in Talladega, and was a circuit judge. The firm still exists today and is one of the oldest continuous law firms in the state.

"The town of Heflin, Alabama, is named for this John T. Many people in Heflin think their town was named for my grandfather since he traveled there from Louina, about 25 miles away with a horse and buggy to deliver babies and practice other medicine. He delivered a lot of babies in Heflin. In fact, the book *Alabama* says that. But as I understand it, the town was named for my grandfather's brother because he was a railroad lawyer. The railroad was going to open a station in that location, and they decided to name it for him. He had gained some fame as a member of the Alabama Constitutional Convention of 1875."

The other John T. Heflin, Howell's uncle, was the probate judge of Randolph County and was a member of the state legislature and the 1901 Alabama Constitutional Convention.

"I had three uncles in politics," Howell says, "and I'm sure they had some influence on my decision to go into politics. My father was interested in politics. He was proud of his family's tradition and their political activities. He was much more of a moderate in his own thinking than his brother Tom, but he was proud of the offices that Tom and others in the family held. . . . Several family members were delegates to the State Constitutional Convention in 1901. My wife's grandfather and his brother were both members of the Constitutional Convention. I sometimes tell my son Tom that politics is in his blood. I don't know if he's proud of having all those relatives in the Constitutional Convention because they disfranchised the blacks." Sarah Stell Heflin's brother, John D. Stell, obtained fame as president pro tem of the Texas Secession Convention of 1861.

THE IMMEDIATE FAMILY. *Marvin* Heflin, Howell's father, was born in Louina but moved to Roanoke when Dr. Wilson took the family there. Marvin became a Methodist minister. He married Louise Strudwick on November 6, 1912. Her family had also been in America many generations. Louise's great-great-grandfather came to North Carolina from Scotland about 1750 and fought on the American side in the Revolutionary War. Another great-great-grandfather represented North Carolina in the U.S. House of Representatives in the 1790s.

During the Civil War, grandfather Wilson Heflin served part-time as a surgeon in the Confederate Army. Doctors were allowed to come and go during the war. They would serve in a battle and then return home to continue their practice, to be called up again when needed.

Howell's maternal grandfather, Samuel Strudwick, lived in Demopolis, Alabama, and in 1884 married Julia Reese Clarke, whose forebears were from Virginia. Julia's father, William Edward Clarke, was elected to the Alabama Secession Convention in 1861 and signed the Secession ordinance. In a letter he wrote to his children about 1895, he said he believed in the right of secession and had felt the South should act promptly "to show the determination of her people not to submit to Abolition, or Black Republican rule, as the Lincoln party was called then."[5]

An inclination for public service and achievement was also shown by other family members. A famous cousin, Julia Strudwick Tutwiler, was a pioneering woman leader in Alabama and wrote the official state song, "Alabama, Alabama."

COTTON TOM. One of the most colorful Alabama politicians in the twentieth century was Howell's uncle, J. Thomas "Cotton Tom" Heflin, who was born in Louina in 1869. After finishing the equivalent of high school, Tom Heflin enrolled in normal school and received the standard preparation for teaching. A short time later, he enrolled in Southern University at Greensboro, Alabama, the forerunner to Birmingham-Southern College. He also attended Alabama Polytechnic Institute, now Auburn University.

To become a lawyer in those days, people read law with a practicing lawyer and then took the bar exam. Young Tom left college after three years to read law in LaFayette, the county seat of Chambers County, thirty miles south of Louina. He was admitted to the state bar in 1893, at the age of twenty-three, and set up practice in LaFayette. He started right off spending time in the courthouse square and swapping yarns with the locals. He honed his speaking ability, and within a year, he was elected mayor.[6]

In 1896, at age twenty-six, he was elected by a wide margin to the state legislature, and was reelected two years later. In Montgomery, he quickly became a member of the state Democratic Executive Committee, and he was a delegate to the Constitutional Convention of 1901. The 1901 Alabama Constitution was one of a group of "segregation" constitutions adopted by former states of the old Confederacy which legally denied African-Americans many of their basic rights, including the right to vote. The white framers of that Constitution intended it to protect their "Southern way of life," which it effectively did for more than a half century.

Cotton Tom was a leader in the fight for white supremacy. In one debate on the issue he said, "I believe as truly as I am standing here that God Almighty intended the Negro to be the servant of the white man."[7] He ran for Secretary of State in 1902 at age 32 and was elected. In one speech he said:

> The night of Negro suffrage, thank God, is passed. The sable mantle has been torn away and Alabama stands robed in the costume woven in the loom of Anglo-Saxon genius; stands in the morning of a new day, beholding the sun of Caucasian authority ascending the clear sky of civic splendor and glory.[8]

In 1904, U.S. Representative Charles W. Thompson had died in office and Tom Heflin ran without opposition to fill the vacancy. Tom continued to serve in the House until 1920. A sidenote of his congressional career came in 1913 when he introduced and helped pass the Mother's Day Act. According to Howell Heflin, "The idea of setting aside a day to honor the nation's mothers came from a West Virginia woman, Anna Jarvis, who convinced my uncle of the idea's merit. For their efforts, Miss Jarvis came to be known as the 'Mother of Mother's Day' and my uncle as the 'Father of Mother's Day.'"[9]

Tom Heflin was a strong supporter of the progressive movement, which had gained prominence at the start of the century with Theodore Roosevelt and then Woodrow Wilson. Progressivism, an outgrowth of the 1890s Populist movement, was a turn away from the hands-off-business policy which had long dominated government and moved toward support of the rights and well-being of ordinary people.

The labor movement established a solid footing during this period, and Tom was a consistent supporter of organized labor and of working people. He supported the eight-hour day and the right of workers to organize. Samuel Gompers, president of the American Federation of Labor, said in 1920, "Labor never had a better friend in Congress than Tom Heflin."[10] He regularly made vitriolic speeches against the Republicans, who he said took advantage of the working man.

Tom was also a strong supporter of Southern farmers, and he got the "Cotton Tom" nickname from his support of cotton, the crop that dominated the Alabama agricultural economy.[11]

After World War I ended, demand and prices for farm products fell sharply, creating a nationwide crisis. Many farmers could not sell their crops for enough to cover the cost of production. Cotton Tom received a letter which said, "There is not today in Alabama a one-horse farmer, white or black, who does not need $75 of clothing and shoes, yet they have nothing to buy with."

The prevailing Republican attitude was that farming should be subject to market forces like other businesses. The most capable would survive and do well, and the weak would drop out. In this way, production would fall, prices would stabilize, and the situation would take care of itself.

The farm community fought back by organizing the American Farm Bureau Federation in 1919 to give farm interests a voice in politics. After Warren Harding became President in 1921, the Farm Bureau worked to form the Farm Bloc in Congress, and many of both parties became involved. Cotton Tom was a Bloc member and a strong supporter of its agenda.

The Federal Reserve Board in the early 1920s pursued policies which favored big business and Wall Street and hurt farmers. Tom Heflin engaged in a highly visible, well-publicized fight with the Board chairman, fellow Alabamian W. P. G. Harding. Harding's term expired in 1923, and Cotton Tom fought against his reappointment. When Harvard bestowed an honorary degree on Harding, Cotton Tom said on the Senate floor:

> Horatius at the Bridge and Leonidas at Thermophylae never displayed such grim boldness and reckless daring as did the members of the Harvard faculty when in defiance of the pride and interest of her honored living and in utter disregard for the memory of her illustrious dead, they conferred the degree of L.L.D. on W.P.G. Harding. . . . Theodore Roosevelt, a brilliant graduate of Harvard in her better and brighter days, used to carry a big stick and terrorize big crooks, but the fates spared him the dreadful ordeal of seeing and hearing the money changers of Wall Street chuckle when Harvard conferred the degree of L.L.D. on W.P.G. Harding.[12]

Harding was not reappointed.

On March 1, 1920, Senator John H. Bankhead died with four years left in his term. Cotton Tom easily won the seat and was sworn into the Senate in December 1920 as Alabama's junior senator. He was fifty-one years old and had been in politics twenty-seven years.

Biographer Ralph M. Tanner says that Tom Heflin carried to his Senate career "a mind of that sort of simplicity which understands in terms of absolutes. He took a passionate spirit capable of deep loves and profound hates. He bore the stamp of a region that was shaped more by backward glances than by forward vision."[13]

In 1924, Cotton Tom was unopposed in the Democratic primary and he won easily over his Republican opponent in the general election. In 1926, Oscar W. Underwood retired from the Senate and was replaced by Hugo Black. Cotton Tom became Alabama's senior senator.

As the election of 1928 approached, New York Governor Alfred E. Smith seemed the likely Democratic candidate for president, and Tom Heflin made known his strong opposition.[14]

Smith was selected as the candidate, and the state party supported him. The chairman of the Executive Committee warned that any person who voted against Smith in the general election would be barred from the

Democratic primary in 1930.[15] Cotton Tom made speeches all over the state opposing Smith, and he pointedly stayed away from the polls on election day.

Cotton Tom announced his candidacy for reelection to the Senate in 1929, and John H. Bankhead, Jr., son of the senator whose unexpired term Cotton Tom had completed a decade earlier, also announced. The State Democratic Committee met in December 1929 with the loyalist faction in control. As a disciplinary measure, they passed a resolution which barred from the coming primary any candidate who had failed to support Al Smith in 1928. Thus, Cotton Tom could not enter.[16]

John Bankhead won the Democratic primary easily, and Cotton Tom announced his candidacy in the general election as an independent. As the election approached, Hugo Black announced his support for the Democratic ticket, dooming Cotton Tom's chances. The 1930 election drew the largest voter turnout in Alabama history, and Cotton Tom lost big. He received 100,952 votes to Bankhead's 150,985. On his last day in the Senate in April 1932, Cotton Tom made a five and a half hour farewell speech. H.L. Mencken wrote of it:

> The new Senate . . . will show some gifted clowns, but there will still be a large vacuum in it where the Honorable J. Thomas Heflin of Alabama used to sit, howl and have his being.[17]

After Tom Heflin left the Senate, he went back to LaFayette and practiced law. When the Democrats nominated Franklin Roosevelt for president in 1932, he made a number of appearances in support of the ticket. He supported Roosevelt and the New Deal strongly, though he disagreed with the repeal of the Eighteenth Amendment and the end of Prohibition. Cotton Tom ran unsuccessfully for public office three more times.

In the 1948 presidential campaign, when many Southern Democrats bolted the party over a civil rights plank in the party's platform and formed the Dixiecrats, Cotton Tom advised Democrats to stay with the national party.

James Thomas Heflin died April 22, 1951. These words were engraved on his tombstone:

> Unawed by Opinion
> Unseduced by Flattery
> Undismayed by Disaster
> He confronted life with antique courage
> And Death with Christian hope.

Cotton Tom was a character from the old school. His silver hair curled up at the collar. He was portly and wore gray-and-black striped trousers, galluses, bow ties, a black Prince Albert coat in winter and a white one in summer, a double-breasted waistcoat, a broad-brimmed hat, and tan shoes. He had a booming baritone voice, and when he spoke, he sprinkled his words with lines from Shakespeare and the Bible.[18] He was also a master of the use of ridicule as a political tactic. One opponent said of him, "If you stick a pitchfork in Tom Heflin and let the wind blow out, a pair of my breeches would swallow him."[19]

J. Thomas Heflin is remembered now as a flamboyant anti-Catholic, virulently racist, Prohibition-pushing demagogue. His nephew notes this is a judgment well after the fact and that Cotton Tom was not notorious among the home folks when he was in office. Howell Heflin reminds us that Cotton Tom did many outstanding things before he was caught up in anti-Catholicism in 1928. "When he was in the House, he was the first Southerner invited to make a speech on the anniversary of the Battle of Gettysburg. He strongly and with considerable success supported farmers throughout his career."

Cotton Tom always seems to have been totally in tune with the attitudes and desires of his then all-white constituency. This is an interesting contrast with his nephew who would follow him to the Senate a half-century later. On many occasions — sometimes in the glare of national publicity — Howell Heflin made decisions which were unpopular with the large majority of white Alabama voters. But by then blacks had regained the vote, and the body politic had moderated.

Cotton Tom's behavior with regard to race undoubtedly influenced Howell, who took the opposite direction from his uncle. Many have speculated that Howell's consistent support of civil rights throughout his career was an effort, conscious or not, to redeem the legacy of racism of his famous uncle.

THE LOUINA SITE TODAY. Today, none of the Heflin family remains in Randolph County where Wyatt originally settled, although they continued to gather for a reunion in Randolph County for some years. An Alabama newspaper, the *Roanoke Leader,* announced on October 11, 1905, "Yesterday began the annual gathering of the family of Dr. W.L. Heflin in camp at their old homestead at Louina. Our readers are aware that this is one of the most prominent families that has been identified with the history of Alabama."[20]

Louina itself no longer exists but the home that Wyatt Heflin built has recently been restored as a historical monument to the Heflin family. The house is of Greek Revival style. The floors are heart-pine, and the original hand-carved doors in the entryways are still in place. A penciled note on the wall by the fireplace says, "This house was built in June by Wyatt Heflin 1829."[21]

HOWELL HEFLIN came from traditions of achievement and public service on both sides of his family, which explains in part the motivation behind his own achievements. He also has deep roots in the values and traditions of the Old South. He says that not all of his family were supporters of the Confederacy, however. "I had Yankee sympathizers in my family. Most were on the side of the Confederates, but one of my great-uncles, Roberts Stell Heflin, was a Union sympathizer. He was elected to Congress for one term during the Reconstruction. He was very independent in his thinking, so we've got things in common."

Perhaps so.

In matters political, Howell Heflin was his own man, defying both family and party traditions when his conscience directed otherwise.

3

The Minister's Son

In Howell Heflin's case, Wordsworth's comment that "The Child is father of the Man"[1] has special relevance. Most of us have our character and our outlook on life formed when we are children, and Howell Heflin is no exception. He grew up in an atmosphere of care and love with family life dominated by the rather strict Methodism of the time. The Reverend Marvin R. Heflin, Howell's father, was a true believer, so the family spent vacations at camp meetings and had group prayers mornings and evenings. Thus, a strong religious belief was instilled in Howell, along with ideals of honesty, morality, and the Protestant work ethic.

Howell's friend Edward Mauldin remembers that "Brother Marvin Heflin was a sweet, dear, kind, gentle, caring person, and everybody in the community loved him. They loved to have him around. Brother Marvin was a small man, not more than about five feet, six inches tall, and I think Mrs. Heflin provided the genes that gave Howell his size." Though the Reverend was a small man, Mauldin says, there was always a big smile on his face to go along with his big heart. However, the big heart did not keep him from being a stern disciplinarian. "Father would wear you out with a belt or a paddle," remembers Howell.

Marvin Heflin attended the University of Alabama and then went into the Methodist ministry. Howell recalls tales that his father was "a wild buck" at the University but apparently "got converted . . . renounced the devil and accepted the Lord." Over the years, the Reverend Heflin continued his education with graduate work in theology at the universities of Chicago, Harvard, Columbia, and Vanderbilt, though he did not obtain an advanced degree. He had pastorships in the North Alabama Conference of the Methodist Church at Fayette, Cullman, Tuscaloosa, and Bridgeport in the years before the First World War. About 1910 or 1911, he was pastor of the First Methodist Church in Tuscaloosa, where he met and married Louise Strudwick and where Howell's older brother Wilson was born.

After the United States became involved in World War I, the Reverend Heflin worked with the YMCA, the equivalent of today's USO. He stayed with the YMCA for a year or two after the war. He intended to return to the ministry in Alabama, but there were no churches available, so he moved his wife and two children to a temporary Methodist pastorate in Poulan, Georgia, where Howell was born in 1921. Howell recalls an interesting coincidence from those years:

> We didn't live in Poulan long. We moved first to McRae and after a short time to Montezuma. McRae was the home of Gene Talmadge. Gene was a lawyer, and he ran for the state senate and was defeated. He was later elected state Commissioner of Agriculture, and then he became Governor. He would campaign wearing red suspenders. He said that the poor man only had three friends: Jesus Christ, Sears and Roebuck, and Gene Talmadge.
>
> Gene's son, Herman, and my brother Wilson were in the same class, about the fourth or fifth grade, and sat together. Remember that this was in the 1920s. When I went to the Senate, I served with Herman Talmadge, and he asked me, "Did you have a brother named Wilson Heflin? Did y'all live in McRae?" I said, "Yes," and he told me he and Wilson were classmates. I'd always heard it from Wilson, but I thought it was interesting that Herman remembered it all those years later when I went to the Senate.

In 1934, Marvin Heflin moved his family back to Alabama and took a church in Red Bay. He later served churches in Attalla, Leighton (where Howell graduated from high school), Fairview in Birmingham, Oneonta, and finally Pell City, where he retired. Howell recalls:

> In his ministry, he had his ups and downs with parishioners. It's hard to please all the people, and sometimes disagreements would lead to a move. I think some of his career was influenced by the popularity of his brothers. When they were on a high, he was accepted at First Church in Tuscaloosa, a pretty fancy assignment. Later on when Uncle Tom fell out with the Democrats and was not elected, I sense that some of the people in the Methodist church said, "We don't want that. We're mighty different from Tom on political views, and we don't want his brother preaching here." After Tom's defeat, Father's church assignments were not as good as those he had before.
>
> My father was the youngest child. From his oldest brother Wyatt to my father was about seventeen or eighteen years difference. So he was the baby of the lot. He was always an excellent speaker, just like my Uncle Tom. He loved to tell stories and jokes just like Uncle Tom.
>
> As a parent he was probably more dominant than my mother. It was the typical family of the era. The husband was more dominant, and the wife was more motherly. My mother would stand up to him in arguments if the children were involved. Mother and Father were well suited to each other, and I think very happy.
>
> One thing in our family history controlled my father, and through him, it made a great impact on me. My grandfather was a doctor, and he did well. He owned about six thousand acres of land, but he endorsed some notes for some members of his wife's family, and he lost it all. My daddy used to say, "Don't sign anything." He didn't believe in putting a mortgage on anything. I have never had a mortgage on any real estate, including my home, in my life.
>
> My daddy always kept up with current events, and he was alert to things which were happening. In March of 1932, the Lindbergh baby had been kidnapped in New Jersey, and the police were searching for the kidnapper and the baby. Cordele, Georgia, where we lived then, was

on the main highway going north and south to Florida. Daddy had been looking at pictures about the kidnapping. He saw some people at a filling station. They had a New Jersey tag, and a baby was in the car and was crying. They were suspicious looking, and Daddy was convinced it was the Lindbergh child. He notified the police, but by the time the police got there, the car was gone. Daddy got a big write-up in the paper about being on the alert to help find the Lindbergh baby. He was convinced all throughout his life that it was the Lindbergh child, and if other people had listened to him, he could have saved its life.

Howell's mother was Louise D. Strudwick of Demopolis, who gave up teaching to marry Marvin. In those days, it was an unwritten rule that you didn't ask your girlfriend to marry you until you were able to support her, so she could stay at home and raise a family. Consequently, they courted a long time.

My Mother, who was the third child, was a twin. Her twin brother, Carter, was deaf and stayed at home. He had various businesses during his lifetime. He had a store for a while. Then he had a brick yard, and he looked after some of the farming interests. But his biggest joy was making wine. He would come up to Florence to visit his sister, Mrs. Helen Norvell, and he'd bring a suitcase full of good scuppernong wine.

My mother went to Livingston State Teacher's College. At that time, the president of Livingston was Julia Strudwick Tutwiler, who was related to the Strudwicks of Demopolis. The family has a letter signed by Julia Tutwiler which says, "Louise has become a good student, and I know you are proud of her." After graduating from Livingston, Mother went to Tuscaloosa and taught two or three years before she married my father.

Mother was very kind and lovable and took good care of us. She was a preacher's wife, and she supported him well. She liked people and people liked her. She was a big woman. She must have weighed as much as two hundred pounds back as far as I can remember. She was too fat, and she had diabetes, which caused a lot of problems. She would fight her weight and fight eating, but she loved sweets.

Her mother was what I would call an old-time aristocrat. She was proud of her family and background. Mother didn't put on airs like Grandmother Strudwick, though Mother was interested in family and would spend time with genealogy. She had six family lines back to the DAR. Lord have mercy, she would correspond with all of her relatives everywhere!

Grandfather Samuel Strudwick was dead, and my grandfather Heflin was dead. My grandmother Heflin died when my father was six years old, so the only grandparent I knew was my grandmother Strudwick.

Some summers, we would go over and spend a week or two weeks in Demopolis. Demopolis has the Tombigbee River and these white chalk banks. I remember swimming down there in the Tombigbee, and I remember all those good meals, especially breakfasts with her in Demopolis.

When I visited my grandmother, Sunday breakfast was a great event. She'd have spoonbread and roe herring, which she got in big containers that were shipped in. It was salted down. She'd also have salt mackerel. We'd have eggs with salt mackerel or eggs with roe herring along with the spoonbread. When my Uncle Carter came up to visit, we'd always have him cook spoonbread. Spoonbread is about gone from the menu of most Southerners. You know breakfast is a fast meal now. Lord, I remember back in those days, we sometimes had a cook, and she'd cook biscuits and eggs and pork chops for breakfast.

Howell Heflin was famous throughout his career for his appetite. This was well in evidence in his youth when as a minister's son he was often a dinner guest of a family in the church following Sunday morning services.

That was back when most families had cooks. Nowadays, you couldn't get anybody to do a home meal. If you're going to feed a preacher and his family today, you have to take them to a restaurant. Typically, fried chicken was the Sunday dinner. I grew up talking about fried chicken being the "sacred bird of Methodism." I could eat more fried chicken than anybody.

It's hard to find good fried chicken now. In those days, families raised their own chickens. A fryer was small so you had fairly small pieces of breasts or thighs or drumsticks. Until I was about fourteen, I sat at the children's table where we ate the wings and the backs and the necks. I never got tired of good fried chicken.

Howell was the youngest of three children. His sister Julia was six years older, and was killed in an accident in her early 20s. His brother Wilson was eight years older and was a typical big brother.

He used to kid me terribly. When I was very young, probably four or five, I had a billy goat, an angora with a beard. I was greatly infatuated with that billy goat. My brother started talking about making goat burgers out of my billy goat. I started crying, and my mother and father told him, "Don't you say anything about goat burgers any more." Then he'd sneak around and tell me, "We're going to have billy burgers," and I would go to crying again. They made him stop doing it. He was mischievous and was deviling me all the time.

My friend Billy McKenzie and I had what we called the Billy McKenzie-Howell Heflin Circus. The goat was the center of the circus. Billy had a rabbit or something, and we'd have a dog and a cat and a bunch of other things. These were our circus animals, and we'd get them all together and play. I remember having them all on the sidewalk. I don't know if my brother and his friends called it the Billy McKenzie-Howell Heflin circus or not, but they'd make fun of us and all our little animals.

When we moved to another parsonage, they wouldn't let us bring the goat, and I had to leave him. And oh, to separate from that goat was a searing experience. That is one of my earliest recollections.

Wilson Heflin had a successful and interesting career. He went two years to Young Harris Junior College in Georgia. Then he transferred to Birmingham-Southern and earned his bachelor's degree. At Vanderbilt University, he earned M.A. and Ph.D. degrees in English. He taught at Vanderbilt and at the University of Alabama. During World War II, he went into an officers' program in the Navy. The Navy found out he taught college English, so he was transferred to the Naval Academy at Annapolis where he taught a short time as a naval officer. At the end of the war, he accepted a position as a civilian faculty member, and he spent forty years at the Naval Academy. He died in 1985.

Howell remembers Wilson fondly. "My brother got more of our mother's literary skills. He got a flair for writing from her, and he wrote several books. He got into *Moby Dick* and did a lot of research on Herman Melville. He married a Birmingham girl, Mary Catherine Rochester, and they had two daughters, Ann and Kitty."

Growing up a preacher's son had a big impact on Howell Heflin's life.

> When I was growing up, the morning and evening prayers were a way of life for us. It was a custom I was used to until I went to college, and then, you know, you get away from it. We'd get down on our knees in the family prayers. We had family prayer every day before breakfast. It was the same thing at night before we'd go to bed. I still pray daily, but we don't have family prayers.
>
> Since my father was very religious, we spent our vacations at camp meetings. Indian Springs Meeting Grounds was a big Methodist camp in Georgia we went to, and in those days the people who went there were charismatic types. Only in those days, it was called sanctification. You had to be born again and sanctified. You could believe in God, renounce the devil, and accept the Lord, but then you had to have the second blessing.
>
> We'd go over to Indian Springs and spend a week or ten days. I had to go to the altar and get sanctified several times during the course of my life because I would backslide. There were some people speaking in

tongues. I never did understand that. Others had still different religious experiences. I remember a lady that had long hair. Her neck would jerk back and forth like a whip. I reckon she was sincere.

We would travel to camp meetings at other places. Sometimes my Uncle Bob, who had a great singing voice, would be along. My father had a good singing voice, too. I remember one of the highlights in our traveling was singing along with them. They'd sing songs like "Working on the Railroad" and "Dinah." I remember one they could sing was, "I wandered today to the hills, Maggie." They would sing "The Bells of St. Mary's" and other songs of those days. I remember I'd try to join in, but I couldn't carry a tune in a bucket, as they used to say.

I remember the first girl I ever kissed was at a camp meeting. I was probably about a senior in high school. I remember that it worried me as to whether I'd sinned. Her name was Josephine. I had known her and had lived close to her for a time. She was very attractive. Anyway, we were at that camp meeting, and someway or another the mood to kiss her came over me. So I did, and she was very receptive.

I remember when I was six or seven I fell and broke my arm. We were playing some game like hide and seek. Whoever was "it" would go out and hunt you, and you would try to get back to your base and touch it ahead of them. After I broke my arm, I came back by the base when they were leading me away, and I said, "Let me touch it." I touched my base to win. My daddy bragged on that. He bragged on me because, "He didn't lose sight; he was supposed to get back and touch the base, and he did." That has sorta stuck in my mind. I reckon it's because he would say, "Now, he's going to be a fine young man. He's coming along."

One time we were living somewhere in a parsonage, and some way or another the sewage system stopped up. It was a nice brick house. They put a fire hose in the main sewer line to clean it out. Well, somehow or other the fire hose got misdirected. It went through the sewer line that was connected to our house, and it blew stuff everywhere, all over the house. You never saw such a mess in your life. We had to get it cleaned up, and it still smelled for weeks.

I've never been mechanically minded or ever wanted to do things around the house. For some reason or other it stuck in my mind that I'm going to make a mistake like that man with the fire hose, and it's going to have a devastating effect on the whole family. Luckily, my wife is very mechanically minded. She can fix anything. She can build anything and can repair as long as it's not electrical. So I've always been thumbs, and I think it goes back to that experience. On the other hand, it may just be an excuse to let her do the work.

Another childhood event had an effect on me. I was a cub scout, about eight or nine years old, and we were out somewhere sleeping in tents. It was cold; my tent-mate got pneumonia and died from it. I never was an outdoorsman after that. I have never been a hunter or fisherman. I know later when I was in the Marines, I was in a fox hole, and a bomb fell and killed the fellow in the fox hole with me, but it didn't hit me. That revived the feeling I had when my tent-mate died."

When we lived in Columbus, Georgia, my father was pastor of St. Luke's, which was sort of in the ritzy-rich section of the Methodist church. My mother had some cousins and other relatives who were fairly well off, and we'd go down to Apalachicola [Florida] with them and go fishing. I was pretty young, about six or seven, and I remember catching jelly fish. You'd fish for them with a bucket-type thing which had kind of a seine in the bottom where the water would go through. I also remember catching crab. I thought going to Florida was a great thing.

Howell was interested in politics long before most children pay any attention to it. He began developing the speaking ability which would later be one of his strengths. He remembers attending a political rally in Cordele, Georgia, when he was ten or eleven:

There was a Senate race with Richard Russell running against a Congressman named Charlie Crisp, and they had a debate in the courthouse. I evidenced an early interest in politics by going by myself to listen to two politicians debate as they ran for office. I had on my best clothes, a white suit. I had to get up to go the bathroom, and I stumbled over somebody and fell flat out into the passageway between the two sections of the courthouse. You remember how they used to put oil on the courthouse floor? My suit was stained. And when I came home, my mama raised cain. They had been proud of it. They had bought it for me, and we didn't have a lot of money. About all you had was your Sunday go-to-meeting clothes.

Once, Uncle Tom came and made a speech. This was the first time I remember seeing him. He spoke to the Chamber of Commerce in the town where we lived. I remember he quoted a poem, and he said it was by an anonymous poet. I was pretty young, but I had read the poem. After he made his speech, I ran home and looked it up. I ran over to the train station to give him the name of the poet he had quoted. I had to run like everything to get there before he left. I was trying to make an impression on him.

When I was growing up, I used to quote a lot of poetry and practice talking. I would imagine myself a speaker, and I would make speeches by myself in the garden. Some of them used to say I made speeches to corn stalks.

A Georgia politician named Benjamin Hill made a speech that impressed me. I've forgotten it now, but it was very patriotic. I memorized the speech, and I memorized Longfellow's "Footprints on the Sands of Time." I memorized some other poetry and things so I could make good speeches.

Howell recalls his first job.

When we were living in Pelham, Georgia, I had my first job. I worked at a place called the Hand Trading Company. The family that owned it was wealthy, and some of them were members of Daddy's church. A fellow named Fred Hand was the Speaker of the Georgia House of Representatives.

I worked down in the fish market on Saturdays selling and cleaning fish. They'd sell these great big buckets of fish, mostly a good Gulf fish called mullet, but they had others like salt mackerel.

I'd get up early and go to work about 5 a.m., and I would work until about 12 at night. That's how you used to work. Big crowds would come to rural towns on Saturday. All the field hands would get off at noon, and later they didn't work at all on Saturday. I remember I made a dollar a day at the Hand Trading Company. It was a small amount, but they'd let me drink all the cold drinks and eat all the cheese I wanted. They had hoop cheese, and I'd drink seven or eight peach and strawberry soda pops. Being a Methodist, my daddy had conflicts about this because the "Co-cola" industry was tied to the Methodist church, but he thought when I was growing up I ought not to drink "Co-colas."

Daddy had a lot of ideas about food and reactions. I can remember he had the idea that if you ate pineapple or watermelon, you couldn't drink milk with it. It would make you sick. So we had watermelon and then couldn't drink any milk the rest of the day. Someway or another it was going to cause you problems.

Marvin Heflin pastored a church until he reached the mandatory retirement age of 72. After he retired, he and his wife lived in Pell City, Alabama, and he continued to preach in small rural churches.

The people built my parents a home, and my parents lived there about twenty years until they decided to go to a nursing home. He was in his nineties and she was around eighty, and they were getting pretty feeble. They had been living in a nursing home about six months when my mother died. We got Dad to come and live with us in Tuscumbia nine or ten months a year. He was very independent. We had arranged it so he couldn't get his driver's license because he was a road menace at that age. But he'd get a taxi and go wherever he wanted. He didn't have any old folks to talk to in our home, so he visited all the nursing homes in the area and picked one out. He moved there and lived to be ninety-eight. He was very happy because he'd picked out his own nursing home.

Daddy mellowed a little bit as he got older. I remember how he would preach the evils of the "demon rum," but after he retired, he changed a little on that. He began to feel that a little bourbon would be medicinal for his aches and pains. So he got to sipping a little bit when he was about eighty.

Marvin R. Heflin died in March 1976. He was the oldest living member of the North Alabama Conference of the United Methodist Church. The funeral was at the First United Methodist Church in Tuscumbia with burial in Oneonta Cemetery. He had served in the pulpit for more than sixty years.

4

School Days

METHODIST MINISTERS are assigned to churches by the district conference. Those in charge follow a general rule that ministers shouldn't stay with the same congregation too long; they are routinely moved to new pastorates every two to four years. Young Howell Heflin thus attended a number of different schools, beginning in Columbus, Georgia.

I also lived and went to school in Cordele and Pelham, and I believe we lived in Jackson for a year. My last school in Georgia was in Pelham. Being a minister's son, the biggest thing was moving. You'd made friends, and then all of a sudden, in the middle of the school year, you'd be moving and have to leave them.

Georgia had eleven grades in their public school system. In Alabama they had twelve. When I moved to Red Bay, I was in the eighth grade, and there was the question of whether I would stay in that grade in the Alabama system or go into the ninth. They decided I would go into the ninth grade. So in effect, I skipped a grade in the Alabama system. This meant that when I graduated from high school I was sixteen years old. The others in my class were seventeen or eighteen. I finished college when I was twenty rather than twenty-one or twenty-two like most of the others.

RED BAY. In 1934, when Howell was twelve, the Heflins moved to Red Bay, Alabama. Times were hard.

> I think the Great Depression had a sizable influence on me. The first cuts in salaries were for preachers, you know. The offerings in churches were voluntary, and the preacher's salary depended on what was given. Many would pay the preacher partly in eggs, produce, home-canned vegetables, and fruits. I remember I used to go get milk, and I'd walk about a mile with a gallon jug and get a gallon of milk for thirty cents.
>
> [Also in that time a terrible storm] hit Tupelo, Mississippi, and killed about five hundred or six hundred people, and it touched down in Red Bay and killed about ten. Then it touched down in Gainesville, Georgia, and killed about six hundred people. It was the same tornado at all three places, or at least that's what they thought.
>
> Before the storm hit, we left the parsonage and went next door to the church basement, and it blew the roof off the kitchen of the house. After that, everybody built storm cellars. It's about like the fad after World War II, when the Russians got the atomic bomb. Everybody started having bomb cellars. You'd put all the groceries down there and a radio, and you could live for a week or two.
>
> One of the bootleggers' homes was hit and some of his family, including the bootlegger, got killed. I remember my daddy preaching their funeral. Daddy thought bootleggers were the greatest sinners in the world, and he had always preached strong against whiskey and "demon rum." He struggled mightily to come up with a sermon for the funeral that didn't make the family feel bad but at the same time didn't praise the deceased too much. You know, ministers always have that as a task when there's a notorious person to be buried. Some preachers have made saints out of devils at funerals, but my father felt this was wrong.

Howell was in Red Bay at a formative period of his youth, long enough to make some lasting memories:

When we lived in Red Bay, I was bad to fight with other boys. I'd fight about anything and everything. Sometimes it was about a ball game. I got black eyes and even had a tooth knocked out. This caused me trouble in school. I was never expelled or suspended or arrested or anything really terrible, but I got whippings. I got spankings in school, and when I got a spanking at school, I got another when I went home.

They used to say that the minister's son was the meanest boy in town, and we always came back with, "Look what he has to associate with." But I don't think being the preacher's son had a great deal of influence on me in terms of my fighting and trouble-making. I was just a typical boy. I don't think I would ever stop and consider whether anything I did was going to embarrass my father. If you had a pretty good upbringing, you knew you'd get a "whupping" if you did things that were wrong.

I was big, and the group of boys I ran around with would play football or baseball when we weren't in school. This was what we did in the summer in particular. James Robert Cashion was about as big as I and was a raw-boned, tough guy. He and I would end up fighting. After we finished the fight, we'd go back to playing ball, and we'd play again the next day. But we'd fight. Fred Bostick and his cousin Lebert Harold Bostick were great boyhood friends of mine and both have been very successful in business.

When I was in Red Bay, we played baseball on a vacant lot or in a cow pasture or wherever we could, and we had a great rivalry with Vina. But we never did want to go over to Vina because in those days, the home team furnished the umpire.

Once when we were playing in Vina, the score was tied two to two. It was the ninth inning, and there were two outs. Red Bay was up to bat, and the batter hit a home run. He just knocked it forever, but in doing so, he got turned around, and he went to third first, then to second, then to first and then home. The umpire says, "You're out. Vina wins 1-2. You untied the score!" I admit this story may be just a little bit embellished.

When I lived in Red Bay and was playing ball, I associated with some fine young people who were later right successful. There's a doctor named Walker Dempsey who is still alive but sick. I recently went over and made a speech at a dinner honoring him. He built a hospital and has contributed a lot. The story was told that somebody phoned him and said, "Mother's terribly sick; please come." He went over to the house which was several miles from town, and she had a toothache. He said, "She's got a toothache. You should have called the dentist." The caller said, "Yeah, but I knew you'd come." I thought that story was typical of his life.

By the way, there was a section close to Red Bay called Freedom Hills, and Freedom Hills was in the really rough hill country, about as rough as there is in Alabama. It got its name about the time of the Civil War because it was a sort of staging area for slaves who were escaping. When they were going north, they would come into the area where some people were friendly to them. From there, they'd go north trying to reach Paducah, Kentucky. That area of hill country in Franklin County had very few slaves, and Winston County, which is close by, seceded from the Confederacy. Most of the people in the area were split on their loyalties to the Union and the Confederacy.

Later on, that area was so rough that the revenue officers couldn't catch people tending their stills. There were a lot of bootleggers there and a lot of moonshiners. It had a good strategic location. They were close to the Mississippi line, and were fairly close to Birmingham, Memphis, and Nashville. They did a lot of reducing their corn to the liquid stage in order to transport it. They had a poem that went something like this:

The preachers may preach,
And the owls may screech,
And revenue officers may ever be so sly.
But there'll be stills in Freedom Hills,
When the rest of the world goes dry.

ATTALLA AND LEIGHTON. Howell began high school in Red Bay, but his father was transferred to Attalla in 1936, so he moved to Etowah County High School. After one year, the Heflins moved again, this time to Leighton, a small cotton farming town. Howell made a number of friendships in Leighton that have continued over the years. One particular friend is Ed Mauldin, whose future wife Mildred became friends with the future Elizabeth Ann Heflin when they were in high school. Mildred went to school in Leighton and Elizabeth Ann in Tuscumbia. Ed Mauldin became a prosperous farmer and banker.

Mauldin was born in Sylacauga, but both his mother and father died when he was still in elementary school. He and his sister moved to Leighton in 1938 to live with an uncle, Edward Fennel, a cotton farmer. Mauldin remembers that a large number of farm workers lived in the immediate vicinity of his uncle's home. "A gravel road or lane ran beside his home," Mauldin says, "and there were wooden frame houses on the lane. They were filled mostly with black folks, so I grew up in the country with blacks." Mauldin graduated from elementary school in Leighton in 1938, the same year Howell graduated from high school, so they were acquaintances rather than close friends at the time. Over the years the friendship has deepened.

Ed Mauldin remembers his early days in Leighton fondly and gives a vivid description of what life in the rural community was like. "When I got home from school," he recalls, "I went to the cotton patch to help weigh the cotton picked that day. I had the responsibility of weighing it and paying them for their day's harvest. They were paid by the pound. The going rate was fifty cents for a hundred pounds of seed cotton. That's cotton and seed the way it comes off the stalk. A good picker could pick in the neighborhood of two hundred pounds, but a real good picker could get close to three hundred pounds, or about $1.50. That was pretty good for the times. Many people worked for a dollar a day.

"It was not an easy job, and women were sometimes the better pickers. They had more dexterity with their hands and could operate with two hands getting the cotton out of the bolls into the sack.

"A rather large black fellow named Edgar Ricks was about the best that I recall. I used to enjoy watching him, and when I wasn't otherwise employed in the cotton patch, I would sometimes get out in front of him and back up as he came forward and watch him. I wondered how in the world he was so good. For a long time he would pick two rows at a time. Later on I noticed he quit picking two rows at a time but would straddle one row and kind of squeeze the plants between his legs. That would put the open bolls closer together, and he could get to them faster. He would get over two hundred pounds almost every day."

Like other schools in the South in those years, Colbert County High School started in August and ran until cotton-picking time. Then there would be a harvest recess of some six weeks so that people could harvest the cotton crop. School would start back in October.

THE HEFLIN FAMILY. Howell's father was the minister at the First Methodist Church in Leighton where Ed Mauldin and his family attended.

The Depression was still going strong in the late 1930s, and Leighton had suffered tremendously. According to Ed Mauldin, the main social activities were family meals. "These were held many times after church," Mauldin says, "and sometimes in the early evening. Families would invite the preacher's family into their home, and they were always glad to have Brother Heflin. Most of the time Mrs. Heflin was at the hospital caring for their sick daughter. So the parsonage family was pretty much Brother Heflin and his youngest son, Howell. The older son was in graduate school or teaching at this time. When the Heflins were invited to the family lunches, Howell would come. He was a large, energetic fellow who had a good appetite, which pleased the church ladies. A story was circulated that Brother Heflin would make Howell eat a loaf of bread before he went out to dinner so that he wouldn't embarrass them by eating so much.

"Howell," Mauldin continues, "was always in a good humor and, like his father, pleasant to be around and a joy to have in your home. I have been fortunate to have known and been associated with Howell from that time forward."

Howell worked for Claude King and Son, a general store, in Leighton before he went to college, and later on he worked for them in the summers.

I'd work from about 6 in the morning until 7 at night, and on Saturdays it was all day long from 6 a.m. to midnight. I made a dollar a day. I figured I was making six cents an hour. I look back on that and say, Lordy, mercy. But I thought then it was big money. That was when we were coming out of the Depression, and most of the wages were low.

In the summers, I worked some on the farms. Among other things, I hoed and worked in the hay fields. I can remember working in a barn, up in the hayloft, and it was terribly hot. When it was that hot, you would perspire and get hay all around you and down in your clothes, and it would itch down your back. Of course we wore overalls, which helped a little.

One time, I was sent out to thin the corn. Anyway, I didn't know how to thin corn. I had a hoe, and I'd cut it off right above the root but still leave the root. Lord, I got blessed out! I had to go back and do it all over again. That was on a day when they came and watched me. They said, "Get out there and thin the corn." You know, we all learn by experience.

I remember when I was working on the farms I would sometimes try to pick cotton. I wasn't very skilled at this and couldn't pick much, maybe about 150 pounds a day, and I couldn't make any money.

HIGH SCHOOL YEARS AT LEIGHTON. The state passed a law in the early part of the century to establish a high school in every county, and through the efforts of people in Leighton, the Colbert County High School was established there. It was a consolidated school serving a large area, and many students rode to school on buses. The school had twelve grades and occupied two adjacent buildings, one for the elementary school and the other for the high school. There was no kindergarten. The controlling authority was the county board of education, of which Ed Mauldin's uncle was a member for many years.

Howell played high school football at Leighton. He was a center and, according to Ed Mauldin, was feared by the opposing teams because of his size and his aggressiveness.

"Contrary to what one might think, looking at his size and proportions now," Mauldin says, "he was really a good athlete. He played basketball and football and engaged in other sports."

> I was a pretty good-sized boy, and I started playing football when I was a freshman in high school. I was just a substitute, and I remember one of the first times they sent me in I got the breath knocked out of me the first thing. I thought I was dead!
>
> The boys I'd been playing with had all reached puberty, but I had not. In the locker room, I'd hide myself behind a towel so they wouldn't see that I hadn't matured as much as they had. I was big with a lot of baby fat. I remember how embarrassed I'd be to take a shower.
>
> I played football at three high schools because we moved around so much. When my last year in high school started, we were living in Attalla, and I was playing at Etowah County High. In those days, the Methodist preacher would move in November, and that's when we moved to Leighton. The cotton-split session delayed the football schedule, and as a result, I got to play at Leighton. All of the schools around there did the same thing. I earned letters from two different high schools in the same football season. I always thought that was unusual.
>
> A tragedy happened at one of my football games with Red Bay. A fellow named J. T. Page got his lung punctured some way or another, and he died as a result of it. This stayed with me a long time.

During his high school years, Howell became more aware of politics. He also had opportunities to develop his speaking talents and the storytelling abilities for which he would later be famous.

> John Sparkman came to visit when I was at Colbert County High. This was when he was a Congressman and before he went into the

Senate. He spoke to the student body, as politicians used to do a lot. His visit made a big impression on me. Later, when I went to the Senate, I made it part of my plan to visit as many high schools as I could, and I visited some five hundred of them over the state. I think Sparkman created in me the idea of what I called High School Town Meetings. You usually speak to the students about how important their education is, the federal programs available to assist them, and the fact that everybody can go to college or to a technical school if they want to. Then you open it up for questions and they ask you all sorts of things.

We had some oratorical contests when I was in school and I got into them. One year, I was in two contests, one in Etowah County and one in Leighton. I memorized a lot of speeches for that.

I won at the local level, but that was it. We didn't go against other schools at that time. Now, the American Legion has an oratorical contest with district winners who go on to the state contest. I memorized a patriotic speech by Senator Benjamin Hill of Georgia and would quote it in those oratorical contests.

I don't think there was any question that my father wanted me to become an office holder. He encouraged me. He was alive when I was sworn in as chief justice of Alabama, and he was very proud. He and Uncle Tom both would have greatly enjoyed seeing me in the Senate.

After War World II, stuff like quoting long speeches and telling stories was considered a little mushy. We went through a period of attitude change. After storytelling ended, they came along with the one-liners. When I went to Washington, everything was one-liners. My stories would take a minute and a half or two minutes.

Howell graduated from Colbert County High School in Leighton in 1938. He took away from the school a fondness for some of his teachers even though he would subsequently recognize that education in rural Alabama was not equal to the need. He also learned to supplement his schoolwork with reading and with listening to and observing interesting people.

I had some great teachers in elementary and high school. One in Red Bay was an English teacher, Cass Johnson. She actually taught with my wife later at Deshler. Then in Etowah County High in Attalla, I had some really good ones. One was Mr. Snead, who taught physics, and I became all interested in that. Maud Floyd Herndon was a really excellent teacher at Etowah.

Some of the teachers I had were really good, but in most of those small schools, teaching and education weren't the best in the world. When I went to Birmingham-Southern, the student body was about ninety percent from the city schools. That was back before integration, so they were all-white. If you'd gone to some country school, students who attended urban high schools were so far superior to you in their education that you really had to work like everything to try to catch up. It was a matter or studying night and day, because the competition with most of those city school graduates was tough. That was a problem I had going to country schools during the 1930s. I wasn't anywhere close to having the equivalent of a good high school education. I had to study like everything to catch up. I started out playing football, and when Southern quit the sport, it helped me more than anything else. I spent more time studying after that. I had good grades in high school. At Southern I didn't start out so high, but I had higher and higher grades each year I was there. I had troubles with foreign language. I started out taking French, but I got out of that class soon. Then I took Spanish and did all right, but I didn't make very good grades in it. I improved as I went along.

I remember when I was in high school in Leighton I read *Gone with the Wind*. It is the only book I ever read where I didn't stop. It was so interesting, I just read it straight through. I think maybe I stopped to eat. I think it took it me about twelve to fourteen hours.

One thing I found really interesting when I lived in Leighton was a Confederate veteran, Captain James Spangler. His granddaughter, Nancy Pride, was in school with me and was a friend. When he was up in his nineties, I would go sit with him. I can particularly remember cold wintry days when we were before a hearth with a fire. He would recite tales about the War Between the States — or the Civil War or the War of Northern Aggression — depending on how you wanted to refer to it.

Spangler had been with Nathan Bedford Forrest in this area when Forrest and his troops went after a group over in Etowah County. It was called the Streight Raid. A young girl named Emma Samson directed Forrest's cavalrymen. Emma Samson High School near Gadsden was named for her.

Captain Spangler would tell about Forrest and his raids, and I loved listening to him. There was a college near Leighton on the mountain, LaGrange College, and the Yankees burned it down. Then there was a battle over around Town Creek, and he'd tell about it.

A good part of Alabama didn't have any fighting during the Civil War, but north Alabama did several times. The Yankees would occupy Tuscumbia, and the Confederates would take it back. Locust Hill, an old beautiful home, was occupied about five different times as a headquarters for the Yankees.

I used to make speeches to veterans' groups as well as to young people, and I would tell them they ought to talk with World War I veterans about their experiences. Most veterans never did much talking about their war experiences until they got to the age of sixty-five or seventy. I still don't do a lot of talking about my war experiences unless somebody asks me. Captain Spangler had reached the age that he would talk about his war, and I just sat enthralled listening. I'm sure he embellished a little bit, but that comes about naturally.

FRANKLIN D. ROOSEVELT. Growing up during the Great Depression and observing the New Deal in action had a significant effect on Howell Heflin. It gave him a view toward social needs and the responsibilities of government in meeting them. This was to mark his later career as a public servant.

When we moved to Alabama, the Depression was going full blast and poverty was widespread. Then Franklin Roosevelt came along.

Roosevelt had a big influence in the United States and in the world but especially on those of us in the South. He gave hope to the farmers and to the citizens of this area. He established the TVA which created jobs and helped rural people. When Roosevelt came along with his programs, he represented the idea that government could help people.

My father wanted to see Roosevelt. The Indian Springs Camp where we went wasn't far from Warm Springs. We'd go over to Warm Springs just on the chance we would see him, but we never did. Once the President came to Barnesville, Georgia, and made a speech. He was really there to try to defeat Georgia Senator Walter George, who was the chairman of the Banking Committee and giving him some trouble. We drove over to Barnesville, and I saw Roosevelt. Daddy wanted us to shake hands with Roosevelt, but we never did get that close. But we did shake hands with Jim Farley, who was both the chairman of the National Democratic Party and the postmaster general.

Everybody was giving Hoover the devil for the Depression. I remember that people used a tobacco called "Golden Grain" and would roll their own cigarettes. They called it Hoover Dust, because they couldn't afford to buy ready-made cigarettes in those days.

Roosevelt, along with Senator Lister Hill, was largely responsible for Reynolds Metal Company constructing an aluminum plant near Tuscumbia. At the time, Alcoa was the only company that made aluminum metal in the United States. This particular Reynolds was making aluminum foil for Camels and the other Reynolds Tobacco Company cigarettes. Mr. Reynolds was trying to get a supply of aluminum, and when he went to Europe in the early 1930s, he found out that Hitler was using all of the aluminum to make airplanes. He came back and got the attention of Senator Lister Hill, and Hill in turn got the attention of President Roosevelt. America needed to concentrate on getting more aluminum for planes. At one time, before America went into the war, Roosevelt said we had to build 50,000 planes a year to be ready to defend ourselves. He helped establish Reynolds Metals Company outside of Sheffield, and, of course, it created a lot of jobs in this area.

I always felt that Roosevelt cared a lot about the South, and I really had a great admiration for him. I remember when I was in the Marine Corps and had been discharged from hospitals, I was on a special assignment in some universities and colleges. I was at the University of Texas at Austin when I heard over the radio that Roosevelt had died. I cried liked a baby. You just felt like he was a member of your family. I was spellbound by Roosevelt's fireside chats.

5

Birmingham-Southern College

I N 1938, IN KEEPING with his Methodist upbringing and family tradition, Howell Heflin entered Birmingham-Southern College. The school was founded as Southern University in Greensboro, Alabama, in 1856 as the "seminary of learning" for the General Conference of the Methodist Episcopal Church in Alabama. In May 1918, it was combined with Birmingham College, which had been founded in 1898 by the new North Alabama Conference. The combined institution was located in Birmingham. From its beginning, Birmingham-Southern sought academic distinction.[1] When Howell Heflin enrolled, it was considered the top academic institution in Alabama. It still is.

Howell's father and brother both attended Birmingham College. His uncle Cotton Tom had attended Southern University. Because Birmingham-Southern was a Methodist school, Howell, as the son of a Methodist minister, received a tuition discount.

The Heflin family still lived in Leighton, about 125 miles northwest of Birmingham. As a preacher's family during the Great Depression, the Heflins did not have a lot of money. One way Howell could get home from college was to hitchhike.

COLLEGE LIFE. Howell had a difficult time at first. He had to be frugal during his undergraduate days and he lived in the dormitory with the football team his first year at Birmingham-Southern.

For meals, I'd walk about a mile to a boarding house because it was less expensive than the cafeteria. I could get three meals a day for twelve dollars a month, though the food wasn't all that great. They had great big ole lima beans. We'd also have fat back, fried, of course. I was accustomed to eating that sort of menu at home. They also had fresh turnip greens and other vegetables.

I lived in the dormitory several years. Then I lived for one year down in the basement in a lady's home. About four of us were there. Her name was Mrs. Bell, and she was a great cook. Her husband would watch us eat, and he'd think we were eating too much. Then he'd lecture me about it. "You're eating too much," he'd say. "You're going die before you're twenty-five years old." I always felt he was self-serving with this advice, wanting me to cut down on the grub! He was some sort of accountant out at the TCI, which U.S. Steel was called in those days. ["TCI" stood for Tennessee Coal and Iron Company.]

Howell was straight-laced as a boy, avoiding many things his religion taught were sinful, but as time went by in college, he learned some of ways of the world with his college buddies.

My father had always preached the evils of alcohol. Every now and then when we were juniors and seniors, we'd sneak off over to the Plaza Grill or some other restaurant and drink beer. It was something we couldn't do anywhere around campus because it was a church college. Birmingham had street cars in those days, and when we went downtown, we'd ride the street car. A few students had cars. If my daddy had known I had my first beer when I was at Birmingham-Southern, he would have probably taken me out of school. I didn't smoke at Southern. My cigar smoking started when I was overseas in the Marine Corps.

Part of the religion was that you couldn't dance. When I grew up, dancing was sinful and evil. Lord, when I went to Birmingham-Southern, you couldn't dance anywhere on the campus. I learned to dance at Southern, but we did it over at the old Pickwick Club, where the Pickwick Center is now. There was a big dance hall there where the sorority and fraternity dances were held. Finally during our senior year, they allowed us to have a dance on campus.

It wasn't until my second year that I finally joined a fraternity. I joined one called Theta Kappa Nu, and then it merged into Lamba Chi Alpha. It's no longer there. It was sort of an unusual fraternity. A lot of the members of the fraternity were preacher's kids, "pks" as they said. My roommate Sam Pruett, who was a grade ahead of me, was a preacher's son. Another one named Tom Dill was a preacher's son, and so was Charles West. We called him "Happy." "Happy West." He was a character. He was a little fellow and he'd go around asking everybody, "Are you happy?" I think my attraction to them was probably the affinity with preachers' sons.

You had friends that you sat around and talked to and had all sorts of arguments about this and that. I had a friend named Paul Kassouf, who later had a big CPA firm in Birmingham. He was Lebanese and a brilliant student. Another good friend was Dick Blanton, who was this long, tall, Ichabod Crane type of fellow with a brilliant mind. He could quote poetry. At that time I was interested in memorizing poetry and such. Dick would make an A in the subjects he liked, but if he didn't like something, maybe chemistry or another science, he'd flunk it. He had a little coterie of friends around him. One of them was Joe Kiger, who became head of the history department at Ole Miss. Another one named Hobson Adcock had a great career with the FBI.

Later on, the Huddleston family became friends of mine. George Huddleston, Sr., had been a Congressman and had served with my uncle, Tom Heflin. He was elected to Congress from Birmingham about 1914 with labor and liberal support, and he stayed in Congress for twenty-two years. Then in the Roosevelt days, he turned and was much more conservative. I think he probably had misread Roosevelt. I was in school with George Huddleston, Jr., John, Jane and Mary, and then Nancy later on. They were all friends. George Jr. later got elected to Congress. They were all progressive minded when they were in school, but George, Jr., was very conservative after getting elected to Congress. When I came back from the war to Birmingham, I spent a lot of time with the Huddlestons. Every one of them was highly intelligent, and each was diverse in his or her thinking. Nancy later was professor of creative writing at Stanford in California and has been named teacher of the year there.

Howell did not have any serious girlfriends at Southern.

> I dated several girls. When I was president of my fraternity we had a lead-out at our annual dance. As my date, I selected Lucie Ford, who was a buddy. She was very popular on campus. I dated several, but I didn't have any particular girl friend. I wasn't interested in getting serious. I may have been a little afraid of the girls. I'd date a few three or four times, but I was not thick with any of them.
>
> We all worked at various and sundry things to help pay expenses. I worked at the post office and at other things, and during some summers I came back home to Leighton and worked at a store. I helped pay my way through school, and I tried to save money every way I could. The first three years, I worked enough to pay about half of my college expenses. I paid for all of them in my senior year. In those days, Southern was relatively expensive when compared to state institutions. As I recall, the last year cost about $600. I was business manager of the Annual my last year, and that helped me pay my expenses.

COLLEGE POLITICS. Heflin became active in campus politics at Birmingham-Southern and was elected to the school senate for several years.

> A group I was with would run people for political office. We jazzed it up by putting up political signs on campus, and we collected money to support our candidates. Our group was very successful in electing candidates. Sometimes fraternities were lined up against fraternities and other people and independents.
>
> Then we made the mistake. They wanted me to run for president of

the student body, but I needed money to get through college. So I ran for business manager of the Annual because you earned fees sufficient to pay your college expenses. We decided to run a very popular young lady, Virginia Evins, for president. No woman had run up to that time, and we thought she'd go in with a breeze. The candidate on the other side was smart, but he wasn't very friendly and wasn't as well known.

All of a sudden the other side told all the other sororities that if Virginia were elected, they wouldn't be able to "rush" successfully. If she were president of the student body, it would give her sorority an advantage during "rush" season, when sororities were seeking pledges. Well, they convinced all the other sororities to vote against her because of that. Even some of her close friends said they had to stick by their sororities. I said, "Ohhhhh my goodness, I'm going to learn something about politics here." Virginia was exceedingly popular and smart and should have won. We started out doing well, but somebody on the other side thought up the idea of going around to the other sororities and saying, "You're cutting off your nose to spite your face." And all women voted against their fellow feminist.

A GOOD EXPERIENCE. Howell's interest in public speaking was honed by participation on the debate team his junior and senior years. He was able to go on several trips to debate other schools, including one trip to the University of Toronto.

Birmingham-Southern College was obviously a good choice for young Howell Heflin.

> I think my education at Southern probably was the most influential part of my life. Southern had an excellent faculty and student body. The interplay between students and faculty was challenging, and it helped to formulate ideas and philosophical beliefs that stayed with me. The faculty would stimulate you and get you interested in ideas. I think it was the incubator for my philosophical thinking. I became much more progressive in my thinking, race-wise and problems-wise, through my experience at Southern.

Birmingham-Southern was a small school with about 600 or 700 students. There were a few large classes, but most classes were small. You could talk to professors privately, and you could sit around and talk in the bookstore where people drank coffee. A professor would be there with three or four students chatting. Everybody knew everybody.

I had an excellent history professor, Dr. Henry Shanks. James Saxon Childers, an English professor, spent a lot of time in England. He always carried his handkerchief in his sleeve, and he'd pull it out with a flourish. Professor Childers was sort of a prima donna. He'd have no more than about ten students in his classes, and you had to be selected to get into his classes. I managed to get in one year with him. Usually, if you took one of his classes, you would have tea each day about four o'clock in the afternoon in his office. He'd gone to Oxford.

We had an English professor named Richebourg Gaillard McWilliams. He was dapper. He had a little white mustache, and he made literature live. There would be maybe twenty in McWilliams' classes. Not long ago, Southern asked many of its graduates to give recollections of their favorite professors. I picked McWilliams as my favorite professor, and it is interesting that former Southern student Howell Raines, who is now Executive Editor of *The New York Times*, also picked McWilliams.

I had a speech professor, Marcie Fred Evans, who was exceptionally good, and I had excellent teachers in political science. One was Dr. Bill Jefferies, who later went to the Naval Academy and taught with my brother. A young professor named Jake Ward, who was later the vice president of academic affairs at Emory, made the study of government intriguing.

The college decided to create an unusual class my last year. It involved placing some seniors in sort of a seminar-class setting and having an organized collegial relationship between faculty members and students. They picked about ten students, and I got in. We would meet every two weeks or so, and sometimes would have dinner meetings. The theme was "The South Today." We read a study that Roosevelt had commissioned about the South and its economic potential. It told about the discrimination that existed in such things as steel prices, particularly in Birmingham, which was known as "Pittsburgh Plus." We'd sit around at night or sometimes in the afternoon and discuss the problems of the South. Each had to write a paper at the end of the course. The students were basically very bright, and the interaction was enlightening and intriguing. Reading this and discussing it had an influence on the philosophy that I developed later. I greatly admired Franklin Roosevelt.

I think the students as well as the faculty at Southern were intellectually stimulated, and they were also progressive minded on the race issue and other human issues like improving poverty conditions. At Southern I got an education and an outlook on a lot of different things that stayed with me. I modified some of my ideals later on for political purposes, as most politicians do to some degree, but I never fully compromised them.

I had pretty much decided I would be a lawyer, and at Southern I had a joint major in history and political science and a minor in speech. I never seriously entertained the idea of going into the ministry.

While Howell likes to be modest about it, he made quite a splash at Birmingham-Southern. He was business manager of the student newspaper, president of Lamda Chi Alpha Fraternity, president of Tau Kappa Alpha, an honorary speech fraternity, chairman for varsity debate, president of International Relations Club, and a member of Omicron Delta Kappa, a national honorary leadership and scholarship fraternity. During his senior year, he was named in "Who's Who in American Colleges and Universities."[2]

THE WAR STARTS. World War II started during Howell's senior year at Birmingham-Southern, and it disrupted a lot of lives.

We watched during the late thirties as the situation developed in Europe, and in 1939, the Germans attacked Poland and started World War II. There was a lot of debate around campus as to whether the

United States should get involved. Like most of the other students, I was opposed to the United States entering the war. It was not that we liked Hitler, but we had real questions as to whether we could win. I had a course in European history, and I saw that, in one sense, it was a history of wars. We had been to Europe in the "war to end all wars" not many years before, and here was another European war coming along.

Then, in December of 1941 when I was a senior, the Japanese attacked Pearl Harbor. That raised the ire in my blood, and people's Americanism blotted out our doubts. All of us had an immediate change of attitude, and I was ready to volunteer and do my part.

Conrad M. Fowler came along and told us about an officers' training program in the Marine Corps called the Platoon Leaders Class. I didn't know him then. He had graduated from the University of Alabama. He was called to active duty as a marine officer and was assigned to recruiting duty in Alabama colleges. You could sign up for the special officers' program, and if you were a senior, they'd let you finish college. Then you'd go to officers' training school, and if you were successful and graduated, you'd be commissioned a Second Lieutenant in the Marine Corps. I was accepted in the Platoon Leaders Class, and I was allowed to stay and graduate from Southern with the class of 1942.

Howell almost did not make it into the marines. His friend, Conrad Fowler, remembers that Howell was a senior and had not had advanced military training. "As a soon-to-be graduate he was concerned about the draft situation. At that time it was not unusual for a person to lose his deferment from the draft board when he graduated from college and had to look for something to do. Howell was in that position in the spring of '42 when I recruited him.

"All my recruits had to be approved by the marine recruiting station in Birmingham," Fowler continues. "They had called back to active duty a navy captain, a medical officer, who was quite strict in his interpretation of the regulations of the Bureau of Medicine and Surgery. Given the situation at that time, to my way of thinking, the restrictions were unreasonable. This medical officer was giving the regular recruiting officer quite a chore in trying to get recruits in the Marine Corps."

Howell came in for his examination on the last day of March 1942, and Fowler was present. "It was a Saturday, and I had been worried about getting Howell by the medical examiner because Howell was a big man. He was obviously overweight and not in the greatest shape. The medical officer explained to him why he couldn't take him into the Marine Corps. Then he turned to the chief and said, 'Chief, how many more do we need to make our quota this month?' The Chief answered, 'Doctor, that's him.' So the doctor slapped him on the rump and said, 'You're in the Marine Corps.'"

Howell continued at Southern the remainder of his senior year and graduated the following May of 1942. As he left for officer training, the war was going badly for the United States, and he was anxious to get involved.

6

The Marines

FOLLOWING JAPAN's surprise attack on Pearl Harbor on December 7, 1941, most Americans felt that the United States would exact a quick retribution. However, the Japanese swept rapidly across Southeast Asia and the South Pacific. They attacked Hong Kong the same day as Pearl Harbor and captured the British crown colony on Christmas Day. They marched easily through Malaysia and Singapore, and they attacked the Philippines, then an American possession. General Douglas MacArthur, U.S. commander in the Philippines, escaped just before the Japanese took Corregidor in May 1942. By mid-1942, the Japanese had captured most of the Dutch East Indies and were poised to strike Australia. To the western world, things seemed desperate, and Americans were fearful of another attack on Pearl Harbor or the Panama Canal, or even the U.S. west coast.

Meanwhile, the Japanese people were euphoric over their military successes, and the Japanese general staff believed the war was practically over. They envisioned an American capitulation on the Capitol steps in Washington.

One person who knew better was Admiral Isoroku Yamamoto, Commander-in-Chief of the combined Japanese fleet. Yamamoto had studied at Harvard and served as Japanese naval attaché in Washington, and he was aware of America's industrial strength. He initially opposed a war with the United States but was overruled by Prime Minister Hideki

Tojo and the general staff. Yamamoto knew that if Japan were to win a war, it had to do so quickly. On this basis, he planned the attack on Pearl Harbor and the strategy to control the Pacific.[1]

However, the "day that shall forever live in infamy" had united America as never before, and Yamamoto's fears of being overwhelmed by an adversary with greater resources proved well-founded even though his plans had achieved temporary mastery of the Pacific and had fundamentally changed the strategic balance of the world.[2]

This was the situation when twenty-one-year-old Howell Heflin joined the U.S. Marines in July 1942, shortly after he graduated from Birmingham-Southern College.

TRAINING. The United States had begun a rapid military buildup in 1940 as the crisis in Europe worsened and relations with the Japanese deteriorated, but the country was far from ready for all-out war. Among other things, there was a desperate need for more men in the armed services. Conrad "Bulley" Fowler, who recruited Heflin into the Marine Corps, recalls that there were fewer marines than New York policemen when the war started. As a result, the training of new recruits was compressed. Howell was sent to the marine base at Quantico, Virginia, for Officers' Candidate School. His training was approximately sixteen weeks in two phases. First, he was in basic training as an officer candidate. After graduating and receiving his commission, he completed the second phase as a second lieutenant.

Part of Officers' Candidate School resembled the marines' traditional and legendary boot camp.

> We called it boot camp. The regular Marines who went through boot camp in Parris Island or San Diego would probably say, "Those officer candidates got off lighter," but I don't think we did. I think it was pretty well the same. The platoon instructors were tough as nails. They would do everything in the world to embarrass you and make you think you were the dregs of the earth. I remember when I first got there, I had to ask somebody something. I walked into a room and said,

"Might I ask a question?" They said, "You knock before you come in." So I knocked on the door.

They'd find fault with everything I did and then give me some humiliating task. I had the job one weekend of cleaning the floor of a large bathroom. I had to use a toothbrush and clean it immaculately. I scrubbed and then wiped with a cloth. I spent the whole weekend doing this, cursing and raising cain. "What in the devil am I doing here?" The drill instructor said, "You're not doing too well." You couldn't argue with him. They made life miserable.

You'd put on a big pack, and they'd make you run and trot. Then you'd drill. You learned how to break down rifles and put them back together, and you learned the same thing with machine guns and mortars.

Near the end of Heflin's training, he developed a painful ingrown toenail, a condition which would plague him off and on over the years. He continued to drill despite the inflamed and swollen foot, cutting the toe out of his shoe to relieve the pressure. By this time, his hard work and attitude had earned the respect of the other marines, and he remembers that his captain cut him some slack until the foot got better.

Conrad Fowler says it was obvious that Howell was a natural leader. "For Hef just to go through the training routine with the bulk he had to carry was really pretty tough. He did everything anybody else did. The fact that he was as large as he was but fulfilled all the training missions was always of interest to the men who served under him."

Heflin's size, as always, attracted notice. Fowler tells of a conversation between Bill Shockley, the assistant battalion quartermaster, and Howell. "Bill and Hef had many things in common and spent a lot of time talking. I overheard them talking about their families. Hef told Bill, who was about five-feet nine, 'My father is about your height.' Shockley threw up both hands in mock dismay and said, 'Good Lord, Hef, you mean something like you could happen to me?'"

Howell was commissioned a second lieutenant and entered the second phase of his accelerated training. "They said we were officers and gentlemen," he recalls, "and they didn't treat us like they did in boot camp. We learned tactics and how to be a platoon leader."

After boot camp, the OCS trainees also received weekend liberty and a pay increase — up from the $21 a month as raw recruits to $150 to $200 a month after commissioning. Heflin remembers weekend trips to Washington including visits to the Occidental Restaurant and seeing all the pictures of presidents. Sonja Henie's husband was in Heflin's class, and he got to meet her.

After OCS, Howell was sent to Camp Pendleton near San Diego where a new unit of the Marine Corps was being organized. He was assigned first to Fleet Marine Force Pacific, then in turn to the Third Division, the Ninth Regiment, First Battalion, and finally A Company. By coincidence, Conrad Fowler, who had recruited Heflin at Birmingham-Southern, had also been transferred to A Company. He and Howell both served as platoon leaders in the newly organized marine units at Camp Pendleton. They began training for amphibious warfare in the Pacific. After a few weeks, they shipped out. "We didn't know where we were going when we left," Howell says, "but it turned out to be New Zealand. I remember crossing the equator and being initiated into the Order of Neptune. Crossing the equator was supposed to be a big deal."

ON TO NEW ZEALAND. Second Lt. Howell Heflin, with only a month of combat training under his ample belt, arrived in New Zealand with the Third Marine Division in January 1943. The company commander was promoted to major and Conrad Fowler, who had seniority, became a captain and the new company commander. Fowler was commander of A Company and Howell was leader of the Third Platoon the remainder of the time they were together in the Pacific.

The division continued training:

> We were in a little community south of Auckland. Our battalion commander was a Puerto Rican, Lt. Colonel Jamie Saboteur. He had graduated from the Naval Academy and was a character. The regimen-

tal commander was Lemuel Sheppard who had been in World War I. He later became a four-star general and commandant of the Marine Corps. They were all spit-and-polish marines. They wanted everything perfect, and I never was a tidy individual.

We went through all sorts of training in New Zealand. Saboteur would take us on twenty-mile hikes. All the people had blisters, but we'd still go with full packs on, and it was hot. He believed in hikes. I wrote my father and mother to the effect that we had hiked a total of three hundred miles. Well, my father misunderstood what I said, and he got in touch with Conrad Fowler's folks who lived in Columbiana. They wrote back and asked Conrad, "Have you been on this three hundred mile hike?" Fowler laughed and asked, "What did you tell them?" I said, "Well, I just added it up, and we had been three hundred miles. We were going something like twenty miles a day, and if we went five days a week for three weeks, it amounted to three hundred miles." Then we got some training on landings to prepare us for amphibious warfare.

At the time, most New Zealand males of military age were in the army, and most were in North Africa, along with the Australians. As part of the British Commonwealth, they had been in World War II since 1939, and they were involved with the desert war for control of the Middle East and the Suez Canal. Very few servicemen were left in New Zealand. Along with everyone else, the Australians and New Zealanders had not anticipated the Japanese thrust across the Pacific. Howell sensed that the New Zealanders and the Australians were seriously considering withdrawing their troops from North Africa and bringing them home. That would have had a disastrous effect upon the Allied North African campaign.

The Australians and New Zealanders were very appreciative of the fact that the Third Marine Division and other Americans were there because they feared the Japanese were coming to Australia and on to New Zealand. Japanese troops actually landed at one place in Australia.

New Zealanders were very friendly to us and would invite us into their homes. They had steak and eggs often. They spoke with their British accent, and it was "stak and aggs." They'd always have tea and crumpets in the afternoon, according to their English background.

We saw a lot of interesting things in New Zealand. They raised a lot of sheep. We'd have mutton to eat, and if you don't cook mutton right, it can have a terrible flavor. I got to the point I never wanted to see a mutton chop again in my life. Later on, when we were in combat eating C-rations, we would have loved mutton. While we were in New Zealand, we went down to see the aborigines, the natives who had been there before the British came. They were called the Maori group.

We stayed there for a few months working with weapons and learning how to break down and then fire machine guns and rifles. We would go through maneuvers, like taking hills. I remember that no two people were supposed to be close together as we moved. I got to thinking about Civil War tactics when they'd have masses of people moving, like Pickett's Charge at Gettysburg, and my Lord, they just shot them down. If an artillery shell hits and is going to kill or injure somebody, hopefully it won't be more than one if you are dispersed.

Conrad Fowler relates how Howell got a nickname in New Zealand. "Our little camp was thirty miles from Auckland, the principal city," he says. "There were no overnight passes, but the fellows could catch a train to Auckland about 5:30 p.m. The timing was just right to spend the evening and be back before 10:45. Hef's hutmate was a fellow named Bill Pfeifle.

"Bill located a little girl whose company he enjoyed, so he was going to Auckland regularly. The lady suggested, 'Why don't you bring your hutmate? I'll get him a date.' So it worked out. There were Bill and Hef, and Bill's girlfriend brought this nice little nineteen- or twenty-year-old lass, a New Zealand cracker. She didn't have a tooth in her head. They had about a 25-year lag on dental work down there, and they didn't fill teeth. They just pulled them and waited until maturity to give them a plate. When she saw Hef, she said, 'Wy, Hef, you es as big as a musse.'"

To his war comrades, Heflin was thereafter known as Moose, even after he was a successful lawyer. Fowler said that when Heflin became the chief justice of the Alabama Supreme Court, he let it be known that he thought the nickname should be dropped, and most of his friends stopped calling him Moose — but not all.

Bill Pfeifle had became a successful California banker. According to Fowler, "He had not seen Howell in some years and was in Washington. He told the receptionist in Howell's office, 'I want to see Hef. Go tell the Moose that Bill is here.' She said, 'He's busy. He has appointments and all.' 'Well, go anyway and tell the Moose that Bill is here.' Howell came out when he got the message that Bill wanted to see the Moose."

GUADALCANAL. The Third Marine Division arrived in the South Pacific at a critical time in the war. The Japanese had made it to New Guinea just north of Australia, and there appeared to be no stopping them. If they went on to Australia and New Zealand, America and its allies would be in an extremely difficult position because there was no other land base from which to oppose them for thousands of miles. The situation was desperate as the Japanese prepared to take Port Moresby, New Guinea, just a few hundred miles north of Australia.

Even though the U.S. Navy was badly crippled from the Pearl Harbor attack, in May 1942 it mounted an attack on the Japanese fleet which was supporting the Port Moresby invasion. The Battle of the Coral Sea was a tactical draw, but it was a great strategic victory for the United States and its allies because it stopped the Japanese advance, at least temporarily.

In that same month of May, in response to President Roosevelt's feeling that the American people desperately needed a morale boost, General Jimmy Doolittle headed a surprise carrier-launched air attack on Tokyo. This had the desired effect in the United States, and it also produced a large unanticipated shock in Japan. The Japanese decided to extend their control perimeter in the central Pacific several hundred miles east to prevent a recurrence, and they made Midway Island their target.

The United States won a critical and surprising victory at the Battle of Midway in June, just six months after Pearl Harbor. Americans had broken the Japanese code. With only three aircraft carriers, they totally surprised a large Japanese fleet headed for an invasion of Midway, and they sank four Japanese carriers. It was a blow from which the Japanese never recovered.

With the battles of the Coral Sea and Midway, the Japanese advance was halted, but there was still a question whether they could resume the offensive. Great danger still existed in the area north of Australia. To end the threat and gain air supremacy so that the long advance back westward over the Pacific could begin, the United States invaded Guadalcanal in August 1942. Guadalcanal was the first offensive action on land that America and its Allies took in the Pacific.

The battle for Guadalcanal was desperate for several months, with victory not certain. As late as mid-October, General MacArthur warned President Roosevelt, "If we are defeated in the Solomons, the entire Southeast Pacific will be in gravest danger."[3] By the end of the year, the Americans had finally gained control, and the ultimate defeat of Japan was assured. The Japanese evacuated their troops from Guadalcanal in February 1943.

When the Third Marine Division arrived at Guadalcanal early in 1943, the island was secure, though a few Japanese remained in the hills. Americans patrolling would sometimes run into them. Howell says he felt two or three times that a sniper was firing at him.

"The Japanese would bomb sometimes," Howell remembers. "One of them would always come in the middle of the night, just to irritate people I think. We called him 'Washing Machine Charlie.' The plane would fly at a high altitude and drop bombs, but it sounded like a washing machine. Sirens would go off almost every night, and we would get in bomb shelters. A lot of times, Washing Machine Charlie would come over about the time the movies were showing."

The First Marine Division had been in Guadalcanal before Howell's group. Henderson Field, the airfield there, was of great strategic importance. The Japanese had built it originally, but Americans enlarged it so their aircraft could use it. The objective was to gain control of the air and the sea in that part of the Pacific. The Japanese would send bombers and try to put Henderson Field out of commission.

Guadalcanal was important, not only because it made invasion of Australia impossible but because Americans could take off from Henderson Field and strike Japanese fortifications in places like New Britain and Truk. Different naval excursions, involving submarines, raids on various islands, and PT boats, were run from Guadalcanal.

Howell may have met John F. Kennedy, a PT boat captain, in Guadalcanal.

> I remember one time I was at an officers' club and sat at a table with some PT captains. We talked about the coast watchers, a group of New Zealanders and Australians who had radios. They would watch for Japanese activities in the islands and report back to headquarters. One of the coast watchers helped in the rescue of John F. Kennedy. Later I talked to Kennedy about it and he said, "I may have met you on Guadalcanal. I was at that officers' club frequently."
>
> We stayed in Guadalcanal several months training for amphibious landings. Holland M. Smith, a marine general they called "Howling Mad Smith," is known as the "Father of Amphibious Warfare." He was an interesting fellow. He had graduated from Auburn, then he went to law school at Alabama, and then into the Marine Corps. He was from Seale, Alabama. There's a bust of him that the family gave to the law school at the University of Alabama.
>
> Guadalcanal was a big island. From one end to the other it was fifty or sixty miles, and it was about thirty miles across. It had a lot of big coconut groves, and there were also a lot of jungles and other types of terrain.
>
> When we first got there, we had to find a creek or go out in the ocean to bathe. Then they got these big fifty-five-gallon cans which had had oil in them. After they cleaned them up real good to get the oil out, they would pour water in, and we could take a shower. When we first got there, we were living on C-rations, but then they set up what the

Marines and the Navy call a cooking galley and we began to get decent food.

A lot of people got sick, and some of them would get hurt in training and in other ways. Our battalion had a medical officer named Dr. Branch, who was a surgeon. We hadn't been in a lot of combat at that particular time. The word went out if you got a stomach ache or something wrong with your penis, don't see Dr. Branch. Dr. Branch would either operate on you for appendicitis or circumcise you. The men would stay away from Dr. Branch. They figured that he wanted to practice with his hands and not lose his surgical skills.

There were all sorts of things like mosquitoes and jungle rot, an athletes-foot type of thing you would get all over you. There was malaria, and a lot of people developed yellow jaundice. Some in our division had been at Samoa, and they had developed elephantiasis, which makes the extremities real large. But there were just a few cases like that.

A fellow I knew there was Captain Lewis Wilson, who was a great friend of Fowler's and became a great friend of mine, too. On Guam he won the Congressional Medal of Honor. When I went to Washington, he was Commandant of the Marine Corps. His wife and my wife were great friends when I was in the Senate.

When we were out training, we were not seeking Japs, but we were still cautious because there could be some. We were coming down a trail one time, and I made a curve. Lo and behold, right in front of me was a human leg standing up. We went up to it and had no idea what had happened. We started looking around trying to find a body, and then we saw some other marines. They told us that this fellow was carrying a dynamite cap in his pocket, and the cap exploded and blew his leg off. We found out later that he got to the hospital but died. Coming around a curve like that and seeing a leg made a lasting impression on me.

Our battalion had a tent city in a coconut grove. Most of the floors were dirt. The rainy season would come because Guadalcanal was close to the equator and in a tropical area. I went to bed one night and left my shoes right at the end of the cot. During the night the rain came in such volume that it caused a virtual river to come through, and it washed the shoes away. Next morning when I got up I didn't have any shoes. About a foot and a half of water was running through my tent. That was an instance to remember.

BOUGAINVILLE. Howell was among the marines who landed on the island of Bougainville, at the west end of the Solomon Islands about 600 miles northwest of Guadalcanal, in November 1943.

Bougainville was fortified by the Japanese, but it was big enough that a landing place could be selected where not too much resistance would be anticipated. There would eventually be trouble, however. There was sure to be a battle over the beachhead which had been established.

The idea of a beachhead was to move inland far enough that enemy artillery couldn't hit landing crafts and couldn't hit the beaches. Usually a beachhead would give you protection for a radius of fifteen miles or so. The size was determined by the range of the Japanese artillery. We wanted to be able to land safely and protect the beach as supplies came in. Our particular mission was to take an area where the Seabees could put in a landing strip for our aircraft. This would advance our forward base several hundred miles from Guadalcanal.

We landed at Princess Augustus Bay and had very little resistance. There was a small group of Japanese nearby, but they had anticipated a landing some other place. So we landed and moved forward.

There's a humorous story that Fowler likes to tell. He claims that I held up the invasion of Bougainville. After we'd moved in several hundred yards and secured our objective area, we were relaxing. The island was muddy, and when I hit the beach I got sand and mud all over everything. I went back to take off my shoes and wash out my socks and pants. I put my shoes down and a big wave took them out to sea. I had a duffle bag with another pair of shoes on the ship we came from. They had to radio and have somebody go down in the hold of the ship, get the shoes out of my duffle bag and bring them to me. Fowler says I held up the invasion of Bougainville until I could get my size twelve-and-a-halves.

By the fourth or fifth day, the marines had moved well toward their objective of securing the beachhead.

> We were three or four miles in, close to the apex of the beachhead and we were moving on up.
>
> We had dug foxholes, and a redheaded marine was at the forward part of our perimeter. We were in the front line, and every now or then a Japanese sniper would fire. Well, the redhead developed diarrhea one night. There were no toilets, and he had to use his helmet as a pot. His area was fairly clear, without too much jungle, and the tropical moon was shining down. As he did his business, the white, pink skin of his exposed extremities was showing in the tropical moonlight. Some Japanese sniper spotted it and fired, and the bullet went in and out both cheeks. It made four holes. "Red" was a humorous sort of fellow, and the next day he said, "I want to put in for four purple hearts." We both laughed. I said, "I want to ask you one question. How is your diarrhea?" He immediately answered, "It was the fastest cure I ever had."
>
> When people had diarrhea or something like that, they couldn't get up and wander around. We were on the front lines, and there were Japanese snipers and patrols out there. The next morning, they'd find some water and clean out the helmets.
>
> By Thanksgiving Day we had moved pretty well along and thought we were fine. Some way or other the cooks had gotten a turkey from the ship, and they were going to fix turkey and dressing. Well, about the time we were getting ready to sit down to eat, word came to move out to a battle at Piva Forks. We had to leave our turkey dinner. In two or three hours we got to the battle location. As we moved forward, we saw that the Japanese had dug in, and this was a battle line where they wanted to fight.
>
> We started moving up this hill. There were surrounding hills, but this was the highest. The Japanese were there, and we were at close

range. It was thick jungle, with vegetation and other things, and even when we were close to the top of the hill we couldn't see them. When we stood up, they could spot us, but we couldn't spot them. They waited until we got nearly to the top of the hill and opened fire on us with machine guns and everything else.

It later became known as Grenade Hill because you were close enough to throw grenades and hit the Japanese. This was all in the jungle with big banyan trees. My sergeant, Harvey Carbaugh, and I and the others were pinned down. We were throwing grenades, but when we'd fire bullets they'd go up the hill and over the line of fire. The only way we could be effective was to get on the level where we could spray them.

Carbaugh and I decided that he would create a diversion, and I would take a Browning Automatic Rifle and fire. If you didn't have some diversion and move, they'd fire their machine guns at you. His people threw hand grenades and attracted the Japanese's attention, and I got up with a Browning Automatic Rifle and sprayed the area. The next day when we charged up the hill, we found we had destroyed several machine gun nests and a large number of Japanese soldiers.

I got some hand grenade fragments, but I wasn't hurt enough to go to sick bay. I picked them out because they were just skin deep. That was a major battle in Bougainville. It was called the Battle of Piva Forks, but our outfit always called it Grenade Hill.

The record indicates that Heflin is probably understating his role. As Harvey Carbaugh described the incident some fifty years later, "The Third Platoon was pinned down two-thirds of the way up a hill by small arms fire and grenades coming from both sides of a large Banyan tree. I consulted with Heflin and decided to try and take cover behind the tree trunk. I made it, and Hef came soon after. I spotted a sniper about 10 feet from the tree and took him out with a short-fused grenade. Nips started firing into the tree trunk with Nambu. We needed a B.A.R. (Browning Automatic Rifle), and Hef got it. We decided I would reach around the trunk on the left side and throw a short-fused grenade, and Hef would rake the area with B.A.R. from the right side. A sniper raised up, and I beat him to the draw. I fired right across Hef, and he cried out that the muzzle blast broke his ear drum. The combination of the B.A.R. and the grenades silenced the Nambu. We tried making contact with the First Platoon before we made an attempt to overrun the position but had no success."[4]

Conrad Fowler remembers that Howell had a particularly fine performance in Bougainville. "The Japanese were supporting their own effort with aircraft and ships," he says. "Hand Grenade Hill was a prominently designated battle area. Howell's platoon was right in the middle of it and was the assault force on an intensively prepared Japanese position. Howell and his platoon sergeant employed the appropriate tactics. They built up a base of fire and then deployed an enveloping force to go around and hit them on the flank, using smoke, hand grenades, rifles, and Browning Automatic Rifles. They were successful in eliminating a position that had the whole front held up, and they did it with high casualties for the Japanese and very few in their platoon. Hef and his platoon sergeant, Harvey Carbaugh, were each awarded a Silver Star for their efforts on Hand Grenade Hill."

Howell discovered that some men in combat have a premonition of death.

> We had a fellow in our outfit called Groggy Glass who was from Massillon, Ohio. He had been a good football player at Tulane. He had a premonition that he was going to be killed, and he'd talk about it all the time. Groggy was killed in the battle of Iwo Jima. It's unusual how many just kept saying, "I'll never get home again," or something like that. They had a premonition they were going to be killed, and it usually happened.

GUAM. When Bougainville was secured, the Third Marine Division went back to Guadalcanal and continued to train. By this time, a grand strategy in the Pacific was being followed, both by Admiral Nimitz, who had command in the northern part of the battle area, and General

MacArthur, who was in command in the south. The strategy was to island hop in a large movement northward and westward, and to pick and choose carefully, using surprise when possible. This strategy was working. It not only saved American lives, it stranded thousands of Japanese soldiers on isolated islands.

After Bougainville, Howell's unit returned to Guadalcanal for more training.

> When we got back, I had lost about fifty pounds and was down to something like a size thirty pants size. It was the end of the year, and the New Zealanders we'd known before were there and invited us to come over and celebrate New Year's Eve with them. I had to get some khaki pants. You know, we'd been wearing dungarees and rough clothing like that. My khakis wouldn't fit, so I borrowed a pair of Fowler's. That's when I knew I'd lost all that weight; I could get into his clothing. The C-rations were terrible. The only decent meal we would have had was that Thanksgiving dinner that we didn't get to eat.

After a few weeks, the division was loaded on another ship. At the time, American forces were in the battles for Saipan and Tinian. A lot of resistance was encountered on Saipan, and leaders thought they might have to deploy the Third Marine Division there. The division was held in reserve for sixty-two days, and the men stayed on board the ship. Heflin remembers that conditions were confining, especially for the enlisted men stuck down in the hold on tightly jammed hanging cots. Many became seasick.

The leaders finally decided to have the Third Division go ahead with its regular mission of landing on Guam, which was some 1,500 miles north of Bougainville in the Mariana Islands. When Guam was invaded in July 1944, Americans had driven the Japanese back all across the Pacific and were preparing to launch an attack on Japan. The first step was to get air bases close enough for bombing. Japanese troops were still fighting desperately and ferociously, but there was no question that Japan faced certain defeat.

The Japanese knew we would try to liberate Guam because it had been American territory, and they fortified it pretty well. Guam was the first American territory liberated in the Pacific. We had acquired Guam at the end of the Spanish-American War, and it was a focal point in the trans-Pacific trade. We had air fields and some naval bases there before the Japanese took it.

The strategic plan was to use Guam, Saipan, and Tinian to launch bombing raids against mainland Japan. The long-range bombers sometimes had difficulty going the distance from these locations to Japan and returning. Iwo Jima was close enough that they could bomb and return, and it also provided a place for planes from Guam or one of the other places to land if they got into trouble.

My outfit was to land on Guam at a designated area, and we would be among the first to hit the beach. On the day we were to land, Fowler, our company commander, called a meeting and then had to leave for a few minutes. One of the lieutenants had a bandolier of hand grenades. He was throwing it over his shoulders, and one fell out and the pin broke. We were in a state room, which is what they called a sleeping room for officers. The thing went off. There must have been four or five or us in that room, but not a single one got hurt. It was remarkable. Some way or another the Lord must have been taking care of us.

Guam was a much bigger operation than Bougainville. On Guam, our mission was to recapture the whole island. The landing was pretty heavily opposed. Again it was the idea of taking a beachhead and moving inland. The Japanese were well fortified and were firing artillery. They knew pretty well where we would land, and their artillery hit the shore and sank some of the landing craft in the harbor and on the beaches. We had to move forward and get to high ground as fast as we could.

We got over the first hill, and there was another hill up ahead. I got hit in the hand going up the next hill. The bullet went through my thumb. They fused it later, and I still have a stiff thumb. I kept going. A short time later, I was hit in the leg. I was pretty well immobile, but

I could still move forward. We got to the top of that hill, which was the immediate objective. From there, we could move up our mortars and begin to blow up some of their artillery. Our planes hit them, and there was some naval gunfire.

Conrad Fowler tells what happened next. "We had a lot of casualties," he says, "and Hef was one of them. You could put a nickel through the bullet hole in his thumb. Then he had a bullet wound in his right leg, not too far below the hip, that was disabling. Howell said, 'I'm not bad hurt. Get the men out first, Bulley.' 'Ok, Hef.' About four o'clock in the afternoon, Hef was ready to go. We wanted to make sure we got him on board the hospital ship before dark. It wasn't far to the beach, maybe six or seven hundred yards. We got four of the biggest men of his platoon to handle the stretcher to get him back to the beach. They had been gone fifteen or twenty minutes, and I turned around with the field glasses to see how they were doing. They were about to go over that first ridge in from the beach, and Hef had a limb of some sort and was using it as a crutch. They were following him carrying an empty stretcher. I can understand that; Hef was a pretty good load on a stretcher, no question."

EVACUATION AND RECUPERATION. Howell was placed on the hospital ship, *USS Solace*, and shipped with a lot of other casualties to Aiea Heights Naval Hospital in Hawaii, where he stayed about a month. The hospital was well up on the heights overlooking Honolulu.

Howell recalls that the last week or two, he was able to get around on crutches and go to Honolulu. The bone in the leg was chipped, and the bullet was still there.

> They put a cast on my right hand and I remember I'd salute left-handed. Everybody would look at me and wonder what I was doing, but that was a way of doing things rather than not saluting.
> When I was at Aiea Heights in Hawaii, this fellow Shockley shows up. He was not wounded but was covered with jungle rot. It was over his whole body. Imagine having that all over your body. Oh Lord! He

was in terrible itching pain. I never saw anybody with so much fungus growth all over him. Every time I have athlete's feet or the jock itch or something like that, I remember him.

Howell was transferred from Hawaii to Oak Knoll Naval Hospital in Oakland, California, and he stayed there a few weeks.

I wanted to get closer to home and I kept asking to be transferred to some other naval hospital. They transferred me to one in New Orleans. A couple of things that happened while I was in Oakland are worth telling.

One fellow was shot in both arms and both legs, and they had him in a solid cast, all the way from his neck down his legs. His arms were out, and he had two other openings, one in front to urinate and one in the rear where he could use a bedpan. While he was in that cast, he got gonorrhea, and they had to give him penicillin to get rid of it. I reckon human beings will be human beings regardless of their circumstances. I don't know how in the world he did it.

I had grown up in Leighton with a young lady named Virginia Lile. Her brother was a good friend of mine. During the war she would occasionally write me letters. When I got to Oak Knoll she was in that area, and I had two or three dates with her. Some of us marines coming back were looking for more, but I tell you she straightened me out. She showed she was a perfect lady. You know, you were coming back from a rough time and hadn't seen girls for a long time. That had a good influence on me, and I have always had the greatest admiration for her and felt indebted to her for being a lady.

I was transferred to New Orleans Naval Hospital which was out on Lake Pontchartrain. I could move around fairly well by then, and after I was there a few days, they gave me leave to come to Alabama. I took a commercial flight, and I remember flying over Alabama and flying over Birmingham-Southern's campus. Seeing landmarks like Munger Hall and experiencing the reality of coming home gave me a great feeling of nostalgia. My folks had moved close by to Oneonta, and I stayed some with them. I had an uncle, Dr. Wyatt Heflin, in Birmingham who was an old bachelor and up in years. While I was on leave, I stayed a lot with him and visited friends and former schoolmates at Southern. Later, when I got out of the Marine Corps, I stayed with him whenever I was in Birmingham. Uncle Wyatt was a great old fellow and was an excellent surgeon. He'd been sort of a pioneer in surgery and had performed one of the first hysterectomies and splenectomies in the nation.

I went back to New Orleans after leave and stayed there five or six months. They operated on me and removed the bullet from my leg, and they put another cast on my hand. The bone didn't grow back right or something. While I was there, Hobson Adcock, one of my close friends at Southern, came in. He had some sort of illness. By that time I was pretty ambulatory, and we'd go into New Orleans, and, Lord have mercy, we would go to all the restaurants and eat! I was a captain by then and making fairly big money. I'd accumulated a couple of thousand dollars because I figured I was going on to law school and would need it.

Alabama played Duke in the Sugar Bowl on New Year's Day while I was in New Orleans. This was in 1945 and it was the first team Alabama had since the war started. Dr. Raymond Paty had been president of Birmingham-Southern and had moved to Tuscaloosa as president of the University of Alabama. I was very fond of him at Southern. I went down to Alabama's headquarters for the game and ran into him. He gave me some tickets, and Hobson and I went. Duke finally beat Alabama, but Harry Gilmer, a freshman who would leap when he passed, had almost a perfect record passing that day. He later made All-American.

Over in the army hospital close by was a friend I had known at Birmingham-Southern, Hugh Locke. He had been wounded in his legs and was really butchered up. He had to wear braces the rest of his life. He went on to law school at Alabama. Those hospitals were one of the places we learned so much about sulfur drugs and penicillin. I think that experience had an influence on me later when I was a strong supporter of the National Institutes of Health and a great admirer of the remarkable progress at UAB.

CONCLUDING MILITARY SERVICE. When Howell was discharged from the hospital, he was assigned to help in the Naval Reserve Officer Training Corps programs at five universities. Participants in NROTC were not subject to the draft, but at the end of the college program they received a reserve commission and would go on active duty.

Howell's job was to lecture on Marine Corps subjects like amphibious warfare, and he would recruit the seniors for the Marine Corps rather than the Navy. He was headquartered at Tulane University, but he spent two to three weeks each at the University of Oklahoma, Rice Institute in Houston, the University of Colorado, and the University of Texas.

> Seeing all those schools was a broadening experience. When I finished that program, they assigned me to Purdue University in West Lafayette, Indiana, to be the officer-in-charge of the Marine V-12 unit, a college program to train officers. I was there when the war ended. At Purdue they had the only black V-12 unit, and they probably wanted a Southerner to be in charge. The fellow I succeeded was from Louisiana.
>
> I figured I'd be sent back overseas because I had recuperated enough to return to combat. But V-J Day came, and Lord, we had trouble with the students! The Marine Corps always wanted to keep discipline and order, and we had to figure out how to do that the night the war ended. The students wanted to break loose and go on the town and celebrate. We finally decided just to turn them loose and to be back at a certain time.
>
> After V-J Day was announced, a fellow named Ernie Jones and I went to church. The churches were open, and people could go in and pray, thankful that the war was over. It was quite a day of celebration.

The Japanese surrendered on August 14, 1945, ending World War II. Germany had surrendered the previous May.

After the war, Howell was transferred to Camp Lejeune in North

Carolina where he taught in the officers' training program. Several blacks were in the program, and Howell believes they were the first commissioned in the Marine Corps. The armed forces were moving forward with plans to integrate the officers' corps. Before that, blacks were not allowed to volunteer for officer programs, and there was not a great deal of integration in World War II.

After the war ended, Howell wanted to get out as quickly as he could and go to law school.

> They began to process us while I was at Camp Lejeune. They had offered a regular commission to a few of us after Bougainville. I took it because I figured it might help me get promoted. This meant I had to be transferred back to reserve status, and it delayed me a little.
>
> They sent me to Millington Naval Air Station in Memphis, Tennessee, but I didn't stay there very long because I had accrued leave. I started law school at Alabama in January of 1946 while I was on leave. I was discharged in February. I stayed in the inactive reserve, but my marine service was finally terminated after I was promoted to major.

AFTERTHOUGHTS.

> There was a saying throughout the war in the Pacific that there were no atheists in foxholes, and I think that's true. When I left for the marines, my father gave me a Bible. It was a little New Testament, and I carried it in a breast pocket. I had heard of somebody who was shot right over the heart, but it went through his New Testament and saved him. So I said, "That's a pretty good idea. I think I'll keep my New Testament there, and I can read it." We did a lot of praying in combat. There was no question about that.
>
> My experience in the Marine Corps greatly broadened my views. When I went back to law school, I was asked to speak at a banquet. I told them that the outfit I headed in the Marine Corps had an American Indian and a man of East Indian background. There was every denomination and all sorts of people, Italians, Irish, northerners, farm boys,

city boys, and everything else. I said that the war experience had given us a pluralist approach towards problems and the realization that people from other parts of the country and from other races were all human beings. We should profit from this, and we should spread the beauty of diversity.

I hadn't been around Catholics very much when I was young. Bill Shockley, my friend in the Ninth Marines, didn't think much of our Protestant chaplain, and I wasn't very much impressed with him, either. Bill said, "If he's a sky pilot, I'm a hunk of crap." He used another word instead of crap. But we all had the greatest respect for and revered our Catholic chaplain. I learned that Catholics were not demons but were just like me. That gave me some thoughts about all the anti-Catholicism things, particularly in regards to my Uncle Tom's position on those. While I had great love and respect for Uncle Tom, I developed a conviction that he was wrong on all that.

Howell's war experiences led him to question the need for most wars.

You have all emotions in a war, and you see your friends and companions killed. In retrospect, you always wonder whether wars accomplish anything. Of course we were attacked in World War II, and there was no question that we were dealing with a bad situation with Hitler desiring to conquer the world and the Japanese wanting to control everything in the Pacific and the Far East.

I just wonder whether many of the wars we've participated in were caused by hotheads and not justified. I'm not sure that our participation in World War I was really justified. What were America's interests, and what did we need to protect? I don't say we were not justified in doing it, I just think it was a close call. I'm not an isolationist; I know you have to go to war at times. I supported Desert Storm, but I did a lot of soul-searching before making the decision. I supported going into Bosnia, but I did a lot of soul-searching on that, too.

Regarding the atomic bomb, Howell has no doubt about the wisdom of using it. "If Japan hadn't surrendered when they did, I would have been back in the Pacific when we landed on Japan. I give credit that I'm alive today to Harry Truman and his decision to drop the bomb. I think a lot of marines and a lot army people do, too."

Howell had a great experience related to his war days when he was in the Senate. He was on a trip to the Philippines with some other senators, and they had to refuel in Guam. The House of Representatives member from Guam had been in the Marine Corps and had retired as a Brigadier General. He let some people in Guam know that the plane would stop. Howell recounts what happened. "Lord, we were met with a band and a big delegation. They started making a big fuss over me as the 'Great Liberator.' They said they wanted to show me where I landed and the place where I was probably wounded. Then we went down to the beach. The governor of Guam was there, and they had a big sign that said, 'Lieutenant Howell Heflin, Liberator of Guam, 1944.' There must have been 300 or 400 Guamians. They made speeches and had a big ceremony. It was very touching."

Howell Heflin was awarded the Silver Star, the nation's third highest military honor. The citation, signed by Secretary of the Navy James Forrestal, reads:

> For conspicuous gallantry and intrepidity as Commanding Officer of an Assault Platoon attached to a company of the First Battalion, Ninth Marines, Third Marine Division, during the Battle of Piva Forks, Bougainville, Solomon Islands, on November 25, 1943. When his men were subjected to intense fire from hostile mortars and automatic weapons while advancing on a strongly organized and defended Japanese position, First Lieutenant Heflin promptly and skillfully deployed his platoon and courageously led it through difficult jungle terrain under a barrage of grenades and gunfire to the edge of the enemy's position. Directing his troops in a vigorous, prolonged battle, he frequently exposed himself to devastating fire at close range in order to control the attack more effectively and, by his unflinching determination and aggressive fighting spirit, contributed materially to the defeat of

the enemy and the attainment of his company's objectives. First Lieutenant Heflin's expert leadership and fearless conduct under extremely hazardous conditions were in keeping with the highest traditions of the United States Naval Service.

7

Learning Law

IN THE CLOSING MONTHS of World War II, Congress passed legislation that changed American society forever. The Servicemen's Readjustment Act, known more popularly as the "GI Bill of Rights," was signed into law by President Franklin D. Roosevelt on June 22, 1944. The GI Bill was a major factor in turning America into a postwar economic superpower.

The GI Bill of Rights created the largest middle class in the world, and many famous people have credited the program with providing an opportunity they would otherwise have missed. Among those helped by the GI bill are Robert Dole, Harry Belafonte, Art Buchwald, Nobel Prize Laureate Martin Perl, historian William Leuchtenberg, and economist Andrew Brimmer. The GI Bill of Rights has been called the greatest piece of American legislation in the twentieth century.[1] In supporting the GI Bill, the government paid some $14.5 billion in benefits.

One effect of the GI Bill was to put tremendous pressure on the nation's colleges and universities. In the late 1930s about 160,000 U.S. citizens had graduated from college each year. In almost four years of war, the colleges and universities had made few changes because a great proportion of the country's energy went into the war effort. Higher education remained as it had been in 1941, when it had relatively small enrollments.

Fifteen million veterans had served in the war in the United States, and the GI Bill provided them with one free year of higher education for each ninety days of service, up to a total of four years or forty-eight months in school. It also guaranteed housing and business loans.

In 1947, veterans accounted for 49 percent of U.S. college enrollments. By 1950, total college enrollment had increased to 500,000. Schools were short of space and faculty, and they used all manner of temporary structures, including no-longer-needed military barracks. This was the situation at the University of Alabama in January 1946 when Howell Heflin arrived to attend law school. The school offered a year-round program to accommodate returning veterans, and he was able to graduate with an L.L.D. degree in March 1948.

Howell had known that he wanted to go to law school since his undergraduate days at Birmingham-Southern College. He believes that his small-town upbringing helped lead him into the legal profession. There was less entertainment in those days, and he spent a lot of time at the courthouse listening to trials. Another influential factor was the fact that he had three uncles who were lawyers, and one had been a U.S. Senator.

THE SCHOOL AND STUDENT BODY. When Heflin arrived at law school, Dr. Raymond Paty was president of the University of Alabama. Paty had been at Emory before becoming president of Birmingham-Southern College, and then had been selected as president by the University. Heflin thinks it is interesting that he had the same president for undergraduate and law school at two different institutions. He thought highly of Paty and felt that the law school at Alabama had excellent professors.

> When I first arrived, we had Dean William Hepburn who was a philosopher, and then Leigh Harrison became the dean. He was as fine a teacher as you'd ever have. Another professor who comes to mind was Jay Murphy who provided an atmosphere for legal education that was rare. He was very liberal. On the other hand, we had Dr. John Masters and General Morrisette, who were of the old school and very conserva-

tive. A wide variety of professors provided a great atmosphere for returning veterans, most of whom were serious minded.

Heflin recalls that the law school used the honor system, which was rigorously enforced by the students. Exams could be taken wherever the student chose.

Most of the students in law school when Howell entered were GIs who were back from the service. They were in their mid-twenties or later, and they were serious students who wanted to get on with their educations. They had been in service four or five years, and they wanted to get out, make a living, and get on with life.

Still, they were veterans, and they'd go off and have big parties. Sometimes we would come unprepared to classes. But we had a remarkable group of people in law school, including Frank Samford, Jr., who was later the head of Torchmark Corporation, and Ryan de Graffenried, who became a popular politician and opposed and might have beaten George Wallace, except he was killed in an airplane crash. John Patterson was elected Attorney General and Governor.

Several of my classmates became Congressmen, including George Huddleston, Jr., and Armisted Selden. Selden later served as Ambassador to New Zealand. A number went on to become circuit judges, justices and judges in the Alabama appellate system. J. Foy Guin and Bert Haltom became federal judges. They were all successful. Others who did well in law included classmates like Frank Dominick, Doug Corretti, Herndon Inge, Richard Poellnitz, Ralph Gaines, Drew Redden, Bob Smith, Pat Richardson, Gordon Rosen, Bill Moore, Charlie Adair, Sam Earle Hobbs, Jane Kimbrough Dishuck, and many others. Roy Green, who lived upstairs from me, ended up in Phenix City owning a television system, a newspaper, and two or three banks. He's done exceptionally well and is a good friend. Camille Cook became a professor at law school. Conrad Fowler became a district attorney and probate judge, and he served as president of the National Association of County Officials.

The University of Alabama, like other colleges and universities in the post-war period, was short of trained faculty, and to fill the gap, the administration turned to returning veterans who had a college degree, partly because they knew the veterans were mature. Starting after his first semester, Howell taught two political science classes to undergraduates.

> I'd been a political science major at Birmingham-Southern. A lot of law students were teaching, including Sam Earle Hobbs who was later President Pro Tem of the Board of Trustees of the University Alabama, Hobson Adcock and Drew Redden. I taught two years at Alabama and was happy for the experience. Also, it provided extra income.
>
> Nelle Lee, later known as Harper Lee, was in law school with us. She went by Nelle then. Her sister, Alice, has been a great lawyer down in Monroeville, and their father before them was a lawyer. Harper wrote *To Kill a Mockingbird* with its story of Atticus Finch, and her legal background helped. She was editor of the monthly magazine, the *Rammer Jammer*, while she was at Alabama. She had a lot of writing ability.

Two college presidents and a law school dean came out of Howell's class. Jeff Bennett was later president of The University of the South in Sewanee, Tennessee, Robert Guilott became president of the University of North Alabama, and Tom Christopher was later dean of the law school at Alabama. Howell says that all were great friends.

> Tom named his son Thomas Heflin Christopher. He built the new law school building at Alabama. It's a lovely building, and they have really kept it up. It was designed by Edward Durell Stone, a famous architect. It is well appointed and has many portraits. Tom Christopher was also dean of the law school at the University of New Mexico.

STUDENT LIFE. The GI bill paid enough that a student could live on it and pay tuition.

It wouldn't be a high type of living, but you had enough to eat three meals a day and pay for a room. I qualified for enhanced benefits from the GI Bill because I had been wounded, and I had savings bonds plus money I had sent home from overseas. That was the richest I'd ever been, and I thought I was in real good financial shape. A lot of times, if I had a date or something, I'd rent a car. I didn't own one. They were an expensive investment, and you could hardly buy them for a while. I was flying high then, but it didn't last too long.

His first roommate at Alabama was George Huddleston, Jr. He and George found an apartment in a house.

There was an upstairs, and two of my friends, Roy Green and Peyton Finch, lived there. George and I lived downstairs. The owner, Mrs. Lamont, had a double bed in our bedroom. George was a small fellow, and I was as big as the double bed. When I'd lie down, he'd be on an incline and would roll down. After about two days of sleeping in that double bed, he told Mrs. Lamont he was going to have to move unless she got some twin beds. She got twin beds.

Huddleston and I finally bought an automobile for $125. It was an old Buick. We called it "Oklahoma," because it burned more oil than there was in the state of Oklahoma, and it looked like the cars the Okies used to get to California. Also, it had a much greater variety of sounds than the musical "Oklahoma." We would use Oklahoma to drive down to Nick's at Knoxville. That was the beer joint in Greene County. We had to go there because Tuscaloosa was dry in those days. We'd go down to Nick's at Knoxville, and sometimes we'd go on down to Eutaw and to the Cotton Patch and few places like that.

In school we'd play poker and drink a little bit. Only once or twice did any of us drink too much. When he was overseas, Fowler would play poker. I don't know if it was at the end of law school, but at some stage of his life, he changed. He never drank anything else, and he has never played any poker. I never did have much of a gambling streak in me, so that's probably the last time that I played, too.

I also smoked cigars while I was at the University. When we were overseas we'd sit around playing poker or shooting the bull or something, and we'd smoke cigars. That got me started. I smoked cigars for 40 years till I had my heart problem, and my cardiologist at UAB, Dr. Gerald Pohost, made me stop. Now I chew them.

After Huddleston graduated, Howell moved to the Lamba Chi fraternity house and roomed a while with Bill Brown, who later became a minister. Another roommate was Tom Christopher, who had graduated from Washington and Lee, had taught in the Army, and was teaching in the ROTC program at Tuscaloosa. He and Heflin were in the same law class.

At the same time, Howell had some cousins who were students at the University of Alabama. One was Samuel Strudwick Norvell, known as "Tut." Another was Martha Thigpen from Tuscumbia, who introduced Howell to Elizabeth Ann Carmichael, an undergraduate student in the School of Education.

The late Bob Morrisette, who was in undergraduate school at the time, became a good friend. He was editor of the *Atmore Advance*, a small town newspaper, and he owned and operated a printing company. Later, he was office manager for Heflin's Senate office in Mobile.

CAMPUS POLITICS AND ACTIVITIES. Howell made quite an impression on his fellow law school students, and he continued to develop the speaking skills which would later serve him so well. Bill McDonald, a law school classmate and former editorial page editor of *The Montgomery Advertiser* recalled Heflin as "a magnificent raconteur."[2]

Howell was well thought of by the law school faculty. In the summer of 1947, he co-edited a law school handbook, and he was named Alabama's "Student of the Week" on March 14, 1948, when he was a senior.[3]

During an annual spoof with skits put on by various campus student organizations, Howell took the role of Governor "Big Jim" Folsom drunkenly presiding over a University of Alabama Board of Trustees meeting. Howell's high-pitched hill country twang brought the house down.[4]

Classmate Bert Haltom remembers Howell impersonating Folsom. "The first time I ever remember seeing him was on the steps of a building right in the heart of the campus, and he was doing a take-off on Big Jim. He had a great big black hat on, and he was talking like Jim did in all of his speeches. Heflin did a pretty darn good imitation on the steps before all the students."

Howell's longtime casual interest in politics was nurtured by his popularity in the service and in law school. He became active in campus politics at Alabama and he and classmate (later to be attorney general, governor, and judge) John Patterson worked together in the campaigns of slates of successful candidates for Student Government Association offices.[5]

Howell became friends at law school with Marc Ray Clements, a lawyer in Tuscaloosa who was very astute politically and who later became a behind-the-scenes mover on the statewide Alabama political scene. "Foots" Clements, as he was known, was a political advisor to Lister Hill, John Sparkman, and many others.

Howell says that he was sympathetic with the philosophy of Foots Clements and his group against the "big mules," as the big industrialists and land owners in Alabama were called. At the time, James E. "Big Jim" Folsom sometimes called "Kissing Jim" for his propensity to kiss every pretty girl in sight, was governor.

> I liked Big Jim's philosophy and some of the things he did, but I thought he was a disgrace to the state with his drunkenness, his female activities, and all of that. Several times I portrayed Big Jim in skits, and once I did it in a parade. Later I came around and supported him in some races.
>
> An interesting character in campus politics was Richmond Flowers. Richmond was an SAE and his fraternity brother and close friend was Claude Kirk. In the 1948 election, Claude was chairman of the Young

Democrats of the University of Alabama and was for Harry Truman. Richmond was the chairman of Republicans for Dewey. Claude and Richmond did a lot of fussing and made speeches. Richmond and Claude went to political rallies all over the place. The irony is that they switched parties in later years; Richmond made a big success as a Democrat, and Claude was Republican Governor of Florida.

In the 1948 national election, race was a major political issue. President Truman had integrated the armed services and had appointed the Fair Employment Practices Board, moves which highly incensed Southerners. The Democratic platform that year had a strong civil rights plank, and Democrats in Alabama threatened to pull out of the party.

Heflin was in his last term in law school as these events were unfolding, and he followed them with great interest. There was a big battle in the Democratic primary in Alabama as to who the national presidential electors would be. Loyalists had a slate of electors pledged to Truman, while Dixiecrats, who were mad about the civil rights stand of the national Democratic party, offered a different slate. Heflin was in the loyalist Hill-Sparkman group.

> I appeared with a panel group on some state-wide radio network supporting Truman. But the Dixiecrat movement won and got their slate on the ballot. You couldn't vote for Truman in Alabama in 1948 because the Democratic electors were pledged to support Strom Thurmond.
>
> Some friends and I went up to Birmingham to the Dixiecrat convention. We were up in the balcony, and they were all carrying on in the convention manner. Later some friends who were hot Dixiecrats said, "I watched you. You wouldn't clap or do anything." I answered, "I'm a Truman Democrat." Strom Thurmond and Fielding Wright carried Alabama that year. George Wallace, who was just getting started in Alabama politics, was against that Dixiecrat slate. He was at the Democratic National Convention in 1948 when a bunch of the Alabama delegation walked out. George didn't walk out.

ELIZABETH ANN AND TUSCUMBIA. Howell met his future wife, Elizabeth Ann, while he was in law school. They had several dates, but the relationship didn't get serious. He says he went with several girls at the time.

Elizabeth Ann remembers meeting him at a sorority house which was next to the Alpha Delta Gamma house where she lived. "Howell's cousin, Martha Thigpen, lived next door. We had grown up together in Tuscumbia. Her mother was there, and I went over to see Big Martha. Howell was either there or came about the same time I did to see Big Martha, and that's when I met him.

"It never entered my head that this was the guy I was going to marry. No, no, no, no, no. That never entered my head. It was not love at first sight. At that time everybody dated everybody else. You know, nobody dated anybody special all the time. You dated around. I dated around until I got engaged."

After he graduated, Howell had the task of selecting where he would move and set up law practice. Leighton, where he graduated from high school, was a small town with limited possibilities, and his father and mother had moved from there to Birmingham. He was looking for a location with good possibilities for building a law practice, and in the back of his mind was involvement with politics.

He thought of Birmingham, the state's largest city.

> I had a friend in Birmingham, Douglas Arant, who was a remarkable individual. Arant was in one of the big corporate law firms, and he influenced a lot of young people. He had been the editor of the *Yale Law Review*. I talked with him about what to do after I finished. Arant helped a number of people, including Paul Hardin, who was recently interim president at UAB; David Vann, former mayor of Birmingham; Jim North; and Dayton Nabers, who is now president of Protective Life.
>
> Arant was very conservative on business matters, but he was very progressive on race and matters generally of social importance. He offered me a position in his law firm, but he told me that I would

eventually go into politics and should select some place which would be good for that.

I talked to Foots Clements, and he gave me what I think was excellent advice. He said, "Don't worry about where you're going to practice law, whether there are too many lawyers or not enough or whatever. Go where you think you want to live and be happy." I had lived in Colbert County, and I had some relatives here. I liked North Alabama. Clement said, "Don't worry about it. You'll develop your law practice. It will come to you wherever you are." He was right. If you have your roots in an area and you like the community and the people who live there, that's where you ought to live.

He and George Huddleston checked the Tuscumbia area with a survey of sales tax increases over the years and some indices of growth. It looked to them like a growth area. Another plus was that his Aunt Helen Norvell and two cousins lived in the area.

He had friends in Leighton, and had roots in that section of Alabama. He ruled out Birmingham and finally narrowed his decision to Talladega County or Tuscumbia, and then he chose the latter. Howell admits that Elizabeth Ann also influenced his decision to locate in Tuscumbia.

While Elizabeth Ann influenced him in locating his law practice, getting married was not on the immediate horizon.

> I grew up believing you ought not to think about marriage until you could support a wife. In those days wives didn't work. Oh, a few put their husbands through law school or medical school. Those who put them through medical school often ended in divorce. The doctors get "wandering eyes" for the nurses.

In the fall of 1948, Howell Heflin, fresh out of law school, moved to Tuscumbia, Alabama, to set up his practice and get on with life.

8

Debut of a Country Lawyer

Howell Heflin did not move to Tuscumbia immediately after graduating from law school, for he was still not absolutely certain where he wanted to settle permanently. He visited various locations from April to the end of August in 1948, and he entertained offers from several law firms. Then he visited Tuscumbia to look around and talk, and he decided it was the place. He also decided to open his own law practice rather than joining an existing firm.

In the interim, he worked with Karl Harrison, a lawyer and banker in Columbiana, Alabama. Harrison was executive director of the Alabama Crusade for Children. Howell worked as Harrison's assistant on the Crusade and had the title of field director. He describes the organization as "sort of a United Way," which was raising money. "I traveled over the state visiting lawyers and friends that I knew," Howell says, "and I tried to get them involved in raising money. We raised a little, but not any tremendous amount."

Settling in Tuscumbia. In the fall of 1948, Howell Heflin, age twenty-seven, set up practice as a "country lawyer" in his new home. Tuscumbia is in the northwest corner of Alabama, about ten miles west of Leighton where Heflin had graduated from high school. It is part of the Shoals area, which includes Colbert and Lauderdale counties and is home of the "Quad Cities" of Alabama: Florence, Muscle Shoals,

Sheffield, and Tuscumbia. The Shoals takes its name from a rocky stretch of the Tennessee River where mussels were plentiful and river traffic was restricted much of the year. The completion of Wilson Dam in 1925 opened the river to year-round navigation.

The Tennessee River has played an important role in the area's history and development. Florence, the largest of the four cities, is north of the river in Lauderdale County, and the other three cities are south of the river in Colbert County. The four cities, which have contiguous borders, form the Florence metropolitan area (the most recent census data showed populations of, respectively, Florence, 36,426; Tuscumbia, 8,413; Muscle Shoals, 9,611; and Sheffield, 10,380).

Tuscumbia is the smallest of the four and was the birthplace of Helen Keller, who was born on June 27, 1880. A childhood illness in 1882 took her sight and hearing. Through the work of teacher Anne Sullivan, Helen grasped the meaning of language, and she learned to read braille and to speak. Helen Keller graduated from Radcliffe in 1904. Her writings, charitable works, and unbelievable ability to overcome deafness and blindness made her world famous.

Charles Carmichael, Elizabeth Ann's first cousin and a prominent attorney in Tuscumbia, notes that Tuscumbia was a railroad town when Heflin started practice. The Southern Railway was powerful and important because the river was not navigable due to the shoals.

THE START OF PRACTICE. Howell remembers that first year of practicing law was tough. There were about fourteen lawyers in Colbert County then; now there are about sixty.

> I had an old office upstairs, and I paid fifteen dollars a month rent. It had an old-timey oil heater. We didn't have air conditioning in the summertime, and it was hot! I had an old circular fan trying to keep a little cool. There was a cotton gin about two blocks away, and in ginning season, the lint would come in. I'd open the windows, and that lint would just cover my desk and papers. And I was breathing the stuff!
>
> At first we didn't have any screens, but we finally put some up. The

people who managed the building didn't want to make any improvements. It was old, and they didn't want to spend money on it. The fellow who owned it was Louis Rosenbaum, who owned the theaters and a lot of real estate in the area. He had turned it over to a fellow who wouldn't spend a dime. Good Lord, he was tight! I finally went to Rosenbaum, and he told the manager to make some improvements. Rosenbaum turned out to be a good friend of mine.

In 1964, when Howell hired future partner Charles Rosser, he was still in the same office. Rosser says, "You had to climb up long steps to get to it. The building was very old, and the rooms were not well lit. The lights were big ol' 100- or 200-watt bulbs hanging six to eight feet down on a cord from the ceiling, and they were right up over your head with no shade. There was very little control over the temperature. The place had four offices: a library, Mr. Heflin's office, the secretary's office, and an office used by associates. Across the hall was an old dark room with no lights where we stored dead files and other things. Dust was an inch thick. It was a real pain to go into that old room and retrieve anything, mainly because there were no lights. Everybody in town made fun of our offices, but they didn't make fun of the lawyers in them."

A beginning lawyer doesn't ordinarily get cases until he or she is known in the community. Meantime, something has to be done to survive. It helps if the beginner starts in his or her home town, of course. Howell wasn't at home, but Leighton was only ten miles away, and his first fee came from a high school acquaintance there.

> I wrote a deed for a friend from school named Milan Smallwood. As I recall I charged him four dollars. I wrote a few deeds for other people I went to high school with. Jim Kirk Fennel, a farmer I knew out in Leighton, was comparatively wealthy. He told me, "I'm going to give you my business." He gave me a good deal of work, with more deeds and things like that.

Howell's friend Ed Mauldin says the people in Leighton welcomed

Howell back with open arms. "Everybody in Leighton thought, 'Our lawyer has come back to take care of us.' He had done his part in the war overseas and came back as a hero. He was a graduate of Birmingham-Southern and the University of Alabama Law School, and everybody was very proud of him.

"If people in Leighton had a problem, they would go to Howell. He did a marvelous job for everybody. Of course, in Leighton there was not much law practice because folks were not very litigious with each other. They were mostly friends. What litigation they had in their business and personal lives was usually with people outside the community. I regarded Howell's service to the people of Leighton as more of a service than a revenue producer for him, and I expect he did, too.

"During that time, when we both came back and were getting established, we spent time together and really got acquainted. Anytime I needed any legal work done, I enlisted his help. We used his assistance in legal work before the bank actually needed much help. My uncle had a rather sizable estate for the times, and there were a lot of affairs to attend to."

Bert Haltom, a local attorney who was becoming a good friend, also helped. "He opened up solo and didn't have much law practice," Haltom recalls. "I was with a firm here which handled a lot of collections. We had worlds of collections in Tuscumbia, so I called Heflin and asked him if he would like to handle those and take whatever fee was permissible. Boy, he took it eagerly and did it for a good while. It was a tedious, dry kind of work. People get a letter from a lawyer and it scares them into paying."

Heflin's first litigation cases were court appointments, and as he notes, lawyers didn't make much money on appointed cases.

> The first year I'm sure I took in less than $1,200. Under the GI bill, if you were starting a business, they guaranteed you something like $100 a month. A couple of months I drew the difference between what I made and the $100. The first year wasn't much.
>
> I was the first president of the Alabama Law School Alumni Association in 1949, and I went back and made a speech to the students

urging them to join. I told them I brought them "greetings from the very active practice of law. I've made some good fees, including one for five dollars and a few smaller ones." That got a big laugh, but in those days, five-dollar fees were pretty good.

Charles Rosser, later Howell's law partner, recalls rummaging around the office after Howell became chief justice. "I found some old account books where he recorded his early fees, and those books were right interesting. During the early periods of his law practice, he would record a fee of $2.50 or $6.50 or a payment of $3 on an $8 fee."

In time, things began to improve. Howell had some success with the appointed criminal cases. He began to develop a reputation as a trial lawyer, and this helped him get civil cases. "People began to recognize his effectiveness with the jury in the criminal cases he handled," Bert Haltom says. "Those cases got a lot of publicity."

SUPPLEMENTING THE INCOME. Howell's experience teaching at the University of Alabama helped him in his first years at Tuscumbia. Florence State Teachers College (now the University of North Alabama), was just a few miles away, and it had a shortage of trained teachers. From 1948 to 1952, Heflin says he "kept the wolf away from the door" by teaching early-morning classes in government and political science, as he had done at the University of Alabama while in law school. By mid-morning, he would be back in his office practicing law.

A big break came when he was appointed executive director of the Tuscumbia Housing Authority.

> This was fairly early in my law practice, about 1950. The people on the housing authority picked me out and wanted to know if I was interested in it. At that time there were not a lot of young lawyers here. The chairman of the Housing Authority was Dr. Loren Gary, and there was a druggist named A. E. Ray on it. I was always friendly with Dr. Gary and his wife as well as with the Rays. Working with the Housing Authority helped me financially.

The government had a public housing program during Truman's administration. There were a lot of questions about socialism at the time and whether or not this was a step in that direction. The city government appointed five people to the Housing Authority, and they appointed me as executive director. We ended up building housing projects in the black community and in the white community. One housing project was named Dr. Davis Homes after a very fine black physician.

I operated those units for several years as the executive director. We had to file applications to build the units, and then we would issue bonds on the authority. Part of the job was collecting rents, and it had its down side because you would have to evict some. The ones evicted were the types of people that would have problems and get in court, and it may be that being involved with them helped my law practice. The work supplemented my income. It paid me $85 a week, which was big money then.

About 1952 we issued some bonds, and we had to go to New York to sign the bonds and finalize the transactions. Dr. Gary drove, and the party included his wife, me, and my wife. He was a character. If he was riding in the car and not driving, he'd get car sick. So he drove all the way up and all the way back. On the way back home, we got on Highway 20 which comes from Decatur to Tuscumbia. We were crossing a bridge at Town Creek, which is the dividing line between Colbert and Lawrence County, and lo and behold, a large number of mules ran out into the highway. Gary just plowed into them. He didn't kill any, but it damaged the car some. He had to phone and get his brother, who was another doctor, to come and take us in. It didn't hurt any of us, but the car just wouldn't run. I remember I was asleep in the back seat, and all of a sudden, I heard his wife holler, "Loren, Loren, Loren!!!" I woke up, and all I could see were the rear ends of mules.

The Housing Authority was just one of several appointments that Howell received early in his career, and it is obvious that he was making a good impression in Tuscumbia. He was civic-minded and active in the community, and he was elected president of the Kiwanis Club in 1952. Howell was appointed chairman of the Tuscumbia City Board of Education in 1952, and he served ten years.

His financial condition was improving, and he finally bought a car, a new Ford which promptly burned up during a trip to Mobile for a football game. He recalls that he had Traveler's Insurance and the car burned up in the yard of the Traveler's lawyer in Mobile.

ELIZABETH ANN. Tuscumbia was the hometown of Elizabeth Ann Carmichael, whom Howell had met in college, and she was back in north Alabama teaching school when Howell moved there. Like Howell's, Elizabeth Ann's family had a history of public service. Her great-grandfather, J. M. Carmichael, was a circuit judge in the Wiregrass section of Alabama. Her grandfather, Archie Carmichael, was a member of the 1901 Alabama Constitutional Convention and was Speaker of the Alabama House of Representatives in the 1920s. From 1933 to 1937, he served two terms in Congress. Elizabeth Ann's father was Jesse Malcolm Carmichael, and her mother was Elizabeth Mary Weille. Elizabeth Ann was born in New Castle, Pennsylvania, where her father was working at the time, but the family then moved back to Alabama.

She had an unusual experience visiting an uncle in Boston. The uncle was a pioneer in otolaryngology. He had a private practice, and he also taught at Harvard Medical School. He had many famous patients such as Helen Hayes, Katherine Hepburn, and Spencer Tracy.

"I had spent the summer with them," Elizabeth Ann recalls. "I went up in June when school was out, and a polio epidemic broke out here after I left. It still was going on at the end of summer, and my uncle said, 'No indeed, you're not going home.' I said, 'I've got to. I've got to go to school.' He said, 'No, you can go to school here.' He called Mother and told her that he wasn't letting me come home.

"I was a junior in high school, and he wanted to enroll me in a private school with his children. I said, 'No, Uncle Francis. I don't want to go to private school. If you ever get me in private school, you'll never let me out of here.' So, I insisted I go to public school. He nearly had a fit. You didn't go to public school in Boston if you could help it. But I did.

"I went in and dumb me, I thought, 'This is the biggest school I ever saw in my life for so few people.' The first day there were not a hundred people in the school. The Jewish students were all out for the Jewish holiday. When they came the next day, I nearly got trampled to death. I was really caught in a big crowd. The student body was at least 90 percent Jewish.

"My uncle's chauffeur took me to school every day and picked me up every day, and if you think I didn't cause conversation! Everybody wondered, 'What's she doing here?' But I went, and I stayed until frost. I went in a month late, and everybody was way ahead of me. I took what I would be taking here, basically, but I had to play catch-up. Then when I came home, I was ahead in the classes.

Howell says he had his eye on her after he moved to Tuscumbia.

> I was in pursuit pretty good. She would come back home on weekends, and I would date her then. Sometimes I'd go over to Huntsville where she taught. She was there a couple of years, and in 1950, she came back home to Deshler High School. I might have had dates with other girls, but I don't remember anybody in particular. Well, I did have dates with some girls in Florence, but I was primarily in pursuit of Elizabeth Ann. We dated a year or two until I'd made some money.

Howell had become executive director of the Housing Commission before he and Elizabeth Ann married. Women ordinarily did not work after they were married, and Howell felt he had to be able to support her before they could marry. Howell had lived in a garage apartment from September 1948 until he got married. It had one room and a bathroom with a shower. His law practice was increasing, but he wouldn't have had what he considered enough to support a wife without the Housing Commission position.

Howell remembers proposing after the Alabama-Auburn football game in 1951. "We were parked on a street up on Red Mountain in

Birmingham. You could park and see the valley with all the lights on and neon lights. It was beautiful, and I got romantic and proposed right there."

Elizabeth Ann recalls, "He gave me my ring on my birthday, December 5, and we got married the next February. Howell wanted to be married in December. He wanted me to be a tax deduction, and I said, 'Nope.'"

"I figured it was a way to save," Howell explains. "I could have filed a joint return if we had married before the first of the year and could have saved enough money to pay for the honeymoon and a few other things."

Howell and Elizabeth Ann were married on February 23, 1952. "I can remember the date," he says, "though she has to remind me every once in a while. Our son, Tom, reminds me if I've forgotten." After Howell and Elizabeth Ann were married, she resigned her teaching position.

They moved immediately into their own home. He explains:

> We bought a little house up in Carmichael Terrace, a little development which was named for her folks. The G.I. bill helped me get a loan. It wasn't a mortgage. I never did have a mortgage on any house or property or anything else. The loan was at four percent interest. I still had some money in savings from World War II; there was some other money from my earnings in a savings account. I pledged the savings account as security for payment of the loan. We bought the house a month or two before our wedding, and we'd already put things in it. After we came back from our honeymoon, we just moved in.

"I remember the first dinner party we ever had," Elizabeth Ann says. "Howell didn't show. He was at a church meeting."

Howell recalls that he was chairman of the Pastoral Relations Committee of the church and there was opposition to a candidate to be the new pastor. The Methodist conference, meanwhile, was meeting over in Huntsville, and Heflin was involved in the lengthy negotiations. In the midst of this, Elizabeth Ann had asked him to pick up some pies in

Courtland for her dinner party. He did, and then promptly returned to the negotiations.

"Chess pies were to be picked up by him and brought home. He brought them home, all right. He walked in the front door and out the back. Just never slowed down. Gone. I could have killed him on the spot," Elizabeth Ann remembers.

The newlyweds had another problem. Howell came from a long line of Methodists, and Elizabeth Ann's maternal side of the family had just as long a history as Episcopalians. Elizabeth Ann decided initially that she would become a Methodist, but she decided otherwise in a short time. Howell explains why:

> I was elected to be a delegate to the General Conference of the Methodist church. This was in 1952, right after we got married. We went to San Francisco where the general conference was meeting. All the preachers were there, and they were all politicking. There was a lot of in-fighting among them. She said, "I am not going to get into that. I'm going to stay an Episcopalian." So I think I made mistake in carrying her to San Francisco and letting her see all of the in-fighting among the preachers. She thought they were all men of God and above internal Methodist politics and all of that, and she found out that they weren't. She didn't think it was Christ-like. So she decided then that she wasn't going to join. She may have been hunting for an excuse. I wouldn't be a bit surprised.
>
> She and her mother had gone to the Episcopal Church in Tuscumbia and in Sheffield where she grew up. They didn't have good cars because of the war effort, and they'd ride the streetcar to church. I think she had a feeling that her mother wouldn't be able to go to church, and she ought to stay with her mother.
>
> I never considered going to the Episcopal Church. My father was a Methodist minister, and I was active in my church here. I was a Florence-district lay leader and was a delegate for several years to the Jurisdictional Conference at Lake Junaluska where they elect bishops. My daddy was still alive at that time. If I had gone over to the Episcopal

church, it would have killed him. He didn't like the idea that our son, Tom, grew up in the Episcopal church. We've adapted well. I go with her some, and she goes with me some. She reads my bulletin to see who's sick and in the hospital and who is this and that.

The Heflins had an unusual cook.

Her name was Annie Mae Peters, and she was big, fat, and black. If I was defending some black in a criminal case, Annie Mae would have an opinion one way or the other. She'd go down and listen to the cases. She cooked our main meal, which we ate at night, and she was supposed to be at our house at four o'clock. Well, she'd go to the courtroom and listen to cases, and she wouldn't get to the house on time. If I was trying a case, she'd listen in on it for sure. She knew all about them, and she'd give me hell. She didn't like some of the blacks I was defending and thought they were guilty as the devil. "Why are you defending that sorry, no-good . . ." She tried to tell me what to do.

"Annie Mae just died recently," Elizabeth Ann recalls. "She never hesitated to tell you what she thought. Every time I went to the nursing home to see her, she'd look to see what I had on. I'd ask, 'Do you like it?' She'd say, 'It's fine. I like that.' I said, 'And if you didn't, you'd sure tell me, wouldn't you?' She said, 'You know I would.'

"One time she whopped our son Tom on top of the head when he came home from school and asked her what a nigger was. She said, 'Where did you hear that?' He'd heard it at school, and he wanted to know what it was." "The remarkable thing," Howell adds, "was that he had never heard that at home. He had never heard that word until he went to the first grade in school."

"Once he was sitting on the side steps, the Cave Street side of our house, watching the traffic and all," Elizabeth Ann recalls. "There was a wreck on the corner. Annie Mae came charging out to get Tom. He said, 'I saw it! I saw it!' He was just screaming. She said, 'You didn't see a thing, Tom. Come on in the house with me.' He kept saying, 'But I saw it Annie

Mae.' She said, 'I'm not having that child go to court.'"

EARLY CASES. Howell remembers the first case he tried. He was appointed to represent a black man who was accused of murdering his wife. Howell calls it the "scissors case."

> My client was from somewhere around Cherokee in the west end of the county. The prosecution was making a case that he'd killed his wife, and he claimed was that it was self-defense. She had come at him with a pair of open scissors, he said, and he was fighting her off and hit her over the head. The members of her family said she wasn't the type of woman who would ever fight and that he was mean and everything else. She was examined in death by a doctor who testified she had the scissors in the hand, but the prosecution argued that the defendant had placed them there.
>
> To get around the claim that my client planted the scissors, I had to establish that she was clutching the scissors and that, after rigor mortis had set in, they could not have been placed in the position in which she was holding them. I did this through the doctor who examined her body. My client was charged with first degree murder, but we ended up with a jury verdict of manslaughter with eight years. This was a big victory. It was my first case, and it got people saying, "He's going to make a good trial lawyer."
>
> A little later, I had a case which involved a woman named Lucinda Moore. She was a great big, fat woman and was known as "Big Mamma." She was one of the most foul-mouthed women I have ever known. She was charged with assault to commit murder, and we got her off light, but she still had to serve some time. They were short of space in the state penitentiary, and Big Mamma had to spend the time in the Colbert County Jail. Well, she was the only person in that cell, and she came up pregnant. I asked her, "How in the world?" She says, "We did it through the bars."
>
> She said, "I put myself in a position." Can you imagine having intercourse between bars? I don't remember too much about her case,

but I remember her getting pregnant. Old people may need Viagra, but young people don't. Big Mamma had a baby, and I think she got out of jail about the time she had it. Human beings are going to get together one way or another. You can't stop it.

When I'd been in practice a few years, I had a criminal case which involved a place out here they called the Log Cabin. It was a beer joint and everything else. The fellow who ran it was Willie Young, and the Budweiser distributor was named McGee. They got into some sort of feud, and there was bad blood. McGee and his two sons came over to Young's place. The word went out to Young that McGee and his two boys were after him, and he went and got a shotgun. McGee came in, and they had a gunfight. One of the McGee boys was killed and another one wounded. Old man McGee, the Budweiser distributor, was not injured. Lord, it was the hot topic of Colbert County. The courthouse was crowded during the trial. Colbert County has gone wet and dry at various times, and it was wet at that time. This case was probably one reason it went back dry.

I defended Young in the case, and we ended up trying it several days. The Judge wanted to finish the case, and we ended up with the jury returning a verdict at four o'clock in the morning. They were out about three hours, and they found Young not-guilty. The Youngs had money, and they had paid me a pretty good fee to defend him. After the case was over, Willie Young's brother came up, congratulated me, and shook my hand. He had a $100 bill in his hand. That was the first time I ever had that happen. He was well satisfied with the way it came out.

One of the McGees had a knife, and it was lying up on the jury railing at the trial after being admitted as evidence. I got to speaking, and I came down hard on the jury railing with my hand to make a point. A juror later told me the knife jumped up in the air, and all the jurors begin to think the knife was going to hit them. Sometimes, you get sort of intense, and you don't realize what you're doing.

Howell's friend Ed Mauldin recalls an after-effect of the Young case. "One day about lunch time, I was up at Howell's office. The restaurant where we were going to eat was around the corner. Howell and I were walking two abreast, and we occupied most of the sidewalk. We went around a corner, and coming the other way was H. C. McGee, the fellow whose son had been killed. When we got next to him, McGee just growled, "Grrrrrrrrr." I wondered if I wasn't in the line of fire, because I was between McGee and Howell. I was very glad to get around the corner and up the street."

The scissors and Young cases and some others of my early cases attracted a lot of attention, and my practice developed from that. I had a country law practice, which is a little of everything. You try criminal cases; you try civil cases. You try divorce cases and child custody cases, and you represent some businesses. I would be the plaintiff in civil cases, particularly where there were personal injuries, and I would also do some defending. Sometimes I defended individuals, and sometimes I defended some of the insurance companies. So I had a good cross section of law practice. I tried a lot of criminal cases, and some of them were interesting.

First Steps Toward Politics. Charles Carmichael, Elizabeth Ann's first cousin and Howell's long-time lawyer friend, says that when he and Howell first started practicing law in the late 1940s, they were all involved in local political races. Politics were hot in Colbert County in those days, Charles says, and he tells of an early probate judge's election when he and Howell were on different sides. "Howell supported a fine lady who had been the clerk in the probate judge's office. I was just out of school. That woman lived in the same block I did, and she was passing out cases of gardening items and things to people and wasn't giving me any. Heflin organized all the lawyers and got all the doctors, and he would have a meeting in this building down below me and invite them.

"When I had a client come in, I'd talk politics with them. I'd ask, 'Did Howell invite y'all to the party down there?' They answered, 'No.' I said, 'Well, I guess they don't want your vote then, do they?' We lucked out and won the race, and it liked to have killed ole Howell.

"We had a cartoon portrait made, and we put it in front of a casket in the courthouse yard. The cartoon showed Howell and the probate judge and some others who had been involved. Somebody who worked at the post office put up another cardboard sign with 'the slush hogs' written on it. Lord, they got so upset over that race, it was something. Our little stunt was just a joke."

Howell had been very active in the American Legion and through this had become known among veterans around the state. In July 1949, he was a speaker at the Legion's state convention. At the time, he was vice chairman of the Department's 4-H Club committee.[1] He urged the Legion to "drive the Ku Klux Klan out of business. The Klan so often desecrates the symbol of Calvary with the fire of hate."

He was elected senior vice commander of the Legion over W. M. Beck, former Speaker of the Alabama House. He had been junior vice commander the year before. He ran for the post of state commander in 1952, but he lost. Big Jim Folsom was governor, and the winner, a man in the automobile business in Folsom's home town of Cullman, was one of Big Jim's buddies. This was the only political race that Heflin ever entered and didn't win.

Former Federal Judge Bert Haltom, a close friend of Howell's, says that none of his friends knew he was going to run, and he adds, "He got the whey beat out of him." Haltom adds that it was a foregone conclusion that Heflin would run for something big at some point.

THE UNIVERSITY OF ALABAMA. Howell's continued involvement with the University of Alabama Law School and its alumni association would prove a great help in his later political career. Not long after arriving in Tuscumbia, he became more active in building support and raising money for the school. Howell had organized the Alabama Law School Alumni Association in 1949 and was its first president.

Law school dean Leigh Harrison liked Howell and knew he could help in building loyalty and encouraging support among alumni. The University had a plane, and Dean Harrison would use it to attend functions in different parts of the state. If Harrison thought Howell could help with a meeting, he would have the plane fly to Tuscumbia to get him. The plane was used on weekends to haul the football coaches on scouting and recruiting missions, so Dean Harrison and Howell would have to drive at those times.

> They were trying to raise money as all educational institutions do. I believed in legal education, and thought it ought to be fully supported. I was happy to do it.
>
> I was on good terms with Dean Harrison, and he wanted an alumni association very much. In those days, they didn't get much money from the state, and they wanted outside money to do such things as attract visiting professors. So we started raising money. Then we created the Law School Foundation in 1961, and I was involved in that. Later they had the Farrah Law Society, started in 1969, which is named for former Dean Albert Farrah. We solicited graduates to give $100 a year, and if they did, the Farrah Law Society gave them a plaque. Over the years, it has produced a good deal of money.
>
> The Law School Foundation also went to wealthier people, and they got a substantial contribution from General Holland M. Smith who was in the Marine Corps and a law school graduate. A good number of other wealthy people contributed. I even went on a trip to Denver, Colorado, with Tom Christopher when he was dean. We visited Barney Whatley, the former partner of Supreme Court Justice Hugo Black, to see if he would make a contribution. He gave a fairly substantial amount to the law school. We went to see the Kellogg Foundation up in Battle Creek, Michigan, and traveled other places. Over the years the law school has raised enough to create some endowed professorships. They just recently finished a capital drive, and they raised $21 million dollars.

Howell's work with the law school was a fine contribution to his alma mater. It also helped him become known in other parts of Alabama. He traveled around the state a good deal doing this work, and his connection to the Alumni Association and the Law School Foundation put him in good standing among lawyers from one end of the state to the other. Howell made great strides in a short time in getting known and in building a solid reputation.

FRIENDSHIP WITH ED MAULDIN. Howell developed a deep and lasting friendship with Ed Mauldin during the first years in Tuscumbia. The association was both business and social. They were both unmarried at first, and they began to spend time together at parties and other events and to travel together to such things as football games.

The uncle who raised Ed, Edward Fennel, was a very successful farmer and a director of a bank in Decatur that had a branch in Leighton. After the war, bank management decided that business opportunities in Leighton were too limited, and they should move the charter somewhere with greater potential. Fennel knew the community needed a bank, and he decided that, if they moved the bank over his protest, he would assist the community in organizing its own. When Ed returned in 1946 after two years in the Navy, Fennel was helping the community to organize.

Fennel was getting older and was in declining health, so Ed Mauldin acted as his uncle's agent from time to time even though he was only nineteen. "I did the things he would have done if he had been physically able," Ed says. "I contacted the regulators and the community leaders and businesses, and I was involved in all of the work of organizing. My uncle died in 1947, and they went ahead and formed the bank. I was administrator of his estate, and I pursued the organization of the bank as best I could, because that is what he had wanted."

Fennel's partner, Leonard Pruitt, who became Ed's father-in-law, was the new bank's president. Three years later, Pruitt died, and as Ed notes, "that left a little fledgling bank with the prime organizers out of the picture. It didn't really have the management and talent and all to make it prosperous."

Despite his youth, Ed was asked to be a director and to help the bank survive. "I kind of had a tiger by the tail," he recalls. "I couldn't turn loose, and I couldn't get off. I had to be more and more involved. Finally I realized that we would have to put in a better facility to meet the needs of a community that was growing and producing income other than cotton revenue. We did that, and that's how we gradually grew one location at a time."

Ed Mauldin became chief executive officer, and the bank prospered. Now known as Bank Independent, it has ten locations and a base of $300 million. Mauldin continued to operate the farm and was very successful with that, too.

Ed Mauldin was a delegate for Lyndon Johnson at the 1960 Democratic National Convention. In 1961, President Kennedy appointed Ed to the National Agricultural Advisory Commission. He remained on the Commission after Johnson became President and became a highly respected member. Bert Haltom says that Ed Mauldin has one of the brightest agriculture minds in the country. Mauldin was a help later when Howell became a member of the Senate Agriculture Committee.

After just a few years in Tuscumbia, Howell Heflin was on his way. He was earning a reputation as an outstanding litigator, and his practice was growing. He had an attractive wife and was active in church and community affairs. His friendships with good people were expanding, and his work with the University of Alabama law school was helping him become known throughout the state. The path to political office was being set.

9

Success and Recognition

Howell Heflin was coming into his prime as a lawyer at a prosperous time in American history. The GI Bill was helping to create a large middle class. In 1952, Dwight Eisenhower, the great hero of World War II, was elected the first Republican president in twenty years. He helped to end the Korean War in 1953, and while the Cold War with the Soviet Union intensified, Americans took it in stride and did not really think anything would disturb their peaceful existence. The Cold War probably contributed to the general prosperity because it meant heavy government spending to keep up the military. Eisenhower's amiable and easy-going appearance contributed to the positive mood. Everybody loved Ike.

In December 1955, Rosa Parks refused to vacate her bus seat for a white person in Montgomery, Alabama, and the modern Civil Rights Movement was born. Politics in Alabama would never be the same. Civil rights issues dominated the political scene in the state for the next twenty years, and it paved the way for dramatic Republican gains and the end of the old Democratic one-party system in which the primary was the only election that counted.

The Civil Rights Movement widened a split between "states rights Democrats" and "national Democrats" in Alabama which had existed since Dixicrats made their big splash in 1948. States righters reasoned that they could exert control in presidential races by refusing to pledge the state's electors, denying any candidate a majority of electors, and possibly throwing the election into the House of Representatives.

The most famous and powerful states righter was George Wallace. He waged political war against the federal government in his first term as governor and in his presidential campaigns. Howell Heflin was a loyal national Democrat, and he was a racial moderate. This, and his growing political potential, made him the natural enemy of George Wallace even though they never personally ran against one another.

Alabama is divided geographically into four horizontal sections: North Alabama, which is defined by the Tennessee Valley and by farms which generally were not suitable for slavery in antebellum days; North Central Alabama, which includes the state's largest city, Birmingham, and has hilly, sandy soil better suited to fruit trees and garden crops than to cotton; the Black Belt, low country characterized by rich black soil and big cotton plantations which depended on slavery; and the Gulf Coast, again with soil not suited to large cotton farms. The proportion of blacks is highest in the Black Belt, where it far exceeds fifty percent, substantial but less than half in the North Central and Gulf Coast areas, and lowest in North Alabama.

North Alabama has traditionally been the most progressive part of the state on racial matters. This is the area that nurtured Howell Heflin and contributed to his outlook on life. Thus he came naturally by his relatively liberal stand on race issues, his loyalty to the National Democratic Party, and his aversion to George Wallace.

SIGNS OF GROWING RESPECT. Respect for Howell Heflin in the Tuscumbia area continued to grow, and it was demonstrated again in 1959 when he was named attorney for the County Commission.

> It was then called the Board of Revenue. They ran the business of the county and had charge of the roads. I was called county attorney. Mostly I was concerned about what the commissioners could do legitimately, and you had to watch some of them. If the sheriff wanted an additional deputy, he had to have the approval of the commission. They voted on the number of new clerks and other employees in all

courthouse departments and on salary raises. I never did get involved in the merits of what they were doing and tried to stay out of their politics. I had to go to meetings every week. Sometimes I couldn't attend because I was in court, and they'd understand. It didn't pay a lot.

Howell also got a boost at the state level during this period. While he was chairman of the Board of Education from 1954 to 1964, he was appointed to the Alabama Educational Study Commission created by the legislature to study the state's educational system. It was more familiarly called the Edwards-Lackey Commission.

It was an interesting commission with a lot of business people. It included Mervin Sterne, a rather remarkable man from Birmingham who was with a well known brokerage house. Hugh Kaul, who was then a Big Mule, was a member. This was during the second Folsom administration, and Big Jim called all the big corporations "Big Mules." Another fellow on the Commission was Joe Dawkins, who had been in the legislature and was a known friend of education. He was a leader. He was in the Folsom administration and had been head of the state Alcoholic Beverage Control Board.

It was an effort to improve education. Folsom had tried before, but the Big Mules and the Black Belt had an alliance and controlled the legislature. The fact that Sterne and Kaul, both of whom were well respected in the business community, were for it was very important. In its report, the Commission recommended a substantial increase in revenue for education. It included a $100 million bond issue for school buildings, which was a lot of money in those days. There was a lot of opposition because it would mean new taxes.

Bill Nichols, who was in the legislature and a Senate floor leader for John Patterson, pushed it. Later when I was in Congress, we were talking about it, and he mentioned Avondale Mills and all the textile companies. It increased taxes on their machinery, and it increased other taxes. Nichols's district included most of the textile mills, such as Russell Mills, Avondale Mills, West Point Pepperell, and some others, and they were all greatly opposed to this tax. He always told them, "Well, you didn't say anything to me until I was committed." He survived, though I think they talked about running somebody against him for awhile. Later, he was a great proponent of anything that the textile industry wanted. It was tough to be elected to Congress in that district if you didn't have the textile support.

Sterne, Kaul, Lackey, and Edwards got a good deal of support from the business community. They lobbied for it and convinced the new governor, John Patterson, to support it. I testified before the House and the Senate in support of it. Patterson got the bond issue and an increase in taxation to support schools though the legislature. Local communities were called on to increase their millage, and many did, including Jefferson County (Birmingham) and Tuscumbia. It was the first big movement for education in the state that succeeded. If those business people had not supported it, it never would have passed. Patterson pushed it, and he still had a tough fight.

THE NATURE OF LAW PRACTICE. By this time, Howell had shifted from the criminal cases of his early years more to the civil side which was more lucrative. He also did a lot of estates and other types of practice.

An unusual job involved a "lie bill."

> I have asked lawyers everywhere, "Have you ever written a lie bill?" And they say, "No. What is a lie bill? I never heard of that." Well, I never heard of it either until this man who lived in the country came in to see me and said, "I want you to write me a lie bill. This man out in the neighborhood claims he's been running around with my daughter and sleeping with her. It's a lie, and I told him I was going to do this. I also told him what I'd do if he didn't get up in church and admit to the congregation that he had lied. I want you to write a lie bill that he'll get up and read." He got the man to come in and sign it, and it was basically to the effect, "I, whatever his name was, do admit that I have lied by making statements about the fact that I was running around and sleeping with whatever her name was, and such and such." He made the

man pay me, and I remember I got $35 for writing a lie bill.

He never liked divorce cases, which could involve vindictive parties.

Word kept coming back from those divorce cases, "You'd better be careful. He said he was going to get you." When I had associates and then a partner, I told them, "Y'all handle all the divorce cases." I just didn't want to listen to all that hoo-ha. The women would cuss the husbands, and the husbands would cuss the wives. Lord have mercy! Tim Milan, a fellow who works with my son Tom, specializes in divorce cases and loves them. All these secretaries love all that. Lord have mercy! Husbands wouldn't bring their children back on time when they had visitation rights, and wives would phone you at any time of the night and day. So I didn't handle divorce cases my last ten years of practice. Civil cases are where you make the money. I was doing quite well, and I just said no more, no more to divorce cases.

In criminal cases, Howell sometimes handled the defense and other times he prosecuted. People interested in a case could hire a lawyer to be a special prosecutor who would work with the district attorney.

I lost a lot of cases, you know. You win some, you lose some. You don't talk about the ones you lose. You feel you've had a victory if somebody's charged with first degree murder ends up with manslaughter. I never did have anybody convicted of first degree murder in a criminal case. You'd settle a lot of cases. Sometimes people didn't want to gamble, like if you had a bad case or if the state figured they had one. That's more true in civil cases. If you had an automobile accident or an accident at a plant, you'd end up settling the vast majority of them. If the plaintiff had insurance, you'd usually reach a settlement with the insurance company. But you'd try a lot of them, and sometimes you'd lose. I was fortunate to be a winner most of the time.

I tried lawsuits all over this section of the state. You almost ride the circuit. I tried them in Lauderdale County where Florence is located. I went into Lawrence and Franklin Counties and got up into Tennessee and over into Mississippi. You could practice in other states if you had a licensed lawyer from that state with you. You weren't admitted to practice, but people would hire you, and you'd associate with a lawyer there to help you with the case. It was a matter of reciprocity. Lawyers from Mississippi and Tennessee would try cases here the same way.

STUDYING THE JURY. One of the most critical skills a lawyer needs in trying a case is selecting people for the jury who will be swayed by the arguments he plans to give. Attorneys representing each side are presented a list of prospective jurors called a venire. They can question those on the venire, and they have a number of preemptive strikes; that is, they can eliminate candidates without giving a reason. Howell spent a lot of time selecting juries. When he left his practice to become chief justice of the Alabama Supreme Court, he had a card index file with about 10,000 names of people in Colbert County who had served on juries. The file also included names from Lauderdale and Franklin counties. It included information about each case on which the person had served and the way the case was decided.

He explains his method.

> I investigated them beforehand. I would get the jury list a week in advance, and I'd check it out in communities like Leighton, Poplar Creek, Cherokee, and Allsboro. You'd know somebody there, and you'd ask them about people they knew on the list. You made notes about what type of people they were and whether they were tight with their money. It was a great resource in picking juries.
>
> In Franklin, there was a fellow I would meet on a Saturday afternoon and go over the jury list. He was the tax assessor, and he didn't want it to be known that he was helping me. But he liked it because he'd know everybody who came in the courthouse, and he'd go up to them and ask, "John, how are you doing?" "Mary, how are you doing?" He thought it helped him politically, because it helped him recall the names. Bill Gardiner, the mayor of Tuscumbia, would help

me go over the lists. A group of people at different places spent a lot of time trying to find out about jurors for me. In big cities they have so many they can't do it, but in places like this, you can.

SOME INTERESTING CASES. One of Howell's most interesting cases during this period of his law practice had to do with a dog, "Old Buster." The case involved a retired highway patrolman, Bert Robinson, who was running for sheriff of Lauderdale County.

> He was out canvassing and going house-to-house in the country, and these people had Old Buster, who chewed on him when he came to their house. He claimed that he lost the sheriff's race because of Old Buster. Old Buster's owners had insurance, and I represented the insurance company. Robinson wanted something like $100,000. We tried to settle it but couldn't. He had high figures in mind.
>
> Frank Potts, who represented Robinson, was asking prospective jurors questions, and he inquired if anybody couldn't give a fair trial to any of the parties. A lady stuck up her hand and said, "I can give a fair trial to all the people, but I don't know whether I can give a fair trial to Old Buster." The court excused her from the jury after Potts asked her, "What was your problem?" She answered, "I went out there, and Buster chewed me up."
>
> The law was to the effect that you're not responsible for the first bite of your dog. But if you had knowledge that the dog was ferocious, then you had the responsibility of taking steps to confine him where he won't hurt people. You're negligent if you don't. Well, Potts had two or three other witnesses who had similar experiences, and this woman came back and testified against Old Buster.
>
> There I was trying this case, and what in the world should we do? Potts made a pretty good case against my client. I decided I had to appeal to the emotions of the jury. I had a friend who said, "Why don't you get up and quote that *Ode to the Dog*." So I found it, and I quoted *Ode to the Dog* about how faithful dogs are and how we ought to love them.

We had offered something like $5,000 to settle the case since he had some serious injuries, and the jury came back in with $5,000, exactly what we had offered. Robinson, the highway patrolman who was running for sheriff, would have been defeated anyway. He was mad at me for awhile, but when I ran for the Senate later on, he supported me.

Another interesting case was the "Taxicab Preacher" case. As the son of a Methodist preacher and a person active in the Methodist church in this area, I knew all the preachers and other church people. I wrote a lot of deeds to churches and did other transactions, and I did it *pro bono*, for free. When a preacher got into some sort of trouble, I'd help and wouldn't charge anything.

Well, one of them was in the used car business. He was being sued, and he was talking about how he was being mistreated. During the case the opposition brought out that this man of God had gone down to Birmingham and found a lot of old taxicabs. He bought the taxicabs and brought them to Florence. He repainted and changed them around and got them running, and he was selling them to people and not telling them the truth, that they were just worn out taxicabs. He kept insisting that he make at least one of the speeches to the jury. I couldn't get him to settle down. He got up and preached to the jury. We lost that case.

Another rather unusual case in Lauderdale County involved an optometrist, Dr. Herbert Bryant. He was charged with murdering a man named Joe Moore. Joe was sort of notorious around the Shoals area for running around with women including the optometrist's wife. Joe had a trailer somewhere out on the lake near Florence. Dr. Bryant went over there and discovered them in the trailer. Bryant lived here in Colbert County, and he drove all the way across the river and got his shotgun and went back to the trailer. He claimed that Moore, who was much bigger than he was, lunged at him, and as Moore did, he shot him and killed him. It was a tough case with premeditation since he went after his shotgun and had all that time to think about it. Our defense was that he was driven by passion, as well as by self-defense.

I made a big to-do over the fact that everything was pink inside the trailer. It had pink sheets and a pink lavatory. Everything was a different color pink. We talked about Moore and his love of pink. Bert Haltom, who was working with me on the case, reminded me a while back that during the case, I took a lunge at the jury, and you know, I was big. I scared Haltom as well as the jury.

It was a long trial, and we had Dr. Bryant examined by a psychologist and a psychiatrist. The psychiatrist wouldn't help us much, but the psychologist would. We got the judge to allow us to use the psychologist. The psychologist testified that in his judgment, Bryant was insane, and passions had controlled his reason. He went into a long recitation of medical terms explaining it. The jury came out with a verdict of not-guilty by reason of insanity, which is unusual. As far as I know that's the only one around here. Under the law Dr. Bryant had to go to the state insane hospital. He was under observation and stayed for several months until the psychiatrists felt he was not a threat.

Former law partner Charles Rosser describes another of Howell's cases which was "funny as hell. Howell was defending a little, skinny fellow on a rape charge. The lady who had the guy charged was big, strong, and healthy. Heflin was cross-examining the lady. He said, 'Well, you say he had you in your car and y'all were parked out on the creek bank, on a moonlit night, and he turned the radio on and put his arms around you and got to petting and hugging on you. What did he do next?'

"The lady answered, 'Well, he put my right leg up behind the driver's seat and my left leg up on the dashboard.' The jury laughed, and that pleased the witness. Heflin asked her, 'What happened next?' She said, 'He pulled off my drawers.' The jury laughed again, and when they laughed, the witness giggled, and everybody was getting rather jovial. Heflin then asked her, 'What did he do next?' She said, 'He throwed it to me.' This generated the biggest laugh of all and suggested strongly that she was a willing participant."

Howell helped his case with some courtroom dramatics. The deputies had gone to the exact spot where the rape allegedly happened, and the lady's panties were found a considerable distance away. During the trial,

Howell took a pair of panties and threw them as hard as he could across the courtroom. They didn't go very far. He proved it was impossible for this guy to have thrown the panties from where she said he did to where they landed.

The testimony and the dramatics were enough to cast doubt that the robust woman couldn't have been raped by the skinny little man. The jury quickly brought a verdict of not-guilty.

As his lunging at the jury and his throwing the panties shows, Howell would engage in courtroom dramatics when he conducted trials. He recalls an embarrassing incident which resulted from his dramatics. It was a murder case where his client was accused of shooting somebody through a window.

> Whoever committed the murder had sneaked up to the window and killed a person. There had been some bad blood between my client and the victim, so they charged him. They showed that the assailant ran off after he did the shooting. It was sort of muddy, and they had the shoe prints and a measurement of the stride between the two. They were never able to identify the shoe print with this man's shoes, and there was an issue as to how long his stride was. In arguing to the jury, I poured powder all over the floor in front of the jury box. My client was short, and I was in the process of trying to show that the killer had to be a long-legged man. I ran across the jury room, and lo and behold, my feet went out from under me on the powder, and I crashed to the floor. That created quite a scene. As I remember, my client got off because they couldn't prove the case sufficiently. There was linoleum right in front of the jury box where I was trying to prance around and show off.

One of Howell's cases set a precedent in Alabama law that stayed in effect several years. It involved a situation where two men were working as employees and excavating a big ditch twenty feet deep to lay pipe. The ditch collapsed, and it killed one and buried the other for several hours, seriously injuring him. The only remedy at the time was workman's compensation. There was evidence that the superintendent was negligent. He should have known that the soil was the type that could fall in, and he didn't take the proper precautions. Howell and his associates went into detail about the safety measures that could have been followed.

> The law in most states is that the workman's compensation is the exclusive remedy, and you can't sue a superintendent. In Alabama, it had never been determined. The other issue was whether or not the company's insurance would cover. As the trial was about to start, the company filed a declaratory judgment suit which asked the court to rule whether or not the superintendent could be held liable and whether or not the insurance policy would cover it. A lot of litigation was involved, and we ended up winning it. That law suit went to the Alabama Supreme Court and established in Alabama what is known as the Co-employee Suit, which became very controversial. I was the forerunner in establishing a principle that a lot of people used to recover damages. Workman's compensation then was very limited as to how much you could recover. Finally the legislature worked out an agreement with the labor unions, and they substantially raised the workman's compensation benefits.

Charles Rosser says that Howell established what are called "third party suits" in this case. "Heflin pioneered the theory that, while you cannot sue your employer, you can sue a fellow employee such as a superintendent, a supervisor, or a foreman who negligently caused your injury. He discovered that most of the time the fellow employees were insured under the company's policy. That case was called the McCormick case, and it became famous."

Howell was opposed in court many times by his friend Bert Haltom. "They used to close the courthouse offices over in Tuscumbia when we were trying a case over there," Haltom says. "Everybody knew how friendly we were and man, I'd just lambast him with everything I could lay hands on that was ethical. He was a great trial lawyer, I'll tell you the truth. We never got mad at each other except temporarily. We had some real tough cases some times."

ELIZABETH ANN AND THE COURT. Howell was famous for his courtroom style, but Elizabeth Ann never saw him demonstrate it. "My granddaddy had told me years and years ago that I was not to go to the courtroom," she recalls. "It was not a place for ladies and young women. I wanted to go hear Granddaddy, and he said, 'No, indeed.' I decided one time I was going anyway, and he met me at the door and said, 'I told you, this is no place for ladies.'

"I was called as a witness in Florence after we married. It was about the Service League and a lady who had stolen us blind. There was a case preceding the one that we had been called on, and all of the members of our Service League were in the witness room. It was a carnal knowledge case or something like that. Judge Hill came in and said, 'I'm sorry the case preceding this one has taken so long.' He said, 'Please do not come in and listen to the case that's going on. It is a nasty, ugly case, and I don't want you to be embarrassed.' Well, some of them had planned to go on in there anyway, and they did. I mean they came out of there in a hurry, and their faces were red as beets."

WORKING WITH BLACKS. The Civil Rights Movement significantly allowed the concerns of blacks with the judicial process to be heard. Blacks had always known that there was white justice and there was black justice and the two were different.[1] Black citizens had been systematically excluded from Alabama juries since the 1901 Constitution. As a result, whites who were primarily concerned with preserving their own privileges and prerogatives and keeping blacks in "their place," decided cases. Howell Heflin became involved in many cases involving blacks. In a time of extreme racial stress, he was a moderate.

Howell recounts a case in which all the blacks in his area got involved on one side or the other.

> There was a black funeral home here, Thompson Funeral Home. Thompson and his wife ran it. They had a son who drank and was always into something. He was accused of shooting his wife with a pistol about four or five o'clock in the morning, and the state had a

strong case against him. I was his attorney.

Several unusual things were involved. He had shacked up with a woman over in Sheffield that night, and the woman he shacked up with was mad at him about something when he came to trial. The prosecutor asked her what time he arrived that night. "Well, he got there about ten o'clock." "Was he drinking?" "Yeah, he was drinking and kept drinking and I drank some with him, but we went to bed." She kept on talking like that. The prosecutor asked, "What time did he leave? About one o'clock in the morning?" And she growled, "No, he left at four."

My client was really squirming. While this witness was testifying he kept whispering, "I got to go to the bathroom. I got to go to the bathroom." I said, "You're not going to the bathroom. You're not getting up. You don't do anything until this witness gets off the stand." He kept on, "I got to go to the bathroom." He wanted to get up and go to the bathroom in the middle of that woman testifying, and I wasn't fixing to let him go. Finally she finished, and we crossed examined her to show that she was mad at him over something after all this had happened. When the Judge did call a recess, my client shot to the bathroom.

His wife was found dead with a gun in her hand, and it looked like she might have committed suicide. He contended he wasn't home, that the gun went off just as he drove up. She had been shot in the face, and the prosecution's contention was that no woman will commit suicide by shooting herself in the face. The theory was that she wants to be a pretty corpse.

I got a fellow who had been a state toxicologist, one of these experts who had performed autopsies. The toxicologist and I went through the house, and then we went over all the coroner's reports and other reports. She had spots on the back of her hand, and there was a wall in the house that had stucco sticking out. We visioned that she went to the window to look out when his car came in. There was some sort of cord that connected an iron, and we figured that she tripped and hit the stucco and the gun went off and killed her. This former toxicologist made a pretty good witness, and my client was found not-guilty. Our cook, Annie Mae, thought he was so guilty. She just raised immortal Cain with me about defending him.

Blacks in the Tuscumbia, Quad-Cities area appreciated the fact that Howell Heflin, a prominent white attorney, would take their cases and work with them in the 1950s. They remembered that years later when he entered politics, and they supported him with their votes.

PARTNERSHIP WITH CHARLES ROSSER. The first few years Howell was in practice he worked alone. Then as his practice grew, he hired other lawyers, called "associates," to work for him. After sixteen years in practice, he formed a partnership with Charles Rosser. Charles Rosser was a student in law school in the early 1960s, and he had met Heflin at various bar and law school functions. "I had heard him speak," Rosser says, "and I had a great deal of respect for him." Rosser finished law school in January 1963 and was a clerk for Judge Walter Gewin on the Fifth Circuit Court of Appeals for eighteen months. With the clerkship ending in the spring of 1964, he was searching for a new position.

"I heard the lawyer who had been with Mr. Heflin for a year or two was pulling out to go on his own," Rosser recalls, "so I decided I would try to get a job with him. I came up and talked. He said he was interested in having me come, but he never called me back to give the final yes or no. A week or so before my clerkship ended, I was getting desperate, so I decided to push him for an answer. He finally said, 'Yeah, come on up.'"

In 1967, Heflin made Rosser a partner, and they were partners until Heflin went to the state Supreme Court. When the term as chief justice ended in 1977, Rosser and Heflin became partners again, along with Stanley Munsey who had joined Rosser in the meantime.

As the senior member of Heflin & Rosser, Howell Heflin continued to gain a reputation as a highly successful "country lawyer," specializing in both civil and criminal cases. His reputation for humor and for wry comments and observations grew. His success in the courtroom before a jury led a writer from the *Florence Times* to refer to him as "the Perry Mason of North Alabama," and other people picked up on this.

Howell Heflin's reputation continued to spread beyond his immediate practice area. He was elected a fellow of the International Academy of Trial Lawyers, the American College of Trial Lawyers, and the International Society of Barristers. These groups would meet once or twice a year. "You'd get together with lawyers from all over the country and talk about cases and brag about them," Heflin says. "You never tell about the ones you lost. It was an interchange of ideas of what was happening across the country that was important."

INVOLVEMENT IN POLITICS. With a growing statewide reputation, a penchant for humor and making friends, his own family history, and a well-developed and improving speaking ability, it was inevitable that Howell Heflin would run for political office. He was tempted a number of times, but he practiced twenty-two years before entering his first campaign for public office.

He explains that he had an interest in politics early, but Elizabeth Ann didn't like the idea and had pretty well kept the possibility out of his mind.

> I had a good law practice going, and I was involved in civic activities like the Board of Education. I just didn't feel like the time was right. Wallace came along, and during his first years I felt you had to be a racist to run. I was not going to get involved in that.
>
> Still, I was interested in politics. There was a state senate race in the early days, and a number of people encouraged me. Our senate district had three counties: Colbert, Franklin, and Marion. Under a gentleman's agreement, each county would take a turn. When it came Colbert's time, I was urged to run, and I thought a good deal about it. Lawyers up here who got involved in politics would lose their practice unless they were in a firm that could carry them and it was for the benefit of the firm. They'd be gone from Monday till Friday night, and they couldn't take care of their business. Paul Coburn, a friend who had been in the legislature a long time, wanted to run, and one of my wife's Carmichael kinsman wanted to run. Both ran and got beat. Sometime earlier,

somebody tried to get me to run for the Alabama Public Service Commission. I listened a few times to that, but it didn't appeal to me.

But I stayed active and was involved in some of the state politics. I supported Sparkman and was active in his campaigns. For his first election in 1948, he ran against Phillip Hamm from Dothan, and I traveled some over the state with young people for Sparkman.

Sparkman ran as vice president on the Democratic ticket in 1952 with former Illinois Governor Adlai Stevenson. Heflin stumped for them in the Shoals area, which went Democratic over Eisenhower by a huge margin.[2]

Howell soon was active in the governor's races. In 1958, as the Civil Rights Movement was gaining steam and dominating Alabama politics, he first supported Jimmy Faulkner for the Democratic nomination.

> He was a bright, young fellow who was very progressive and for education. I supported him in the primary, but he didn't do well. In the run-off between Wallace and Patterson that year, I supported Patterson. I had been in school with him, and, after he was Governor, he appointed me as president of the Alabama Teacher's Tenure Commission. I was on the Board of Education, and they had to select a board of education member. I didn't get very active in that campaign, but I did support him.

Howell was more actively involved in a statewide political contest in 1962 when he served as campaign manager for his friend, Bert Haltom, who was a state senator and was running for lieutenant governor. Haltom recalls that there were about nine people in the race, including one Ku Klux Klan member, and Bert thought of himself as the front-runner. "Then all of a sudden," he says, "Jim Allen, who had been our lieutenant governor before, hopped in and qualified. I was feisty and full of myself, and I was just as happy as a lark. I thought I could beat Jim Allen. I did pretty well in the primary, but he beat the hell out of me in the run-off."

After the first primary, Allen was only leading Haltom by 3,000 votes statewide. Allen told Haltom, "Bert, why don't you go ahead and concede and not force me into a run-off. If you do, I'll make you this promise: I'll commit to you that you'll be lieutenant governor of Alabama four years from now. I made that same commitment to Guy Hardwick, and I made him lieutenant governor four years from then." Haltom thought about it a minute and finally said, "Jim, I just can't do it. Too many people have put up money for me, and there are others I'm responsible for. I just can't turn my back on them."

"I couldn't cut the mustard down in the Black Belt or the counties around Gadsden," Haltom says. "People there would smile and be very nice and courteous to me, but I knew they weren't going to vote for me. I wasn't a pinko by any means, but I was much more liberal than Jim Allen. I was much more of a Democrat in the national sense."

During the race, Elizabeth Ann was one of eight women who traveled Alabama extensively in an automobile. "They had red, white and blue jackets, white skirts, and straw hats with a great big Haltom band around them," Haltom says. "I picked up that idea from President Kennedy when he was running. It was the first time it had ever been done in Alabama. The first place they'd go when they hit town was the newspaper. The papers always loved to take their picture because most of them were good looking. They did a great job."

When Elizabeth Ann was helping in the Haltom campaign in 1962, she ran into a Wallace group who was against Haltom. "There were four of us out campaigning, passing out literature," Elizabeth Ann says. "It was the bumper sticker group. We had our jackets, hats and all, and were very evident in towns where we went. The Wallace supporters physically threatened us, and they scared us. They told us not to go to our next stop. We went right ahead, and just dared them. But you know, it was scary, because they looked like they meant business.

"Nonnie, Bert's wife, called George Wallace's brother 'Sag,' who had been a school friend of Bert. 'Sag' called George and said, 'You better call off the dogs. That bunch of women are going to do some serious reporting.' We never did have any more trouble with them, and we went all over the state."

Howell impressed a number of people in the 1962 race. Ed Horton, who ran for the state senate that year, was with Heflin and Bert Haltom on many occasions during the campaign. Horton says, "I was impressed with Howell Heflin, his political savvy and the way he conducted himself at rallies, the impressions he made on people."[3]

When Senator Lister Hill seemed in trouble in 1962, Heflin joined hands with long-time Hill supporter, *Decatur Daily* publisher Barrett Shelton, to rally voters for Cotton Tom Heflin's old enemy. As North Alabama returns were counted, Heflin's work began to show. "If Hill hadn't carried our area seven or eight to one, he would have lost," Heflin says. "Polls showed that the election was close, and Hill was worried. Republican James Martin came within 5,000 votes of beating him. All the doctors were against Hill because he was supporting the Medicare program. They considered it socialism. It was just two years before the Goldwater sweep in Alabama."

In 1968, Lister Hill decided not to seek reelection to the Senate. Armistead Selden, who had been in law school with Howell and was a close friend, was running, and so was Jim Allen. Howell was urged by a lot of people across the state to get in the race.

> Selden and Allen were both felt to be strong Wallace people, and some people wanted Alabama to have something different than a Wallace spokesman. I came to the conclusion that it would be very difficult to raise money. Also, Wallace was very popular. I knew he wouldn't support me. Selden came to me and asked for my support. I said, "I will unless I run myself." I then told him later when I'd made my decision that I would support him. He got beat. I had a lot of urging to run from Barney Weeks, who was then the head of the state labor council. I had the urging from some of the blacks to run. They weren't happy with either of the others.
>
> I had been active for Brewer, and when he was governor, he appointed me as chairman of the first Alabama Ethics Commission, which was created under executive order. We started some things about disclosure, established some sort of rules, and had an interesting

commission. Guy Hardwick from Dothan was on it, and so was Eris Paul who was a circuit judge in Coffee County, Enterprise. We met a number of times, and I was active with that.

Brewer, an early Wallace supporter, had been lieutenant governor and took over when Lurleen Wallace died in 1968. As governor, he was moderate on racial issues. Wallace promised to support Brewer in the 1970 election, but then he decided to run himself. After Brewer came out ahead in the primary, Wallace and his crowd gave him immortal hell in the run-off, with a lot of dirty tricks and Ku Klux involvement. Wallace won and became governor for a second term.

THE NEWSPAPER BUSINESS. Howell and Ed Mauldin had become close friends over the years. In 1959, they started a newspaper, *The Valley Voice*. Friend Joe Ware says they were not looking for a political voice; it was just a couple of young men feeling their oats and wanting to try something else. They saw it as a business opportunity.

Howell says they started the paper because of a gifted writer named Ben Knight.

> He had been a friend of ours, and he talked us into it. He had the idea of creating a newspaper and not selling subscriptions. Just give it to everybody. It would come out once a week. Ed talked to me and got me interested in doing it along with him. All we did is furnish the money. We put in about $10,000 each, and we lost it all before it was over.
>
> It went on for several years. Ben had a propensity to hit the bottle. You had to publish every week. If you missed a week, you lost some sort of accreditation on national advertising, and you would also lose the legals. I had to put out the paper once or twice. Bless his soul, he's dead and gone now. Charlie Granger, who was with the *Birmingham News*, succeeded Ben as the editor. We did pretty good for awhile, but we finally ended up selling out.

10

Prelude to Office

BY THE MID-1960S, American society was being torn apart by civil rights struggles and by involvement in the Vietnam War. The assassinations of President John F. Kennedy in 1963 and of Martin Luther King and Robert F. Kennedy in 1968 added to the malaise.

In Alabama, firebrand segregationist George Wallace was elected governor in 1962. The state was rent by such events as demonstrations and bombings in Birmingham in 1963, Wallace standing in the schoolhouse door trying to prevent integration of the University of Alabama the same year, and the Selma-to-Montgomery March in 1965.

White backlash set in. While Lyndon Johnson won a landslide victory over Republican Barry Goldwater in the 1964 presidential campaign with 61 percent of the popular vote, Alabama, along with four other Southern states and Goldwater's native Arizona, went Republican. Goldwater won 69.5 percent of Alabama's presidential vote. Race had turned the tide in Alabama politics, and Republicans, playing the race card with little subtlety, were winning offices throughout the state for the first time since Reconstruction. Five Republicans were elected to Congress in 1964, and 94 local Republican candidates won.[1]

George Hawkins, Howell's high-school classmate at Attalla, was a Democratic nominee for Congress in 1964. He ran against Jim Martin, who had almost defeated Lister Hill two years earlier, and was defeated in the Goldwater sweep of Alabama.

> George was an old friend from Gadsden. I went to school with him at Etowah County High. He practiced law and was in the state senate, and he became Folsom's legal advisor. He had run for governor in 1958 and had taken a right progressive stand on race matters. Hawkins attracted a lot of young idealistic people like Chuck Morgan, David Vann, Erskine Smith, Vic Gold, and some young lawyers who really wanted to do something about the race issue. I was really active in that campaign and made a number of speeches.

In 1966, Alabama politics was in turmoil. The state constitution then barred governors from succeeding themselves, so George Wallace was out of the race. There was also the question of whether the 1964 Republican gains would hold or whether the state would revert to the one-party system of the past. Wallace's wife Lurleen, with no qualifications other than being wife of the popular governor, won the Democratic primary against ten male opponents. Howell recalls that election.

> Jim Martin ran in 1966 as Republican candidate against Lurleen. The two big names in the Republican party then were Jim Martin and John Grenier. Grenier had reorganized the Republican party in 1962 and was mastermind of the race against Hill. He had been Alabama campaign manager for Goldwater in 1964, and all the Republicans were high on him. John Sparkman was up for reelection that year. Some of them say that Martin wanted to run against Sparkman, but Grenier was smart enough to put him off on Lurleen. Grenier thought he could win against Sparkman and entered the general election as Republican candidate for Senate. Grenier lost.

One of the candidates defeated by Lurleen Wallace in the Democratic primary in 1966 was former Congressman Carl Elliott. Elliott, a New Deal liberal, had served with distinction, and in 1958 had been joint author with Lister Hill of the National Defense Education Act*, one of the seminal pieces of American legislation since World War II. Alabama lost a congressional seat after the 1960 census, and after new congressional districts had been drawn, an election was held in which the eight existing congressmen ran for the seven remaining seats. Heflin knew Elliott and his family and had many clients in Elliott's home county, Franklin. So he supported Elliott. But conservatives in south Alabama had targeted Elliott to be defeated, and he was.

In 1990, Carl Elliott was the first winner of the John F. Kennedy Profiles in Courage Award, which is presented annually by the Kennedy Library Foundation. The award honors elected officials who, acting on their conscience, risk their careers by pursuing a larger vision of the national, state, or local interest.

WINNING THE BAR PRESIDENCY. A great honor came to Howell Heflin in the mid-1960s when he served as president of the Alabama State Bar Association.

> Running for Bar Association president is a story in itself. I'd been going to the State Bar conventions and was active in pushing some of the judicial reforms. But generally the presidency of the State Bar was reserved for the older members who were in their 60s. It was sort of an accolade to them. The fellow slated to be elected vice president of the bar that year and then president the next was being investigated by the Internal Revenue Service for some gambling issue. The rumor was that he had been playing cribbage out at the Birmingham Country Club and hadn't reported his winnings.
>
> I had no idea of running. The convention was in Mobile, and we drove down there Wednesday afternoon as we usually do. As soon as I walked in the hotel door, I was hit by three or four people, "Why don't

---

*The National Defense Education Act authorized federal funds for all levels of education to help develop as rapidly as possible those skills essential to the national defense.

you run to be president of the State Bar?" To do this, first you were elected first vice president, which was in fact president-elect, and you automatically moved to the presidency the next year. I said, "Well, I hadn't thought of it."

It started big on Thursday. More and more people urged me to run. Some of my closest friends, like Francis Hare, were committed to Winston McCall, the man who was running. It turned out later that Winston didn't have any real problems, so it was really an unfair situation. But at the time they thought he would embarrass the Bar Association if he got into problems with the Internal Revenue Service. By Friday afternoon, I finally decided, "All right, I'm going to run." I phoned some of my friends up home and said, "I'm running to be president of the Bar, and I need. . ." They weren't coming to the meeting. Well, they got a plane, and something like six or seven of them flew down on Saturday morning. A bus load came in from somewhere. The election was on Saturday morning, and the people had to get there between Friday afternoon and Saturday morning. The people who wanted me organized a whirlwind campaign, and I was elected.

Running for first vice president allowed you one year before your term as presidency began. That year allowed me to get more active and to travel and talk to others about what was going on in Bar Associations, in legal education, and in legal and judicial reform.

The fact that the Goldwater candidacy swept many Republicans into office in 1964 had created concern about the future of the appellate courts. If there had been a Republican candidate with the name of John Doe running for chief justice of the Supreme Court of Alabama in that election, there is little doubt that this candidate would have been elected, regardless of his background, experience, or ability. In those states where partisan politics frequently cause change, members of the Supreme Court are not elected or retained on the basis of the individual candidate's qualifications.

The popularity or the unpopularity of a national political party should not be the controlling factor in the election of the justices of the Supreme Court of a state. There was a great feeling among the lawyers that the legal profession ought to go through a cleansing process and straighten up and also should try to move forward with judicial reform. That set part of the tone when I went in as president of the Bar.

I took office as Bar Association President in 1965. We had a big scandal in quickie divorces that had been going on for a number of years. The way the law was written in Alabama, people could submit themselves to the jurisdiction of the court. If people from other states wanted to come in and were not going to contest a divorce, they would get the divorce fast. In other locations, in those days before no-fault divorces, the grounds for divorce were very limited. It had to be something like abandonment or adultery, particularly in some states where the Catholic church was very predominant, and a twelve-month waiting period was required. Geneva County was a big divorce mill, and so were Marion County and several other places. They were giving more divorces in those counties than Birmingham or Mobile or anywhere else, and they were very small with populations something like 20,000 people.

People would fly in from out of state, but the party moving for the divorce would have to swear that he or she was a resident of the state of Alabama. Well, the quickie divorce lawyers were interpreting residence as a matter of intent, and you didn't have to be here for any length of time after residence. The legislature wouldn't do anything about the scandal because a number of the legislators were involved and were making big money out of it. The State Bar decided that it was unethical to be involved in quickie divorces and that something should be done. When I was president-elect it started, and in my term as president, we tried ethics cases against certain lawyers. It usually ended up that there were pleas, and they were suspended from the practice of law for two years. That was the way the quickie divorce scandal was cured in the state.

When I took over as president, I appointed a number of committees. Most did excellent work. I had seen committees work; you appoint them and they meet one time. So we had all the committees meet on the same day, and we scheduled at least three committee meetings during the year. We met in the courthouse in Birmingham in the big courtroom, and we had 300-400 people present. Those attending felt like they were involved in a movement to get something done. The vast majority of them ended up doing a lot of good work.

We had a Bar Discipline Committee. There was at the time a very cumbersome way of disciplining lawyers. The general counsel of the Bar would take a deposition of the witnesses, and the defense would do likewise. Each of the thirty or so members of the Board of Bar Commissioners would get a transcript of the evidence and would read it. Then they would get together for a meeting, and the lawyers on both sides would make arguments. But there weren't any actual witnesses before the Bar Commission, so it was very cumbersome.

What we ended up with was a three member panel that heard all the evidence, saw all the witnesses or heard the arguments of the lawyers, and determined whether the accused had violated any of the canons of ethics or been guilty of criminal conduct or any conduct that is punishable. The panel could reprimand them, suspend them, or disbar them. There was also an appellate process.

There were Committees on Congestion in the appellate courts and in the trial courts. The Committee on Congestion in the trial courts was small at first, but they expanded to have a member from every judicial circuit in the state.

Another committee dealt with judicial salaries. Judges were making some amount that was very low. Even when I went on the court as chief justice, the salary was just $22,500. I'd had a very lucrative law practice with an income in six figures, so I took a tremendous cut.

We had a Committee on Legal/Medical Relationships between the lawyers and the doctors. There's a lot of friction between doctors and lawyers. Doctors don't like to come to court and testify, and the committee's purpose was to try to ease the strained relationships.

There was a feeling at the time that in legal education students were given a lot of theory and a lot of law principles but not much clinical education on how to practice law. There was a big gap between law school teaching and the actual practice of law. The Committee on Legal

Internships was appointed to address this, and they brought about some changes in legal education.

We also had committees on Law Clerks for Circuit Judges, Rules of Civil Procedure, Discovery in Criminal Cases, and Revision of the Canons of Ethics. The Code of Alabama was vastly out-of-date, and the Committee on Alabama Law Books recommended that we have a new code. Another committee dealt with a Client Security Fund. If a lawyer embezzled money from a client, the lawyer would be prosecuted and disciplined, but the client wouldn't get anything.

A move which was quite successful was founding the State Law Institute, which is housed at the University of Alabama Law School. It takes technical laws such as the Alabama Partnership Law and Alabama Corporation Law that are not necessarily controversial but ought to be updated, and it recommends revisions to the legislature.

We advocated that a statewide courthouse commission be created to assist the counties in having adequate facilities for women on the jury. Every courthouse in the state needed to be rearranged or remodeled to some degree.

That year the Bar Association decided they would have a Citizens' Conference on the judicial and legal systems of the state, and that was really the nucleus of the reforms which later took place. A Uniform Commercial Code, which was a national movement, was adopted during my administration.

The 1966 Citizens' Conference was supported by the American Judicature Society, an organization which promotes efficient administration of justice. The Conference recommended creation of a judicial administrative office, abolishment of the Justice of the Peace system, a uniform statewide system of inferior courts, merit selection of judges, and an independent judicial commission. The conference had some 100 participants and represented the starting point for the judicial reform effort which culminated later during Heflin's term as chief justice in the adoption of a new Judicial Article for the state constitution, and most of its recommendations were later adopted.[2]

Howell ended his term with the President's Address on July 23, 1966. In the address, he noted that the past year had witnessed study activities of intensity and variety never before experienced by the Bar Association. Overall study of the judicial system had been undertaken because the matter of improving the administration of justice in Alabama could no longer be delayed without damage to the public's interest.[3]

Howell spoke of the large and difficult problem of court congestion which remained. "Never before in the history of our state have our courts affected so many of its people. In some localities congestion in courts deprives the people of their constitutional rights to a prompt determination of the disputed issues."[4]

At the end of Howell's year as president, the Alabama Bar Association was given the American Bar Association's coveted Award of Progress for having the most progressive state bar organization in the nation.

A Bar Association member remembers, "President Heflin let all of the chairmen of the various committees know that he would not tolerate a dormant committee, followed by a perfunctory innocuous report. Under his gentle but constant prodding of all committee chairmen . . . there was created a ferment that permeated the entire bar."[5]

Partly as a result of issues raised by Heflin and by the Citizens' Conference, and at the urging of then Governor Albert Brewer, the state legislature in April 1969 passed a resolution calling for a Joint House-Senate Constitution Revision Committee. The Alabama Constitutional Commission was established September 1969 with Howell's friend, Conrad Fowler, as its chairman. The commission had twenty-one members, including the senate president, the speaker of the house, three designees of the speaker, two designees of the senate president, and fourteen appointed by the governor. The commission's work would later be very important when Heflin was chief justice.

ASSESSMENT BY HIS PEERS. Perhaps the best measure of a man is the way his peers at home see him. Friends from his lawyering days in Tuscumbia have many things to say about Howell Heflin.

Charles (Charlie) Carmichael, Elizabeth Ann's first cousin who is a lawyer in Tuscumbia, has known Howell for many years. Charlie is the son of a Tuscumbia lawyer who served as probate judge of the county at the same time that Marvin Heflin was a minister in Leighton. Charlie's father and the Reverend Heflin were close friends. Charlie is the grandson of Archie Carmichael who helped write the 1901 Constitution and was later in Congress. Charlie has been on the State Democratic Executive Committee for some thirty years, and he served on the State Corrections Board and the State Board of Education.

Carmichael worked with Howell on many occasions and opposed him on many others. "He and I used to butt heads on all of types of cases, including divorce," Carmichael says. "We had a little bit of everything back then. When we started practicing law, a $10,000 judgment was about as large as they'd ever had up here. After we started trying cases, we got some larger judgments."

During the time he and Howell practiced in Tuscumbia, Charlie observes, the profession changed significantly. Women and blacks came on the jury, and there were large modifications in the practice of criminal law, civil law, and probate law.

Carmichael calls Howell "a lawyer's lawyer. Heflin's an actor, and he's the best. He knows how to talk to different people, and he knows how to act around them. If Heflin is with people from the country, he knows how to talk with them. If he's with the elite, he knows how to talk with them. He can always say the right thing at the right time.

"They couldn't run over Howell in court. He had the know-how before a jury. If some lawyer tried to get smart with him or something like that, Heflin would be nice to him, but he wouldn't take too much off him. Howell is one of the best lawyers who has ever been in the Bar in northwest Alabama. He is smart. He might call himself a country lawyer, but he is good in whatever he does. Howell's a workaholic. He'd work seven days a week, and if it took it, he'd work seven nights, too. He enjoyed it, and when he had a case, he was prepared for it. The only hobby he had was playing tennis. He'd play with Ed Mauldin and some others."

Carmichael explains how Howell's big appetite and joy in eating worked in his favor. "The Southern Railway used to have a fellow named Shrader who would give chitling dinners. Heflin liked to come and eat those chitlings. The people thought he hung the moon, you know, down there eating those chitlings when he was a young man."

Charles Rosser, Howell's law partner, says that Howell could take a case and do things with it that most lawyers couldn't. "He was a lawyer who could persuade a jury to view things his way and persuade a judge or an appellate court, and he was famous."

Rosser describes three types of lawyers who can successfully present a case to a jury or to an appellate court. One is the lawyer who is so thoroughly versed in the law and the facts of his case that his presentation is overwhelmingly convincing. Another kind has charm and charisma and good looks, and you want to do things for them because they're handsome.

The third kind, the kind Heflin is, exudes sincerity and honesty. "He convinces you right away when you meet him and talk to him that he's not going to tell you a lie. He doesn't have to tell you that he's not going to tell you a lie. Something about his character and presentation makes you know you can hang your hat on what he says. He also convinces you that the cause he's involved in is of utmost importance. Howell's not the most handsome guy in the world and he's not the most charming, but he makes you feel he's not going to lie to you. He's going to tell it to you straight, and he's going to talk to you about important things."

Rosser describes another key Heflin quality as total loyalty to whatever he happens to be involved in. "If it's a friendship, he will be totally loyal to that friendship. If it's a case, he's going to stick to the case and do everything that needs to be done. If it's a political party, he's going to be loyal to that almost to a fault.

"Those are the things that made him a very convincing, persuasive lawyer. The same things that made him a convincing lawyer made him a convincing Senator. Sincerity comes through, and people see it. He's honest. How often do you deal with somebody that you feel is being totally honest? Not often."

Rosser comments on the humor which helped Heflin in trying cases.

"I don't suppose he tried to be entertaining or funny, but in a lot of the cases, he came across like that. Whether he was actually seeking that result or not, it was effective."

Rosser, like Charles Carmichael, remembers that Howell worked all of the time. "He didn't waste time much with sports. One time I asked him to go deer hunting, and he said, 'That's the silliest thing in the world. I tried that once. You sit on a damn stump and freeze your toes off waiting for a poor ole deer to come walking by.' He did like to go to ball games, and he would have lunch with his buddies, but that was about the extent of his wasting time. He'd come to the office early and leave late, and he'd work on Saturday and Sunday. He was a hard worker.

"He was probably the one lawyer in town that everybody in the legal profession, including judges, leaned on and counted on for strength and advice if they needed it. He has more friends than anybody I've ever known."

Rosser comments on one of Howell's habits that later drew the ire of writers, TV analysts, and both friends and enemies in the political world. "He makes you wait till the last damn minute. The first thing he did when he became chief justice was to push everybody to get things moving in a hurry. He did it, and it worked. Local judges throughout the state reduced their dockets from a two- or three-year wait to a few months. I laughed. Heflin never filed a suit until the last day. The statute of limitation meant that most cases had to be filed within one year, and Heflin would file on the 364th day. He got us all in a hurry, but he never was in a hurry."

Rosser notes that a Heflin habit is to pick off of his friend's plates. "If he's having steak and you're having pork chops, he will want a bite of the pork chop. One time Howell and a group of people were at a motel in Florida. Six or eight of them were at a table eating at a breakfast buffet where you got everything you wanted. A woman eating breakfast alone was at a next table. She got up and left. Heflin spotted a muffin on her plate that she hadn't touched. He said, 'Well, I'll just get that, and I won't have to go get one.' So he reached over for it and ate it. About the time he finished, the woman came back. She'd only been to the bathroom. She sat down and looked for her muffin. Howell got up and went on his way, leaving the others at the table to explain it to her."

Several people have commented on Howell's habit of keeping notes on envelopes. Each morning he would reach in a stack of envelopes and get one, and he would jot down the things he had to do that day. "That was his diary," Rosser says. "He might finish this one and use another one today, or he might not finish it and use the same one tomorrow. That was his modern way of keeping up with his tasks for the day."

A close friend, Joe Ware, says that Howell remained a good tennis player. "A group of us played tennis together every Sunday afternoon for something like thirty years, and Howell was in that group when he was in town. People say, 'He's such a big man. How could he get around?' Well, he was so big, he didn't need to get around. He could stay in the middle of the tennis court, and you couldn't get a ball past him. He's a natural athlete and quick. He was a darn good tennis player."

Ware tells the following story about Howell's size. "A grand-dame Southern lady in Florence, Mrs. Mae Ervin, was hosting the Florence Study Club, a very old club. They were meeting at Mrs. Mae's house, and Howell was the speaker. Mrs. Mae had a very dainty, delicate dining room chair for him to sit in, and Howell was a large man. Howell sat in the chair and it broke. There were many apologies and much embarrassment and all that. A few years later when Howell was running for the Supreme Court, my mother-in-law, who was well over 80 at that time, was calling her lady friends to vote for Howell. She called Mrs. Mae, and Mrs. Mae said, 'Indeed I will not vote for him. He broke my chair!'"

THE ETHICS COMMISSION. Another sign of respect for Howell Heflin came in 1969 when he was named to the State Ethics Commission by Governor Albert Brewer. Brewer was a well-liked, bright progressive who was trying to lead Alabama to higher ground after a disastrous six years.

Brewer became Governor by accident. He had been one of a group of energetic "young Turks" who first came to office in 1955 with plans to move Alabama forward. Unfortunately for their good intentions, the civil rights struggle intervened. Brewer supported Wallace for a time because he thought the harsh rhetoric was just political game-playing. He was elected lieutenant governor, the state's second highest office, in 1966 after a career in the state House. By then, Brewer had come to believe that George Wallace was a dangerous man doing great harm to the state.[6] Albert Brewer became governor on May 7, 1968, when Lurleen Wallace died from cancer only sixteen months after taking office.

The ten-member Ethics Commission was set up under executive order by Governor Brewer following indictment of two state senators and charges of Capitol Hill corruption. The same executive order establishing the Commission also spelled out a code of ethics which calls on state officials, including legislators, to disclose their holdings in firms or other financial dealings which may put them in a conflict of interest with the state.[7] The Commission included people like Guy Hardwick who had been lieutenant governor and Eris Paul who was a circuit judge. Commission members elected Howell as their chairman.

In the meantime, Howell had returned to his law practice. He continued to be active in the Alabama Bar Association, the American Bar Association, and the American Judicature Society. He made a number of speeches to other bar associations about Alabama Bar Association reform efforts when he was president.

"We met when the Brewer administration decided to circulate disclosure forms to all state officials," Howell says. "We had some hearings on officials accused of unethical conduct. However, many felt that officials in the legislature would have to pass an ethics law, doubting such an executive order's effectiveness."

POLITICS CALLS. Howell was tempted to run for office in 1968 after Lister Hill decided he would not run for reelection to the Senate. Hill was 74, and his close call in the 1962 election showed that his New Deal liberalism no longer played well in Alabama. "Jim Allen and Armistead Selden were probably going to be candidates," Howell remembers, "and a good number of people over the state urged me to run. I looked at it carefully. Wallace was very powerful at the time, and he could either elect or defeat pretty well anybody he wanted to. I had opposed him and knew he would be against me, so I decided it was best I didn't run."

Charlie Carmichael speaks of Howell's viability as a candidate. "You didn't have to politic for Heflin much after people knew him," Charles says. "They knew what caliber he was. Around here and in the county they'd say, 'Oh, yeah, I know him. That's Brother Heflin's son.' All these Methodists supported Howell. He was a showman. Put that cigar in his mouth, and he'd put on a show."

Howell, of course, had thoughts of public office even in his childhood days when he made speeches to corn stalks. He says that the possibility of office was in the back of his mind in his law school days and the twenty-two years he practiced law. As Ed Mauldin comments, "Howell's got politics in his genes. He came from a leadership family, and he was involved in various campaigns from the early 1950s."

A MAN WIDELY RECOGNIZED. During the twenty-two years Howell Heflin practiced law in Tuscumbia, his reputation grew locally and statewide, and he received many honors and many opportunities for public service.

Howell Heflin was 49 years old, vigorous, and in good health. He had kept his finger in politics, and he was well-known and well-liked among professional people statewide, including educators as well as lawyers and politicians. As president of the Alabama Teachers Tenure Commission, he had met a lot of teachers and administrators, school board members, and officials of the Alabama Education Association.

Howell's quiet but persistent opposition to George Wallace and his progressive stand on racial matters made him a breath of fresh air in a state struggling to overcome the outrageous demagoguery and blatant racism of the Wallace years. Different strands of his history, including his long-standing interest in political office, had converged in 1970 to make Howell's emergence as a political candidate almost inevitable.

11

Judicial Reform Begins

IN 1970, THE JUDICIAL system in Alabama was ranked at the bottom by national observers. The state had what legal expert Charles Cole calls "a non-system of courts of varied jurisdictions that were not subject to any centralized administration or accountability."[1] Alan Tarr and Mary Porter observe in *State Supreme Courts in State and Nation* that the Alabama Supreme Court was "in total control of old men" operating under antiquated, petty, and ludicrous rules, and it was known nationally for the length of time it took to decide cases. The court's reputation outside the state was further diminished by its eager participation in Alabama's fierce resistance to the civil rights movement. . . ."[2]

In Alabama, the state legislature had long been the most dominant branch of government. This was by design. The 1901 Constitution placed power in an alliance of big land owners, Black Belt "Bourbons,"* and industrialists. This alliance controlled the state through the first two-thirds of the twentieth century, and efforts to balance power through one-man-one-vote are still not completely successful. Governor "Big Jim" Folsom challenged the system with some success in the 1940s and 1950s but did not affect the basic political structure.

---

* "Bourbon" refers to a group who, taking their attitudes from the Reconstruction-era white planters of the Black Belt, held that civilization and order depended on white supremacy and total domination of blacks. A related interest was protecting financial and social positions.

In this situation, the Alabama Supreme Court was effectively controlled by the legislature. Justices followed the desires of the legislature in their opinions, and they allowed the legislature to formulate judicial rules of procedure. The question of separation of powers was seldom raised.[3] The idea was non-existent of an independent judiciary unaffected by the whims of momentary political fortune and providing a stabilizing counter to other branches of government.

The 1901 Constitution established the circuit (state level) courts but left it up to the legislature to set up the remainder of the court system. Intermediate courts proliferated, with wide variations from county to county. Different counties could set their own system by having their representatives get a local act passed.

A trial court survey, conducted by the Judicial Conference of Alabama in 1973, revealed that there were eighty-five limited jurisdiction trial courts, apart from municipal and probate courts, under twenty-three different names, each with varying jurisdiction and procedure.[4] Each court had different jurisdictions, and each had its own rules. Even lawyers were confused.

The Alabama Supreme Court was known for stringent application of rules, to the detriment of decisions based on merit. Numbers of appeals were dismissed because transcript pages were incorrectly numbered, margins were not of requisite width, the "inevitable red ribbon" girding the transcript was not arranged according to specification, or counsel had failed to include in the brief the "ritual incantations about the organization of the circuit courts."[5]

The Justice of the Peace system in the state was a travesty. A lot of Justice of the Peace courts were rackets. Justices would be in trailers, and the highway patrol or the sheriff's people would be out on the highways. They would stop somebody, take them to a moveable trailer housing the Justice of the Peace, and collect the fees and the fine right there and maybe split the take among themselves. There was no regulation of Justices of the Peace. Their decisions faced no review, and they were subject to no audit.

The entire judicial system in Alabama was beset with serious delays.

Janie L. Shores, later a justice of the Alabama Supreme Court, commented that the entire court system was several years behind in caseloads. At the appellate level, three or four years passed after submission before opinions were released. At the trial level, it was not unusual in some instances for four or five years to pass from the date of filing to the date of trial.[6]

The Alabama judiciary and its Supreme Court justices reflected the views of the white establishment. The 1901 Constitution legally prevented blacks from voting, and it kept them out of government. The courts went along in assuring that blacks remained virtually powerless second-class citizens. In cases involving black defendants and white victims, the courts unfailingly intensified the race issue.

This system was challenged in 1954 with the U.S. Supreme Court's *Brown v. Board of Education* decision. Response of Alabama courts echoed the state's political leadership and played an important role in the state's counterattack late in the 1950s against the NAACP. Disagreement with the U.S. Supreme Court during this period turned into contempt, fear, and hatred of the federal judiciary.[7]

At Governor George Wallace's request, the court provided advisory opinions sustaining the validity of his closing of the public schools instead of obeying federal court orders to integrate. It helped the state find a way around the U.S. Supreme Court's invalidation of the Boswell Amendment to the state Constitution. The Boswell Amendment denied the ballot to blacks.[8]

PRELIMINARIES TO REFORM. Several attempts to reform the state judiciary had been made in the past, with some change. The Alabama rules of civil and criminal procedure were first adopted in 1852 and had undergone several revisions.[9]

Governor Emmet O'Neal created a commission to study judicial reform in 1912. After receiving a report from the commission in 1915, he reported to the legislature that, "in Alabama our whole judicial system has grown up without harmony, unity of scientific arrangement, each legislature creating different courts, until the whole system has become a patchwork which now demands revision and reform." He made a number of recommendations, but the legislature took no action. "Although Governor O'Neal's Commission recommended and the legislature conferred administrative and supervisory powers on the chief justice, the support staff necessary to facilitate the exercise of such authority was not provided to the chief justice until the 1970s when the Department of Court Management and the Administrative Office of Courts were created."[10]

An Alabama Commission for Judicial Reform was organized in 1955 during the second Folsom administration. Financial support was appropriated, and the commission spent a lot of time studying issues, including rules of procedure. The commission made an effort to have the state legislature adopt federal rules of civil procedure and an up-to-date method of pleadings and practice in the courts. With the help of consultants, including the famed Charles Allen Wright, whose works on Federal Civil Procedure and Practice were considered outstanding, it prepared new rules of civil procedure in 1957. It tried to get legislation adopting them, but the legislature did not act. In the meantime, there was a "law explosion" in Alabama and the rest of the country. State procedures were very detailed, cumbersome, and time consuming, and there were too few judges to meet the need. Cases quickly became backlogged.

Some progress was made in the early 1960s when the legislature established a Judicial Conference to conduct a continuing study of the system and to present reports to each regular session of the legislature recommending improvements.[11]

THE FIRST CITIZENS' CONFERENCE. The Citizens' Conference Howell Heflin had planned when he was president of the state bar association was held in Birmingham December 8–10, 1966. More than 100 delegates from all over the state attended. Birmingham lawyer Douglas Arant served as chairman, and many outstanding people attended. Though Howell had left office as bar association president, he was a leader in the meeting. Justice Pelham Merrill of the state Supreme Court made the keynote speech, and speakers from around the country who had been involved in reform efforts were brought in.[12]

Participants included Monsignor Oscar Lipscomb from the Catholic Diocese in Mobile. Howell calls Monsignor Lipscomb "a great citizen, one who has never been given much recognition for what he's done for the state." Lipscomb later became Archbishop of the Mobile area. The conference included blacks, labor and management. Some prominent Birmingham women were involved, along with the League of Women Voters and the Business and Professional Women.

Howell says that the Citizens' Conference was effective.

> The American Judicature Society had gone through several Citizens' Conferences, and they had a pretty good format. We profited by their experience. The selection of judges was discussed, as was ways to eliminate as much politics as possible. It discussed the Missouri plan, the Illinois plan, and other state plans, and then it discussed the federal rules and how they needed to be adopted.
>
> When the legislature met in 1967, it was very supportive. People who attended the conference formed a nucleus of lobbyists for adoption of recommendations of the Conference. C.C. "Bo" Torbert, later to be chief justice, was in the state senate then and was supportive, as was Lieutenant Governor Albert Brewer. They introduced a package of bills that had the endorsement of the Citizens' Conference and the state bar association. We were all enthusiastic that we could get these passed.
>
> But George Wallace was ranting and raving against federal judges and, of course, he was opposed to all of this all along. The opponents were saying, "You're just trying to have a federal court system in the state." Well, the Speaker of the House was Wallace's man. Instead of assigning the bills to the Judiciary Committee, he assigned them to the Highway Safety Committee. They got buried and never got out of committee.
>
> When Albert Brewer became governor after Lurleen Wallace died, the Citizens' Conference interest was still there. Justice Pelham Merrill was the legislative liaison. He and Bill Younger, librarian and marshal

for the Supreme Court, went up to the governor's office and met with Hugh Maddox, who was then the governor's legal advisor. Maddox later became a justice of the Supreme Court.

The Citizens' Conference people wanted several bills, but they decided they had better concentrate, so they asked for a bill that would increase the membership of the Supreme Court from seven to nine. They wanted to enlarge the three-man Alabama Court of Appeals, but finally agreed as a compromise to a Court of Civil Appeals with three members and a Court of Criminal Appeals with three members. Brewer supported this, and the two bills were passed. Conference people were also pushing for a new judicial building, but Brewer wouldn't go along with that, for he felt that reform had to pass in small doses.

A great deal of interest in judicial reform had been raised by the Citizens' Conference and some progress made, but much remained to be done. Alabama Supreme Court Justice Hugh Maddox says, "In my opinion, (the Citizens' Conference) was the catalyst for the judicial reform that would later occur."[13]

CONSTITUTIONAL REVISION COMMISSION. In 1968, Governor Brewer appointed an Alabama Constitutional Revision Commission and charged them with rewriting the entire state Constitution. Conrad Fowler, Howell's friend from the marines and law school days, was appointed chairman. Fowler was then probate judge of Shelby County. Leigh Harrison, retired dean of the University of Alabama Law School, was hired as the executive director.

According to Conrad Fowler, the membership included some very able people. "We had consultants brought in, and we worked at it diligently," he says. "We finally drafted a new Constitution for Alabama, and we published a small book that included the Constitution and an explanation of what we had done. However, there was no positive reception at all from the Wallace administration for what the Commission was doing."

Howell says that the Commission did a rather remarkable job, with

Harrison's legal expertise and Fowler's law experience and leadership ability. In 1971, after the work had been underway two years, George Wallace again became governor, and he did not support the work. He had toned down his racist rhetoric since he had presidential ambitions, but he was still against any change in the balance of power in the state and anything that resembled cooperation with the federal courts. Efforts for a new Constitution and judicial reform stalled until a strong reformer became chief justice.[14]

DECIDING TO RUN FOR CHIEF JUSTICE. As the 1970 election drew near, people wondered if Ed Livingston would run again for chief justice. Livingston had held the position for twenty years (1951-71) and was 78 years old. Howell says that everybody assumed Livingston probably would not run, so they began looking around for another candidate.

Former Governor John Patterson was testing the political waters for a chief justice campaign.

> The lawyers didn't want Patterson. At that time, much of the leadership in the legal profession dealt with companies, lawyers, and people in other parts of the country. The image of Alabama was bad with George Wallace all ranting and raving, plus we had the quickie divorce scandal. There was also the feeling we ought to do more about judicial reform.
>
> The lawyers looked around for somebody they might get to run. I was happily practicing law, making substantial money, and I didn't have much interest in it. But they started talking to me, and a lot of momentum began to grow. If I didn't run, they argued, Patterson would go in with his name, having been governor. He and Wallace were now friendly, and the lawyers wanted somebody to do something. They were hunting somebody who could beat him.
>
> I had lawyers from all over the state urging me to run. You know the name "Heflin" was still known at that time, and the bad parts of Tom had been forgotten. I figured if I were ever going to get in politics, this was probably the time. It may have been a little selfishness on my part.

I didn't think my wife was *really* all that opposed. She had a tone to her protest that you could read between the lines, and she had some relatives and friends down in Montgomery.

Elizabeth Ann counters, "I thought all of the politics thing was over. I relaxed. Then when he started getting serious about chief justice, I asked, 'What in the world are you doing?' I was like a tiger against his running. Timing was very bad; he never realized it was so bad."

It paid $22,000, and I was making well over $100,000 a year at the time practicing law. I had been president of the Bar, and I had some standing among the lawyers and in the community. I had recently formed a partnership with Charlie Rosser. We had an associate or two, so things were going pretty good.

For years, I had in the back of my mind that, if the right opportunity came, I would like to jump into political waters. I still had the idea of doing something more about the judicial system and the legal system. I got broad-based urging, and I finally agreed to run. I don't say I was drafted, but it was pretty close to it. I had a lot of lawyer support.

THE CAMPAIGN. Heflin ran for chief justice against John Patterson, who had gained notoriety as governor during the Civil Rights Movement by trying to defy federal authority with his strong stand on segregation. At the beginning of the race, Patterson was considered the odds-on favorite. It was Heflin's first try for political office, and, while he was well known in the legal profession, he was relatively unknown among the voters.

We started out with the idea of getting my name around. I had help from Jack Voorhies, who was a radio announcer and was very clever. He could mimic in a country voice a fellow named Luther Appleby, who had a mule named Chilton. "Getty-up, Chilton!" was his trademark. He'd mention something about Heflin. He'd bring in Tom Heflin, Heflin, Alabama, and then have something about heifer. "No, it's Heflin. H-E-F-L-I-N." Then he said, "Well, you'd better elect him. I'll guarantee you one thing, he'll clean up the court system, and I want to tell you right now every courthouse in the state needs to be cleaned up. The pigeons have about ruined 'em." It was humorous as the devil.

We raised about $75,000 for the race. When you look back, that was small potatoes. We had some television ads, and I had a lot of support locally.

Elizabeth Ann and some of her friends resurrected an idea they had used when Bert Haltom ran for lieutenant governor. The girls from the Shoals area formed a group called "Howell's Angels" and campaigned statewide. They wore straw hats, vests, and striped jackets, and they wore little buttons with Howell's picture on them. Ed Mauldin's wife, Mildred, was one of Howell's Angels. Ed says that his wife abhors politics but was very excited about Howell's campaign, and she wanted to be involved with her friend Elizabeth Ann. Joe Ware's wife was also a member. "They'd get in their outfits, and they'd take off," he recalls. "I think they loved Howell and Elizabeth Ann so much they were willing to do anything that they were asked to support him."

Howell was aware of the need for statewide organization, which he didn't have when the campaign began.

> Patterson had his machine, and he had the group that had been with him as governor. But I knew lawyers in every community in the state, and this gave me a nucleus like most people who are successful politically. I'd been all over the place trying to solicit money for the Farrah Law Society. My motivation in being bar president was judicial reform, and I wanted to improve legal education when we organized the Farrah Law Society. As a by-product of these, I had made a lot of political friends. The Law Society had 500 some-odd members.

Howell did his best to keep racial matters out of his campaign. The governor's race was between George Wallace and Albert Brewer. It was very nasty, with heavy racist overtones and documented dirty tricks by Wallace supporters. Heflin acknowledges that some of those overtones got into the chief justice campaign because the Wallace people wanted Patterson. "But we tried to keep out of their fight. It's a fundamental rule that you do not get into somebody else's politics when you're running."

The black vote had grown rapidly in Alabama since 1965 and was now a substantial force. To take advantage of their growing power, blacks had organized the Alabama Democratic Conference (ADC), which was headed by Joe Reed, associate executive secretary of the Alabama Education Association.

> Everybody who was running wanted the black vote, but they didn't want to be identified with it. The ADC had screening committees, and they wanted candidates to go to the Whitley Hotel in Montgomery and meet with them. Then they would make their endorsements. The only two who would go were Bill Baxley, a candidate for Alabama Attorney General, and myself. We appeared before the screening committee, and we got the endorsement. Later the blacks talked about what a courageous step it was.

Joe Reed remembers the 1970 race. "I had just been elected chairman of the Alabama Democratic Conference. We thought John Patterson was strong in the chief justice race, and getting behind Heflin was a thrill, a thrill for more than one reason. It was a thrill for us to help pay back John Patterson. As Attorney General and Governor of Alabama, Patterson had not been very kind to issues of concern to blacks. I had taught school in Tuscumbia, Senator Heflin's hometown. I didn't know him when I was teaching, but I always heard positive things about him. At that time folks called him 'Lawyer' Heflin."[15]

During the election, *The Huntsville Times* characterized Heflin as "a man of intelligence and integrity. Steeped in the best traditions of the legal profession, he also is a creative, innovative practitioner of the law ... with a wide repute as a brilliant attorney." Heflin received the endorsement of most of the larger dailies of the state. Before the election, polls revealed Heflin was on a rise and in the lead.

The Birmingham News, reporting the day after the primary (May 6,

1970), said that Howell never mentioned Patterson's name in any of his speeches or appearances during the campaign. They said, "Patterson said the race was a choice between 'a lawyer's judge and a people's judge.'"

Heflin won the Democratic primary by a two to one margin. He told the *Birmingham News*, "I am indeed grateful to the voters for their support, particularly to the people of the Muscle Shoals area where results indicate I received about 95 percent of my neighbors' votes." He was proud of the local folks' support. "I thought I'd made a lot of enemies practicing law. They must have gone underground or something."

Asked if he had enjoyed the campaigning, Howell replied, "Yeah! Oh yeah!" For sure, a politician had been born.

George Wallace narrowly defeated Brewer in the governor's race, assuring that the new chief justice would face opposition in trying to proceed with judicial reform.

On April 19, during the election, University of Alabama law students gave the first Daniel J. Meador Outstanding Alumnus Award to Heflin. The award, created by members of Bench and Bar, a legal honorary fraternity, is named for former law school dean, Daniel J. Meador. It is given annually to a graduate who was outstanding during the previous year.

THE WORK BEGINS. Howell Heflin took office as chief justice of the Alabama Supreme Court on January 18, 1971. His friends Bert Haltom, Bob Cox, and Charlie Rosser helped to robe him at his investiture. Drawing on his twenty-three years experience as a trial lawyer and his work with the bar, Howell was ready to strike out for reform.

The Heflins rented an apartment in Montgomery, but their son, Tom, did not move there with them. He was still in high school in Tuscumbia and playing football. So Elizabeth Ann's mother moved into the Heflin's house in Tuscumbia and took care of Tom. The Heflins would go home most weekends, with Elizabeth Ann driving and Howell reading. Heflin had already found that keeping up on the court took a tremendous amount of reading and studying.

Elizabeth Ann reports that she enjoyed living in Montgomery. "I really did. Everybody thought I hated it, but I enjoyed it while we were there. I was real active in St. John's Episcopal Church. I belonged to a garden club, which was hysterical. I said, 'I don't garden.' And they said, 'We don't either.' We had a real good time, and they were sweet to invite me. I also played bridge with a foursome."

Howell was snubbed by Governor Wallace at the inauguration in January 1971.

> It had been customary for the chief justice to give the oath of office to the Governor. Well, he didn't ask me; he asked his brother, Jack Wallace, who was a circuit judge in Barbour County. The next day, Taylor Hardin of the governor's staff phoned and asked me to come up to the capitol. He had me give the oath of office to the appointed heads of departments, like the highway department and industrial relations. I didn't see much of Wallace in the beginning. Fortunately, I had strong support from the state legislature. Jere Beasley, who had been elected lieutenant governor, was very supportive of judicial reform throughout and was very helpful in the state senate. The Speaker of the House, Sage Lyons, was very supportive. His law partner, Sam Pipes, was an old-time friend of mine and was very supportive of judicial reform. He had been chairman of one of the committees when I was president of the bar association.

Work on reform began immediately, and in less than a year, Howell had the first bills through the legislature. At his urging, the state legislature in 1972 gave the Alabama Supreme Court authority to establish its own rules pertaining to appeals and practice in the state appellate courts, and the Supreme Court was given exclusive power to promulgate rules of procedure, practice, and pleading for the trial courts. This delegation of power prevented the legislature from haggling over each rule and meant that a filibuster couldn't kill rule reform. Legislation was passed to provide for a continuing judicial training and educational program and to create a Department of Court Management and a permanent Study Commission on courts.

Despite some strong opposition, Howell persuaded the legislature to set up statewide referenda on two Constitutional amendments, one which created a commission to handle complaints about judges and provide for a retirement system and a second which abolished the Justice of the Peace courts and authorized a new small claims court. These passed in a statewide vote in January 1972 by more than a two-to-one margin.

The amendment which created the Judicial Commission charged its members with responsibility for the discipline, removal, and retirement of judges, and it proved an effective way of dealing with judges whose conduct required disciplinary action. Previously, they could only be disciplined through the cumbersome method of impeachment, and no judges had been impeached in many years.

In 1971, the legislature, at Heflin's request, created the Permanent Study Commission on Alabama's Judicial System. The Commission was given broad power to study any matter which directly or indirectly affected the administration of justice, including prisons and criminal rehabilitation methods and procedures. Heflin directed the Study Commission to consider the judicial article which had been formulated by Conrad Fowler's Constitutional Commission, and the Committee became very active in the formulation of a comprehensive plan for Alabama's judicial system.[16]

DEPARTMENT OF COURT MANAGEMENT. When Heflin came to office, state law gave the chief justice responsibility for seeing that the business of the courts was carried out with proper dispatch, but no administrative help was provided to do the job. Heflin asked the legislature to create a Department of Court Management for this purpose, and it did.[17] The chief justice was designated as the chief administrative officer of the trial courts of Alabama and was furnished with personnel, including a Court Administrator.

The Department of Court Management and new rule-making power made it possible to eliminate procedural delays. To help with disposition of cases, the chief justice was given authority to assign circuit judges temporarily to the Supreme Court, the courts of criminal and civil appeals, and within the circuit courts.

ELIMINATION OF BACKLOGS. One of the first orders of business was to attack the huge backlogs in the courts. Heflin noted that it wasn't a new problem. He remarked he had read that Emperor Claudius in 42 AD requested the Roman Senate to pass a law creating a special summer session for the Roman court to ease its backlog.

Progress on eliminating backlogs was made quickly. When the October 1972 court term began, the Alabama Supreme Court was current in its docket for the first time in memory, and it was one of the few state supreme courts in the nation to be so.[18]

The Court of Criminal Appeals had a heavy backlog. In 1971, the presiding judge of that court, with the help of the chief justice, sought and obtained authority for the court to be increased from three to five judges. Also, arrangements were made for a number of circuit and retired judges to assist in reducing the heavy load. New authority from the legislature was used to transfer cases from the Court of Criminal Appeals to the Supreme Court. By November 1973, the Court of Criminal Appeals had reduced its huge backlog so that only six cases were pending at the beginning of the session.[19]

Before Heflin came to office, Jefferson County, with Birmingham, the state's largest city, wouldn't hold court in the months of June, July, and August. This led to great court congestion. People in criminal cases who couldn't make bail waited in jail as long as eighteen months for trial.

> **We brought in about twenty judges from other counties and other circuits in the state and cleared the docket. This cleared the jail of all those people who were waiting for trial. All the lawyers fussed because they didn't want to work in the summer, and the judges didn't want to work. A lot of the cases were not serious. They were felonies but not capital cases.**
>
> **Two of the judges came from down around Auburn, and they were tough. They had a judge down there called "Long-Time" Tiner.**

Another one was named "Spud" Wright. Somebody would enter a plea and expect to get a year and a day or something like that, and Spud would give them ten. Lawyers from Jefferson County came to me in a group to get rid of him. I said, "All right. I'm willing to, but I'm going to substitute Long-Time Tiner in place of him." They said, "Awww, no!" They didn't want Long-Time Tiner 'cause he was even tougher. That brought about a lot of plea negotiation.

Tiner was the one they brought the son of a congressman before. The young man was caught at Auburn with some marijuana. Tiner was going to give him ten years, but they finally talked him into probation. Well, I'll tell you, those students down there thought a long time before they smoked marijuana cigarettes.

Elizabeth Ann adds, "Interestingly enough, Judge Tiner's niece was a very good friend of mine, and poor Betty Jane suffered at what her uncle would do. Everybody was cussing him. She'd whisper, 'Do you think they know he's my uncle?'"

JUDICIAL TRAINING. In a 1972 speech Heflin said, "My first step as chief justice was to order an orientation program for all new circuit judges. Within a few days after I took office, a four-day training program for fourteen newly elected circuit judges and eight circuit judges who had served less than two years was undertaken. This orientation program, a first for a state court system in the United States, proved to be exceptionally beneficial for these twenty-two judges."[20]

An expanded judicial training program was launched for all state judges, and during the first two years of Heflin's term, he persuaded 30 of the 87 circuit judges to attend courses at the National College of the State Judiciary.[21] With the exception of New York and California, there were more judges from Alabama attending this college than any other state.

"Actually, most of the judges wanted to go to Reno," Howell relates. "We had one that wanted to go all the time. We finally had to tell him, 'No. You've been enough. You're over educated.' He'd go out there, and then he'd go to Las Vegas. When some of these judges get away from home, they're not as dignified and church living and upright as they are back home."

Howell went to outside sources for funding to support the training and other work.

> About that time, Congress had funded the Law Enforcement Assistance Program (LEAA) which was designed to improve law enforcement and the criminal laws, and it had a lot of federal money. We prevailed upon national agencies to give us some money to help with our Department of Court Management and with other things. I received monies for the courts to have assistants. We were able to get a lot of resources we couldn't get from the legislature.
>
> Judge Ingram Beasley of Birmingham was the original chairman of a committee on pattern jury charges and then was succeeded by Judge Bill Sullivan of Talladega. The Supreme Court approved these charges in 1972 or '73. Before the pattern charges were used, a lot of cases got reversed because the judges instructed the jury incorrectly on the law. They were useful thereafter.

NEW RULES OF PROCEDURE. Heflin led a successful move to change rules of procedure in Alabama courts. In 1971, shortly after he took office as chief justice, the Supreme Court appointed an advisory committee to prepare suggested rules of appellate procedure for its consideration. This culminated in new Alabama Rules of Appellate Procedure.[22]

New rules of civil procedure were adopted on January 3, 1973. They revised pleading, practice, and procedure in all civil matters before state courts, and they represented an effort to make justice faster and less expensive for the litigant. The state ETV network beamed 144 telecasts throughout the state to help in educating the legal profession and citizens about the new civil procedures.[23]

CIVIL RIGHTS. In 1974, Elaine R. Jones of the NAACP Legal Defense Fund, was representing an Alabama death-row inmate, Johnny Daniel

Beecher. Jones notes that Beecher was entitled to due process under the law no matter what his crime. The case was taken to the U.S. Supreme Court twice, and both times Jones and her group prevailed. But Alabama kept retrying Mr. Beecher. A cousin of Hugo Black was the prosecutor.

Jones recounts, "The third time Beecher was tried, it went up through the state court system. My petition before the Alabama Supreme Court was denied, and I was on my way back to the U.S. Supreme Court for the third time. Meanwhile, Howell Heflin became chief justice." Jones decided to file with the state Supreme Court again, and the Court voted to reverse the conviction. "The Alabama Supreme Court didn't need the U.S. Supreme Court to tell them what to do," Jones says. "The Alabama Court issued a carefully-written opinion, following the law. Judge Heflin is a lawyer's lawyer. He understands how the law is supposed to work, and he's not afraid of tough issues."[24]

MIKE HOUSE JOINS THE STAFF. In September 1972, Howell added Mike House to his staff. House would be with Heflin some fourteen years altogether, both in the chief justice years and the U.S. Senate years. House, who had recently graduated from law school, was working in Dallas for a Texas congressman but wanted to return to Alabama. He wrote a letter to Chief Justice Heflin. Howell and House had met when House was a law student at the University of Alabama. Heflin knew House was smart, and he wanted somebody who knew something about politics and about legislation, so he hired House.

Mike House was born, raised and attended public schools in Birmingham. He received a BA degree from Auburn University in 1968 and a J.D. from the University of Alabama Law School in 1971. House was in law school when Howell was elected chief justice, and was president of the Student Bar Association his senior year. Howell Heflin gave the speech at the Student Bar Association Bar Day activities that year.

Mike House, who became Howell's administrative assistant for legislative liaison, commented, "I don't think I've ever met a man who was as focused as he was as chief justice; he was a man who really knew what he wanted to do and who had the energy and the ability to do it."[25]

GETTING SUPPORT FOR THE FIRST CHANGES. "We were able to pass all of these first things during the honeymoon you get after taking office," Howell says. "There wasn't a lot of opposition, and we had support from the Citizens' Conference."

Some of the judges in the state supported the change, but a substantial number were opposed at first. Howell won them by offering them a carrot related to retirement. Mike House explains how this was done.

"They had this supernumerary system," he explains. "It was an old system that developed because of the Constitutional provision that no elected official could become part of a retirement system. To get around this problem, elected officials created the supernumerary position. For example, if a sheriff after finishing his term had so many years, he could qualify to become a supernumerary sheriff. That meant that he was on call to do sheriff's work in his county or any other county. The same was true of tax assessors, tax collectors, and circuit judges. The supernumerary would draw some type of annual salary. It was pretty inadequate, but they didn't make any contributions to their retirement system like the state employees, and their wives received no benefits after the office holder's death."

Howell came up with a retirement system for the judges. "We had all the judges and their wives in," House recalls. "We had this dinner, and Heflin was telling them about the system. As he talked about the changes he was going to make, he said, 'We're going to put a retirement system in, and guess what? The retirement system's going to have widow benefits.' The wives heard that, and by the next day, we didn't have a problem because the wives had all talked to their husbands. If you're taking something away from somebody, jurisdiction or whatever, you've got to give them something. It took a lot of thought to get there, and it was absolutely incredible."[26]

Howell remembers that several judges took the lead in supporting reform. This included Judges Jim Haley in Birmingham, Bill Sullivan in Talladega, John Snodgrass in Huntsville, Jerry Vanderhoef in Tuscumbia, and J. Edward Tease in Florence.

They were younger and were real supportive. Judge Joe Hocklander from Mobile was a real champion. Retirement was the carrot that got the judges, but we still had to sell them on all of it. Any time you change anybody's *status quo* you run into great difficulty.

When I went there, the attitude of the state Supreme Court was to find a way not to follow the decisions of the United States Supreme Court. Of course, the Constitution of the United States and the decisions of the United States Supreme Court are the ultimate law. The United States Supreme Court was highly criticized for its liberal stance and criminal law matters such as Miranda warnings and search and seizures.

Many people wanted to move forward and stay in step with what the law required in regards to the Constitution, but a lot didn't. Several of the justices were old, and when I first went in they would write opinions that would find a way to get around U.S. Supreme Court decisions they didn't like. During the first year, I wrote something like thirty or forty dissenting opinions from what they wrote. That shook some of them up, but at the same time it gave support to some of the others who wanted to dissent but hadn't spoken out.

We went through a period of trying to educate. Of course, the other justices were feeling pressures and were running for office. At that time, the John Birch Society had billboards all over the state that said, "Impeach Earl Warren."

Warren was chief justice of the U.S. Supreme Court. Hugo Black was considered to be a traitor to Alabama. Bill Mitchell, a friend over in Florence, told me that when he was in law school, some bright young lawyers wanted to bring Hugo Black down to speak and said something to some of the older lawyers about it. The older lawyers said, "We'll ride you out of town on a rail if you bring Hugo Black to Alabama to speak." We were at a time when a transition was needed, but this required some push and leadership.

We started encouraging some young people to seek election to the court, people like Janie Shores, a young woman, and Red Jones and some others. They eventually ran and got elected. We had to go through a transition period internally, and in time we changed the attitude of the courts.

Looking over all that had happened in the time since he took office, Howell Heflin said in a 1973 speech, "Perhaps the most important change which has taken place in the past two years is the atmosphere of cooperation on the part of judges, lawyers, legislators, and citizens throughout the state to improve the administration of justice. At all levels there is now an awareness of the need to improve the operation of our courts system so that cases may be speedily and justly decided."[27]

A great deal had been accomplished during the first two years of Howell Heflin's term as chief justice of the Alabama Supreme Court, but even more remained. The Constitutional Commission headed by Conrad Fowler was continuing its work, and changing the state Constitution would be a far bigger fight because it would threaten powerful interests which were long entrenched.

12

The Judicial Article

LEGISLATIVE ACTION IN 1971 and 1972 had assisted Chief Justice Howell Heflin in beginning judicial modernization, but he knew that the real answer in reforming the state's judicial system lay in rewriting part of Alabama's 1901 Constitution. Heflin began work immediately on a revision of Article VI, the Judicial Article.

Rewriting the Constitution was fraught with difficulty, for it involved a complex mix of conflicting feelings and interests. The 1901 Constitution was the crowning victory in restoring white supremacy to Alabama after the bitter years which followed the Civil War. "Wrote one observer of the Alabama and Southern scene 'the Negro vote has made political progress exceedingly tedious. Reforms and more timely laws have come tardily, lest their suddenness might divide the white vote.' "Lily White" Republicans joined the disfranchising movement because they believed 'that the only hope of the Republican Party and of political progress in the South' lay in the elimination of the Negro vote."[1] For years, special interests played the "Southern Way of Life" theme with great skill and portrayed anyone who questioned the state's way of handling legal matters as a traitor to holy memories.

By the end of World War II, the "Lost Cause" theme had faded somewhat, along with memories of the Civil War. The total effort thrown into defeating the Axis powers — mental, physical, and economic — established a new outlook and gave hope that Alabama was ready to put the past aside and join the New South in a progressive future. The early 1950s were a time of great hope as bright young men, veterans who had fought for freedom and democracy, entered politics and took leadership in business and legal affairs. Such hopes were dashed by the state's reaction to the Civil Rights Movement and the politics of discord, reaction, and bitter resistance followed by Governors John Patterson and George Wallace from 1959 through 1968.

When Howell Heflin became chief justice, lawyers throughout Alabama knew that the judicial system was in desperate need of reform, and businessmen knew that their own future depended on generating a better image for the state. Still, politicians were able to sway the people with allusions to the "Southern Way of Life" and suggestions that trying to change the 1901 Constitution was somehow traitorous. No one else had been able to change the document in any fundamental way in the 70 years since its adoption, and Howell Heflin faced a mighty task. Fortunately, he had strong allies in the fight, and he could build on a work in progress which showed that the change was not just his idea. The Alabama Constitutional Commission continued working under the leadership of Conrad Fowler, and plans were made in 1973 to present the Commission's report. Fowler relates that members of the Commission would attend meetings with Howell, and Howell's staff members were prime movers. "They were building public sentiment to support what we had offered," Fowler says. "Howell's influence was very noticeable throughout the state meetings. The needed sentiments were developed among voters so that the legislature took the thing seriously."

For better or worse, a decision was made not to try to adopt a complete new Constitution. The Constitution Commission felt it would be impossible for the legislature to deal with an entire new Constitution in one session, and it decided to submit only the portion which dealt with the judiciary.[2] Conrad Fowler says that the article submitted to the legislature was very close to what the Commission had adopted. "The Judicial Article was not precisely what the Commission approved," he recalls, "but I felt the changes strengthened rather than weakened the article."

OPPOSITION TO CHANGE. A lot of opposition to the new Judicial Article developed in 1973. One reason, Howell says, is that Alabamians just naturally don't like change. Women were coming on the jury for the first time in Alabama, and that was a big change. "Ye Gods," Heflin exclaims in mock horror, "there was terrible opposition to putting women on the jury. My Lord!" Blacks were coming on juries for the first time in the twentieth century, and the old line segregationists didn't like that.

Among the many groups who were initially opposed were farmers, timber owners, and some business interests. There was also opposition by non-lawyer judges, by Justices of the Peace whose positions were to be eliminated, and by others in the old power structure who liked the *status quo*.

A major opponent was the League of Municipalities, which feared the proposal would take away city funds from court costs and fees.

Governor Wallace took a dim view of reform, and although his opposition was muted, people who supported him were considered a serious threat. Wallace was quietly doing everything he could to undermine the Judicial Article.

> He didn't want to come out too vehemently against it because it wouldn't look good, but he wasn't for it. Sage Lyons, one of Wallace's legal advisors, had helped us before, but he didn't help us any now.
>
> One reason Wallace was opposed was that I had never supported him, and he didn't want me to gain any strength. Some of Wallace's opposition was based on "Heflin's got a political name, and you better be careful about him. He'll be running for something one of these days, and you don't want him to get too much publicity."

Tarr and Porter commented in *State Supreme Courts in State and Nation* that there were lingering resentments in Alabama against the federal government and the rest of the country generally, with opponents contending that the proposed new rules of procedure would "federalize" the state courts. "The creation of a Department of Court Administration headed by a court administrator raised apprehensions about 'some liberal

New York professor' riding herd over judges elected by the people of the sovereign state of Alabama," Tarr and Porter relate. "Heflin himself was a target, accused by some as being engaged in a 'personal power grab.'"[3]

One compromise involved appeals courts.

> We wanted to consolidate the Court of Civil Appeals and the Court of Criminal Appeals. National consultants told us we didn't need to have two separate courts. The clerk of the Court of Criminal Appeals was a woman named Mollie Jordan, and Mollie was very influential with the legislators. She was utterly opposed to changing her court. She got the governor and John Harris, the governor's legal advisor, to oppose and to delay a lot of things. Finally, we had to compromise with her and keep the Court of Civil Appeals and the Court of Criminal Appeals separate. She was a powerful woman.
>
> Many older lawyers also did not favor the change. The lawyers who had vested interests were strongly opposed. The astute lawyer back home, if he was over 50, was generally opposed to it because he knew ways he could win a law suit not on merit but on a technicality, and he didn't want to give that up. These young lawyers had all the zip and vinegar and go, and they'd have the facts on their side, but there would be some technicality. Well, you know, the older ones could see that their castles were going to be destroyed.
>
> And then the judicial staff was slow in supporting the change. At first the clerks didn't know whether they were going to support it or not. You had to give them a carrot. You had the registrars who wouldn't go along at first. Most of the judges were opposed at the start, so you had to make compromises.
>
> Forty-four of the circuit clerks were on a fee system before the change, and their income would be converted to a salary. Some clerks on the fee system were making $75,000 to $100,000 a year. They opposed it, and they got some of their legislators to oppose.
>
> One old clerk, an old time tough politician in Autauga County, would get up in the clerks' meeting and oppose it. He called me "the great white father" in these meetings. Later on when I ran for the

Senate, he fought me, as did several of the clerks who had been on the fee system. Someone claimed my Autauga County friend was one of those clerks making $75,000 a year.

I would always go to the courthouse in all the counties when I was in the Senate, and I'd go by to see him. I jokingly called him "the great white father." He was an old curmudgeon of the first order. He didn't want any changes.

Another issue was the cost of the new system. Heflin knew it would be substantial.

We had national consultants who came in under LEAA (Law Enforcement Assistance Administration) monies, and they knew something about the costs of other judicial systems and what ours would be. Since it would be a unified court system, the state would assume all the costs. The consultants made estimates. Actually they made errors, because it cost more than they said. A good bit of opposition was based on cost. We made the argument that the entire judicial system of the state would only amount to one percent of the entire budget of the state. This was very small compared to other branches of government.

BUILDING SUPPORT. Heflin knew that he faced a very large task in winning support for the Judicial Article. Support from all segments of the state's population would be necessary to overcome the governor's foot-dragging, entrenched interests in the legislature, and certain elements of the legal establishment.

The corporate world was for the change, and we got the Farm Bureau to support it. A lot of corporate lawyers had a good deal of experience in the federal courts. In those days, if somebody filed a suit against General Motors in Winston County and it was for more than $3,000, you could remove it to the federal courts under the diversity of citizenship theory. Most of the corporate people knew they would end up having a fairer deal and less "home cooking." You know, in rural counties you could get a lot of "home cooking" then. The judges and the jurors took care of their own and in some places still do. Sometimes I represented the local person, so it depends which side you are on whether you are for or against "home cooking." But from a theory of justice viewpoint, it is certainly improper.

To approach the people of the state, Howell reached back to a strategy he had used successfully when he was president of the state bar association. He convened a new Citizens' Conference and included respected citizens from every city and town. They were the opinion leaders in their communities, and having them involved gained publicity from local newspapers.

He contacted the American Judicature Society and arranged for the Second Citizens' Conference on Alabama State Courts to convene in Birmingham April 5-7, 1973, less than a month before the legislature would convene in Montgomery. Over 200 citizens attended the three-day conference.[4] The Citizens' Conference became the vehicle through which wide-based support for the judicial article among the citizenry was gained.

Mike House played a key role in the 1973 Citizens' Conference. He was the person in Heflin's office in charge of arranging for the conference. He was also the legislative contact in 1973 and was in charge of the referendum campaign that year.[5] "Heflin would never go to the legislature," House says. "He felt it would hurt him as a judge. So I was it."[6]

Howell's friend Conrad Fowler was a leader at the Citizens' Conference and made a major presentation in which he explained the work of the Constitutional Commission he had headed and how it related to the proposed Judicial Article. After hearing Fowler and a range of other speakers, the Conference recommended strongly that the legislature allow the state's citizens to vote on the Judicial Article.

The Associated Press reported on the conference as follows:

> A citizen's group Saturday recommended sweeping changes in the state's judicial system and urged the legislature to let the voters decide

the fate of a proposed Judicial Article for the Alabama Constitution.

The Second Alabama Citizens' Conference on Courts said in a consensus statement that vast improvements have occurred in the judicial system in the past two years, under the leadership of Chief Justice Howell Heflin.

But the group said it found additional improvements and reforms necessary for the judicial branch to function properly.[7]

What the legislature was being asked was to approve a statewide referendum so citizens could indicate whether they wanted the change. The legislature was not asked to decide itself whether to adopt the rewritten section of the Constitution. Putting the matter directly to voters was the democratic approach and a process legislators could not openly oppose. Howell explains how he got important help from a respected justice on the Supreme Court

> A conservative judge who was very supportive of the Judicial Article was Justice Hugh Maddox. He is still on the Supreme Court of Alabama. He had been Wallace's legal advisor, and then when Brewer came in, he was Brewer's legal advisor. Brewer appointed him to the Supreme Court. He was probably the most conservative member, but he saw the advantages of the change.
>
> I remember when Justice Maddox was making a speech. He held up a penny and said that, out of each dollar that goes to the cost of operating the state, this was what the new court system would cost. One penny for the state to have a modern, unified judicial system.

The Second Citizens' Conference, the backing of the Farm Bureau and other businesses, and help from respected officials like Hugh Maddox had created a positive atmosphere for change in the state. Pushed by Justices Merrill and Maddox, the entire Supreme Court of Alabama supported the adoption of the new Judicial Article. Still, the opposition, though muted, was strong, and legislative maneuvering to defeat the measure could be expected.

GAINING LEGISLATIVE APPROVAL. The Judicial Article was formally submitted to the legislature as a part of the Constitutional Commission's report on May 1, 1973, and it was introduced in a bill in the Alabama Senate on May 22. Two days later an identical measure was introduced in the House. Heflin chose two Florence lawyer-legislators, Senator Stewart O'Bannon, Jr. and Representative Bill Hill, Jr., to sponsor the bills.[8]

Mike House recalls that, to handle the legislative process, Heflin put together a legislative team called the "Muscle Shoals Mafia," composed mostly of individuals from the northwest corner of the state. "William F. Gardiner, mayor of Tuscumbia and president of the Alabama League of Municipalities, played the lead part in securing a compromise agreement over the municipal court issue," House says. "Circuit Judge Ed Tease from Florence, a member of the Constitutional Commission like O'Bannon, would take one of the lead roles in lobbying efforts in the legislature. Robert Martin, former editor of the *Florence Times*, handled the media campaign throughout the legislative session and the ratification campaign."[9]

Heflin tells of the fight to get a referendum approved.

> O'Bannon got it passed in the Senate first, with the help of many, including Lt. Governor Jere Beasley, Bo Torbert, Joe Fine, and many other senators. We had all sorts of problems in the House. We couldn't really get going over there, and they delayed and delayed and delayed. They thought they'd kill it in committee, and there was one key vote. Casey Downing, a lawyer from Mobile, was the key vote on the House Judiciary Committee. The day before the vote, Mike House, my administrative assistant who handled legislative liaison, came to me and said, "We're going to lose it if we can't get it out of committee. Casey's going to vote against us." I said, "He's Catholic, and he's from Mobile. I'm going to get in touch with Monsignor Oscar Lipscomb."
>
> So I phoned Oscar Lipscomb and told him that Casey was the key to it and asked would he contact him. Well, the Archbishop-to-be couldn't get Casey at first, but he talked to him after midnight and

convinced him to vote for us. The Monsignor phoned us and said, "He's committed; he's going to vote with us." The next day when the vote came up, Casey voted with us, and we got the bill out of committee. I always told the Archbishop that he was the reason we finally were able to adopt the judicial article.

According to Mike House, when the bill was finally reported out from committee in the House, it had been placed so far down on the calendar it could be brought up for consideration only by a special order. "As was the custom," House says, "the legislature adjourned for a week, so the bill would come up for consideration, if at all, on the last day of the session. To get the judicial article up for consideration the last day, a four-fifths vote of the entire House was required to suspend the rules and bring it up out of order. The first time Rep. Hill moved for a suspension of the rules to bring it up, the move failed. About 8:00 p.m. Hill tried again and this time was successful."[10]

Mike House worked hard and so did House members Bob Hill and Ronnie Flippo, who later became a congressman. They really took the lead, and they got that four-fifths vote. Jerry Vanderhoef was a stalwart among inferior court judges.

Opponents put up fifteen amendments, and nine were adopted. Since these were changes, you had to send the bill back to the Senate. The Senate then had to approve the amendments the House passed. On the final House vote, the article was approved 77-22. Then it had to be signed by the speaker of the house and the lieutenant governor before midnight. It was somewhere in the neighborhood of ten o'clock by the time they finally adopted it, and we were running against time. It went over to the Senate and Lieutenant Governor Jere Beasley helped get it passed immediately. Then we had to get it all redrafted. C. C. "Bo" Torbert, who would later serve as chief justice of Alabama, was one of the leaders in the Senate who helped. Another who was intimately involved was Robert Martin, director of administrative services in the Office of Court Management.

We had anticipated what the amendments would be, and we had about seven or eight different versions ready on memory typewriters. We were able to pick the version that matched the amendments the closest, and we made a few changes and got the bill with House amendments back to the Senate quickly. Beasley got the Senate to approve and then sign it, and Mike House got it back over to the House. It was getting close to midnight, but the speaker of the House signed it. As a constitutional amendment, it did not have to be submitted to the governor. It takes a two-thirds vote for a constitutional amendment to be adopted by both houses, and it is then submitted to the people for a vote.

A four-fifths vote was needed to suspend the rules, and they never thought we'd ever get it done. But Mike House and the others worked hard on it. We had all these Citizens' Conference people, particularly in the Birmingham area, working tirelessly. They were phoning people, and they had contacted their legislators beforehand. The opposition thought they could use all the tricks of their legislative skills to defeat it in committee. There's no question that Wallace and all the Wallace people were telling their legislative leaders to defeat it. But they didn't want to get caught doing it. We had great newspaper support.

We had to figure out the amendments that would probably be adopted. Some hadn't been filed, but the word was out that there would be some amendments. For example, if Senator Joe Doaks had asked to file an amendment, we'd go to the legislative drafting service, the agency in the legislature that drafts bills and amendments. Legislators tell them what they want, and they put it in proper legal language. So, knowing what the amendments were, we could pick their language. As soon as the drafting service finished their work and gave it to Senator Doaks, it was in the public domain, so we'd pick it up. Now Senator Doaks might not introduce the amendment for two hours in the legislature, but in the meantime we would have it typed in our memory typewriter in the proper place. You anticipated; this one will be adopted, this won't be adopted. Mike House was smart and knew how to do it. He would get all of the amendments, and then, in Lieutenant

Governor Beasley's office, we had their typewriters going. We had a couple of secretaries up there working and drafting language so we would be ready to meet the deadline.

Mike House remembers, "It was incredible that it even made it. I think of getting it out of the Committee by one vote and passing it on the floor with about two minutes to go. When it actually passed, we surrounded Ronnie Flippo, who had the bill in hand, and we took it across to the Senate side. Flippo was surrounded so nobody could steal the bill. If you lost the bill, you lost the issue. The House figured that if they passed it with only a few minutes to go, we could never get the changes made in time for the Senate to act before twelve o'clock. They never figured that out."[11]

According to Charles Cole, the bill was approved approximately fifteen minutes before the close of the session.[12]

Mike House says staff had quite a night after the vote. "We stayed up till about four o'clock that morning just raising hell and partying."[13]

Getting the Judicial Article through the legislature was a remarkable feat. Even with the narrow escapes in the legislative process, however, it was evident that the great majority of state lawmakers wanted court reform. The total vote in the House and Senate reflected this. The Amendment passed by a total vote of more than four to one. The leadership, under the influence of the governor, had used parliamentary maneuvering to try to have their way, but Chief Justice Heflin and his aides outworked and outsmarted them.

THE STATEWIDE REFERENDUM. Heflin then launched a political campaign on behalf of the Judicial Article, and he literally stumped the state. A speakers bureau was organized, and more than 100 talks on the amendment were scheduled at civic clubs throughout Alabama. Heflin made more than fifty speeches and TV appearances.[14] Members of the Alabama Supreme Court and others joined him in speaking to civic clubs. Ultimately, some forty-five organizations, over twenty of them statewide groups, endorsed the revised Judicial Article.

Citizens' groups were organized throughout Alabama, and more than 15,000 citizens were involved in the campaign. Mike House says, "We had businesses, professional women, Jaycees, young lawyers, the Junior League, the League of Women Voters, the Alabama Women for Highway Safety — we had every group under the sun. Justice Janie Shores was extremely helpful in the legislature and with women's organizations. We organized the women as much as we organized the men. They'd get on the phone and make calls."

The amendment was supported by such diverse organizations as the Alabama Congress of Parents and Teachers, the Alabama State Chamber of Commerce, the Alabama Farm Bureau Federation, the Alabama Education Association, Alabama Business and Professional Women, the Alabama Labor Council (AFL-CIO), the American Association of University Women, the Alabama Democratic Conference, and the League of Women Voters.[15] In all, according to Robert Martin, Heflin energized the support of nearly fifty diverse organizations in support of the reform effort. Even the Alabama Motorists Association spent $10,000 on advertising to support the work.[16]

News media in the state played an important role in the campaign to inform voters of the advantages of the new judicial article. Before the December 18th vote, twenty of the state's twenty-five dailies, including all the major papers, gave editorial endorsements and printed numerous commentaries explaining the content of the article. Seventy percent of the state's 116 weekly papers gave editorial approval.[17]

Howell recalls a clever campaign device that was used.

> The Alabama Farm Bureau wanted a promotion fee to support pork, and they wanted to charge all the farmers something like a $1.00 for every pig or hog that was sold. According to the old Constitution, this had to be voted on as a Constitutional amendment. So we went together, and we advocated "Pigs and Judges." That was sort of a motto: Support the Pigs and the Judges. It caught the eye, and people thought it was funny. Pigs and Judges.

The statewide Constitutional amendment election was held on December 18, 1973, and it passed with 62 percent of the vote. The people of Alabama approved a sweeping change in the court system as Amendment Number 328 to the Alabama Constitution of 1901.

An Incredible Feat. The new Judicial Article was a complete revision of all the laws pertaining to the judiciary in Alabama. It impacted the local and intermediate courts as well as the state Supreme Court. One of the most significant things it did was to end legislative control of the judiciary and adhere more closely to the principle of separation of powers.

The revised Judicial Article made these major changes:

1. A unified state judiciary was adopted, with a two-tier trial court system composed of a circuit court (high trial court) and a district court (inferior). Municipal courts were retained but were given the option to merge into the district court.

2. General rule-making power for the judiciary was conferred on the Supreme Court, subject only to the power of the legislature to alter such rules by general law.

3. The legislature was obligated to fund the court system.

4. All judges, except county probate judges, had to be licensed to practice law.

5. Strong professional standards were established, with a judicial inquiry commission which had the power to make complaints against judges and a court of the judiciary to hear the complaints.

6. A commission with power to recommend judicial salaries was created. The recommendations became law if not overridden by the legislature.

7. The article required the Supreme Court to advise the legislature on changes needed in the number of judgeships and jurisdictional procedures. The legislature was not allowed to make changes in these matters until the court had rendered its advice.

8. Broad administrative power to run the court system was vested in the chief justice.

One of the most important substantive changes was the transfer of funding for all courts from county to state level. This ended the practice of local courts using fines and other judicial income for their own, sometime questionable, purposes.[18]

Originally, the proposed Judicial Amendment abolished all municipal courts and transferred their functions to the district courts, but a compromise was necessary. The cities and the League of Municipalities were greatly opposed. In 1973, Tuscumbia Mayor William F. Gardiner, Heflin's close friend, became president of the League. Gardiner laid the groundwork for the compromise that satisfied the League. Through Gardiner's efforts, the requirements that all municipal judges be lawyers and that municipal courts be brought under the supervisory authority of the Supreme Court were retained.

> We finally compromised so that cities could keep their city courts, but their judges had to be lawyers. They would have to conduct the court with decorum and with dignity, and we made them wear robes. They also had to be under control of the Department of Court Management at state level. For awhile the cities wouldn't give up on the thing. Senator Stewart O'Bannon stood on the floor one day when the head of the League of Municipalities was sitting in the balcony. Stewart pointed to him and really low-rated him about how "you are stopping the wheels of justice." He shocked them so much that I think they decided to see if they could work out something.
>
> Another important change we only partially got. There was a national movement for the defense of the indigent and poor, and we tried to help provide for that. At one time we recommended that the state have public defenders, but that's never been adopted. The federal government finally created the Legal Service Corporation, and Reagan tried to kill it. We started on this matter with a committee which included Paul Johnston who was very much a liberal on the race issue. He left his firm because he came up with a major defense of one of the civil rights bills and was not popular with his partners.

The new Judicial Article expanded membership in the retirement system. A previous Constitutional amendment had allowed judges to contribute to and become part of the system. When the Judicial Article was passed, clerks, registers, and other employees also became eligible. A clerk could draw a supernumerary salary for himself under the old system, but he might have ten employees in his office who couldn't qualify. The change opened retirement as well as widow's benefits to all.

Tarr and Porter speak of the incredible feat that had been accomplished. "Schooled in the ways of Alabama politics, Heflin had little difficulty juggling, deflecting, and doing end runs around the opposition. . . . One way or another, as one justice succinctly noted, Heflin managed to 'outfox them all.' Additionally, Heflin's immense energy, personal charisma, and dedication were decisive. He was a constant goad to all the groups working for voter approval of the judicial article . . . . Working with him and for him was, it seems, regarded as a privilege; one hears him referred to as a 'hero.'"[19]

Mike House says that Howell knew he had just one six-year term as chief justice to get judicial reform accomplished. "He knew that if you come in and blow a system apart, the person that blows the system apart is not likely to be the person that stays and puts it back together. You've irritated too many people and created too many hard feelings. If you change a system, you move on and let somebody else put up a wall to make sure it doesn't go back. That's what (future chief justice) Torbert did. I think the state was incredibly fortunate to have Howell Heflin."[20]

The ultimate result of the Judicial Article was a unified court system, standardized rules and procedures, efficient administration and record-keeping in the courts, an end to non-lawyer judges in other than probate courts, and a significant decrease of backlogs in civil and criminal cases. Robert Martin, one of those involved in the fight, points out that, in the broadest context, the fight was about the independence and power of the judicial branch of state government and about the fundamental American concept of separation of powers.[21] Through the effort of Heflin and his aides and supporters, Alabama moved from possibly the worst judicial system in the country to being hailed as a national model.

13

Implementation and National Attention

As 1973 DREW TO A CLOSE, Howell Heflin had reason to feel great pride in what he had accomplished in just three years as Alabama's chief justice. In the face of opposition from popular Governor George Wallace, he had maneuvered revision of part of the state Constitution through the legislature and had managed to persuade almost two-thirds of the voters to support comprehensive change in the state's courts.

Still the job wasn't finished, and major change was not assured. The Judicial Article was written in broad Constitutional language and did not go into particulars. Legislation to add the necessary detail and to flesh out the article was necessary. Furthermore, legislation was necessary to fund implementation of the new system. Howell and his staff knew they would again have problems with the legislative leadership in getting the needed bills passed.

In 1972, Wallace had been left paralyzed after an assassination attempt. Gaining sympathy votes and with only token opposition, Wallace was easily elected governor a third time in 1974. States rights and suspicion of everything federal, particularly the courts, remained a major theme of his political rhetoric.

THE IMPLEMENTATION BILL. Howell Heflin faced the enormous task of drafting a legislative implementation package for the new Judicial Article of the Constitution. The amendment the voters had passed gave the legislature four years to implement its provisions, but Chief Justice Heflin wanted it done in two. He obtained federal LEAA funds and in April 1974 established an Advisory Commission on Judicial Article Implementation to draft the policy recommendations and legislation needed. The Commission had fifty-five members who represented the courts, clerks, registrars, district attorneys, lawyers, members of the legislature, and local government.[1] Heflin named Joseph F. Johnston, a leading Constitutional lawyer, as Commission chair, and Cumberland Law Professor Charles D. Cole was named full-time executive director.

The first meeting was held June 23–25, 1974, and five working committees were named: District Court Organization, Personnel and Administration, Fiscal and Budgetary, Municipal Courts and Court-Related Agencies, and Prosecution Services. Following much committee work, full Commission meetings were held again in October and November 1974, with a final meeting in February 1975. The Commission's report was transmitted to the legislature on March 28, 1975. It was 198 pages long and contained 66 recommendations.[2]

Heflin says that Cole spent a lot of time on the task. Cole also acted as a lightning rod in the legislature, taking a lot of hits that would otherwise have been aimed at Heflin.

The implementation bill was introduced to the House on May 25, 1975, and to the Senate a week later. Opelika Senator C. C. "Bo" Torbert, Jr., later to be chief justice, sponsored the legislation in the Senate. Heflin says that before the legislation was introduced, he and his staff made a real effort to get as many sponsors and cosponsors as they could. The House bill was sponsored by 72 of the 105 House members, and the Senate bill was sponsored by 25 of the 35 senators.

> When they are cosponsors they can still change their vote, but it's a pretty good indication that they will vote with you.
>
> I sort of stayed away because of the separation of powers. I never would go up and lobby. If I lobbied some lawyer legislator and got him to agree to help, then he'd be suspected of having a *quid pro quo* on

some case that might come up. Judicial lobbying has to be conducted with certain dignity and restraint. I would never go up and lobby, but we could send Mike House and then Bo Cole, and some other law clerks would help.

Once more there was trouble getting the legislation passed in time, but according to Mike House, the Heflin team was more sophisticated than before in its approach. "We would come out of the session on Thursday, and by that night or Friday morning we would have 10,000 pieces of mail going out with what people needed to do before the Tuesday session. This went primarily to the group which had been involved in the Citizens' Conference.

At one point we had just about every major group in the state involved — labor, the Farm Bureau, the PTA, the Jaycees. I was the state Jaycees Governmental Affairs chairman and Young Lawyers Governmental Affairs chairman, so we had those organizations. We had the League of Women Voters, the AAUW, the Women's Political Conference, the Alabama Federation of Women, The Alabama State Chamber of Commerce, the Alabama Education Association, the Alabama Labor Council (AFL-CIO), and the Alabama Democratic Conference. In all, some forty-five organizations, over twenty of them statewide, had endorsed and worked for the Judicial Article. In 1975, the same groups were strongly behind us, so we had an organization of 10,000 people out there really committed and working."

In essence, House says, they succeeded by running a statewide political campaign for three years. "The only way to pass the Constitutional or Judicial Article or anything like that is to get the whole state behind it, then go to the legislature. You don't go to the legislature first. What made it all successful was the Citizens' Conference and the involvement of all of the people and groups."[3]

After considerable debate, mainly over funding aspects, the bill was approved by the House of Representatives 100-1 and by the State Senate 30-0 on the final day of the 1975 regular session of the legislature.[4] The bill was signed into law by Governor Wallace on October 10, 1975.

Again, Mike House, Bob Hill and Ronnie Flippo were key players in the process.

Almost two years had elapsed between approval of the Judicial Article and adoption of the implementation legislation. Howell says this time was useful in one respect because he and his staff got information from other states and learned some corrections that were needed.

Heflin's group received federal financial help through the Law Enforcement Assistance Administration (LEAA). The LEAA was designed to help police departments and sheriff's departments. But LEAA would also finance novel judicial system improvements that would affect criminal cases. Heflin's team argued that the Judicial Article was very important to criminal cases. Working through Bill Herndon in LEAA's Atlanta Regional Office, Heflin's group got monies to finance the advisory committee and its studies.

After the implementation legislation passed in 1975, Mike House went into private practice, though he still did legislative work for the court as a consultant.

TRANSITION. WHEN the implementation legislation was passed, Heflin had about fifteen months remaining in his term as chief justice. While a number of steps required for transition to the new system occurred under Heflin, the major implementation task fell to his successor, Bo Torbert. The new chief justice encountered financial problems as the legislature attempted to "sunset" the Department of Court Management. "Torbert changed the name to the Administrative Office of Courts, moved the employees under constitutional protection, developed a continuing dialogue with the legislature, and brought in a new Administrative Director of Courts. Within two years 1,100 county employees were transferred to the state, the new district court was placed in operation, and most court operations had been streamlined and simplified."[5]

> A lot of cooperation between the federal courts and the states courts developed in the years I was chief justice. At the same time, Wallace was ranting and raving about federal judges. He said they ought to give

some of the judges barbed-wire enemas and all that sort of thing. He said some of them didn't have sense enough to try chicken thieves. Wallace's fight with Judge Frank Johnson was earlier in the '60s, but he continued to oppose any decision that chipped away at states rights or did something that was considered liberal. Wallace was running for president in 1972 and again in 1976.

In the years after 1971, there was a complete change in the philosophy of the court. Not all of the justices had been trying to find ways to get around the United States Supreme Court, but a majority had. In the end, it was a progressive-minded court that was interested in following the Supreme Court. Actually, we created a Federal-State Council. The members of the appellate courts would meet with federal judges in the state once or twice a year. We adopted an agreement that was called the certification rule. Under the rule, if there were a case that involved state law and it was a case of first impression, the federal circuit court of appeals would ask the Alabama Supreme Court to determine the law and then certify it back to the federal appeals court.

The year after my term ended, Chief Justice Torbert had a lot of problems including funding since the new court system proved to be more costly than our consultants had predicted, but he finally convinced Wallace to help him. He had gotten along with Wallace, and he was a friend of Fob James, the next governor. Torbert and James were both from Opelika. James supported Torbert in regards to the appropriations. Torbert did a good job of getting money for the new court system. I don't think I would have ever gotten it. I think that I would have had real problems with Wallace and the others. They would have liked to see the judicial system fall on its face because of a lack of funds. Torbert had been very supportive in the state Senate, and he really was the logical person to be chief justice and get the new system functioning effectively. He knew well in advance that I was not going to run again, and he was ready to run. He was elected chief justice, and then he was reelected.

When you go through a shake-down cruise and you're in charge, you have to be a good manager. He hasn't been given the credit due him for his role in getting the amendment and the implementation legislation passed and then following up as chief justice.

Mike House agrees that Howell would have had trouble with implementation. "It was the combination of Heflin and Bo Torbert which pulled it off, and it worked extremely well. We're fortunate in Alabama we had that combination. Heflin's a bulldog. When he got hold of something he wouldn't let go. He would personally stay on the phone for hours at night calling people. We really went after them, and this caused some resentment, which would have carried over year after year. That's why Bo was so important. He could go to the legislative leadership and say, 'Gentlemen, look, I didn't pass the Judicial Article. Howell Heflin did that. My job is to implement it.' It worked beautifully. Bo has the personality to do that. Heflin blew the whole system apart and came back and completely restructured it, and he made all of the enemies you make when you do that sort of thing."[6]

In a move to open up court proceedings and give the people more information on its operation, Howell had the Supreme Court hold a session before over 1,000 students at the University of Alabama's student center auditorium. It was a historic first since the 1901 Constitution mandated that the court sit only in the capital city.

PERMANENT JUDICIAL TRAINING. The Alabama judicial system was being completely overhauled, and this huge change brought with it the problem of how to prepare the judges and lawyers who worked in the system.

> We really had quite an educational task trying to get the lawyers and the judges in the state knowledgeable about the new system and how to operate under it.
>
> In speaking about the need, I used a quote from C. K. Chesterton. He said something to the effect that, "all legal officials, judges, sheriffs, bailiffs, policemen, do their job as if it were by rote." They are accustomed to it, and they just want to keep doing the same routine

over and over. "But," Chesterton said, "members of the jury, with the sweet smell of the law fresh in their nostrils, do not try cases by rote, and they judge the facts with no taint of routine." Anytime you change judges from anything they've been doing for five or ten or more years, they don't like it. To get them to change, you have to have people they respect within their ranks to urge and lead them.

One such person was Judge James O. Haley. Seminars were held all over the state, with one attended by nearly 1,000 lawyers and judges, and Haley, who believed strongly in the educational program, helped make them a success.

He understood the need. Judge Haley practiced in the federal courts, and he was on the advisory committee I appointed in 1971. Later he was on the Implementation Commission. He was one of the keys in getting the rest of the judges to go along. Others who played an important role were John Snodgrass, Bill Sullivan, Joe Phelps, Perry Hooper, Joe Hocklander, Ed Tease, and a district judge named Jerry Vanderhoef.

Judge Haley was an interesting person. He was the son of a Mississippi tenant farmer, and he had only one year of college and a degree from a night law school. He started in Birmingham doing various things, and got a job in one of the big corporate law firms, as a sort of runner, I think. The firm decided he was pretty good and could take notes, but he had to be able to take shorthand. So he took a shorthand course and became secretary to the head of the firm. He got interested in the law and he went to Jones Law School, which offered a four-year course at night. After a year and a half he took the bar exam and passed. But he wanted to achieve, so he finished the prescribed course and became a lawyer with the firm. Later he became a judge, and then he went to Cumberland Law School as a professor. He really taught the law students how to practice law — trial advocacy and tips that you don't learn in academic studies but have to pick up in the actual practice. He received all sorts of awards.

To prepare for the long term, Heflin and his staff created an Alabama College of the Judiciary, with financial help from the LEAA. It was made mandatory that judges in the state attend the judiciary college. Eighty-two out of the eighty-seven circuit judges attended within a year. Heflin admits that some didn't want to participate, but they did.

The Alabama Judicial College still operates under the chief justice. Seminar-like sessions are held in different locations around the state, including the University of Alabama Law School, Cumberland Law School at Samford University, Jones Law School, and the Birmingham School of Law.

RECOGNITION. Court reform in Alabama drew nationwide attention, and the list of Heflin's recognition and honors grew rapidly. He traveled around the country and became well known as a judicial figure, and he received various honors. A *Birmingham News* article in 1974 stated,

> The name of Alabama Supreme Court Chief Justice Howell Heflin is almost a household word in Alabama today, a synonym for activism in court reform. Before his landslide election in 1970, few could tell you anything about Howell Heflin except that he was a big wheel in the Alabama Bar Association and that he was some kin to the late U.S. Senator (Cotton Tom) Heflin. . . . Heflin's name is now known not only in his home state, but across the country as the catalyst for a dramatic overhaul of one of the most antiquated court systems in the nation.[7]

In 1973, Howell Heflin was named Distinguished Alumnus of both Birmingham-Southern College and the University of Alabama, and he received the Herbert Lincoln Harley Award of the American Judicature Society for meritorious service in court reform. He was inducted into the Alabama Academy of Honor in 1974.

On January 18, 1975, a *The New York Times* headline proclaimed, "Alabama Praised on Court Reform." The article stated that, "Alabama has become the most dramatic example in the country of what can be done, without undue delay, to improve the quality of justice in state courts. . . . It's really attributable to the personality and leadership of Justice Heflin." On November 14, 1975, *The Nashville Banner* headlined, "Judicial System in Alabama Nation's Best."[8]

Howell Heflin received the "Award of Merit" of the American Judges Association in 1975. Previous recipients were Judge John J. Sirica, Chief Justice Warren E. Burger, and Justice Tom Clark.

He was named "Alabama Citizen of the Year" by the Alabama Cable Television Association in 1973 and by the Alabama Broadcasters Association in 1975.

He was selected as the country's most outstanding appellate judge by the Association of Trial Lawyers of America in 1976.

Howell became involved in the Conference of Chief Justices of the United States, and during the last year of his term as chief justice in 1976, he was the president.

Howell was also active in the National Center for State Courts. He was vice-president/president-elect at the time he went out of office, but he did not move on to the presidency. He explains, "Since I was no longer in office and was about to run for the Senate, I didn't advance my position in the National Center of the State Courts."

In 1977, he was selected as an honorary fellow of the American Bar Foundation, and, with Eric Sevareid, he was awarded the James Madison Award by the National Editorial Broadcasters Association.

At the sesquicentennial of The University of Alabama in 1981, each school selected three living graduates as "Sesquicentennial Professors," and the law school faculty selected Howell, Federal Judge Frank Johnson, and Federal Judge Sam Pointer in Birmingham.

The new Alabama court system became a model for other state courts to follow. Janet Reno, later to be U.S. Attorney General but was then staff attorney for Florida's State Senate Judiciary Committee, visited Alabama to study the reform movement. Florida later enacted some of the elements of the Alabama system. When Bill Clinton became Arkansas's Attorney General, that state copied some of Alabama's model.[9]

In the late 1970s, New York State was engaged in improving its court system. An article about the Alabama experience, written by Janie L. Shores, associate justice of the Alabama Supreme Court, was carried in the *New York State Bar Journal.*

In the Winter 1997 *Alabama Law Review*, Janie L. Shores wrote, "Heflin had the wisdom and the vision to see the needs of the court system and the determination to devote his time and effort to see that they were met. With very little support in the beginning, he determined not only to change the system but also to make Alabama's judiciary a model for the nation."[10]

A study of state supreme courts, published in 1988 by the Yale University Press, used Alabama as one of three courts for case studies. The study focused on judicial reform, on similarities and differences among the state courts and between them at the U.S. Supreme Court, and on the broader factors producing change in all courts.[11]

"Once the movement for reform was under way, progress was unusually swift; and whatever the assessment of reform in other states, in Alabama it did make a difference," the study concludes. "While one can only speculate about the extent to which the success should be attributed to Howell Heflin alone or to his role in conjunction with the more moderate social and political climate that followed the turbulent fifties and sixties, we believe that credit is largely due to Heflin. The critical first steps were taken at a time when black protests, federal intervention, and massive resistance dominated the public agenda. During this period Heflin managed, quietly and persistently, to divert attention to another issue. . . . In 1975, when the new judicial article and new rules of procedure were operative, when new blood came on the court, when Heflin had assumed the leadership of the Conference of Chief Justices, times had changed in Alabama and aspects of other cultures emerged from the shadows. . . Heflin took on what, by any lights, might be regarded as a hopeless task in a period of turmoil. In this sense, his achievements, even when compared with those of other chief justices who have been reform leaders, were the more remarkable."[12]

"For whatever reasons," Tarr and Porter state, "the culmination of reform efforts and advent of the 'New South' coincided, and nothing — nothing — was the same on the Alabama high court after Howell Heflin completed his first and only term as chief justice."[13]

Two changes in the composition of the Supreme Court can be directly attributed to effect of his leadership. First, Janie L. Shores became the first female associate justice in Alabama history and the third in U.S. history. Second Oscar Adams, Jr., was appointed the first black associate justice in Alabama. In 1983, in a statewide election, Adams became the first African-American to be elected statewide as a constitutional officer for the state of Alabama since Reconstruction.

When Howell announced he would not seek reelection as chief justice, *The Mobile Register* editorialized, "No one really believes that Howell Heflin is going to be content to go home and practice law in Tuscumbia after having become such a national celebrity."[14]

BACK HOME. Howell did not seek reelection as Alabama's chief justice. There were a number of reasons, and one was frankly financial. He had made substantially more money practicing law than he was paid as chief justice. More importantly, he felt he had accomplished what he set out to do as chief justice. A lot of work remained, and he believed someone else could complete the job more effectively, and he had in the back of his mind to either run for governor or for the U.S. Senate.

> As things developed and I got accolades and felt I had made a success and was well known, other thoughts came to mind, but I really didn't have a plan. I had completed what I set out to do in the court system, and I had to look to the future. We had put language in the new Judicial Article that you could not continue to serve as a judge if you were in a political race other than for your own reelection. Under the canons of ethics, judges are not suppose to be involved in politics other than in the judiciary. That's to preserve the integrity.
>
> Anyway, after I left the court, we had to make a decision of where to live. Some big law firms in Birmingham made me offers to practice law with them when I announced that I wasn't going to run again. I

could have gone there and made substantial money. I considered this for a while, but my wife and I decided we wanted to go back to Tuscumbia. It's a matter of where you want to live and be happy as opposed to making big money.

Howell and Elizabeth Ann returned to Tuscumbia, and he went back with his old law partner, Charles Rosser. In the meantime, Rosser had taken Stan Munsey as a partner. Munsey had come to Alabama originally as director of a regional office of local governments, and he became active in the campaign when Howell ran for chief justice. After Howell's return, the firm became Heflin, Rosser and Munsey.

One thing Rosser had done was move out of the upstairs offices in the old building where Howell practiced before. "As soon as I left," Howell says, "Rosser built a building fairly close to the courthouse. When I came back they had new offices, and it was really a delight. Even the Supreme Court building in Montgomery was old. That was the first time I had a decent office in all the thirty some-odd years of work. I started in with a number of different activities."

Howell also took on a new teaching job. When he was chairman of the National Conference of Chief Justices in 1977, he became acquainted with Bill Spong, dean of the law school at William and Mary, the oldest law school in the United States. Spong had been in the U.S. Senate and had been defeated. As vice chairman of the National Center for State Courts, Howell was on the committee that located the Center in Williamsburg.

Spong had received a grant from Virginia's prominent Taylor family and had established a visiting professorship named for one of their members, Tazewell Taylor. After Howell left office in 1977, Spong appointed him the Tazewell Taylor Visiting Professor of Law at William and Mary.

Howell explains, "I basically taught seminar classes on judicial activities, decisions, administration, and subjects like that. A co-professor worked with me. I would go up for class on Thursday, and I'd usually stay two days and then come back on Saturday or Sunday. Sometimes I was there other days of the week. Each class would last two or three hours. The students were mostly seniors, and sometimes we had a dinner meeting with them. They'd gone through most of the fundamentals of law school. I think there were a few historians in graduate school in the class, too." The co-professor who worked with Howell was Alex Aikman, who was with the National Center.[15]

NO-TIE HAWKINS MAKES HIS BOW. During his tenure as chief justice and the time immediately following, Howell developed a fictional character, No-Tie Hawkins, for whom he became famous.

As the Alabama system became a model for other states, Howell made speeches at various conferences and meetings all over the country.

> I told them my "No-Tie" jokes. Wherever I'd go, people would talk about No-Tie, and even today some lawyers and justices remember those stories. Stories about No-Tie Hawkins got spread all over the United States.
> No-Tie was a country lawyer over in Russellville. He lived in Vina, Alabama, and he wouldn't wear a necktie. He was very effective with the juries. I said he was an ear lawyer rather than as an eye lawyer, because he learned his law through what people told him rather than reading.
> One time No-Tie lost a case and he had to take it to the Supreme Court of Alabama. All of his friends told him, "Now, No-Tie, if you go down there before the Supreme Court and you don't wear a necktie, you're liable to lose your case." He said, "Nah, I've been right successful with my cases over the years. If I were to wear a necktie, I believe it would hex me, so I'm not going to do it." He came down and argued his case before the Supreme Court, and he didn't have a necktie on. Some of my more dignified colleagues on the court gave him some hard looks, but they didn't say anything. They let him try his case. A few weeks later, he received his opinion, and he had lost. He ran into me and said, "You know, all my friends tell me that the reason I lost my case was because I didn't wear a necktie when I argued the case before the

Supreme Court." I answered, "Now, No-Tie, I want to assure you that the Supreme Court wouldn't let an extraneous matter like that creep into their opinions. They go by the law and the facts." "Well," he said, "I want to tell you this. If that had been the reason, it would have been a damn sight better than the one you gave."

Later No-Tie became a judge, and the waiter who waited on him was asked, "What do you think about No-Tie becoming a judge?" The waiter answered, "Looord! He'll make a fine judge. If he don't fine no more than he tips, he'll make the greatest judge in the world."

No-Tie would be trying cases as a judge, and he wasn't sure how to rule on objections. So he finally got a deck of cards, and he'd get the cards out and cut the deck when somebody made an objection. If it were a spade or a club, a black card, he'd sustain the objection. But if it were a heart or a diamond, he'd overrule the objection. Finally the local bar association said, "That's just horrible. We can't have that." They came to him and said, "No-Tie, we're going to send you to the Judicial Inquiry Commission for unethical conduct if you don't rule according to the law." No-Tie answered, "Well, I'll try. I don't want to go to that Judicial Inquiry Commission." So for six months he tried to rule with the law. Finally, the bar association committee came back and presented him with a new deck of cards.

POLITICAL OPPORTUNITY CALLS. When Howell Heflin left office as chief justice, he was obviously a hot political commodity. Among the people with whom he had become well acquainted was chief justice of the United States, Warren Burger, who was promoting judicial reform throughout the United States and was involved in the National Center of State Courts. The Conference of Chief Justices was working for a separate independent approach toward the judiciary, and this included removing control of federal LEAA money from governors' offices. Heflin testified before Congress on behalf of the Conference of Chief Justices on this matter.

Howell was one of the speakers at the American Conference on the Judicial Systems of the Future, which was sponsored by Columbia

University and held on the campus of Stanford University at Palo Alto, California. Howell recalls that one of the participants was a professor of constitutional law from the University of Arkansas named Bill Clinton.

> That was the first time I met him. Afterwards, Clinton was elected attorney general of Arkansas, and he had me come to Little Rock and speak to a criminal law justice seminar for sheriffs, police chiefs, district attorneys, and other law enforcement officials. I was in Washington the first time I saw him when he was running for president. He came over and reminded me where we first met. Every time he sees me, he talks about how we're old friends. He'll say, "We go back to the days when I was a law professor."
>
> I also met Warren Christopher, later Secretary of State for Clinton, at the Stanford conference. These are the kinds of connections that came about because of our judicial reform activities and recognition. At South Carolina, they wanted to have a judicial reform meeting, and the leader of the judicial reform group there was Richard Riley, who later became governor of South Carolina and U.S. Secretary of Education. At that time, he was a state senator. I spoke at that conference, and they had me back in South Carolina for another event.

Howell was considered for appointment as U.S. Attorney General by Jimmy Carter. Carter was elected President in November 1976, after Heflin had announced that he wouldn't seek reelection as chief justice.

> My term of office would be up in January of 1977, and that would be the beginning of his term. After the election, he began to consider who he would have for his cabinet. I had become a friend of Griffin Bell who was close to him. There was some talk that Griffin would be the attorney general. For some reason, Griffin first said he didn't want it, and he recommended that I be appointed to the position. I went over to Atlanta and talked to Charlie Kirbo, Carter's appointment chairman, and with Bell, and I flew to Washington for an interview. I never did talk to Carter personally at that stage.

Anyway, the rumor got around Washington, and a couple of articles in the *Birmingham Post-Herald* said that Ted Kennedy had actually come out and said I'd make a good attorney general. Kennedy was chairman of the Judiciary Committee, and his staff director was Kenneth Feinberg, who had been working with the Conference of Chief Justices. I got to know Feinberg, and he recommended me to Kennedy. In the meantime, things got straightened out with Griffin Bell. When I found out that, I withdrew my name and recommended Bell be appointed. When I heard he had changed his mind, I didn't want to be pitted against my friend.

In Alabama, Howell was being urged to continue his political career.

The publisher of the *Mobile Press-Register*, William Herring, came to Montgomery to urge me to run for governor. Later when I was in the Senate he'd give me the immortal devil. When I voted against (Jeff) Sessions, he had an editorial calling me the "Benedict Arnold of Alabama." Several other folks, like Joe Reed, gave me encouragement to run for the Senate.

Mike House was urging me to run, and he really wanted me to run for governor. He was very alert. He'd been in Washington with a congressman, and he knew all the ways of using media and pollsters. So we analyzed the governor's race and the senate race. I decided to look hard at the senate race rather than the governor's race, perhaps because Uncle Tom had served in the Senate. The three B's, Baxley, Beasley and Brewer, were in the picture. They and other people like Sid McDonald ran for governor in 1978, and Fob James came along and beat them all.

Howell Heflin clearly would not stay in a quiet law practice in Tuscumbia very long.

14

Defeating Wallace in the 1978 Senate Race

Late in 1977, Governor George Wallace announced that he would be a candidate for the U.S. Senate race in 1978. Writers speculated that John Sparkman, seventy-eight and in his thirty-second year as a Senator, would not run again, and Wallace would be the strong favorite to replace him. Even if the aging Sparkman ran, Wallace was expected to give him a close race and possibly defeat him. Heflin meanwhile had completed his term as chief justice and was considering other options, including political office. Many friends and advisors urged Howell to oppose Wallace for the Senate seat, but he hesitated because he thought Wallace was almost certain to win. A potential Heflin campaign was looked on with interest because, as one of the rural newspapers noted, it would be a head-on contest between two powerful men of different persuasions and images.[1]

According to Mike House, there was a big debate inside Heflin's group on whether he should run for the Senate or governor. "An early Peter Hart poll tested possibilities," House recalls, "and it showed Heflin couldn't be elected governor but could be elected Senator."[2]

Though Howell had not made the final decision to run for the Senate, he and his staff were preparing, just in case.

> We started to court the business community towards the end of my term as chief justice, and I got a lot of encouragement from business

people to run for the Senate, especially after George Wallace announced he would run. One of their primary concerns was what it would do to the image of the state if Wallace got in the Senate and used it as a forum to promote his presidential aspirations and other parts of his agenda. They were very concerned about Alabama's image.

Mike House, my former administrative assistant who was practicing law, arranged a dinner in Birmingham to honor me. Judicial and legal figures from around the country were invited. The fellow who succeeded me in the Conference of Chief Justices came, as did the chief justices of Colorado and Ohio. It was well attended with about 1,500 people from every walk of life, including Citizens' Conference groups, lawyers, business people, and even sheriffs and probate judges. It sent out the word that "Heflin has strength."

Before my speech that night, this fellow comes out of the blue without a tie on and country-looking as everything. He had a lot of wild looking hair. He hollowed out, "I'm tired of being maligned." He says, "I'm Jim No-Tie Hawkins, and I've heard that Heflin's been telling tales about me across the country, and they are all damn lies." He berated me before all the crowd for about ten minutes. Even these chief justices had heard my No-Tie stories. The man was a country lawyer friend of mine from Hamilton named Nelson Vinson and was an act Mike House and some of the others cooked up.

Senator John Sparkman called Howell late in 1977 and asked him to come to Washington. Howell went, and Sparkman said to him, "You know I haven't made up my mind whether I'm going to run for reelection, but I'm going to tell you what happened to me. The Congressman that I succeeded was named Archie Carmichael. I had been his campaign manager in Madison County, and we were friends. He called me to Washington and said, 'Now John, I don't know whether I'm going to run or not, but my advice is you get ready to run for my seat. You'll know in advance whether I'm going to run.' I told him that Archie Carmichael was Elizabeth Ann's grandfather, and he said, 'Yeah, I know, and that's the reason I'm telling you like this.' He was telling me to get ready to run, that he probably wouldn't run."

Sparkman announced that he would not seek reelectio 21, 1978, and Howell formally announced his candidacy or "I knew a couple of weeks in advance when he was going announcement, and I made the decision to get in the race," "We were ready to send out a press release the next day after his announcement. We had to get ready fast because we didn't have a press secretary or any campaign staff at that time."

One of the reasons Howell gave serious consideration to the race was his belief that Alabama should be represented by a senator who believed in the improvement of race relations and progress in civil rights.

DEFEATING GEORGE WALLACE. It was essential for anyone seriously making a run for the Senate to build a statewide organization. Howell started by naming Mike House the primary campaign manager. Bill Gardiner, a long-time Heflin friend, also helped with managing the campaign. Gardiner had been mayor of Tuscumbia for eighteen years, and past president of the League of Municipalities. He knew mayors all over the state. The two remained close until Gardiner's death due to heart failure in 1995.[3]

Howell had strong support from lawyers in every county of the state, and he was able to build a nucleus around them. "They were my foundation in campaigning and elections and were very helpful. Since we got the probate judges a retirement system, some were active in the campaign, and the circuit clerks and registrars were all happy because the Judicial Article had improved their financial condition. People in the Sparkman group were also very helpful."

Also important, Mike House says, were the people involved in the Citizens' Conference they had conducted during the Judicial Article campaign. Also the courthouse crowd in every county was critical.[4]

Several old friends in Washington came down and helped with the election. One was Vic Gold, a writer who had been active in Alabama politics in the 1950s and 1960s but had moved to Washington, changed parties, and become press secretary for Vice President Spiro Agnew.

A JUDGE IN THE SENATE

Chuck Morgan, an Alabamian who had been Southeastern Director of the American Civil Liberties Union, was also involved with a sort of think-tank that would meet and devise strategy, first against Wallace and later in the campaign against Walter Flowers. They all contributed good ideas.

With the help of many friends, Howell and his immediate aides were able to put together a good staff and an effective statewide organization for the race. Bert Haltom recalls that Howell called a few close friends together after he decided to run, and all helped. Haltom says his job was to be the fundraiser, and he served principally as Howell's money man in north Alabama.

Raising money was critical.

> When I ran for the Senate the first time, you had to have at least a million dollars to have a chance. Now it is much more. Some of the home builders, realtors, and other people who had always been supportive of Sparkman started supporting me. Business people in Birmingham raised something like $200,000. Bert Haltom raised about $100,000 over in Lauderdale, using the idea of a "home area candidate." Bill Gardiner, Ed Mauldin, Gene Crump, F. S. Winford, Mitch Self and some others in Colbert County raised about $150,000. Barney Weeks, then the head of the AFL-CIO state labor council, and Hobert Williams, head of the building and trade unions, helped by bringing some national labor money into the race.

As the campaign was beginning, Mike House was intrigued with what was going on nationally with media consultants. He traveled to Washington and other places to learn more about the process, and he interviewed a number of media persons to find the best one to retain for the race. Howell, House, and the staff decided on Bob Squier, who helped later in Clinton's campaign and was an Al Gore adviser until Squier's death in January 2000.

The staff raised some money, and they decided to start an early TV campaign.

Squier made some commercials I didn't like at first. He came down and filmed and went back to Washington. He was trying to do it by telephone. He phoned me and asked, "What do you think of the films?" I answered, "They are piss-poor." Well, that shocked him. Squier had a large ego. He had me walking like an old man in two or three of them, and there was too much from a side view. When you're as big and fat as I am, with my under-chins, you don't have a good side view. Squier actually didn't have to make many changes. He just hadn't noticed some little things. I think that made Squier a much more careful TV film maker than he had been before. He had great ideas, and I felt without him I wouldn't have been elected.

Luckie and Forney, an advertising agency in Birmingham, was also for me. They had always done Wallace's TV and public relations work in campaigns, but they had had some kind of falling out with him. I had been in school with Bob Luckie and John Forney. Forney was actually a cousin of mine. We worked it out so both they and Squier would be involved. Frank Lee of that firm was a great political consultant. They did the brochures and the billboards and some other materials, and Squier did the television.

Early in the campaign, Heflin hired a national pollster, Peter Hart. The initial polls showed Wallace ahead by about 45 percent to 17 percent. Discouraged, Howell said, "I can't win. All he's got to do is pick up a little of the undecided vote and he wins." The pollster answered that was the way it looked at the moment, but he had found a lot of negative feeling against Wallace. Things were changing in Alabama. The black vote had increased and was a major factor in state politics. This significant group was anti-Wallace. Also, the polling showed that a significant segment of the people joined the business community in worrying about the state's image.

Squier told Heflin there was a good possibility they could eliminate Wallace from the race.

He was a pretty good political analyst, and he'd watched as some of the poll results changed. He said we ought to focus on Wallace's deafness and make an early effort to get him out of the race. Of course, Wallace would have a lot of sympathy because he had been shot and was in the wheelchair. Squier also said, "We should start doing some very positive things about you and do them real early." I said, "Well, I am in this race, and one of the things I would like to be remembered for is being the person who kept Wallace out of the Senate." We were campaigning actively much earlier than a lot of people thought advisable, and we began a series of TV spots which were positive. We had a big task in facing Wallace.

Squier succeeded in getting a Sunday magazine supplement to write a story about Wallace's deafness and the fact he was growing weaker. The deafness issue began to make people realize its seriousness and the importance of good hearing during Senate debates.

The race against Wallace was heated for several months. Heflin began traveling the state and explaining his views, and he gained steadily in the polls as he met with more and more people. One of his major campaign promises was to support a constitutional amendment that would require the government to operate each year with a balanced budget.

Various polls conducted during the first part of the year showed Heflin's strength. In February, student polls taken at the University of Alabama and Samford University's Cumberland Law School showed Heflin way ahead. In March, polls taken around the state showed Heflin and Wallace running all the way from neck to neck to a Heflin lead of 61 percent to Wallace's 20 percent. In a statewide poll conducted by Universal Systems in April, after several months of the campaign, Heflin led Wallace by a margin of 47 percent to 36 percent. It was clear that Wallace had lost momentum and that Heflin's lead was growing. Over the years, Wallace had developed a good polling operation and was known to pay close attention to polling trends. Shortly thereafter, on May 16, Wallace made a speech in Mobile at the annual convention of the Alabama League of Municipalities, and Bill Gardiner was there as a past president of the organization. Gardiner phoned Howell with the news that Wallace announced he was withdrawing from the Senate race. Howell asked, "What did he say was his reason?" and Gardner answered, "He didn't say."

Wallace never gave an explanation for withdrawing. He told reporters, "I just decided I didn't want to run." He was withdrawing, he said, "for reasons known to me." He said that, in spite of adverse poll results, he was sure he could win.[5]

Howell disputes that. "I expect the possibility of losing a political race in his home state preyed on his mind, though he would never admit that he was afraid he would lose." Some have expressed the opinion that the only Alabamian or political figure that Wallace ever ran away from was Heflin. Others reasoned Wallace dropped out because of his health. Whatever, Heflin and Wallace had a race and Wallace withdrew.

Some observers of the Alabama political scene feel that the withdrawal was the turning point in Wallace's career. They contend that Wallace recognized the growing black vote would be a major factor in any political race. As a result he had to lower his rhetoric and change his attitudes toward race if he were to continue to be elected in Alabama.

THE RACE AGAINST WALTER FLOWERS. After Wallace withdrew, Congressman Walter Flowers entered the race with Wallace's blessing and the support of the Wallace organization.

Everything changed the week of June 1 when Alabama's other Senator, James B. Allen, died suddenly. He and his wife were in Gulf Shores vacationing, and he had a heart attack. Allen's death meant that there would be two Senate races in the 1978 election, one for the regular six-year term and one for the two years remaining in Allen's term. By law, the governor would appoint someone to Allen's seat temporarily, and voters would select the person to serve the remainder of the term during the first election following the death.

Wallace appointed Allen's wife Maryon to fill his seat. Writers speculated that Wallace might run for the Allen seat, and Wallace admitted he considered it. On June 21, he said he would not run.

Maryon Allen contends that Wallace wanted the seat and schemed to resign as governor, have the lieutenant governor succeed him, and then be appointed. However, Mrs. Allen insisted that she be appointed. She contended in an article in the *Birmingham News* that "Wallace wanted to succeed her husband but couldn't appoint himself to the Senate. Wallace finally called to offer her the position, apparently hoping she would decline and leave the door open for him to run in a special election." He asked Maryon, "'You understand that I'm going to be running, don't you?' And there was this long, pregnant pause. . . He knew he couldn't run against his appointee." Mrs. Allen later declared, "I want it chiseled on my tombstone that this 5-foot-2 woman who weighs 110 pounds kept George Corley Wallace out of the Senate, and people should come worship at my tombstone."[6] Maryon served as the appointed interim senator, and then she ran for the unexpired term.

At the beginning of the campaign, even before Howell entered, state Democratic Senators Donald Stewart and John Baker were in the race against Wallace for the Sparkman seat. On June 21, Stewart withdrew from that race because he thought Congressman Flowers and Heflin would be the main contenders, and he switched to run against Maryon Allen. Everybody thought that sympathy would be with Mrs. Allen and would make her almost a cinch to win. She started out with sympathy, but her poorly run campaign caused Stewart to gain on her rapidly.

Walter Flowers was well known and popular. He had been on the House Judiciary Committee which investigated Nixon, and he had voted to impeach. This gave him a lot of publicity, but according to Howell, it went against him in many circles because a surprisingly large group of voters in Alabama remained Nixon supporters even after the President resigned.

> Speaker of the House Tip O'Neill, Peter Rodino, and all the big-name Democrats in the House put on a big fundraiser in Washington to help Flowers, and they had their names listed as hosts. We got a copy of the invitation, and we came out with an ad which reprinted it and said, "All the Washington crowd supports Walter Flowers."

Jim Allen had run against the "Washington Crowd," in his Senate campaigns. Maryon got mad and blasted me for what she claimed was stealing Jim Allen's "Washington Crowd" term. That irritated my friends and a lot of others.

Heflin was one of the first Alabama politicians to campaign among blacks in 1970, and in 1978, he made it known from the first that he intended to be a senator of all the people, including blacks.

Flowers was friendly with members of the Black Caucus in Washington, and he arranged for them to try to influence blacks in Alabama to support him. The members wrote a letter supporting Flowers. At that time the Alabama Democratic Conference (ADC), headed by Joe Reed, was the only black group with real political power.

When I was on the Court, I had made friends with many black lawyers, and Joe Reed had urged me to run against Wallace. A lot of black leaders knew that I had been fair in court decisions, civil rights matters, and other issues that were very important to them. So I was in fairly solid with them.

An ADC screening committee scheduled a meeting to which candidates were invited. You appeared before them, talked and answered questions, and they would vote whether or not they were going to endorse you. Their endorsement meant that you got some 85 percent of the black vote, so it was very important. Mike House found out that Walter Flowers had only supported the Congressional Black Caucus twenty percent of the time on issues it considered important. He had a Washington newspaper article which verified it. So Mike and some others got the local black newspaper in Montgomery to reprint this story. It showed the various issues where Flowers had voted against the Black Caucus in Washington. As ADC committee members came to the Montgomery meeting, we were handing out this newspaper which had been published earlier.

In comes Flowers with Victor Poole and his campaign manager. When they saw the newspaper, they didn't know what in the world to do. So we got the endorsement of the ADC.

Joe Reed says that Walter Flowers represented a district which was heavily black. "Some of us encouraged Flowers to run for the other seat and not against Heflin, but he chose to run against Heflin. Some blacks who had told Heflin they were going to be behind him backtracked. I take your word to mean something in politics; your word's got to be your bond. I had encouraged Senator Heflin to run, and my position was, short of Jesus coming and intervening, I was going to be with Senator Heflin."[7]

Flowers was caught in an embarrassing situation in a television debate. President Carter had asked for a three percent increase in military spending by all the NATO nations, including the United States. This was controversial, and one of the issues in the military spending debate was the B2 bomber.

> We found that there were three occasions when Flowers voted against the B2 bomber. He had been stating that he never voted against the B2. When the debate started, an interrogator asked about the B2. Flowers said that he had always supported the B2 and never voted against it. I had a briefcase, and I pulled out three *Congressional Record* excerpts showing his votes. I asked, "Would you like to see this, Mr. Flowers?" He was bumfuzzled.
>
> Squier had an ad that was very effective. Flowers had voted for a $12,000 salary raise, and Squier had this ad where money was added to an already big pile: one thousand, two thousand, three thousand, four thousand, five thousand. "That's what he voted for — a personal salary raise," it said. In those days, a $12,000 raise was big.
>
> Flowers had charged for plane travel on expense accounts a couple of times when he actually traveled by automobile, and he got caught. There was considerable difference in the reimbursement. Squier had an ad which had a little baby playing with a toy automobile and a toy airplane and saying, "Congressman Flowers doesn't know the difference between an airplane and an automobile, or is it the difference

between right or wrong?" My wife saw that and said, "You can't run that. That's too mean and negative." I told them not to run it, but some of my crowd ran it anyway on a few stations."

Mike House recalls that the campaign against Flowers was not always smooth. "At the first of August," he says, "we were about 12 points down. That was when we changed tactics and begin to run against the "Washington Crowd." Prior to that Heflin did not want to run a negative campaign. Necessity required it."[8]

In the primary on September 5, Howell polled 48 percent of the vote to Flowers's 31 percent, and in the other Senate race, Donald Stewart surprised everybody by receiving 35 percent, not far behind Maryon Allen's 44 percent. Both races were decided in a runoff on September 26. Howell received 65 percent of the vote in the runoff, winning big as expected, but Stewart pulled off a big surprise by getting 57 percent. Since Stewart was to fill Allen's seat, he was sworn in immediately and became Alabama's senior senator.

Donald Stewart was only 38 at the time. He had grown up in Anniston and attended both undergraduate school and law school at the University of Alabama. He was president of the Student Government Association while in college. Stewart had been a big labor supporter and was known to be progressive on racial matters. Mrs. Allen called him a "flaming liberal" during the campaign.[9]

Bert Haltom relates an incident of questionable ethics during the campaign. "After the primary, Flowers had his campaign manager call me and say that if Heflin would pick up his debts, he'd withdraw, and we wouldn't have to make a runoff. Heflin and I huddled, and I told him, 'You can't do it. It would ruin you. It might be illegal, too.' Howell agreed."

Howell tells of learning that he would have no Republican opposition in the general election.

> I'd played some tennis and got along well with Winton "Red" Blount, Sr. who was a big Republican. After I beat Flowers two to one

in the runoff, Blount phoned to tell me that Republicans weren't going to run anybody against me. Republican Jim Martin, who almost beat Lister Hill, had started campaigning for the Sparkman seat, but they switched him because they thought he had a better chance of winning the Allen seat. Early on the Republicans figured that Maryon was going to win, and they put up only a token opponent. They were able to replace their token opponent with Martin.

In the November general election, Heflin, with no Republican opposition, received 94 percent of the vote, losing a few votes to minor party candidates. Donald Stewart defeated Martin.

To show his appreciation to neighbors and friends in his home town, Heflin attended an informal ceremony January 11, 1979, where he was sworn in as a U.S. Senator. The ceremony was held at the Deshler High School Gymnasium in Tuscumbia, and more than 5,000 people attended. He went through the ceremony, even though he would be sworn in again in Washington, because "the home folks had been so good to me." C. C. Torbert, Jr., chief justice of the Alabama Supreme Court, administered the oath. Among those attending were Fob James, then Governor-elect, retiring Senator John Sparkman, Judge Frank Johnson, Joe Reed, chairman of the Alabama Democratic Congress, Congressman Ronnie Flippo, and Senator Donald Stewart. In his speech, Heflin promised to "work hard and seek God's guidance."[10]

15

Starting Fast with Ethics and the Judiciary

Howell Heflin was officially sworn in as a member of the 96th Congress on January 15, 1979,[1] and the first order of business was finding a pet-friendly place to live so the Heflins could bring to Washington their beloved cocker spaniel, Honey. "Much to everybody's horror," Elizabeth Ann says, "we lived in an English basement apartment for six years. We went up in November after the election to find a place to live. Oh, everybody was thrilled to death about having a Senator and his wife rent until they found out we had a dog. Then they said, 'Oh no.' Finally I ran out of places to look, and I came back home. I told Howell, 'You go on, and when you find a place for Honey and me, we'll come.' By then he had a staff together, and the staff found us the English basement. After I got back up there, I went out and rented furniture.

"The English basement had two bedrooms, two bathrooms, a living room, and a dining area with the kitchen in one end of it. I didn't complain, and I was the one that was there all the time. It was the ugliest furniture. We kept it so long, we owned it. When I rented it, I said, 'I'm not going for a style show. I want the most inexpensive, the most comfortable for the money, and the least number of pieces I can get by with.' I told everybody, 'I have furniture just like you'd send off to school with your son.'"

Howell countered, "Well, I never did think we could entertain people there."

"Well, Lou and Jane Wilson came. He was the Commandant of the Marine Corps. You can't get much better than that." Lou and Howell had been friends since the Marine Corps days.

Howell answered, "Well, I was embarrassed about it."

"Well, it didn't bother me. If it didn't bother me, it shouldn't have bothered you."

In March 1980, Honey attacked an intruder in the Heflin's Capitol Hill home, and she got a gash on the head in the incident. "I walked in our apartment and found that we had been robbed," Elizabeth Ann says. "The front door was setting wide open. I don't know why I didn't realize it. I walked all the way through the apartment. The police nearly had a fit because I went in. They said, 'You could have been knocked in the head like the dog.' Honey had a knot on her head and had blood on her. I felt sure that she probably bit one of them." The Birmingham Humane Society nominated Honey for the Stillman Award of the American Humane Society for her bravery, and she was named "Dog of the Year."[2]

Howell described some other adjustments that had to be made:

> I wasn't accustomed to big snows. One of the biggest snows in history came in February just after we arrived. Then a second snow came, and it just immobilized Washington. It was about twenty-seven inches.
>
> It is a custom of the Senate to read George Washington's farewell speech on his birthday. I was selected to preside, and John Warner from Virginia was to deliver the speech. And the snow came. John lived in the Watergate with his wife, Elizabeth Taylor. He had to trudge through the snow to get there. Somebody had to chair the Senate, and I couldn't walk in the snow, so they sent a four-wheel drive for me. Just the two of us were there. But George Washington's farewell speech got delivered on his birthday!
>
> I first met John at an orientation program for new senators. We were talking about the committee assignments we wanted, and I said,

"I want to be on the committee where Elizabeth Taylor is rolling bandages."

STAFFING AND RUNNING THE OFFICE. After finding a place to live, Howell's next task was to set up his Senate office. Mike House became administrative assistant. Charles Mitchell, who grew up in Muscle Shoals and had previously worked for Senators Lister Hill and James Allen, was named executive secretary, and Richard Allen, a Montgomery attorney who had been a law clerk when Howell was on the Supreme Court, became a legislative assistant. Another legislative assistant was Mary Stansel, an African-American originally from Bessemer, Alabama. She had a law degree from the University of Georgia.

Tuscumbia native William Mansel Long, Jr., was named to the staff in May as a legislative assistant. Long, an African-American, had been named "Teacher of the Year" in 1968 at Eliot Junior High School in Washington.

> I wanted to have some people who were familiar with Washington, so I took some from Sparkman's staff and some from Allen's staff. Steve Raby came up later, as did Carlton Betenbaugh, an aide on agriculture. Betenbaugh, who had been in Allen's office, knew people. I had a good staff. Suzelle Smith from Birmingham came aboard after she graduated from Oxford in England. She was my old friend Francis Hare's granddaughter.
>
> We had a big debate in the office on whether to go to computers. We inherited these old automatic typewriters. Mike House insisted on using computers, and we did. If we had stayed with those old typewriters, we wouldn't have lasted long. Most of the time I was there, we averaged three thousand letters a week.

By the end of May 1980, Senators Heflin and Stewart had more black staff members in key positions than any other members of the Senate.[3] Both chose to downplay the matter, saying only that they wanted to choose the best people for positions.

It was also necessary to maintain an organization in Alabama. Bill Gardiner ran the state organization from Tuscumbia, and there were offices in Birmingham, Montgomery, and Mobile. Tom Coker, who had been on Senator Allen's staff, ran the Montgomery office and was Heflin's liaison with the state legislature.

DEMANDS ON TIME. Although Heflin had always been a hard worker, he quickly found that the pressures of scheduling a senator's appointments and commitments required a big adjustment.

> Every group comes to Washington, and all of them have a function where they get their Alabama delegation together. You felt like you had to see Alabamians, but there just wasn't any way of seeing everybody. It was impossible.
>
> Trying to have enough time at night was particularly tough. You were so dependent on your staff. You'd go some place, and if they had the location wrong, you'd lose thirty minutes getting to the right place. Sometimes they'd get mixed up as to where the event would be held, even if it was on Capitol Hill, and you could be in the wrong building.
>
> Another adjustment was the large number of issues. The staff would brief you, but it was difficult to feel you were knowledgeable on a lot of issues. It ended up that if I wasn't going to Alabama on weekends, I would work. At first, we had well over a thousand votes a year, but it decreased to about five hundred on average. Overall, I had something like a 98 percent attendance record.
>
> Then you had the mail. I couldn't possibly read all those letters. I started trying to draft answers, but I just didn't have the time. Finally, I turned the mail answering over to Betenbaugh. Members of the staff would look them over and select letters from people they figured I knew or ought to know, or they would pick one that was a good sample on an issue and show them to me. Staff would develop form letters on particular topics. There were some rich folks in the state who had supported me, and they'd write every week raising cain about something. All these people thought they were getting my personal attention

because of Carlton's expertise in letter writing.

A large number of organizations and special interest groups urge people to write their congressmen. The truth is that the letters and phone calls don't have a lot of influence when you know they are generated by a group. If you got a letter from somebody on an old penciled tablet and written in hand and it made sense, you'd pay attention to it. But when you got a letter that was obviously written by some special interest ghost writer, you pretty much ignored it.

Steve Raby says that, while Heflin may have ignored some of the letters, every letter received by the office got a reply, and it averaged something like five thousand a week.[4]

COMMITTEE ASSIGNMENTS. Donald Stewart took office in November 1978, immediately after the election, to fill Allen's unexpired term. Heflin was sworn in in January 1979, and this gave Stewart seniority.

We had some discussions about committee assignments, and I thought he was going to wait until I got there. When I arrived, he already had the assignments he wanted.

I was originally planning to go on the Agriculture Committee because I felt it was important for Alabama, but Stewart got Agriculture. So I put in for the Judiciary, Armed Service, and Commerce. There was some sort of misunderstanding. I got on Judiciary and Commerce. I selected Commerce because it had the science and technology subcommittee which handled NASA's budget, and that was very important to Huntsville. Two years later I had an opportunity to go on Agriculture, and I left Commerce.

THE JUDICIAL COMMITTEE. Heflin's primary area of intellectual and philosophical interest was in the judiciary, where he had received his training and done his previous work. His success as chief justice of Alabama assured that he would receive the Senate Judicial Committee assignment. He remained a member of this important Committee throughout his Senate career, and he served several years as chairman of the Subcommittee on Courts.

Shortly after he took his seat on the Judiciary Committee, Heflin convinced other members to kill the Court Annexed Arbitration Bill, arguing that it violated the constitutional right of trial by jury. This was an unusual accomplishment for a freshman senator, but his reputation as a jurist and court reformer had preceded him. Many of his Senate colleagues, recognizing his expertise, continued to call him "Judge Heflin" throughout his Senate career.

Heflin says he quickly saw that much of the reform which had been accomplished in Alabama was needed at the federal level. Much of his work on the Judiciary Committee focused on improving administration in the federal judicial system and relieving court congestion in criminal and civil matters. This was in line with Heflin's oft-expressed belief that efficient administration is necessary for swift and sure justice — " I have always subscribed to the expression, 'Justice delayed is justice denied.'"

President Carter had a think tank for judicial matters and reform that was headed by Dan Meador, who had been a law clerk of Hugo Black. Later, Meador had been the dean of the law school at the University of Alabama and was a good friend of Heflin.

Meador came to Washington from the University of Virginia, where he was a professor. He later became blind.

> He has a remarkable mind. He retained everything that people read to him and could quote it back verbatim. He came up with many novel ideas about court reform, and I was largely the one pushing these ideas for him in the Judiciary Committee. There was resistance, as there always is with change.
>
> Part of the reform centered on reducing the work load of the United States Supreme Court by giving them authority to turn down appeals from state supreme courts. There were a great number of those appeals, and the Court wanted to have discretion in dealing with them. Meador and I worked on the creation of the United States Court of Appeals for the Federal Circuit.

Chief Justice Warren Burger was a great believer in improvement of judicial administration, and I worked with him. He'd get me to do things that he wouldn't necessarily come out for publicly. With his blessing, I tried to create a National Court of Appeals which would be between the Circuit Courts of Appeal and the Supreme Court.

Conflicts can develop between circuit courts in the United States. One circuit may rule one way on a case, and another one may rule another way. The Supreme Court can decide between them, but they take very few of the conflict cases. The Feeney Study of the Hruska Commission, compiled during the Nixon Administration, showed that about a hundred of these conflicts develop every year. They ought to be resolved because the law should be uniform in the United States. The idea was that a National Court of Appeals would resolve some of them. It was not adopted, but at least it got some discussion going on how to relieve the Supreme Court.

A lot of issues were involved. If you do away with some jurisdiction, it might affect civil rights, so the liberals were really cautious about any change. Jesse Helms and others were trying to take away the jurisdiction of the court to order busing. We later created a blue-ribbon Federal Court Study Commission, and it came out with a number of recommendations and ideas. But getting something adopted even after you point out the need is something else because of the power of special interest groups. Some changes occurred, but there wasn't as much done as we wanted.

Republican Senator Charles E. Grassley, who was a member of the Subcommittee on Courts with Howell Heflin and subcommittee chairman when Republicans controlled the Senate, said, "Heflin does not do his work because he cares about public attention. He does his work because he wants to do the job right and according to the Constitution and what is good public policy."

CREATION OF THE ELEVENTH CIRCUIT. Senator Heflin was instrumental in creation of the Eleventh Circuit Court of Appeals in 1980. This was done by splitting the old Fifth Circuit Court which had ably handled so many important civil rights cases in the Deep South during the 1950s and 1960s. A new circuit was needed because the Fifth, which included Alabama, Florida, Georgia, Louisiana, Mississippi, and Texas, plus Puerto Rico and the Virgin Islands, was badly overloaded. Individual judges in the Fifth Circuit were burdened by excessively large caseloads, and the entire court had accrued the largest *en banc* caseload in U.S. history.

Because of the court's civil rights record, much sentiment remained for keeping the Fifth Circuit as it was. After it was certain the Fifth Circuit would be split, a political battle was waged over how the six states of the old Fifth Circuit would be divided. Senator James Eastland of Mississippi, chairman of the Judiciary Committee, wanted a four-two split, with Texas and Louisiana in one circuit and the other four states and two territories in the other, but civil rights groups strongly opposed this plan because they thought it would leave the four-state circuit with proportionally more judges who had conservative records.

Most of the civil rights cases had originated in federal district courts in Alabama and surrounding states, and their appeals went to the Fifth Circuit (and many eventually on to the U.S. Supreme Court). Some of the judges on the Fifth Ciruit, such as Richard Rives of Alabama, Albert Tuttle of Georgia, and John Minor Wisdom of Louisiana, had handled most of the school integration cases and had become legendary for their strict interpretation of the Constitution in matters of race and other civil rights issues.

Heflin played a crucial role in securing agreement for the three-three split which civil rights groups wanted. He enlisted the help of another Alabamian, Frank M. Johnson, Jr., who had become arguably the most famous federal district judge in the nation through his courageous rulings on one civil rights case after another during the Patterson–Wallace era. Johnson was later elevated to the new Fifth Circuit Court of Appeals himself, but at the time he was still a sitting district judge in Montgomery. Like Heflin, Johnson was a University of Alabama law school graduate, came from north Alabama, and was progressive on social issues and conservative on crime and law enforcement issues. Unlike Heflin, Johnson was a hill-country "Lincoln" Republican, and was appointed to the federal bench in 1955 by Eisenhower. One of Johnson's first cases overturned the segregated bus seating laws challenged by the arrest of Rosa Parks.

> I worked with Frank Johnson and the others, and we finally came up with a split that had Mississippi, Louisiana, and Texas in one circuit and Alabama, Georgia and Florida in another. Philosophically, the judges would keep the same approach as in the existing Fifth Circuit.
>
> It finally boiled down to a matter of convincing civil rights advocates that the split would be fair. Frank Johnson took the lead and convinced people like Ted Kennedy and the civil rights groups. Judge Johnson was the court's spokesman for the split during hearings on the matter in the House.

In June 1980, Heflin introduced a bill to divide the Fifth Circuit into two circuits of three states each. Both chambers passed the House version of the bill by voice vote the following October. Heflin was supported by a formal petition, signed by all twenty-four judges sitting on the court, including Frank Johnson and Joseph Hatchett, the first African-American on the court.

A big affair was held in Atlanta to celebrate the new Eleventh Circuit, and Chief Judge John Godbold was presiding. Heflin was the main speaker at the banquet. Godbold gave Howell a certificate of admission to the Eleventh Circuit made out to the fictitious character No-Tie Hawkins, but he didn't sign it. He made quite a joke about it.

THE STATE JUSTICE INSTITUTE. Heflin was the moving force behind establishment of the State Justice Institute.

> When I was chief justice, the Law Enforcement Assistance Administration (LEAA) provided a lot of funds to fight crime, and they were liberal about how it could be used. Among other things, LEAA pro-

moted education and training. The Warren Court originated a number of protections for individuals like the Miranda warning, and police, particularly in rural towns, had to be educated and really professionalized.

All the Republicans believe in is block grants — give it to the governor and let him do it. Well, the LEAA program was mixed, but it had categorical grants that had to be applied for. You applied to the federal government for a particular project, and if your project had merit, they would fund you. The LEAA program was targeted early during Reagan's first term, and funding for it was eliminated.

There was still a need to provide assistance to state court systems, for they were handling a great number of federal cases. Drug offenses, for example, could be prosecuted in state or federal courts. In many instances, the FBI or the U.S. Attorney would send a case to be handled in state court because the federal courts were overcrowded. This justified federal monies to help state justice systems.

To address this problem, Heflin introduced legislation in 1980 to establish the State Justice Institute. It did not pass immediately, but he continued to push the idea and was a moving force in its establishment in 1984.

> We designed the Institute to assure strong and effective state courts. We sought to provide education for judges and officers of state courts, to teach sound procedures for managing and monitoring caseloads, and to encourage innovative ways of improving the administration of justice. This has become more important because recent federal laws, including the speedy trial act, increased the cases sent to state courts.
>
> The Institute gets around $20 million a year and is free from the influence of the executive and the legislative in states. The President appoints members of the board, but they must first be nominated by the Conference of Chief Justices. The Institute has improved the quality of justice available to the American people.

The State Justice Institute gives the Howell Heflin Award each year to the most innovative program conducted under a state grant.

TORT REFORM AND TRIAL BY JURY. Heflin helped prevent federal product liability (tort) reform from passing. "While I support reasonable tort reform," he explains, "I believe it should be done at the state level and without weakening the jury system. The right of trial by jury is one of the most sacred rights we have as Americans, and nothing should be done to limit that right or restrict a citizen's access to the judicial system." Later Heflin was successful in defeating an effort to take the right of trial by jury from asbestos victims. He also preserved the jury trial right for tort victims in bankruptcy cases.

ANGLO-AMERICAN LEGAL EXCHANGE. The first year Howell was in the Senate, Chief Justice Warren Burger came up with the idea of an Anglo-American Legal Exchange. Howell was one of a small group which went on a two-week trip to England. The group included Bill Webster, who was head of the FBI at the time and later headed the CIA, and several judges, including Sandra Day O'Connor, who was then serving on an Arizona Court of Appeals. Howell got to know her during that trip and thought she was very competent. Later when she was nominated for the Supreme Court, he was one of her strong supporters. Alabama's Chief Justice C.C. "Bo" Torbert was also a member of the group.

> It was an interesting trip. English solicitors, barristers, and judges explained their system. We spent a couple of days at Scotland Yard and learned about their methods of criminal investigation. We went to Old Bailey, where they were trying criminal cases, and we went out in the rural areas. All the judges, even court of appeals judges, were great oralists. We do everything in writing, but even in the appeals courts there, they'd deliver their opinions without notes. The English jurists were very proud of their ability to organize things in their minds and express themselves. We listened to several trials and went for a seminar retreat to Ditchley Park, where Churchill spent weekends during World War II.

Later they sent about ten jurists over here, and we reciprocated and went around with them. I showed them my office. We took them to the Supreme Court, to court trials, went through the FBI building, and did a lot of other things with them.

ETHICS COMMITTEE CHAIRMAN. Heflin's reputation as an outstanding jurist landed him a job he wasn't sure he wanted. In November 1979, just a few months after he arrived in the Senate, he was nominated to be chairman of the Senate Ethics Committee by Majority Leader Robert C. Byrd. The nomination was approved by a vote of the Senate, and it was the first time since 1901 that a freshman senator had been given a major committee chairmanship. In the years that followed, Heflin handled some of the most difficult cases that ever came before the committee.

When charges of wrongdoing were raised against a senator, the Ethics Committee investigated and recommended a course of action. Members had to pass judgment on their peers, a no-win situation. The job was frustrating and time-consuming, requiring an additional twenty to thirty hours of work a week.

This appointment put Howell at center stage much sooner than he otherwise would have been, and in a very short time, he had achieved a reputation for integrity, independence, and wisdom.[5]

The Committee had just finished an investigation of Georgia Senator Herman Talmadge. It cost $670,000 and was the costliest and longest in Senate history up to that time. Talmadge was found guilty of financial transgressions and was formally "denounced" as "reprehensible" in an 81-15 vote.[6] Illinois Democrat Adlai Stevenson, Jr., son of the late presidential candidate, presided over the Talmadge investigation, and he could hardly wait to step down.

There was strong feeling that certain Committee procedures should be changed. The new vice chairman, Republican Senator Malcolm Wallop of Wyoming, favored bringing in a court referee or a retired judge to determine a senator's ultimate guilt or innocence. Heflin agreed on the need for reform, but he believed there would be a serious constitutional problem if outsiders were brought in to judge a senator.

He also felt the same ethics panel should not act both as investigators and jurors. He pointed out that no court would allow a grand juror to serve on a trial jury in the same case.[7]

The Ethics Committee drew on federal election law, the Ethics in Government Act, and Senate rules on ethics in making its rulings. Heflin received Senate authority to review the lists of rules to remove conflicts and compile a single code of ethics.[8] "It is absolutely essential that the strictest standards of Congressional ethics are maintained," he said. "It is equally as essential that actions of members of Congress, as elected leaders of the nation, must be above and beyond suspicion or reproach."[9]

THE WILLIAMS MATTER. In February 1980, the FBI disclosed it was investigating New Jersey Democratic Senator Harrison A. Williams, Jr., and seven members of the House on charges of political bribery. In an operation called ABSCAM, FBI undercover agents, posing as wealthy Arabs or as representatives of Arab interests, paid nearly $500,000 in cash in exchange for promises of political favors and other services. Williams was chairman of the Senate Labor and Human Resources Committee.

The FBI filmed Williams and an agent disguised as an Arab sheik. They were talking about the sheik's investing in a titanium mine in which Williams would own part interest. The senator bragged about his influence in the government and said he would try to obtain permanent resident status for the phony sheik.

Early in February, Democratic Leader Robert C. Byrd and acting Republican Leader Ted Stevens of Alaska called jointly for an ethics committee investigation of the Williams situation "as expeditiously as possible." The Judicial Committee voted unanimously to conduct a preliminary inquiry.[10]

"A big issue," Heflin says, "was whether the Executive Branch and the Department of Justice were making entrapments in the Legislative Branch. Williams was after personal gain, but he claimed he was entrapped and that the FBI had gone beyond their bounds. Under the technical reading of the entrapment statues, we thought we met the requirements for Ethics Committee action."

At first, the Justice Department decided to deny Congressional investigators access to the information it had gathered. It would brief Congressional investigators but not turn over evidence until criminal cases were closed.[11] A possible confrontation was avoided when the Committee reached an agreement with the Justice Department. As the criminal process of grand jury, indictment, and trial proceeded, the Department would pass selected evidence to the Committee with the understanding the Committee would keep it strictly secret and take no action until a verdict was reached.

A federal jury in Brooklyn convicted Williams of bribery and conspiracy on nine felony charges in May 1981. He was sentenced to three years in prison and fined $10,000. By this time, Heflin was no longer Ethics Committee chairman because the Republicans won control of the Senate in 1980. He was, rather, vice chairman and ranking Democrat.[12]

In August 1981, the Ethics Committee voted to recommend that the Senate expel Williams for "ethically repugnant" conduct. He would be the first senator expelled since the Civil War.[13] In his column of September 11, 1981, Jack Anderson claimed Williams was innocent, and the Committee was proceeding like a "kangaroo court." Anderson blasted Heflin and referred to him as "ultra conservative."[14]

The Senate began debate on Williams's expulsion on March 3, 1982, with Vice President George Bush presiding. In more than five hours of debate, Heflin emerged as the chief Senate prosecutor. He spent two and one-half hours outlining Williams's offenses in minute detail. Arguing that "the severity of the sanction must meet the odiousness of the offence," Heflin urged the Senate to expel Senator Williams. "Put most simply, Harrison Williams traded on his office. He traded on his name and position. He acted in an official capacity out of motives for personal financial gain. And in doing so, he sullied both his reputation and that of this institution."

Columnist Mary McGrory wrote that Heflin was a senator with a "man-in-the-moon profile" and "a grinding drawl" who dismantled Williams's defense and again demonstrated "it is always a Southerner, one with a love of the law, the language, and the institutions, who comes forward at such delicate moments in the life of the Senate."[15]

Speaking for Williams, his appointed defense counsel Democratic Senator Daniel Inouye of Hawaii, noted that the only previous expulsions from the Senate have been for treason and disloyalty. The New Jersey Senator's transgressions were far less serious, he said. The videotapes of Williams were disturbing because they showed him bragging coarsely about his influence. Still, Inouye said, "We are here because our egos are immense. What happened to Williams could have happened to any one of us."[16]

Williams resigned early in March, so no vote was ever taken. There was little doubt that if he had not resigned, the Senate would have expelled him.[17]

There had been only three investigations by the Ethics Committee in the ten years prior to Heflin's becoming chairman, and he said he didn't expect anything of such magnitude as the Williams matter so soon. It consumed a great deal of his time.[18]

Heflin served on the Ethics Committee for thirteen years, and he was chairman two different times when Democrats held the majority in the Senate. He later commented, "My service on the Ethics Committee can be described with many adjectives, none of which is 'enjoyable.'"

Heflin was widely credited with excellent performance in a job nobody wants. Senator Fritz Hollings of South Carolina said Heflin did an "outstanding job in a very thankless task," and called him, "A common man of uncommon abilities." Senator David Pryor of Arkansas commented, "In trying to deal with some of the extremely sensitive issues that faced individuals in this body, it was always Judge Heflin who brought us back to the center of the argument and the center of the issue as he said time and again, 'Ladies and gentlemen, we must do what is good for this institution.'"

ALABAMA MATTERS. The first responsibility of an elected official is to represent the interests of the people who elected him. Howell immediately became immersed in three issues of major concern to Alabama: the Tennessee-Tombigbee Waterway Project (the Tenn-Tom), location of the Tennessee Valley Authority (TVA) headquarters; and, a range of defense matters.

Alabama had many waterway projects, including the Coosa-Alabama Rivers System, the Theodore Ship Canal, the Warrior-Tombigbee Waterway, and the Tri-State Waterway, which involved the Chattahoochee, Apalachicola and Flint Rivers in Alabama, Georgia, and Florida. Heflin strongly supported them all. When President Reagan proposed in his budget in January 1982 to close the Coosa-Alabama and Apalachicola-Chattahoochee-Flint waterways and cut back operations on the Warrior-Tombigbee, Heflin strongly protested and wrote the President a strongly worded letter.[19]

The biggest project by far was the Tennessee-Tombigbee Waterway. The Tenn-Tom connects the Tennessee River at Pickwick Lake in South-Central Tennessee to the Port of Mobile, and it saves approximately 800 miles for boats on the Tennessee River headed for the Gulf of Mexico. The waterway is 234 miles long and connects to the Tombigbee River near Demopolis, Alabama, about 120 miles north of Mobile. Forty-five miles of the waterway is a canal, most of which is in Mississippi. Construction began in 1972. It was the largest waterway project ever undertaken by the Army Corps of Engineers in the United States.

The Tenn-Tom was a little more than half finished when Heflin arrived. There was strong opposition from the beginning by people who were against it, because of deficit spending, harm to the environment, and the general claim that it was a boondoggle. Opponents claimed that the cost-benefit figures of supporters were wrong, that the project was a loser which would be fortunate to return twenty cents on the dollar.[20]

Opponents were well organized to cut funds and stop construction in 1980, and Heflin was among the senators fighting to keep the project going. Senate Majority Leader Robert Byrd helped Tenn-Tom supporters in September by calling up the Energy and Water Development Appropriations Bill, the funding measure, sooner than expected and catching the opponents by surprise. In 1980, the Tenn-Tom received $208 million for fiscal year 1981 in a 53-36 Senate vote.

The project was again almost scuttled in 1981.

We had whip counts in the Senate which showed that we were going to lose, so we knew we had a lot of work to do. The Senate was meeting one Saturday night during a time when we were trying to delay the vote and find compromises which could change some minds. Lo and behold, about twelve or one o'clock in the morning Senator Daniel Patrick Moynihan began to make speeches on it and acted like he was going to get it brought up for a vote. If you make a motion to table, it's non-debatable, and you have to vote on it. We were afraid he was going to move to table and thus kill the thing.

Well, Moynihan was speaking, and then I started speaking. I said, "This idea originated with Thomas Jefferson, who said the Tennessee-Tombigbee ought to be built." He pointed on the map where the Tennessee River was shown and where the Tombigbee River started. Moynihan answered, "You're wrong about the originator. George Washington came up with the idea of connecting it, but he didn't know the cost. In fact, there was some discussion among some French explorers about it." He was a great historian and Harvard man, and when it came time to answer him, I didn't want to be outdone. I said, "Senator Moynihan, you have it all wrong. When Moses came down from the mountain top, he said the eleventh commandment was to build the Tennessee-Tombigbee." It got him laughing and got him off of his idea.

Senator Levin, who was new and very friendly with me, wanted to help, and he came up with the Levin Amendment. This said none of the monies appropriated could be used south of Demopolis, which was on the Tombigbee. The Tombigbee River south of Demopolis would eventually have to be enlarged. We agreed with the Levin Amendment because we knew work south of Demopolis would require a congressional enactment anyway. So we picked up his vote.

Senator Donald Stewart and I really worked. We changed a good number of votes and finally won.

In November 1981, the Senate voted 48-46 to defeat an amendment to the budget to remove the Tenn-Tom's 1982 fiscal appropriation of $189 million. This was the closest vote in the history of the project. By that time 71 percent of the Tenn-Tom had been completed, and 81 percent was funded.[21]

Two or three more years of annual appropriations were required, and we knew we could be in trouble. We devised a scheme so that no more votes were required. We set it up so the Corps of Engineers could devote monies from their general appropriation towards construction on waterways that they deemed were needed. Since Jamie Whitten from Mississippi was chairman of the House appropriations committee and Tom Bevill was chairman of the subcommittee that dealt with the Corps of Engineers, we knew that the Corps would go along with what they wanted. We got that passed without any fanfare or anybody really realizing what it meant, and we never had another vote on the Tenn-Tom.

We kept arguing with the environmentalists that if we left it unfinished, we would have an open ditch. The original environmental impact statement called for remediation. Since the canal would go through environmentally sensitive areas, additional land was to be purchased and set aside for wildlife management and other things. Stopping it would have been an environmental catastrophe because it would have left an open ditch.

At that time, the New England states had the acid rain issue. George Mitchell had just come in the Senate from Maine, and he reminded us time and time again that he'd voted for that "boondoggle Tennessee-Tombigbee." He chawed on me to help him on all sorts of things. We finally worked out a pretty good compromise on the acid rain legislation.

TVA. The Tennessee Valley Authority Act in 1933, one author of which was Lister Hill, stated explicitly that TVA's headquarters were to be in Muscle Shoals, Alabama, but in fact they were placed in Knoxville, Tennessee. "They had a little ole building down here that had 'TVA Headquarters' on it," Heflin says, "but all their main offices were in Knoxville."

In 1979, Alabama won a district court decision ordering TVA to move its headquarters to Muscle Shoals. The Fifth Circuit Court of Appeals overturned the ruling, and the Alabama attorney general took the matter to the U.S. Supreme Court in September 1981.[22] In the meanwhile, a fight between Alabama and Tennessee congressional delegations ensued, and Heflin vigorously opposed legislation which would reverse the federal district court order moving the headquarters from Knoxville to Muscle Shoals. However, in the end the circuit court of appeals decision prevailed, and the headquarters have remained in Knoxville.

Defense. Defense was a major concern for Alabama because Redstone Arsenal and the Marshall Space Flight Center were in Huntsville, and Alabama was home to three large military bases: the Air University in Montgomery; the Army helicopter training center at Fort Rucker; and, Fort McClellan in Anniston. From the beginning, Heflin voiced support for a strong defense in the United States, and he fought to see that all military installations in Alabama remained open.

Fort Rucker was the center of a controversy. The Alabama delegation wanted to bring all military helicopter training there. The Air Force had consolidated their training with the Army, and the effort now was to consolidate this with the Navy. In his early years in the Senate, Heflin fought to win and combine all helicopter training at Fort Rucker. Big opposition came from Florida, since the Navy did their helicopter training in Pensacola.

"I was pushing it big. We got Graham Clayton who had been Secretary of the Navy to support us. He became the Deputy Secretary of Defense, and we thought we were going to go forward. But when Jeremiah Denton, an old Navy man, was elected to the Senate from Alabama in 1980, he sided with the Navy. It's still an issue."

In a speech in April 1980, Heflin said that the weak state of the military was one of America's most serious problems. He noted that the USSR had outspent the United States on military matters for ten years. In an impassioned speech on the Senate floor, Heflin said that the Soviet

Union was building up chemical weapons such as nerve gas, and he added they had made great strides in military hardware.[23] In his weekly column in July, he wrote that if military spending were not increased, the U.S. would fall far behind the Soviets in all military aspects.[24]

Heflin feels that Jimmy Carter was never given proper credit for his contribution to defense. "He urged all the NATO nations, including the United States, to increase their military preparedness appropriations by three percent. That began the rejuvenation of military preparedness. Everybody gives Reagan credit, but Carter started it and Reagan greatly accelerated it.

THE BALANCED BUDGET AMENDMENT. Heflin had promised in his campaign to introduce a constitutional amendment to balance the budget, and this was the first piece of legislation he introduced when he became a member of the Senate. He reintroduced it at the beginning of each of the nine Congresses in which he served.

Early on Heflin became a member of an informal bipartisan group of about twenty senators called "The Balance the Budget Caucus." Shortly after Heflin introduced his first bill, his staff realized he was one of five senators on the Judiciary Committee who had introduced proposals for a balanced budget amendment. The five directed their staffs to combine the best features of all the bills into one proposed amendment that fiscally conservative members could rally behind. The consensus bill was approved by the Senate Subcommittee on the Constitution, but it failed in the Senate Judiciary committee by a vote of nine to eight.[25] The consensus bill later became a plank in Ronald Reagan's 1980 presidential campaign.[26]

SALT II. In June 1979, President Carter met with Soviet Premier Leonid Breznev in Vienna and signed Salt II, a second Strategic Arms Limitation Treaty. Salt II recognized the principle of military equality between the Soviet Union and the United States, and its primary aim was to reduce the number of nuclear weapons on both sides. The intended result was nuclear parity. Salt II came under immediate fire from conservatives in the U.S. who felt it did not include sufficient means to verify that weapons had been destroyed. The treaty came up for a ratification vote later in 1979. Heflin remained uncommitted for a long time, saying he had an open mind and wanted to study the matter. By the end of May, he voiced doubts and said somebody would have to do a lot of convincing before he would vote to ratify.[27]

The situation took on a new light when the Soviet Union invaded Afghanistan in December 1979. In January, a motion was made in the Senate to ask President Carter to withdraw the SALT treaty from consideration. At Majority Leader Byrd's request, the Senate voted 50-36 to set aside this motion. Treaties require a two-thirds vote in the Senate, and since only thirty-four senators were needed to defeat Salt II, the 50-36 result meant it would not be ratified. Faced with this result, the Senate did not take up the treaty in 1980.

Heflin said his opposition boiled down to the fact that he "just didn't trust the Russians."

THE PANAMA CANAL. President Carter negotiated a treaty in 1978 to give Panama ownership of the Panama Canal and to return sovereignty of the canal zone to that country. The transfer was to be complete by the year 2000. This treaty created great controversy even though it was widely known that the United States illegally gained possession of the canal zone in 1903. The Panama Canal treaty was approved in the Senate by a very narrow margin in 1978 before Heflin came to the Senate. During his campaign for the Senate he voiced opposition to the treaty.

Georgia Senator Herman Talmadge voted for the treaty. "He supported a lot of Carter things he really wasn't for," Heflin recounts. "He tells about speaking at a gathering in Georgia. In came a little lady with a bonnet on. She was dipping snuff and had a sweet gum stick in her mouth, and she was walking with a cane. She asked, 'Whar's Herman? Whar's Herman? I want to see Herman.' He came up to her and said, 'Sister Such and Such, how are you?' 'Herman, they tell me you voted to give away our canal.' He answered, 'Well, now Sister Such and Such, the facts are . . .' She said, 'Facts my ass, you voted to give away our canal.'"

ENERGY. In 1973, the twelve members of OPEC, the Organization of Petroleum Exporting Countries, cut production of crude oil and raised the price four-fold. This caused gasoline shortages in the United States and a sharp increase in cost. To address the resulting energy crisis, President Carter adopted a broad policy on alternate sources of energy, including solar, geothermal and the conversion of coal into gas. Heflin strongly supported this policy. The alternative which he thought had the greatest potential was renewable sources of energy such as certain agricultural crops.

> Then the Reagan administration came in and just destroyed all of the research and efforts in regards to alternate energy sources. Reagan and his supporters thought it should be left entirely to private enterprise with no government subsidies. Reagan listened to the oil companies who said we have plenty of petroleum and other types of energy.
>
> A central question is the role of government. I believe that government has a role in the development of alternate sources of energy. It's just like the National Institutes of Health. We would never had made the advances in health without NIH. NIH gives grants to companies and universities, and it serves as a clearinghouse. This provides cross fertilization of ideas on cures for diseases. NIH has played a key role.
>
> I had this idea about a National Laser Institute, which would be on the same model as the National Institutes of Health. Laser technology has so much potential. A laser beam travels at the speed of light, 186,000 miles per second, and it is capable of producing great power. It is predicted that some day we'll have a space ship powered by lasers. Lasers are already used for all sorts of things like removing cataracts from the human eye. The inventory systems in supermarkets which let them know when to order a new supply are basically laser technology.

In November 1980, Heflin called for a national commitment to laser technology similar to the commitment President Kennedy made in 1960 to the space program. He introduced a bill in November 1980 to establish a National Laser Institute. The Republicans opposed the bill, saying private enterprise should be the sole developer of laser technology, and the bill died in committee.

TRADE, HELEN KELLER, AND TRACTORS. Heflin attempted to modify the Federal Trade Commission (FTC) reauthorization bill in 1979 to prevent the agency from ordering divestiture by corporations in monopoly cases. He felt that a federal agency should not be able to take property, that only the courts should do it. He lost.[28]

He and Congressman Ronnie Flippo introduced a joint resolution to the House and Senate to proclaim June 27, 1980, "Helen Keller Day." This was 100th anniversary of Miss Keller's birth.[29] The resolution was unanimously approved by the Senate and the House. Helen Keller was born in Tuscumbia and lived there the first years of her life, and Heflin had served as her attorney on some local matters.

Heflin tells of a tractor invasion of Washington in 1980. After the Soviets invaded Afghanistan in December 1979, Carter imposed a grain embargo. This was very unpopular with farmers because the Soviets had been importing large quantities of American grain.

> These farmers came to Washington with their tractor brigade, and were just as mischievous as they could be. They were trying to attract attention and pressure Congress to do away with the embargo. They would park their tractors on the streets and bridges and stop traffic. Lord, we had them from all over Alabama. It came a terrible snowstorm while they were there and because of the snow, the farmers came out smelling like a rose. Cars were backed up to China in all that snow, and the farmers hauled the cars out. They really helped. Finally the President lifted the embargo.

16

Friend of the Farmer

ALABAMA HAS A LARGE rural population and depends heavily on farming for its economy. Because farming is a primary concern, Howell Heflin had asked for appointment to the Senate Agriculture Committee when he first arrived in the Senate in 1979, and he received the assignment in 1981. He served on the Committee the remaining sixteen years of his Senate tenure.

As the twentieth century progressed, there was a fundamental change in farming in the United States. In the old days, a large portion of people who lived on farms were content with a simple life and were happy to survive. Today, farm families want to live the good life with modern conveniences like everybody else. Support of this life style requires a larger operation, and knowledge and management skills have become essentials. Farmers can quickly get in trouble because of things beyond their control.

Agriculture was in trouble in Alabama when Heflin came to office. In December 1981, a Department of Agriculture task force stated that farming and agribusiness in Alabama, Mississippi, and Georgia had been severely weakened during the three preceding years because of drought, inflation, and the soaring cost of borrowing caused by high interest rates.[1]

Heflin started with very little knowledge of the intricacies of agribusiness. "To say Heflin knew nil about agriculture less than a year ago just barely qualifies as an exaggeration," observed reporter Peter Coburn of the *Huntsville Times*. By the time key legislation came up for consideration just a few months later, he was "the most knowledgeable senator on the floor."[2] Associated Press reporter Scott Shepard wrote in April 1984 that Howell Heflin had taken over the role formerly played by Georgia's Senator Herman Talmadge as principal spokesman for Southern agriculture in the nation's capital.[3] This attests to his widely observed habit of working as long as necessary to get on top of matters of importance.

THE AGRICULTURE COMMITTEE. In general, the economics of agriculture in the Carter Administration had been expansive, and American exports of grain and soy beans were increasing. Prices for American farm products were high, and the farm economy was strong. The common thought was that there was no limit to the heights that American agriculture could attain.[4] A change loomed, however, as Ronald Reagan brought a Republican Congress in with him in 1981. This meant tough times in many ways for agriculture, especially for small farmers. With the Republican takeover of the Senate, Heflin was the junior member of the Agriculture Committee on the minority side.

With Reagan came a big change in attitudes toward agriculture. Most Republicans, in their zeal for the free market and for a *laissez-faire* approach to economic policy, insisted that farmers face free-market forces and prove themselves in the same way as other businesses. Support for farm commodity prices came under attack. "They wanted to cut agriculture," Heflin says, "and they started out with food stamps, the school lunch program, the WIC (Women, Infants, and Children) program, the Extension Service, and some others, all of which affected market prices and supply."

Heflin understood that farming is fundamentally different from other businesses and is more vulnerable to forces which are outside the individual farmer's control. Another difference is that increased costs of production cannot be passed on to the consumer as in other parts of the free enterprise system. Farming is one of those areas where the government must depart from a strict hands-off policy and be a partner. He pointed out that, under the old system, American farms had provided a stable supply of food for American families at a lower cost than in any other part of the world. He and his colleagues argued strongly for a balanced farm policy which protected both producers and consumers.

FARM BILLS AND COMMODITY SUPPORT PROGRAMS. Debate on the 1981 Farm Bill was beginning when Heflin joined the Committee. The farm bill passed, but it did not please Heflin in spite of the fact that he won many battles in its preparation. He said it should be called "The Farm Bankruptcy Act" instead of "The Agriculture and Food Act of 1981" because of limited financial support the bill gave farmers.[5]

> In the school lunch program, they were going to cut out the breakfast program, and they were going to do means testing. They had three or four different categories. All the educators said it would be an administrative nightmare and would destroy the nutrition program, which included school lunch. Among another things, means testing would stigmatize the poor. We had big fights trying to preserve the nutrition program.
>
> When farm bills were written over the years, authors had the interest of the farmers at heart, but they had to combine it with a lot of other interests. We received liberal support because the food stamp and WIC programs were tied to the farm bill. In food stamps, we'd have defectors from the Republicans, particularly those from the more populous states. People like Arlen Specter would vote to restore things like school lunch. Even D'Amato would sometimes cross over. Before that, Javits would help. In 1981, we were able to keep the basic school lunch program and the food stamp program with some changes.
>
> Senator Jesse Helms was the committee chairman under Reagan. Helms has a lot of faults, but he was always fair on agriculture and would let people take as much time discussing as they needed. He moved things through, and generally he was a friend of the farmer.
>
> Most types of farm production are restricted to particular geo-

Above, Howell Heflin, in a typically pensive pose at his desk in the U.S. Senate. Among the things he could have pondered was the difference between his legacy and that of his famous uncle, Cotton Tom Heflin, left, who had preceded him in the Senate by a half-century.

Above, the family of Dr. Wilson L. Heflin: (front) Robert Heflin, Mrs. Haden Reid, Dr. Wilson L. Heflin, Rev. Marvin R. Heflin, and Rev. Walter Heflin; and (back) Judge John T. Heflin, Dr. Wyatt Heflin, Sen. J. Thomas Heflin, Judge Harrington P. Heflin, and Dr. Howell T. Heflin, about 1910.

Right, Louise Heflin with her children: Wilson, Howell, and Julia, c. 1925.

Above, Heflin visiting his family cemetery.

Left, all that is remains of Louina, where the Heflins made their first Alabama home, is this historical marker in Randolph County.

Left, young Howell and a beloved puppy, c. 1932.

Below, the Reverend Marvin Heflin with his sons Wilson (L) and Howell (R), about 1936, when Howell was fifteen.

Left, Second Lieutenant Howell Heflin in his United States Marine Corps uniform, November 1942.

Below, Heflin, center, with his platoon at Guadalcanal.

Above, Heflin with Conrad Fowler and Bill Pfeifle at Guadalcanal, 1943. Below, a half-century later, Heflin was received as a returning hero during a Senate trip to Guam. Pictured with him was Governor Joseph Ada.

After World War II, Heflin entered the University of Alabama School of Law. While in law school, he began dating Elizabeth Ann Carmichael. They were married in 1952, after Heflin had established his law practice in Tuscumbia.

Above, with President John F. Kennedy, on the 30th anniversary of the Tennessee Valley Authority, Muscle Shoals, 1963.

Right, Heflin's campaign flyer for his successful entry into politics, 1970.

ELECT
Howell T. Heflin
Chief Justice
Alabama Supreme Court

"There is no guarantee of justice except the character of the judge."

(PAID POL. ADV. BY W. F. GARDINER, CHAIRMAN, HOWELL T. HEFLIN FOR CHIEF JUSTICE COMMITTEE, TUSCUMBIA, ALA.)

Above, Heflin with Elizabeth Ann and their son, Tom, at the victory party after the Chief Justice election in 1970.

Below, the Heflin court: (seated) Hugh Maddox, Pelham Merrill, Heflin, James Bloodworth, and James Faulkner; and (standing) Janie Shores, Richard Jones, Reneau Almon, and Eric Embry.

Above, history was in the making when Chief Justice Heflin gave the oath of office to Justice Janie Shores, Alabama's first female on the Supreme Court.

Below, in another sign of the changing times, Heflin, always a supporter of youth and education, swore an integrated group into "office" at Alabama Boys State, an annual mock government event sponsored by the American Legion.

Above, as Chief Justice, Heflin swore in Alabama's first class of black legislators following reapportionment.

Right, Heflin, shown here voting for it, led the fight to pass a Constitutional Amendment reforming Alabama's court system.

Above, the Chief Justice rubs elbows with Alabama's famous football coaches, "Bear" Bryant of Alabama and "Shug" Jordan of Auburn. Third from left is Senator Jim Allen.

Left, Heflin's campaign brochure for his run to succeed John Sparkman in the U.S. Senate.

Above, as a member of the Senate Agriculture Commuittee, Heflin was a friend of farmers. Here he visits in Muscle Shoals in 1990 with Neal Isbell, L.O. Bishop, and Hollis Isbell.

Below, Heflin at the Senate hearings deciding on funding for the Tennessee-Tombigbee Waterway hearings. Third from left is former Alabama Governor "Fob" James.

Helen Keller was the most famous citizen of Heflin's adopted hometown of Tuscumbia. Here he joins Senator Donald Stewart, Vice President Walter Mondale, and members of Keller's family, at the dedication of a Helen Keller stamp.

Right, after being re-elected in 1990, Heflin took the oath of office from then Vice President Dan Quayle.

Alabama's Congressional delegation during Heflin's second term in the Senate. From left, seated, Rep. Tom Bevill, Heflin, Rep. Bill Dickinson, and Sen. Richard Shelby; Standing, Rep. Glenn Browder, Rep. Claude Harris, Rep. Sonny Callahan, Rep. Ben Erdreich, and Rep. Bud Cramer.

Below, Heflin relied on Chief of Staff Mike House, left, and Campaign Manager Bill Gardiner.

Right, with Mother Teresa at a National Prayer Breakfast of which Heflin was chairman.

Below, chatting in the White House with President Jimmy Carter.

Above, President Jimmy Carter's kick-off campaign for reelection in Tuscumbia, Alabama, Labor Day, 1980.

Below, Heflin's acceptance speech at a tribute given by the Alabama Peanut Producers Association.

Right, Heflin congratulates astronaut Sally Ride on her successful mission as the first American woman in space.

Heflin was an ardent support of the space program. Here he discusses NASA missions with William Lucas of the Marshall Space Flight Center.

Above, with President Ronald Reagan and Vice President George Bush, at the White House, 1985.

Below, with President George Bush, Roy Greene and Bill Moore at one of Heflin's favorite activities, the annual Alfalfa Club dinner.

Above, in Iraq after the Gulf War, with fellow Marines: General Walt Boomer, Senator John Warner, unidentified, and Senator John Glenn.

Right, giving his famous pachyderm speech for the Clinton reelection rally at Birmingham-Southern College, 1996.

Above, an informal discussions with President Bill Clinton and Heflin's chief of staff Steve Raby.

Below, spending some relaxing time fishing with Karl Bradley.

Above, The Heflin family portrait, Howell and Elizabeth Ann Heflin with their son, Tom, his wife, Cornelia, and grandchildren Wil and Mary Catherine.

Left, the loyal and beloved Heflin cook, Annie Mae Peters.

Since Heflin's retirement, he and Elizabeth Ann have settled back into their home in Tuscumbia and have enjoyed spending time with old friends. Above, Elizabeth Ann with Lucy Ware. Below, relaxing and talking with longtime friend, Ed Mauldin.

A recent photo of Senator and Mrs. Howell Heflin, in the garden of their home in Tuscumbia.

graphic regions, and widespread support for a particular crop has to be developed. In the battle to divide up available money, different states look after their own interests, so it can turn into a free-for-all. You had to have coalitions to fight the battles successfully.

We had to keep the Democrats together, and I worked hard on that. We usually had a coalition of sugar, peanuts, cotton, and tobacco. We'd go along with tobacco people on their program, and they'd go along with us on our program. In Alabama, there were about 2,000 acres of tobacco in the low part of Butler County and the north part of Covington County. There might be fifty farmers involved in tobacco but not many.

We didn't have many sugar producers in Alabama but that industry helped in the coalition. Once I helped in getting 67 senators to sign a letter on a GATT sugar issue at the urging of my friends Don Wallace and Macon Edwards.

Republican Senator Pete Wilson was elected from California and came on the Agriculture Committee. He had an amendment on raisins, and he made a good speech about it. Raisins were pretty well limited in their growing area, and they had subsidies and restrictions that Republicans generally didn't like. I made a little speech supporting Wilson's amendment, and I made the motion to adopt it. All the Democrats voted for it, and it got through. After it was over he came up to me and said, "I didn't know you grew raisins in Alabama." I said, "We don't, but we raise peanuts." He got the message. They don't raise peanuts in California, but after that he always helped us with the peanut program. You'd have to do a little trading.

One senator from Iowa who came in with Reagan was against cotton supports. I took him down to Auburn back when senators could make honorarium speeches, and he got an honorarium. I started calling him "Cotton Roger" Jepson. I'd get Cotton Roger to vote with us sometimes. He had a lot of corn in Iowa and was on the Committee. My friend Thad Cochran had solid white hair, and I called him "Cotton Thad."

Out west they had wool. There weren't too many sheep growing states, so we could support each other. The two Alaskan senators always voted for the peanut program, and they never grew a peanut in Alaska. They helped us, and I sure did help them on a lot of different things they wanted in Alaska.

PEANUTS. Peanuts, cotton, and soybeans were the primary crops of concern in Alabama. In the Wiregrass, the Southeast section of the state which adjoins Georgia and Florida, peanuts are grown in fourteen counties and are the mainstay of the economy.

An amendment to the 1981 Farm Bill by Senator Richard Lugar, Indiana Republican, greatly restricted acreage allotments and weakened the section which restricted imports. On the first vote, the Republican-controlled Senate adopted the amendment and practically did away with the peanut program. Supporters had to go immediately to an alternative plan. Heflin walked off the floor with Senators John Warner and Mack Mattingly of Georgia.

> We got with lobbyists Ross Wilson from Texas and James Earl Mobley and Dick Fifield from Alabama and rewrote the peanut program on a yellow pad. Our little group accepted the elimination of acreage allotments and came up with the concept of a "poundage quota," which basically accomplished the same thing. It was based on production instead of acreage.[6]
>
> Warner and I took the lead. We went back on the floor in less than an hour and said, "We've done away with the acreage allotment and made improvements." I correctly said that our program would actually be less costly to the government than the plan proposed by Lugar.[7] That got the program passed. We beat Lugar that time.
>
> We were able to transfer the acreage allotment into a farm quota which allowed the farmer to sell peanuts at the quota price. Farmers could grow peanuts that were not in the quota, but they were not guaranteed a price. We put in an escalator clause that would increase the price of quota peanuts if the cost of production went up. No other crop had an escalator clause.

Peanuts were always being attacked. Many of the free enterprise types opposed any kind of supports, and manufacturers wanted to do away with the peanut program. They always fought any program that raised the amount received by the farmer for peanuts. They wanted to get peanuts cheaper, and they wanted to do away with restrictions on imports.

COTTON. Cotton did not generate the number of battles as peanuts.

We usually worked out the cotton program. The National Cotton Council had everybody together. The manufacturers and textile mills were in alliance with each other and with the producers. But you could still have problems if supporters of other crops thought cotton was getting some advantage compared to theirs.

One protection in the cotton program was the target price. The program established what a farmer should be able to get for his cotton with actual amount varying according to grade, length of fiber, and other factors. If the average market price for all the cotton sold dropped below the target price, the government would make up the difference on a per pound basis up to a limit. They wouldn't pay more than a limit to any one farmer. The target price was something like 74 cents a pound in the 1981 Farm Bill. In a later bill, they cut it to about 72 cents.

Wayne Boutwell of the National Association of Farmers Cooperatives came up with another protection for cotton, the marketing loan.

In the cotton marketing loan, there was a basic loan level, usually around fifty or fifty-one cents a pound. You could put your cotton in loan and draw on it from the government. At the end of the loan period, you could either forfeit and let the government take it, or you could draw it out of loan, repay anything owed, and sell it at the market price. It allowed the farmer to watch the market, and if the price of cotton went up, he could take it out of loan and sell it. Thus, there were two protections for cotton farmers, the target price and the marketing loan.

They were never able to get the marketing loan for wheat or corn or the feed grains.

The cotton loan program worked the first year, and exports of U.S. agriculture commodities went up dramatically in a short time. The cost to the government was less than with alternative programs.[8]

SOYBEANS. In the years before Heflin went on the Agriculture Committee, soybean production had been increasing faster than that of any other crop in the South. In 1980, Alabama had two million acres, making soybeans a major crop, and Mississippi and Tennessee had even more. In 1980, soybeans brought in some $9 billion and were the nation's number one cash crop.

The crop didn't produce as well in some states as in others. Midwestern states produced forty to fifty bushels per acre, while the average in Alabama was about twenty-three bushels to the acre. One problem was that Alabama has cotton weather, which is hot and dry in September, and soybeans need a lot of rain in September to fruit out.

Another problem was that many people who produced soybeans had moved South from the Midwest. They used the technology and seed which had served them in the more northern climates, and they did not employ crop rotations which avoided buildups of the nematode population or other diseases. Yields dropped to as low as fifteen bushels an acre.[9]

For a number of years, soybean producers did not want to be in a government program. Then in the 1980s, when yields dropped, prices got low, and a lot of people were going out of business, there was a change in attitude. Many soybean people wanted to participate in the marketing loan and other commodity programs.[10]

To address the problems, Senator Heflin introduced a Soybean Research Institute in the 1981 Farm Bill. His research showed that soybean production had not had the significant increases which were typical of crops like corn and wheat. He wanted research on such things as stem canker, nematodes, and genetics. To Heflin's disappointment, the Institute was removed from the bill.

The Committee didn't want to have a lot of bills, so they put everything into one bill in agriculture rather than having it separate. They gave us some assurance they would increase the amount of money that went into soybean research, and it ended up in the farm bill as a part of overall research program.

THE FIGHT FOR RURAL DEVELOPMENT AND SMALL FARMS. In addition to farm commodity programs, the Agriculture Committee has jurisdiction over a large number of rural development programs which are extremely important to the millions of people who live in rural areas of the nation.

Senator Heflin strongly supported rural development, and he served a time as chairman of the Agriculture Subcommittee on Rural Development and Rural Electrification. He fought to preserve the Cooperative Extension Service and the Rural Electrification Administration; he was chief author of the Rural Partnership Act; and he sought help for poultry, cattle, catfish, and livestock producers, among others.

Throughout his Senate career, Heflin talked about and fought for the family farm. He recognized early in the Reagan administration that a large number of Republicans were for farm policies that would favor large farmers and the growing conglomerates at the expense of small farmers and the family farm. While he liked Reagan personally and supported many of Reagan's programs, he vigorously opposed the administration's farm policy.

FARM CREDIT SYSTEM. Credit is essential to farmers just as it is to other types of business, but as Senator Heflin pointed out many times, the conditions of agriculture are unique. Farm credit requires special treatment. Heflin was active in continuing the development of a workable and effective farm credit system.

In November 1979, he, Donald Stewart, and Alabama Representatives Tom Bevill and William Nichols, proposed amendments to the Farm Credit Act of 1971. These amendments allowed Federal Land

Banks to make loans in excess of 85 percent of the appraised value of real estate used as security, where guarantees were provided by other governmental units such as the Farmers Home Administration, the Small Business Administration, or state governments.[11]

Later, Heflin pointed out it was essential that the country have a reliable crop insurance plan to provide a safety net for producers, and he worked to increase the amount of the premium the government would pay. "Crop insurance really comes in handy the years you need it," he says. "The years you make a crop, you've got enough money to pay the premium and go on with your business. Crop insurance is very important in keeping farmers afloat, credit-wise."[12]

In 1982, Senator Heflin cosponsored a bill to combat high interest rates on farm loans. The bill extended the Economic Emergency Loan program for a year and created an individual evaluation program to reschedule existing Farm and Home Administration loans at their original interest rates rather than the high rates of 1982.

He cosponsored legislation in 1984 calling on the President to establish a fifteen-member special task force on agricultural credit. The task force was to develop policy recommendations aimed at ensuring the availability of credit to farmers at reasonable interest rates.[13]

EXTENSION SERVICE. The Reagan administration was ready to do away with the Agricultural Extension Service.

> This program has Home Demonstration Agents and Farm Agents in every county. They educate farmers on the latest thing, particularly the research that goes on in universities. At one time, Reagan wanted a sixty percent cut, and it was quite a fight to prevent that. They were saying that in England the Extension Service is operated as proprietary businesses, called agricultural advisory companies. They wanted something like that to be adopted.
>
> Well, the university people and a lot of others were concerned about it and didn't want the Extension Service to be weakened. We ended up keeping it just like it is. Some Republicans from farm states stomached

their free enterprise philosophy and voted with the farmers on this and some other programs.

ELECTRIFICATION. Heflin was especially interested in rural electrification. Electric cooperatives exist in sixty of Alabama's sixty-seven counties and serve one-quarter of the state's population.[14] He was instrumental in protecting programs which provided capital for rural cooperatives. Otherwise, the cooperatives would not have had the borrowing power to operate effectively, and this would directly impact the rates rural users paid. Electric cooperatives serving the most sparsely populated areas of Alabama didn't have access to capital.[15]

Heflin was instrumental in preventing the sale of the Power Marketing Administrations which provide hydroelectric power to public power entities. This would have been another federal assets sale which would have been a onetime benefit to the federal government, but which would have had a long-term impact in increased electric rates for rural electric consumers.[16]

POULTRY. A big battle developed over the poultry industry. Heflin explains that Alabama had developed to the point that it was the number two poultry state.

> I believe Arkansas is number one, and Georgia also had a large industry. Our chickens were being shipped to and sold in California. Generally, they were shipped on trucks. They would freeze or chill them to a certain level and sell then as fresh chickens. A hassle developed as to how low the temperature had to be to label them as "frozen" instead of "fresh." California was developing a poultry industry which was competing with ours, and we were trying to protect the industry in Alabama and the South. The Agriculture Department put in a regulation that, if it had been frozen below 26 degrees Fahrenheit, it had to be sold as frozen instead of fresh. We debated this on the floor. Our folks didn't like it, and we opposed. We felt that the chicken didn't get really hard at 26 degrees, and we wanted it around 20 degrees.

I was talking on the floor about how the temperature varied and how you can't control it exactly. I said, "Just take a human being. The temperature varies according to where you put the thermometer. If you put it in the mouth, you'll get one reading. If you put it in the ear, it will come out with another reading. If you put it in another part of the anatomy, it'll come out with still another reading." Everybody got to laughing. The Department of Agriculture finally prevailed, and we had to concede to their regulation.

Another issue determined whether the Department of Agriculture was going to put in some requirements related to salmonella. It is a serious disease, but if the chicken is cooked to the proper temperature, the salmonella disappears. The farm people didn't want the government telling them what to do, though food safety is of course always the major concern.

DISEASE AND INSECT CONTROL. Disease control programs were very important to farmers, especially in the South.

Cattle farmers had the brucellosis program which was working to eradicate Banges disease. Most cattle farmers were in favor of it, but some were opposed. One of George Wallace's supporters, a big cattle farmer named Red Bamburg, was against it. He tried every way to get me to vote against the brucellosis programs, and I never understood why. Being a Wallace man, he just may have been opposed to the federal government. Over the years, the brucellosis program eradicated that disease among cattle.

Another important program along this line dealt with boll weevil eradication. Farmers tell me it has cut their cost of production down about $100.00 an acre. It had a lot of opposition at first, but the use of chemicals employed in the program has been carried out in an environmentally safe manner. There's been very little opposition to the boll weevil eradication program by environmental groups.

HELP IN A HARD YEAR. Nineteen eighty-two was called potentially the worst for Alabama farmers since the Great Depression of the thirties. Goodwin Myrick, president of the Alabama Farm Bureau Federation, said the state's farm problems had reached "epidemic proportions" and that farmers faced acute financial difficulties. This happened at the same time that the state suffered fifteen percent unemployment, highest in the nation.[17] To try to ease the situation, Heflin successfully prodded the Department of Agriculture into allotting an additional two million pounds of cheese and a half million pounds of butter to distribute to Alabama's unemployed and needy.[18]

Heflin was among a group of senators who defeated Reagan's plan in 1983 to freeze farm target prices at their present level,[19] and in March 1984, he blocked Senate consideration of legislation pushed by the administration which froze cotton target prices. He said he would go along with the freeze if the administration would lower the surplus estimate that triggered the government's acreage-reduction program for the crop. A few days later, after much back-room bargaining, a bill containing many of the concessions sought by Heflin passed the Senate. "I didn't get the whole loaf," he said, "but I got a good chunk of it."[20]

IMPORT/EXPORT CONCERNS. Senator Heflin was interested in doing whatever would help American farmers export more and be more competitive in international trade. He was against both the GATT and NAFTA treaties because he felt they subjected some American industries, including farming and textiles, to unfair competition.

Foreign countries subsidize agriculture commodities, often using loans from the International Monetary Fund or monies otherwise obtained from the U.S. Thus, as Heflin saw it, our government was helping to subsidize agriculture in countries that were in direct competition with our own farmers. Some ninety-five percent of cotton entering world trade does so with the benefit of a subsidy. The net effect is a world price which is often below the actual cost of production. Heflin wanted to help craft a foreign policy which would provide market stability and allow U.S. farmers to aggressively pursue international markets.

> There is always the issue of the meat companies wanting to bring in imports. They can get products so much cheaper than we can get them in this country. Over the years it had been determined that meats coming in would be stamped, "imported meats." I stirred them all up one time. I said, "Hell, all that does is cause the American public to buy more. If they see something marked 'imported' they think it's sophisticated. What you ought to do is change the name. Put on it 'foreign substance.'" And they said, "Oh, noooo, noooo." Then I said, "Well, why don't you put 'un-American substance' or something else like that." But they said, "Oh, noooo, noooo, nooo." But we got one thing through. We prohibited horse meat and kangaroo meat coming in this country being sold as beef.

Heflin relates an incident in which he was instrumental in attacking Japanese restrictions on American agricultural imports.

> I was chairman of the Courts Committee of the Judiciary Committee when the Japanese sent over their Minister of Justice and various court officials. They wanted a bill passed so that Japanese witnesses in the federal courts could have a translator. I took the lead, and we passed the legislation that they wanted. Afterwards, they came to me and were bowing as they usually do and being very thankful. They asked, "Is there anything we can do for you?" I said, "Yes, there is. I'd like to meet with your Minister of Agriculture and your Ambassador and all of the officials dealing with agriculture and trade." At that time, the Japanese had quotas on American beef coming into their country, and they had restrictions on citrus fruit. We had been attempting to negotiate, and just about that time, the negotiations broke down. Then I got some of the American Cattlemen Association's leaders, and we met with them and spent a day talking about these problems. In a fairly short time, the Japanese renewed the negotiations, and they lifted the ban to some degree. The American Cattlemen's Association thought it was the greatest victory they'd had in trade in many a year. I had a little part to play in it.

MORE DIFFICULT DAYS. Alabama farmers continued to have trouble as the 1980s progressed. Weather continued to be unfavorable, and farm prices remained low. A drought in 1986 was called the worst in 115 years in Alabama, and matters reached a crisis stage. Farmers from Colorado, Louisiana, the Midwest and Northeast donated thousands of tons of hay to help their compatriots survive.

Examination of tree rings suggests that droughts occurred in twenty-two year cycles. Heflin asked for this to be investigated more thoroughly and if it proved to be true, to make appropriate changes in policy. He also said that the National Fertilizer Development Center in Muscle Shoals was capable of developing fertilizers for use with less moisture and that Auburn University and the Alabama Cooperative Extension Service could develop better moisture preserving techniques, drought resistant plant varieties, and better livestock handling practices.[21]

In September 1986, as the farm debt crisis grew, the FHA planned to collect on delinquent federal loans, and it hired a New Jersey firm to collect outstanding balances owed after farm liquidations. Some 300 Alabama farmers had declared bankruptcy but still owed a total of $37 million. Another 1,139 Alabama farmers were delinquent in repayment of their loans.[22] The state director of FHA said farmers in Alabama wouldn't be pushed, and the national FHA backed off. Heflin kept track of the situation and was prepared to become involved if necessary.

THE 1985 FARM BILL. A new farm bill was coming up in 1985, and the Reagan Administration was still attempting to make farmers rely more on the market and less on government for their income.[23] In a preemptive move, the Southern Agriculture Act of 1985 was introduced to save the peanut and cotton programs. It also created a Southern Institute for Agriculture Resource Policy to conduct research on improved farming techniques.

Senator Heflin was ready for the battle when the farm bill itself came up, and partly through his efforts, the atmosphere was more friendly than in previous years. As usual, there was extended debate over the peanut program. In the bill, Heflin engineered adjustments in the cost of production formula which allowed the quota support price to reflect more closely the cost of production.

Heflin worked to change the way that premiums and discounts were determined in the Cotton Loan Program. The old system allowed manipulation of quotas so that some grades of cotton could be given arbitrary increases in loan prices by USDA. Heflin offered an amendment which would establish a one-to-one ratio between premiums and discounts in the loan. As the committee was preparing to vote on the amendment, Senator Roger Jepsen of Iowa, in an obvious effort to embarrass, asked Heflin to define micronair (measure of cotton fiber fineness). To Jepsen's surprise, Heflin gave a definition that was textbook perfect. Jepsen then said that the Heflin amendment was the most market-oriented idea offered in the entire bill, and he called for a vote. The amendment passed.[24]

After the vote, a woman from the Caprock area of Texas, which had benefitted from premiums over the loan, came up behind Heflin and said, "Senator, the people of Texas are not going to like you for this." Heflin barely looked back and said, "Ma'am, nobody in Texas votes for me."[25]

Congress passed the new farm bill on December 18, 1985. Heflin said there were a few improvements in the bill but not nearly enough so he voted against it. Rice supports and target prices for soybean farmers had been severely curbed when the Agriculture Committee dropped a provision Heflin had added.[26]

Heflin attached a marketing loan program for soybeans to the Budget Reconciliation Bill in December 1987. He said the program would not cost the federal government any additional budget outlays and would help make the U.S. more competitive in selling soybeans overseas.[27]

THE RURAL PARTNERSHIP ACT. In May 1989, Heflin, Democrat Kent Conrad of North Dakota, and Senate Agriculture Committee chairman Patrick Leahy, Democrat of Vermont, introduced the Rural Partnerships Act. Heflin said, "The Rural Partnerships Act recognizes that rural economic development efforts must begin with local initiative and that it is essential for the federal government to be an active partner in these efforts." He noted that through the bill, rural electric cooperatives, regional economic development groups, and the Cooperative Extension Service would contribute to the revitalization of rural areas.[28]

The main part of the initiative was a $300 million investment fund that would provide $100 million a year for three years to create local, regional, or state revolving loan funds to spur small business development in rural areas.[29] The Senate passed the bill in August.

THE 1990 FARM BILL. A new farm bill would be needed in 1990, and efforts to begin writing it and determining its provisions began in 1989. Congress had been late getting out the 1985 Farm Bill, and members decided to get a head start on the 1990 bill. Heflin promised to be closely involved in writing the new bill and said he would reintroduce his "Southern Agriculture Bill," as he did in 1985, to address specific needs of Southern farmers.[30]

Heflin didn't expect any major changes, though he predicted the usual fight over the peanut support program.[31] Sure enough, in February 1990, the Bush Administration proposed to slash government price supports for peanuts grown for domestic use by twenty percent, beginning in 1991. Heflin said the cut could prove disastrous for Alabama farmers.[32]

The Senate approved the 1990 Farm Bill in July, and it included peanut and cotton programs of which Heflin was the primary author. Heflin voted against final passage in the Senate. In his weekly newspaper column he said the bill represented a good start for Alabama farmers, but he didn't feel it provided enough protection for farmers against inflation.[33] He was left off of the House-Senate conference committee which wrote the final version of the bill. This was surprising and may have been because Heflin voted against the bill. The bill passed in October.

THE SOUTHERN AGRICULTURAL ACT OF 1990. As he promised, Heflin cosponsored the Southern Agricultural Act of 1990 with Democratic Senator Wyche Fowler of Georgia. The Act extended the cotton and peanut titles of the 1985 farm bill. It was a counter to the Bush administration's attempt to reduce peanut price supports to 90 percent of the 1985 level. "What can you buy today that costs 90 percent of what it did in 1985?" Heflin asked. The bill also called for the establishment of a Southern Institute for Agricultural Resources Policy to be located at a land-grant institution, and it provided for the expansion of plant science research.[34]

The Senate Agriculture Committee approved a five-year extension of the government's peanut program after rejecting Bush's plan. Heflin's bill was instrumental in the adopted program. "It gave a yearly increase to the peanut program," he points out. "It was the only farm program in 1990 that got an accelerating clause in it."

Heflin blasted critics of the peanut program, calling them a group of urban and suburban lawmakers who were out to get rural America. He singled out Representative Dick Armey, Texas Republican, who was working to do away with the program. "Mr. Armey regularly fights all farm programs, which, of course, is easier to do when the only green spot in your congressional district is a city park." He added that Armey's suburban Dallas district "couldn't afford to be full of shopping malls and parking lots" if it was not for inexpensive U.S. farm products.[35]

CROP INSURANCE. In 1994, Heflin proposed a crop insurance reform plan that would replace both the existing federal crop insurance program and the annual farm disaster bailouts. The Clinton administration earlier in the year had proposed a comprehensive overhaul of the crop insurance program, and a House-Senate conference committee set aside $1 billion in fiscal 1995 to pay for it. Heflin said his proposal, tailored to meet the needs of Southern farmers and differed somewhat from the administration's, would save taxpayers $750 million over the next five years while lowering crop insurance premiums. The Senate Agriculture Committee approved the bill with Heflin's proposed change in June, and Congress passed it in October.

In another move to help ease the financial burden on farmers, Heflin authored the Rural Electrification Loan Restructuring of 1993.

THE ATTACK ON FARM SUBSIDIES. The attack on farm subsidies picked up steam after the 1994 elections when Republicans gained control of Congress. The government had spent $23.7 billion on farm programs in 1993, with $263 million going to Alabama.[36] Republican Representative Dick Zimmer of New Jersey, who represented an urban district, said, "Farm subsidy programs have been a burden to taxpayers and consumers since they began. We cannot afford them any longer." He used the old argument that farmers should live by the market.

Marion Berry, President Clinton's Department of Agriculture liaison, told a group of Alabama farmers visiting Washington in 1995 that their programs would suffer budget cuts, just like other federal agencies. The only question was how severe.[37] Trying to head off drastic action, Heflin introduced legislation which he said would fine-tune subsidy programs for cotton, peanuts, and soybeans rather than radically restructure them.[38]

The Senate Agricultural Committee, in 1995, agreed to a five-year extension of the peanut program but cut the price support by $50 a ton. Included in legislation was agreement to cut $13.4 billion in farm spending over the next seven years, after which Congress would decide on the future of farm programs. Before the vote, Heflin, who was then known to be a lame duck, delivered a blistering indictment of the agreement. He said, "I was never consulted about the compromise that emerged in the farm bill. I was shut out of all discussions about it and was told it was going to be a Republican bill. Obviously what they told me came true."[39]

In February 1996, the Senate was ready to vote on the bill. Democrats started a filibuster, but it became clear that the Republicans, with some Democratic support, could end it. The Senate passed the Agricultural Transition Act of 1996 the third week in February. Heflin voted for the bill because, he said, the good outweighed the bad. He said he still had reservations, specifically in regard to cotton and peanuts, and he intended to try to remedy some of the worst parts in the conference.[40]

Dick Fifield, director of national affairs for the Alabama Farmers Federation, said the bill had the possibility of throwing American and

Southern and Alabama farmers into a kind of boom-and-bust cycle. He added, "It will be very difficult to take an unsubsidized American farmer and confront him with a totally subsidized world, in which the European Union and other nations protect their agriculture through barriers and internal subsidies."[41]

AGRICULTURAL RESEARCH. Senator Heflin was interested in and supportive of scientific research in general. More than most, he understood its current value to society and its contribution to the future of the country. He supported agricultural research from the beginning and did what he could to get research dollars to Alabama institutions.

He authored the Animal Research Facilities Protection Act, which imposes severe penalties on individuals or groups who interfere with medical and other research facilities where animals are in use. "In a few hours, one or more people can destroy almost a lifetime of research work if they can get into an animal colony," he notes.[42] "The real price of these types of crimes is paid by those waiting for cures and treatments for their afflictions."

With Heflin's help, Auburn University has been especially successful in securing funding for several very important research initiatives for the College of Agriculture and the Alabama Agricultural Experiment Station.

> When I went to Washington, Carter was President, and one of his main initiatives came about as a result of the gas shortage. The various things OPEC did caused shortages, and then the price of oil shot up. Then Iran and a lot of other matters contributed to the situation. Carter started the research initiative on alternative energy sources. He had a background of nuclear energy from being on submarines. Nuclear was not popular, and he didn't really push that, but he pushed research on other alternates including renewable sources like crops.
>
> Carter got things going pretty good. Then Reagan came in and killed it immediately because it was a Carter initiative. I have always been very curious what would have happened if we had gone ahead and

had twenty years of research in finding alternative sources, particularly in regard to renewable sources.

At Auburn University, the dean of the School of Agriculture, R. Dennis Rouse, was a great believer that the future of Alabama agriculture lay in renewable energy crops. Auburn has a lot of research that indicates it can be done, and they developed a plant they call "switch grass." The dean of the agriculture also promoted research in corn, cane, and sugar beets. The use of alcohol in cars had developed in certain countries in South America. In some places, they are running their automobiles entirely on alcohol that is produced from renewable sources.

I always thought that if Carter's research had been allowed to go ahead, we might be well advanced in alternative sources of energy today. You know, there is some talk of returning to nuclear power. It got so expensive because, after Three Mile Island and Chenobyl, they rightly added so many safety devices to protect people.

One issue of particular concern was the management of waste from poultry farms. In cooperation with Alabama's poultry industry, research was conducted and the results used to develop land application guidelines for the disposal of broiler litter and to develop safe procedures for the disposal of dead animal carcasses.[43]

Heflin introduced a bill to transfer aquaculture from the Interior Department to the Department of Agriculture. Auburn University had done outstanding work for some time in this area and was involved with some 100 countries around the world. The long-term work was supported by the Agency for International Development, an agency that Senator Heflin supported. With Heflin's help in securing funding, Auburn developed a fish disease lab. Scientists in the lab discovered technology which allowed the transfer of genes into catfish, and that in turn resulted in much improved growth and feed conversion rates. While aquaculture and commercial fish productions are in their infancy in Alabama, Heflin saw their potential and helped to enhance commercial catfish production. He also assisted in securing funds for other areas such as commercial oyster, shellfish, and shrimp production.[44]

One type of research which was needed and just beginning when Heflin came on the Agriculture Committee was double cropping in the production of soybeans. "You'd plant winter wheat and harvest it," he explains, "and then plant soybeans. No-till farming was involved. You wouldn't plow up after the winter wheat but would plant on top of it. The theory was that the wheat stub and the residue left from it would act like mulch. The chemical companies still haven't developed the necessary chemicals to fight insects in double cropping, and there are environmental issues in the use of chemicals. You have to protect the community instead of just doing something for the benefit of the farmer. Hopefully, there is a middle ground."

Heflin was also interested in water quality research. Alabama is unique in that it has about ten percent of the fresh water supply of the 48 contiguous states.[45] Yet it periodically suffers from droughts. Heflin said there has to be a way to spread the water supply across the year for agriculture. He secured funds for continued water quality research at the Alabama Agriculture Experiment Station. The research involves a team effort by scientists at Auburn and other land-grant universities, the TVA, state and private agencies, and producers. The object is to develop water and crop management practices that both enhance agriculture production and protect and preserve water as an important natural resource.

SUMMARY OF HEFLIN'S WORK IN AGRICULTURE. Senator Heflin remained on the Agriculture Committee until the end of his last term, and he continued to fight hard to protect small farmers and family farms. He was chairman of the Rural Electrification and Rural Development Subcommittee for eight years and was ranking member during the last Congress.

As he prepared to leave the Senate, he summarized his work:

> Over the last eighteen years I am proud to say that I have worked to ensure that electricity and water and sewer systems were extended to areas where they once were not. We have strengthened the family farm

by providing adequate capital to farms and agribusiness. We have passed farm bills that stabilized the family farm, made the American farmer the envy of the world and at the same time, protected the environment and reduced the deficit. We have extended technological advancements into rural America through telemedicine and distance learning initiatives. Foreign markets for U.S. agricultural products have been opened wide, and agricultural research has led to more efficient farming with breakthroughs such as no-till agriculture and precision farming employing satellite imagery.

Heflin was given a range of awards from agricultural organizations. Included are the Eminent Service Award of the Alabama Farm Federation, the Distinguished Service Award of the Alabama Poultry and Egg Association, the Golden Plow Award of the American Farm Bureau, and the National Eminent Service Award of the National Association of Rural Electric Cooperatives.

17

Champion of Equal Rights

P ERHAPS THE MOST surprising aspect of Howell Heflin's Senate career was his consistent and strong support for civil rights causes. His family had been involved in the old Confederacy — in setting it up, serving in and supporting its army, and later working to preserve the values of the great "Lost Cause." Not only this, but he represented a state which had been among the most defiant toward granting equal rights to black citizens.

Lister Hill commented a number of times during his thirty-year Senate career that the two major factors in Alabama elections were race and religion. Hill, a staunch New Dealer and liberal, waffled on race as the Civil Rights Movement gained strength, and he did not dare challenge what he thought was a strong anti-black bias among voters in his state. Heflin did not follow this course. While Heflin took a low profile with the media on these issues, he worked as a strong advocate behind the scenes. When votes were taken, he was always progressive-minded.

"My own personal perspective and conscience compelled me to vote differently than some of my constituents might have liked," he says. The Alabama electorate began to learn of Heflin's civil rights record, and in spite of opponents consistently attempting to use it for political purposes, his fellow citizens elected him to the Senate three times, proving the high value placed on honesty, integrity, and attention to the needs of his people.

Joe Reed, chairman of the Alabama Democratic Conference, a black political group, commented, "Alabama had senators since 1819 when it became a state, but they didn't represent black folks. Senator Heflin was the first to do that. We could go to any meeting and say, 'Senator Heflin's our Senator,' or 'Senator Heflin represents all of Alabama.'"[1]

When Heflin went to the Senate, there were many Southerners of the segregation school there. "But the atmosphere was changing," he says, "and we started working on some of them, like Stennis, Talmadge, Long, and Thurmond. Thurmond changed a great deal as the years moved on. Some of it was a matter of quietly pointing out that it wasn't in the best interest of the South to continue all of the resistance and negative mood. I felt I had a lot to do with this change in attitudes because of my personal talks with each."

The Reagan Administration continued the attacks on civil rights gains of the 1960s that had begun under Nixon. Observers today credit George Wallace with developing and demonstrating the power of many of the positions followed on these matters. Wallace was abrasive and pugnacious and could never have represented the great middle of the political spectrum. Reagan clothed many of the same ideas in soft talk and good humor. "They didn't use the word 'race,'" Heflin notes, "but there were a lot of code expressions."

Senator Heflin had an unique role in civil rights during the Reagan Administration. He was the only Southern Democratic moderate on the Judiciary Committee, and, because of his background and reputation, a lot of other senators deferred to him. During one of the key civil rights battles during the Reagan era, Senator Exon, a moderate conservative from Nebraska, said, "I'm not going to say anything until I talk with my mentor, Judge Heflin. Whatever Judge Heflin tells me to do, that's the way I'm going to go."[2]

Heflin says that in spite of attacks on civil rights during the Reagan administration, congressional action in the civil rights field has been enormously significant since 1979. "During my time there," he says, "the

Senate ensured the continued transition of the South from the 1950s into the next century."

HEFLIN AND REAGAN. The Reagan Administration led the country away from the discord and bitterness of the past two decades. A new sense of well-being developed, and people threw caution aside and indulged themselves, using credit as they never had before. Two years into Reagan's presidency, inflation and interest rates remained high, and the federal deficit was ballooning. The economy began showing signs of improvement in Alabama, but the jobless rate was still 10.9 percent, third highest in the nation, in October 1984.[3]

On March 31, 1981, an attempt was made to assassinate President Reagan by John Hinckley. At the end of Hinckley's trial, the jury voted that he was legally insane, provoking an attack on the insanity defense.[4] Heflin called the verdict "one of the greatest miscarriages of justice in our nation's history."[5] At the time, Heflin was taking the conservative stand, but in retrospect, he thinks that Hinckley probably was insane.

Heflin had hit it off right away with Reagan at a personal level. "Reagan and I got along fine," Heflin says. "He was a great storyteller. Several times when Nancy was out of town he got some of the fellows who were story tellers to come to the White House, have dinner, and spend the evening talking. He was something. He could tell some pretty good stories."

Congressional Quarterly reported that Heflin supported Reagan 67 percent of the time in 1981, placing him among the top ten Democratic supporters. Senate Democrats averaged 49 percent.[6] In 1982, *CQ* reported that Heflin voted with the Democrats 57 percent of the time, while he voted Reagan's way 61 percent.[7]

Reagan often gave the appearance of not quite being sure what was going on, leading to questions about his mental acuity and his ability to concentrate. A writer commented that, though Reagan didn't have the best brain in town, he managed to make the best of the abilities he had — friendliness, likableness, ability to communicate, and trust by the people. Heflin believes this characterization is inaccurate.

I think Reagan was smarter than many people have given him credit for. I think he knew a great deal about overall policy, but he was primarily a delegator. He believed in running things that way, whereas Carter and Clinton were very much engrossed in the details of everything. I don't think there was much question that, from the days when he was a union boss in the actor's guild, he changed in his philosophy on government.

There is no question that the one thing paramount in his mind was opposition to high taxes. Every time we had these Saturday night sessions, we'd get off on taxes. He told me that he had a big income relative to other people after he made it as a movie star. At one time he paid in excess of 95 percent of his income in California taxes and federal taxes. Back in those days, you hit the level of about 90 percent in federal taxes when you were in the neighborhood of $250,000. That was on his mind. His theory was that if you didn't have high taxes, you could put more money into people's pockets, they would invest it, and the average individual, regardless of financial status, would benefit. He really believed that.

His first tax bill in 1982 was basically a modification of the Kemp-Roth bill, and it cut taxes thirty percent over about three years. The 1986 tax bill cut the maximum percent for the rich people, those having net incomes over $250,000 per year, to twenty-eight percent. The bill did away with a lot of sheltering and a lot of deductions and credits, but there is no question that, for a rich man, it contained a big reduction. I went along with the 1982 bill, but I voted against the '86 tax bill.

Generally Reagan cut non-defense programs and increased defense programs substantially, and this was very helpful in breaking down the Soviet Union. But at the same time, he lowered taxes, and the deficit went sky-rocketing. The 1986 tax cut was portrayed as being revenue neutral, but it didn't turn out that way. We lost a lot of money, and military spending was substantially more than he had cut in non-defense spending.

> I was asked by a journalist the three things that Reagan will be remembered for. I think he will be remembered for laying the groundwork for the decline of the Soviet bloc. He'll be known for the biggest tax cut in history, and he'll be known for the greatest deficit in history.

Heflin supported Reagan more than half of the time, as the voting records show, but Heflin was a supporter of civil rights and of some social programs, and he joined the fight against Reagan on farm policies, labor issues, attempts to weaken civil rights laws, and some other issues. One might conclude from the record that Reagan was a far-right ideologue, while Heflin was more of a pragmatic conservative who favored civil rights, Social Security, and Medicare.

EQUAL OPPORTUNITY STAFFING. Mike House says that Heflin's goal always was to have about twenty to twenty-five percent of his staff black. "No other Senator did that," House notes, "not even the Kennedys and other liberals who talked a great game. You can find qualified people. You just have to make an effort to do it. Heflin did that more than anybody else in the Senate."[8]

"Over the years, I have had many black staff members," Heflin notes. "I believe that inclusion of blacks in government helps overcome symbolic and substantive obstacles to equality. However, it just happened that when these staffers applied, they were best qualified to do the job. This is the way is should be in all cases."

BLACK FEDERAL JUDGES. Almost immediately after taking office, Heflin began working with Senator Donald Stewart to find qualified African-Americans to fill vacancies for federal judgeships in Alabama. With the appointment of Frank Johnson to the Fifth Circuit Court of Appeals, Alabama had five federal judgeships to fill, two in the middle district and three in the northern district.

> Carter and Attorney General Griffin Bell were pushing for some black judges, and we came up with U. W. Clemon in Birmingham for

the northern district and Fred Gray from Tuskegee for the middle district. Both of them had been active in the civil rights movement and were highly successful in civil rights litigation. We submitted those two names.

A lot of influential Alabamians resented the thought of black judges, particularly those who had been civil rights activists, and they began to try to dig up dirt on them. They convinced the American Bar Association to rate both of them as unqualified, and this was something we had to overcome. Critics had an income tax matter on Clemon and claimed he hadn't paid a lien. We got a handwriting expert who showed that a federal collection agent had erased some parts of his original report and changed it unfairly. Clemon was a graduate of Columbia University Law School and had a distinguished career as a civil rights lawyer, as did Fred Gray.

>As investigation of Fred Gray proceeded, ethics charges surfaced, and by July, it was evident that Gray would have a difficult time. He denied all these charges and had evidence which supported him. Several hearings here held, hoping that he could overcome these charges.[9]

Heflin took a sounding in the committee and realized that Fred Gray would never survive the hearings. So it was necessary to withdraw support for him if Alabama was to get a black judge for the middle district and to proceed as quickly as possible with a new nominee.

>We had to go with another black nominee, and the black leadership in Montgomery wanted young Myron Thompson, who had been in the state attorney general's office with Bill Baxley. His mother had been the registrar at Tuskegee University, and he graduated from Yale Law School. The American Bar approved Thompson. I submitted his name. He was just thirty-three, and there was a little fight because of his age. He was a good choice and has been a good judge.[10]

I always felt bad about Fred Gray, but you know, you had to do what was possible. By that time the election between Carter and Reagan was in full swing, and chances for confirmation of a Democrat seemed slim. Gray has become one of the truly great lawyers of Alabama and is known for his superbly ethical standards. His son later interned in our office. It was just one of those things I deeply regret.

During the hearings, Heflin stated on the Senate floor his belief that we must make up for years of injustice in this country.

> For many long years, blacks were excluded from the federal judicial nominating process. True equality under the law cannot be achieved under such a system. All Americans must feel they will be treated fairly by the federal courts, but if certain citizens are precluded from serving on the bench, the courts cannot give the perception of fairness.
>
> We got those judges through, and I think they were the last to be confirmed by the Carter administration. It was a tough fight, and we were running against the clock. The Republicans controlled the Senate, and we knew Strom Thurmond was going to become chairman of the Judiciary Committee if the Republicans won in 1980. Strom made a speech at the Republican National Convention in August and said, "We're not going to confirm any more Democratic judges," but we did.
>
> Carter pressed for black judges, but Alabama was the only state that had two black judges appointed to the federal bench. Some states had one. I think there was one in Georgia, one in Arkansas, and one in Louisiana. I don't think they had even one in Mississippi.

There were three other federal district court vacancies to be filled. After some tough negotiation, Heflin submitted his friend Bert Haltom for a vacancy in the northern district. Judge Robert Propst, who was formerly associated with Senator Donald Stewart, was also submitted for the northern district. A middle district nominee was Truman Hobbs, who had been a clerk for Hugo Black. Haltom, Hobbs, and Propst had no trouble going through the confirmation process. They were confirmed before the black judges' fight.

Heflin says that recommending judges can be extremely unpleasant, and you can make enemies. "You have a lot of friends you are close to who want to be federal judges, and you have to make a choice between them."

He received an incredible amount of criticism for both of the black nominations. Peter Cobun, Washington Correspondent for the *Mobile Press*, wrote, "Sen. Howell Heflin has suffered what is thought to be a serious erosion of popular support in this state because of his pivotal role in pushing through the nominations of two Alabama blacks to the federal bench.[11]

SUPPORT OF HISTORICALLY BLACK COLLEGES. In 1862, Congress passed the first Morrill Act, which provided for the establishment of Land-Grant Institutions in the Southern and border states. These institutions were designed to educate citizens in agriculture, home economics, the mechanical arts, and other practical skills. Since the Southern states were uncooperative in funding historically African-American institutions under the original law, Congress passed a second Morrill Act in 1890 which was aimed toward black institutions.

Auburn University is an 1862 land-grant institution, and Tuskegee University and Alabama A&M are 1890 institutions. A stream of "hard" money for research in the 1890 institutions was not created until 1967. Tuskegee was not originally a land-grant college, but Heflin had it added to the permanent list in 1980 to ensure it would receive research funds. Congress created the Chappie James Preventive Health Center at Tuskegee in 1980 and ensured funding in the 1981 farm bill.

The Center was named after General James, the first African-American to achieve four-star rank in the U.S. Air Force. He learned his flying skills as one of the Tuskegee Airmen in the first training program for black pilots during World War II.

> When Dr. Luther Foster was president of Tuskegee, he wanted to build a building in honor of General Chappie James. We got money appropriated during the Carter administration, but by the time it was built, Reagan was President. Dr. Foster had retired from Tuskegee, and the new president was Dr. Benjamin Peyton, who got to be good

friends with Reagan. Dr. Peyton got President Reagan to come down to the dedication.

They called on me to make a speech at the dedication. I gave the history of General Chappie James and the building. I believe that was the first time I flew on Air Force One with Ronald Reagan. He was very pleasant, and my personal friendship with him continued to grow.

In 1981, Heflin introduced a bill which specified that the 1890 land-grant colleges receive money for the purchase of land and equipment and for planning, construction, or renovation of buildings to strengthen the capacity for research in food and agriculture. The bill was folded into the next farm bill and became law.

Heflin served as honorary chairman of the United Negro College Fund for several years and helped assure that black private schools had scholarship money and other funds. He was given the Fund's Notable Service Award.[12] He also received the Alabama NAACP's Appreciation Award. After Senator Heflin retired, he and Elizabeth Ann give the United Negro College Fund monies each year from the scholarship foundation they set up with excess campaign funds.

FAIR HOUSING BILL. In 1979, a Fair Housing Bill which would strengthen and enforce the provisions of the Fair Housing Act of 1968 was proposed. The 1968 Act defined and prohibited discriminatory housing practices, but it failed to include the enforcement tools necessary to prevent such practices and to provide relief to victims of discrimination.

Disagreement on the bill focused on two controversies, whether discrimination should be proven by "results" or "intent," and whether cases should be heard by administrative law judges or federal judges and juries. Civil rights groups supported the "results" standard of proof, while opponents wanted proof of "intent." Civil rights groups supported administrative law judges, and opponents wanted federal judges and a jury.

Senator Heflin proposed a scheme to settle one of the issues. His proposal provided that cases filed by HUD would be heard before administrative law judges if the parties involved chose to do so. If one of the parties did not agree, however, the case would be heard in a jury trial.

A bill which contained Heflin's compromise passed the House in 1980, but it failed in the Senate because of a filibuster. The matter continued to get attention, but legislation to enforce the provisions of the 1968 Act did not pass Congress until 1988.

The 1988 law authorized HUD to penalize those who discriminated in housing sales and rentals. It prohibited discrimination because of race, color, religion, sex, or national origin, and it protected the handicapped and families with young children. This was the first time Congress included the handicapped and families with young children among those to be protected.

BUSING. School busing as a way to achieve integration came under sharp attack in the Reagan Administration. Senator Heflin's voting record suggested that he was ambivalent on the issue. "I reckon I was all over the place on busing," he says. "I voted against a lot of the things on busing that Jesse Helms and Bennett Johnston of Louisiana proposed, and I voted for some of them. It depended on the language."

He wrote in his newspaper column, "In my opinion, court ordered busing has not worked in the vast majority of cases and should be reduced, eliminated, or modified whenever and wherever possible. Experiences with busing have caused broadly based opposition to it among both blacks and whites."[13] The Senate voted in November 1980 to ban the Justice Department from seeking busing as a remedy to end racial discrimination in schools, and Heflin voted against the bill, which failed.[14]

In January 1982, the Senate approved 58-38 the toughest anti-busing legislation passed by either house of Congress. It would prohibit federal judges who were handling desegregation cases from ordering busing for students who lived more than five miles or fifteen minutes from their schools. Heflin was the only Southern senator to vote against the measure.[15]

The following March, a bill which stripped courts of authority to order busing for desegregation was proposed. Heflin sponsored an amendment which allowed the Justice Department to seek the reduction or elimination of existing court-ordered busing on a system to system basis rather than a sweeping one-fits-all approach. He said his amendment made the bill fair to Alabama and the nation as a whole. The Senate voted for the amendment.[16] Heflin first voted against the bill, but after heavy criticism from conservatives in Alabama, he switched his vote in the final enactment.[17] He noted that the final bill had many changes which made it palatable. In explaining his positions, Heflin says,

> There were certain situations in Alabama where busing was achieving the stated purpose and was perceived in a good manner, and there were other situations where it wasn't working well and opposition was strong. The bills introduced in Congress applied to individual lawsuits in other states, but they were sweeping in Alabama. We had good, bad, indifferent all mixed in together. I tried to get an amendment on some of them. In voting, I did what I thought was best for the state and the nation.
>
> Every time I'd vote for busing, I'd catch hell from all the conservatives, and every time I'd vote against it, I'd catch hell from the liberals, though there weren't too many liberals in Alabama. It was one of those things. Unfortunately few people understand language differences.

He explains that Alabama was unique in that the Department of Justice put all of the school systems under one decree. This was a reaction to George Wallace's strategy of delay through multiple lawsuits, and it made it possible for the Justice Department to handle issues in one suit rather than having separate law suits against scores of school systems. Busing was one of the remedies to achieve integration under this scheme. Heflin notes that many of the busing proposals in 1982 would have disrupted the progress of integration that, he believed, were already functioning effectively. He said he felt that other bills and amendments would have burdened many school systems that were pleased with busing.

VOTING RIGHTS EXTENSION. The Voting Rights Act of 1965, the last and perhaps the most important legislation which ended legal discrimination against blacks, expired in August 1982 and needed to be extended. In the fall of 1981, the Reagan Administration vehemently opposed the extension of the Voting Rights Act. In early 1982, in a case involving Bob Jones University, it argued that the government should no longer deny tax exempt status to racist schools. This created a firestorm on Capitol Hill and around the country.[18]

After the 1980 election, Strom Thurmond became chair of the Senate Judiciary Committee and Orin Hatch headed the subcommittee on the Constitution. They took the place of former committee chair Edward Kennedy and subcommittee chair Birch Bayh. Many people thought that this change made it impossible to extend the Voting Rights Act. The House passed the extension on October 5, 1981, and further action was up to the Senate.

The debate in the Senate was very heated. *Congressional Quarterly* reported that Senators Dole and Heflin played the deciding roles on the Judiciary Committee, that divisions on the full committee left them holding the balance of power. Senator Thurmond described the votes of Heflin and Dole as key.[19]

Going into April and May 1982, nine senators on the committee were cosponsors of the extension, seven senators were opposed, and two, Dole and Heflin, were undecided. "Dole and I assumed the undecided position," Heflin explains, "so we could work out something that could get the bill out of committee and get it passed on the floor. We came up with some changes. One time Dole was giving me credit, and I said, 'Don't give me any credit. I don't want to be in the newspapers on this matter.' So, he kept quiet about me." The bill was unpopular with white voters in Alabama. The other Alabama senator, Jeremiah Denton, was on the Judiciary Committee. He opposed extension of the act, and this made it tough.[20]

The compromise which Heflin and Dole worked out contained four essential parts. First, it extended the major enforcement provision of the original act for twenty-five years. Second, it allowed states that could prove a good voting rights record for the previous ten years to "bail out" of the bill's pre-clearance provision after 1984. Third, it amended the permanent provisions of the 1965 act to make it easier to prove violations. Fourth, it extended bilingual requirements for ten years. Mary Frances Berry, chairperson of the U.S. Commission on Civil Rights, said, "The compromise saved the bill and is the basis on which the law has continued to be effective."[21]

The "pre-clearance" provision required nine states, including Alabama, and parts of thirteen others to receive approval from the Department of Justice before they could change their election laws.

On the matter of proving violations, it had previously been necessary to prove the intent to discriminate, but under the new law, it was only necessary to show that the laws had resulted in discrimination. This provision came from a voting case, *Bolden v. City of Mobile*, which was decided by the Supreme Court.

The measure passed the committee in early May by a 17 to 1 vote, and the full Senate was scheduled to vote the week of June 10. On June 15, the Senate voted to limit discussion, cutting off a threatened filibuster. Heflin voted to invoke cloture, and Denton voted against. The vote for cloture was 86-8.[22] Later the same week, the Senate voted 87-7 to extend the Voting Rights Bill for 25 years. Senator Denton first voted against the bill but later changed his vote.[23] The executive director of the Leadership Conference on Civil Rights, Ralph Neas, stated, "We wanted language Senator Howell Heflin would also find acceptable and thus ensure that we also got the moderate and conservative Southern Democrat.[24]

The *Mobile Register* condemned the compromise in an editorial, calling it "probably the most discriminatory legal garbage to ever hit Congress." It claimed the bill would allow any federal judge to change local government's election laws at a whim, and it called on Heflin to lead a filibuster.[25]

The *Talladega Daily Home* later declared that, "The next time he comes before Alabama voters to be reelected or retired, U.S. Senator Howell Heflin may have a problem explaining satisfactorily his vote to extend the so-called voting rights act for another 25 years."[26]

CIVIL RIGHTS COMMISSION. In 1983, authorization of the Civil Rights Commission expired, and Congress began working on a reauthorization measure. President Reagan intruded and tried to restructure the Commission for his own purposes. In late May, he announced he would replace three of the commissioners, Mary Frances Berry, Bladina Cardenas Ramirez, and Rabbi Murray Saltzman. According to *Congressional Quarterly*, Reagan sought to remove these commissioners because they had criticized his administration's policies.

The Senate Judiciary Committee responded by putting off votes on the new nominees. Reagan reacted by summarily firing the three commissioners he sought to replace. Both houses of Congress passed concurrent resolutions declaring their intent to create a new commission whose members would be appointed by the Senate as well as the President. Dr. Berry and Ms. Ramirez won an injunction against Reagan's firings in the D. C. District Court.

The Civil Rights Commission had been formed to serve as a watchdog over the federal government and to assure that progress in civil rights areas were preserved. Until President Reagan's action, the understanding had been that the commissioners were independent from the executive branch and made their own decisions. Otherwise, it would be difficult for them to serve as watchdogs. There was a long fight over this matter, and President Reagan tried to get a number of his choices, most of whom were against civil rights legislation, appointed to the Civil Rights Commission.

Mary Frances Berry, one of the commissioners that Reagan fired, said, "The President had told the press that he fired me because I was serving at his pleasure, and I wasn't giving him very much pleasure. Senator Heflin didn't think it was a very good reason. So he supported the idea that if you're a watchdog, you might bite, and then you shouldn't be kicked in the head for biting. He showed what a stand-up guy he was on this particular issue."[27]

Ultimately there was a compromise which gave the President four appointments and the Congress four, two for each house. The compromise established that the President had to show cause for firings, and it authorized funding for the Commission.

LEGAL SERVICES CORPORATION. The Reagan Administration tried each year to abolish the Legal Services Corporation, which provided legal assistance to the poor in civil litigation. The President also tried to restrict the corporation's activities and reconstitute its board.

Heflin says that the administration cut back on the appropriations and succeeded in forcing a compromise.

> Legal Services was restricted from bringing lawsuits for causes, but they could bring lawsuits for cases. In the past, someone would have a cause and develop it as a pilot case. Under the compromise, the corporation could only handle cases for individuals who had been discriminated against, and it could help with divorce and various other things. If you are going to argue that something is unconstitutional, that is a cause, and Legal Service was prevented from getting involved in it. They didn't get into criminal activities.
>
> I fought very hard to continue the Legal Services Corporation because I believe it is essential to true equality of justice. Given increasing fees and costs, the American system of justice continues to become more difficult for the poor to access, and this unfortunate reality has had a disproportionate impact on minorities. Continuation of the Legal Services Corporation represented a great victory for the Congress and the people.

MARTIN LUTHER KING, JR. FEDERAL HOLIDAY. The Senate voted 78-22 in October 1983 to establish a holiday to honor the birthday of Martin Luther King, Jr. As a federal holiday, it would be an off-day for federal workers. Heflin and Denton both voted in favor, though both voiced concern about the number of paid holidays for federal workers.[28]

When the bill came before the Senate, Senator Jesse Helms led a filibuster against it, saying he objected to King's "action-oriented Marxism" and alleging that King had connections to the communist party. Senator Heflin voted to end the filibuster.

In 1984, Congress passed a bill establishing a Martin Luther King Holiday Commission to encourage ceremonies for the first celebration of the holiday. Five years later, Senator Heflin cosponsored a bill to make the Martin Luther King Commission permanent. It extended the Commission's role to include the promotion of racial equality and nonviolent social change.

CONTROVERSY WITH WOMEN AND PRAYER. Senator Heflin became involved in a bit of controversy on two issues which touch on equal rights and civil liberties. The first concerned his penchant for making innocent remarks which some women considered insensitive, and the second was his stand in favor of prayer in schools.

POLITICAL CORRECTNESS ON WOMEN. "I had trouble getting politically correct on women," he acknowledges. "Elizabeth Ann didn't help, because she wasn't much of a women's libber."

Mike House comments that Heflin was a very strong believer in civil rights and a very strong believer in equal rights. "He believed in equal rights for women, but at the same time, he was from the older generation that didn't quite understand the feminist movement. He believed it and understood it on an intellectual basis. But you know, he was the guy who opened the door for everybody and felt that women should be in the home. That's how he was raised."[29]

In May 1983, the League of Women Voters gave Heflin a 50 percent mark on measures having to do with women's interests. This may seem low, but it was the highest mark received by any member of the Alabama Congressional delegation. Senator Denton received a nine.[30]

When Heflin was on the Commerce Committee, Sally Ride, a great national hero who had been the first woman in space, was testifying before the subcommittee on Space and Technology. "We were all bragging on her being the first woman in space," Heflin recalls. "I made some bright joking remark like, 'Well, were you a pretty good back seat driver?' Lo and behold, a bunch of the newspapers came out against me for making the remark, and I caught the devil. I even caught the devil on that from my wife."

Later in his Senate career, he was to get a great deal of negative publicity because of remarks he made about Fawn Hall, a figure in the Iran-Contra affair.

> There's been a progression on the women's issue, and a lot of things have changed. But back when the movement started, I felt that some of the laws probably were not needed because whatever the Constitution said about men, that held also for women.
>
> Another person and I were speaking at the University of Alabama Law School, and he took the position that the Fifth and Fourteenth Amendments didn't apply to women. I think they did. I wasn't there when the Equal Rights Amendment was up for passage, but the cases in the Supreme Court on women's rights had been based primarily on the Fifth and Fourteenth Amendments.
>
> A lot of people's thinking on those issues has changed. We have two women on the Supreme Court now and are appointing women for every position. But I wish that some of these women who are so active in the movement would put on a little lipstick and powder and make-up and look a little feminine.

PRAYER IN SCHOOLS. In November 1981, Heflin voted in favor of a bill to restore voluntary prayer in public schools. The Supreme Court had ruled in 1962 that prayer in public school was unconstitutional even if the student was given the choice to refuse participation.[31]

When the legislation came up for action in the Senate, a group of liberal senators staged a filibuster, and efforts to invoke cloture failed. Those voting against cloture included a range from Barry Goldwater to Ted Kennedy. Goldwater explained he was for prayer in schools but was strongly against attempts to circumvent the Constitution. Heflin and Denton voted for cloture. The filibuster killed the measure for another year.[32]

Heflin fought in 1984 for the Senate to pass a constitutional amendment which would allow organized spoken prayer in schools. It was carefully worded so that it would only allow "Voluntary Prayer." The proposed amendment fell eleven votes short of the required two-thirds.[33]

In explaining his position on this issue, Howell Heflin points out that the First Amendment to the Constitution actually says two things about religion. First, it says that Congress shall make no law respecting the establishment of religion. In a substantively connecting phrase, it says Congress shall not prohibit the free exercise of religion. He notes that practically no legislative body, state or federal, has ever adopted any laws prohibiting prayer in schools.

> When the Supreme Court came out with some decisions on it in the early 1960s, I think they went too far as to what they thought would tend towards establishing a religion. But they ruled, and we have to comply. I think all this defiance of the Supreme Court is inappropriate, because the only way you can change a Supreme Court ruling is through a Constitutional Amendment. I drafted a Constitutional Amendment that said you could have voluntary prayer in school but no one would be forced directly or indirectly to participate, and it got a lot of support.
>
> Beating the drums on it has made it a much bigger controversy that it needed to be. I told this to some of the ones doing it. I had conversations with Jesse Helms, who's always hot on this issue, and I said, "Y'all are going to keep on publicizing this issue until you're going to run prayer out of schools." This is about what they've done.
>
> When I grew up in school, we had prayer all the time, and nobody thought anything about it. We had it at convocations when I traveled over the state of Alabama holding high school meetings. But at that time, the audience was mostly Protestants.
>
> Now we have greater diversity, and I've always felt that we ought not to do anything to hurt anybody's religion. America has so many Christian denominations, other religions and faiths, I don't believe that anyone has to fear that the government is going to impose a single

religion. But defiance of the courts is a different matter, and if freedoms in America are to survive, respect for our Supreme Court must be maintained. This is a stand I have long advocated.

I think maybe schools can solve some of this controversy by having a course for seniors in comparative religion. There would be a better understanding of other people and what other people believe and think. If people are born in Christian families and grow up that way, that's the basic religion they will follow. I suppose if you grew up as a Muslim, that's what you'd believe. We ought to respect everybody's religion.

A COMMITMENT FROM THE HEART. Howell Heflin was a supporter of equal rights for all citizens throughout his professional career. He handled and won many cases for blacks when he was in law practice, he made sure that blacks were included in decision processes and that they received fair treatment before the courts when he was chief justice, and he worked for civil rights in the Senate. Without question his commitment was real and reflected his deepest feelings.

Heflin's attitudes on equal rights matters stemmed from many factors. First, they came from his family. His father believed in treating everybody the same and with respect. During his Marine Corps experience, Heflin learned to respect people who were different. He had the legacy of his uncle, Cotton Tom, to live down, and he grew up in the Tennessee Valley of Alabama where racial attitudes have mostly been milder than in other parts of the state.

Colleagues in Congress and in the legal profession recognized Heflin's great contribution to civil rights, and this added greatly to the esteem with which they held him. They knew he was taking political risks by standing by his beliefs. Dr. Ralph G. Neas, former executive director of the Leadership Conference on Civil Rights, summed up feelings about Heflin in this statement:

> Judge Heflin is going to be remembered for many things in his long public career, but I certainly would hope that the history books, local history books or national history books, would note his contributions in

the area of civil rights, and take into heart what the Constitution provided, especially in the 13th, 14th, and 15th Amendments, what the Civil Rights Acts of the 1960s provided, and all of those civil rights battles that he was a part of during the '70s, '80s, and '90s that made sure that the Constitution and the Civil Rights Enactments would not be undermined. He is not a flamboyant personality, and there were other Senators who spoke more often and spoke in a louder manner on both sides of the issue, but Senator Heflin, through his knowledge of the issues, and especially time and again by demonstrating his courage, has earned a special niche in the history of this country and certainly in the history of civil rights—standing up for what was right regardless of the political consequences on so many occasions.[34]

18

Into a Second Term

As Howell neared the end of his first term, he and Elizabeth Ann were finding themselves more comfortable in their Washington surroundings. Elizabeth Ann reports that she did not have to make a really large adjustment when they first moved to the nation's capital, that learning her way around was as big a problem as anything.

"I would just get in the car and go. I'll never forget one time, I kept going back and forth across the Key Bridge from Georgetown. I knew there was some way to stay on the Washington side of the river, but I kept going across the river. I thought, 'I'm going to learn this if it takes all day long,' and finally I learned what to do.

"I didn't know anybody when we first moved there. You just sort of sink or swim, I guess. I normally speak to everybody on the street. I always have, and I guess I always will. I did the same thing in Washington, but nobody would respond except the blacks. Nobody else would say 'Good Morning,' 'Good Afternoon,' 'Good Evening' or whatever. I spoke to the people who lived next to us in the English basement for six months, I bet, before I got them to say 'Good Morning.' I guess they thought I wasn't going to give up. If I'm in Washington now and we end up in the grocery store at the same time, I'm the best friend she has."

A New Place to Live. After living in the English basement six years, the

Heflins moved to a larger apartment in the Methodist Building, which was right across the street from the Senator's office. The retired Congressman, Bob Jones, had lived there and told the Heflins that was the place they should live. They were on the waiting list for the Methodist building five years.

Elizabeth Ann reports, "It's an old building, but the rooms are big. The apartment has an entrance way, a reception room of sorts, a dining room, and a living room. There are two bedrooms with a hallway running between them, and in the center of that is the bathroom. Off the entrance is the kitchen, which has the most unusual shape you'll ever find.

"It had a stove and a refrigerator and very little counter space. I went out and found what they call TV carts, which had wheels. When I finished putting one together, I thought, 'Hmmm, that's great. There's room for another one just like it right beside it.' So I bought another one, and the two substituted for a counter. It was a nice big apartment, and we weren't embarrassed to have people over."

Howell notes that the Methodist building was very convenient. "All I had to do was go out the back door and cross the street. Sam Ervin, John Stennis, and Albert Gore Sr. and wife Pauline lived in the Methodist apartments. It is very secure because of the capitol police. The only problem was these old-timey steam heat radiators. It's hard to regulate the heat in those things. You would freeze to death or you'd have to raise the window to get the heat out."

ACTIVITIES. Elizabeth Ann says that she stayed busy in Washington. "I found somebody who played bridge at the Congressional Club. The Congressional Club was a dues-paying organization for all wives of House and Senate members, active and retired, and I think the Supreme Court wives belong to it. I played bridge there on Mondays with a group of little old ladies. The first time I was there one of them asked, 'Oh! Are you kin to Tom Heflin?' I said, 'Well, I have a son named Tom Heflin.' She said, 'Oh no, the Senator.' I responded that my husband was his nephew but I never knew Tom, and I thought, 'Gosh, they ARE old.'

"I went to Senate Wives every Tuesday. When the Senate is in session, the wives are in session, always. The Senate Wives met in the Russell Building and was a non-partisan group, with both parties mixed together."

"What did y'all do, roll bandages?" Howell asked his wife.

"No, they haven't rolled bandages since the Dark Ages, but everybody thinks that's what Senate wives do. It's a Red Cross unit, and we sewed and made puppets for the Children's Hospital. We also did the blood drive."

Howell laughed, "I remember two or three people who would run from you."

"A lot of them in the office would run from me. I always said, 'It's blood drive time.' We had them two or three times a year. Actually, the Senate was the biggest donor in the district.

"I was also active with the Red Cross and on the Red Cross D. C. Chapter Board. I stayed busy."

In recent years things have become more partisan, she says. Most of the last two wives' groups were Republicans. "They would come to the Senate Wives, but they always sat with other Republicans. They never, ever, mixed and mingled with the rest of us. The rest of the Senate wives just couldn't understand them. I know Antoinette Hatfield asked, 'Mike [Elizabeth Ann's nickname], what's the matter with them? Don't they understand why we're friends.' I said, 'Well, that's their problem, isn't it?' and she answered, 'They don't understand that we help each other.' They're as partisan as their husbands."

Elizabeth Ann was also involved in International Clubs. Included were ambassador's wives, Senate wives, Supreme Court Justice's wives, and a few House member's wives. These clubs were just for good will and not for publicity or raising money she says. "We had a number of countries, including Finland, Norway, Sweden, Turkey, Greece, and one time we had Japan, China, New Zealand, Belgium, and Austria."

SOCIAL LIFE. The Heflins didn't host many parties during their Washington years. "We went to a lot of parties, but basically you don't have to entertain. It's hard to entertain, because it's hard to get a night when you can get people together. Howell's schedule was very busy with all the events he had to go to. We went to a little bit of everything. We'd go to the White House for dinner every once in a while, and we went to some State dinners. The Motion Picture Association would invite us to come and have dinner and go to a movie."

Howell added, "Delegations like the Huntsville Chamber of Commerce would come up and give a party, and we would attend. The doctors would come up and the dentists would come, the bankers would come, the farmers would come, all of them."

Howell relates that other members of the Senate and House entertained occasionally.

> Some of them had houses, and we were invited there. Occasionally, we'd have something. We used to give a party at our apartment once a year for the Alabama Congressional Delegation and their wives. Sometimes, we'd just have others in.
>
> There were a couple of parties a week. You'd go to a party, and the next night you'd want to stay home. Usually on Wednesdays and Thursdays you couldn't plan anything because you might be in session until nine or ten or eleven o'clock at night. Maybe some other Senate couple would go out and eat with you during those nights. The social life was pretty full up there, but it was during the week, mainly.

Elizabeth Ann says they found out after the first year that they didn't have to go to everything. "The first year we were there, I said I felt I was on roller skates. We went just every night. We'd go from one to the other, to the other, to the other, and I thought, 'This is going to kill us.'"

INTERESTING PEOPLE. Asked who was the most interesting person she met in Washington, Elizabeth Ann responded, "Well, this is hysterical. The one who turned out to be most controversial was Pamela Harriman.* There wasn't anybody more shocked than I when that book came out about her. I had been to her home several times, and I did not know all those things. I thought, 'They can't be talking about the same person.' She was a very gracious hostess and a very sophisticated person."

Howell adds, "We spent one weekend in a cottage with the Harrimans at a retreat. I got to know her son, Winston Churchill II, in the North Atlantic Organization fairly well. As I recall she put on a fundraiser for me."

Elizabeth Ann says that, of all of the President's wives she met, she liked Barbara Bush best. "Barbara Bush and I were real good friends. I was very fond of Barbara. She was just like your next door neighbor. She came to Senate Wives every Tuesday she was in town, and she didn't come just for the meeting part. She came and, as Howell said, 'gossiped' and sewed with us. She said she was knitting on the same thing the entire four years. I think it was an afghan.

"I knew her first when she was the Vice President's wife. Then when she became President's wife she wasn't suppose to come. We kept telling her to come and she said, 'I can't. I don't want to step on Marilyn's (Quayle) feet.' We said, 'She doesn't come anyway. You might as well.'"

Elizabeth Ann liked Hillary Clinton, too, and Tipper Gore. "I think people are extremely jealous of Hillary, and that's the reason they don't initially like her. It's because of her knowledge and her ability. She's smart, you know. I don't think she puts people down. I think a lot of it is jealousy. I may be wrong, but that is my feeling because she is a very warm person to be around."

> One time I got Hillary's permission to tell Bill to shut up and go to bed. We were at a retreat down in Virginia, and Bill was orating after dinner. It was getting later and later, and he kept on and on answering question after question. Hillary was sitting at the table with us. She said something like, "I wish he would hush so we could go home and go to bed."

---

*Pamela Harriman, Ambassador to France when she died February 1997, was first married to Winston Churchill's son, Randolph, then later married to wealthy diplomat Averell Harriman. Sally Bedell Smith authored a tell-all book about Mrs. Harriman, *Reflected Glory: The Life of Pamela Churchill Harriman*.

I said, "You want me to get him quiet." She said, "Go right ahead." I stood up and said, "Mr. President, I've just been talking with your wife, and she would like to end this and go to bed with you. I think it's time to bring it to a close." You never did see such a room full of shocked people. Later, they all said, "You're the only one that ever told the President to shut up and go to bed."

The next time they had a meeting, George Mitchell, who was the Majority Leader, said, "Now, you do the same thing that you did before. Clinton will go on and on and on. People will ask him questions, and he'll go on answering." This time, after more than an hour of questions and answering I got up and asked him what time his golf tee was the next morning. He answered, "7:30," and went on to the next question. It didn't work. My wife told George he should have stopped it.

Elizabeth Ann was not so impressed with Nancy Reagan. "When she was First Lady, I met her at every luncheon and every dinner until next to the last one, maybe. Each time I was introduced, she acted as though it was the first time. She finally acknowledged that she knew me. I had been seated next to her a number of times, and I thought, 'This is the weirdest thing in the world.' She was friends with her own little group of people, and that was it. The only Senate wife I knew who was friendly with Nancy was Carol Laxalt. That was because Carol's husband and Ronald Reagan had been governors at the same time, and they were from out in that part of the world. It was just weird.

"It didn't matter if you were a Democrat or a Republican. That was just Nancy Reagan. She didn't have a very good press. That was because she was very aloof and class conscious, I thought. She wanted to be friendly with the people everyone was in awe of, people she thought were important."

Howell did not agree totally with this conclusion.

> Well, I don't know. My own opinion was that she was concerned about Ronald, and she was just not a basic, friendly person. Her

meeting of people was mechanical; whereas with Barbara Bush, you came away with a genuine feeling that she was a friend. I think that Nancy Reagan had a lot of things on her mind, and she wasn't able to dismiss them. I think she was very smart and intelligent, but she gave the impression of being mechanical instead of genuine in regards to being nice to people.

The Heflins also had the chance to meet King Hussein of Jordan, and they found him interesting and friendly. "He was his own pilot, you know," Howell says. "We were leaving once, and he was at the airport. He stopped and spoke to all of us, and he took us through his plane. Our whole trip delegation was out there, and we had to wait for him to leave. He knew that, and he said, 'Now I'm going to get on that bird and fly it.' And sure enough, he did."

"By the way," Howell adds, thinking of someone else, "Jesse Helms has a wonderful wife, Dot. She is truly a great Southern lady."

"I like Jesse," Elizabeth Ann confides. "One of the reasons I like him was something that happened right after Howell went to the Senate. I brought the car into the garage not long after we got there, and I parked and got out. Jesse Helms yelled, all the way across, 'Mike! How are you doing today? I'm so glad to see you.' I have never forgotten it.

"Sometimes Howell would have to miss a luncheon, and I would go alone. Jesse and Dot would be there when I arrived, and he'd say, 'Come on and sit with us.' He was always as sweet and nice to me as anybody in Washington. I don't agree with his politics, never have, never will. But I like him, and I don't care what anybody says."

Elizabeth Ann got to know Elizabeth Taylor while she was in Washington as the wife, briefly, of Senator John Warner. Elizabeth Ann says it seems ridiculous and a funny thing to say, but she felt sorry for Taylor in several ways. "There were lots of things where she was completely at a loss. She did not know how to drive a car. I asked her, 'Why don't you come on to Senate Wives? You'll enjoy it. You'll get to know all of us real well.' She answered, 'But I don't drive. I've never learned to drive.' I said, 'That's unreal, isn't it?' She said, 'Well, it is, isn't it?' We were going in to a luncheon one day at one of the women's clubs, and she turned around and said, 'Do you have a bobby pin? I don't know what to do with this hair. I've never had to comb my hair.' I thought, 'How can a woman ever not comb her hair herself?'

"She wore these huge, monstrous dresses, caftans or whatever, to cover up her size, and they made her look twice as large as she was. We all wore our Red Cross uniforms at the First Lady's luncheon. They are princess style and zip up the front. She looked wonderful in one of those, and not half as fat as she did in one of those things she wore all the time. I said, 'You look great in that. You ought to get that style.' I hope she didn't think I was teasing or making fun of her.

"Elizabeth Dole was not active in Senate Wives. I guess she came maybe twice after Bob became majority leader. She had a misconception about what to do and what not to do. She wanted to bring some folks to visit in Senate Wives, and we did not allow even family members to come. Somebody had to tell her she couldn't do that. I like her, but I don't want her to be president."

Howell says, "She was a Democrat, you know. She had to become a Republican when she married Bob Dole."

REELECTION IN 1984. In June 1983, Heflin, then 62, announced that he would seek a second term.[1] The Republicans thought they had a good chance to win his seat. Just twenty-two years before, in 1962, they almost unseated Lister Hill, who was far more entrenched than Heflin. Alabamians learned to split their ticket in the 1960s, and while the Democrats retained control locally, every Republican presidential candidate after Goldwater, except Carter in 1976, won the state. Reagan's win in 1980 and the election of Jeremiah Denton to the Senate showed a continued rise in Republican strength. Heflin was a first termer, and he had done some things in civil rights that went against the grain with some white Alabamians.

He could even appear a little bit liberal to far-right groups. In July 1982, the National Christian Action Coalition issued ratings of Members of Congress on sensitivity of their vote to biblical values. Heflin got

67 percent, lowest in the Alabama delegation. The Coalition listed specific Bible verses which should have been consulted before voting on various bills. Eight senators and 46 representatives received zero. One zero went to Democratic Representative Robert Edgar of Pennsylvania, a husband, father, and ordained Methodist minister.[2]

On the other hand, Heflin had gained considerable influence, and that was obviously an advantage to his constituents. He was one of 293 people listed in *People and Power: Portraits from the Federal Village* by Michael Evans, which was published in January 1985. Others included with Alabama backgrounds were Margaret Tutwiler, executive assistant to the White House Chief of Staff; Howell Raines, national political correspondent for the *New York Times*; and Jack Moseley, chairman of U.S. Fidelity and Guaranty Co., Baltimore; and Congressman Claude Pepper.[3]

BUILDING A REELECTION FUND. An essential for winning high office in American politics is the ability to raise large sums of money, and Heflin proved quite adept at this. He started preparing early for the 1984 race. Several newspapers reported in late 1981 and early 1982 that a group called "Friends of Howell Heflin" were building a reelection fund for him. This was the name Heflin's campaign committee gave itself. By February 1983, the sum had grown to $154,000.[4]

Alabama Peanut Producers held a $100-a-couple dinner in Dothan in 1983 to honor Heflin and raised $50,000 for his campaign. Some oilmen from Texas contributed about $25,000 to the fund, and in Washington, 52 people attended a $1,000 per plate dinner.[5] By the end of June, he had a total of about $400,000.[6]

When election year 1984 dawned, Heflin was in great shape, and his campaign fund had risen to $1.3 million by mid-July. The papers gave his opponents an issue in February 1984 when they reported that he had received $358,600 in PAC money, more than any other senator.[7]

"You had to raise half of your money outside of Alabama because people in Alabama didn't give very much for a Senate race," Heflin says. "There was a limit of $1,000 from any one individual in a Senate race.

We had fund-raisers all over the United States. Jewish people were appreciative of my support for Israel."

Heflin explains why Texas oilmen donated to his fund. "The oil people were interested in Alabama because they were drilling around Tuscaloosa for methane gas. They were drilling for oil in Mobile Bay and off-shore, and there were fields in other locations. Alabama is an oil producing state, so we've supported some of their activities."

THE PRIMARIES. The Republican and Democratic primaries in 1984 were on September 4. Heflin faced two people in the primary, Dr. Charles Wayne Borden, a Moulton dentist, and Margaret Stewart (Mrs. Frank Ross Stewart) of Piedmont. Mrs. Stewart ran regularly for office, always quoting the Bible and telling why, according to her interpretation of it, her opponent wasn't doing right.

Heflin campaigned very little for the primary. He said he didn't want to get into nasty fights, and "Not to take anything from my opponents, but they're basically unknown. I'm going to need their support after the primary's over." Strong Republican opposition had appeared in the first months of 1984 when Birmingham businessman Albert Lee Smith announced that he would oppose Heflin for the Senate. Heflin felt he faced a serious challenge in the general election.[8]

Heflin received 83 percent of the vote in the Democratic primary, and Albert Lee Smith received 59 percent on the Republican side.[9]

THE GENERAL ELECTION. Albert Lee Smith was 53 and a graduate of Auburn. He had worked for Jefferson Standard Life Insurance Company for twenty-five years. Smith became active in Republican politics in 1962 and served for a time as vice chairman of finance for the party in Jefferson County. He was a delegate to Republican National Conventions in 1968, 1972, 1976, and 1984 and was on the Platform Committee in 1976. He was elected to Congress in 1981 but was defeated in 1983.

Smith was not well-known statewide, and in an apparent effort to bolster his campaign, President Reagan appointed him to the Federal Council on Aging in June 1984.[10] An Associated Press article quoted

Smith as saying he faced an uphill battle in the general election. The article commented that it was going to be something like climbing Mt. Everest.[11]

"Albert Lee Smith was as right-wing as anyone," Heflin recalls. "He beat Congressman John Buchanan in the Republican primary. Buchanan went in on the Goldwater sweep but was a moderate. The Alabama Republicans thought he was far too liberal for them. Smith's wife, Eunice, was a big leader of the Eagle Forum for years. They are anti-women's lib and anti-a lot of stuff, you know, and they've been involved in most every Republican right-wing cause. They're the Phyllis Schlafly group."

Heflin formally kicked off his campaign the third week in August, and he opened headquarters in Birmingham, Huntsville, Mobile, and Montgomery. The first poll on September 20 showed him leading Smith about three to one.[12]

The Democrats nominated former Vice President Walter Mondale as their presidential candidate in July. Mondale had been an effective senator and vice president, but he had little chance against the popular Reagan. For Alabamians, Mondale had two big things against him. First, he was intellectual in his demeanor and lacked Reagan's charisma. Second, he was known as a liberal, and Republicans in the state were succeeding in making "liberal" a dirty word.

In his race for reelection, Heflin generally distanced himself from the liberals in the Democratic party. When asked about the Democratic platform, Heflin reiterated that he was independent and had actually voted Reagan's way more than Carter's. He announced his support of the entire Democratic ticket in Alabama. Heflin introduced Mondale on his visit to Alabama, and he introduced Mrs. Mondale twice at rallies. Heflin made it clear that he would not be a "puppet" to the national party and would continue his independence if reelected.

Smith was supported by Concerned Christians for Good Government and by the Eagle Forum. He tried to ride Reagan's coattail. "If somebody votes for Ronald Reagan and Howell Heflin, he is canceling his vote against Walter Mondale and Geraldine Ferraro," Smith said.[13]

President Reagan visited Tuscaloosa October 15 to help in Smith's campaign.

The Alabama League of Women Voters sponsored a TV debate between Heflin and Smith on October 21. Heflin was aggressive from the start, pointing out that he was no "party robot" blindly following the Democratic lead. Smith repeatedly avowed his allegiance to the GOP platform and to President Reagan, and he came across as weak on knowledge of issues.[14]

Heflin followed his usual practice of traveling extensively around the state and appearing before as many people as possible. His folksy manner and humor went over well. He had the support of labor, and Senator John Glenn, the American space hero, appeared at a campaign rally. In the general election November 6, a new record was set in Alabama as 1.4 million people voted. Heflin received 62 percent of the vote and won 62 of the state's 67 counties. Reagan won in a landslide nationally and easily took the state. In Alabama House elections, two Republicans and four Democrats won. The election had clearly bolstered Heflin's standing as a man solidly supported by his people and in control of his own political situation.

Election results in 1984 showed that the South was becoming a region of two political parties. Heflin received a larger percent of the vote in Alabama than Reagan, and analysis showed that there was much ticket-splitting and less one-party voting than in the past. A disturbing aspect of the election was evidence of racial polarization with blacks voting Democratic and whites voting Republican.[15]

FINISHING THE TENN-TOM. Howell Heflin took his seat in the new Senate in January 1985, and he continued working on several matters which began earlier. One was the Tennessee-Tombigbee Waterway, which was almost complete, and supporters were working to assure success in the final push for the waterway. In October 1982, Heflin and Denton announced that the Tenn-Tom would be finished a year faster than expected because of speed-ups in construction.[16] This put big pressure on opponents, from whom supporters expected one last-ditch stand in the fall.[17] After touring the Tenn-Tom in November, Republican Senator Pete Domenici of New Mexico, a long-time foe of the project, said it would be "lunacy" to stop construction with completion only two years away.[18]

Things moved quickly in 1983. In March, the L&N Railroad asked to be dismissed as a plaintiff in a suit, which originated in 1969, to halt construction of the Tenn-Tom.[19] The suit was costly, and the L&N recognized the inevitable and elected not to spend more money. Heflin noted that the L&N had "thrown in the towel" and said he saw the Tenn-Tom battle as won.[20] The Environmental Defense Fund withdrew from the suit in April.

In May 1983, Senator Orin Hatch attached to a budget bill an amendment which would have removed funding for Tenn-Tom, and the Senate defeated the measure 75-23. The Senate voted 91-6 in June to complete the project. Reagan signed the bill, and the long fight was over.

The Tennessee-Tombigbee Waterway was dedicated June 1985 in joint ceremonies in Mobile and Columbus, Mississippi. In gratitude for Heflin's support, the Waterway in March 1997 renamed the Gainesville Lock and Dam the "Howell Heflin Lock and Dam."[21]

There was also progress in other waterways projects. In December 1986, President Reagan signed the first water projects bill in more than fourteen years. It included several flood control projects and the deepening of the Mobile Bay ship channel from 40 to 55 feet.[22] "Deepening of the Mobile Bay ship channel was very important because it made it navigable for any ship in the world," Heflin says.

SUPPORT OF HEALTH CARE. Heflin participated in many efforts to assist the people of Alabama and the nation in health care, particularly in assuring adequate funding for biomedical research.

> The Reagan administration was going to cut a substantial sum from the Cancer Research Center at UAB, and I took the lead on the floor and helped restore the monies. The people at the National Institutes of Health (NIH) were very appreciative.

I made several visits to NIH with Dean Jim Pittman, Dr. Albert LoBuglio, and Bill Croker of UAB. They couldn't get a lot of Senators and Congressmen to come out. We had a dinner which included several high NIH officials, the UAB president, and several professors. NIH had high regards for such UAB professors as Dr. Gerald Povost, head of the department of cardiology, who had a national reputation. The King of Morocco was one of his patients, and when Yeltsin got sick in Russia, Dr. Povost went to Rome, consulted with Yeltsin's cardiologists, and examined him.

PUBLIC HEALTH. In the area of public health education, Heflin sponsored legislation to establish two health facilities at UAB to honor two of Alabama's most outstanding senators. The facilities were the John J. Sparkman Center for International Public Health Education and the Lister Hill Center for Health Policy. The Sparkman Center received $4 million for an endowment, and the Lister Hill Center received $5 million.

Heflin says that the most contentious battles in his fight to improve health care and disease prevention for all Americans involved the Medicaid Program.

> Shortly after I took office, I successfully negotiated a settlement favoring the State of Alabama in regard to the return of $10 million of Medicaid funds. As with cancer research, funding for Medicaid was virtually an annual battle.
>
> I was meeting with a group of doctors one time. I told them that St. Peter and Gabriel were at the pearly gates. A man came up, and they asked what he did. He answered, "Back on earth I was a neurosurgeon, and I saved the lives of many, many people." St. Peter said, "Admit him. He deserves to be in heaven." Another one came along. He was a cancer expert and had saved the lives of many people. St. Peter said, "Admit him. He deserves to be here." Another one came along, and when they asked what he was, he answered, "I'm the fellow who invented managed care, and that has saved a great deal of money." St. Peter said,

"Admit him, but only for three days." I thought the doctors would die laughing. They don't like managed care.

MORE JUDICIARY REFORM. Heflin continued to work hard on major efforts to reform and improve the national judicial system. One of his major efforts was in bankruptcy reform. "The need for major reform became apparent with the record increases in bankruptcy filings," he says. "There was a need to recognize changes in the economy and the different types of financial arrangements faced by consumers and businesses."

In 1978, the Supreme Court had ruled that the bankruptcy law was unconstitutional because bankruptcy judges, who are not appointed for life, should not have the same authority as federal judges who have independence because of life appointments. Having no law would have caused the system for handling bankruptcies to collapse, leaving half a million cases unheard. Temporary measures were passed twice until a major bill could become law.

Heflin wrote several bankruptcy reform bills, and he was the leader in preserving the right of trial by jury in bankruptcy cases. He was responsible for setting up a Bankruptcy Review Commission to review and study the laws and processes related to bankruptcy filings.

> The idea was to try to get people to pay their debts. In Chapter 7, which is straight bankruptcy, they don't pay the debts. Under Chapter 13, they can have a "wage earner's plan" where they reorganize their financial affairs and pay their debts over a three- or four- year period. Unfortunately, most lawyers put them in straight bankruptcy. What we wanted was to require that an official of the court tell the person they had an option to pay off their debts if they wanted to. We had testimony from judges who had met with many people, and something like 90 percent transferred from Chapter 7 bankruptcy to the Chapter 13 when they learned they could pay their debts under a plan.

Later in Heflin's career, passage of the Bankruptcy Reform Act of

1995 brought to a close long years of effort in this area and was seen as a great tribute to his leadership.

WAR ON CRIME. During his first term, Heflin declared war on crime, and he introduced a number of related measures. Elements of his crime package, which became law, included penalties for crimes against cabinet officers, Supreme Court Justices, and presidential staff members; additional protection and assistance to victims and witnesses in federal cases; and penalties for tampering in a law suit. The robbery of a controlled substance was criminalized.

The 1984 Justice Assistance Act provided aid to state law enforcement and created a sentencing commission to establish standards for punishment in federal crimes. It set mandatory sentencing for use of firearms in a federal crime. Federal prosecution was established for murder-for-hire, drug trafficking, labor racketeering, and computer fraud.

The legislation also shifted the burden of proof in the insanity defense from the prosecution to the defendant, a change Heflin had wanted since the attempted assassination of President Reagan. "The burden of proof in an insanity defense was on the government," he explains. "It had to prove beyond a reasonable doubt that the person who committed the crime was sane. The prosecution had difficulty with this in trying Hinckley. He didn't get off scott-free, but neither did he face the greater consequences of his act. I felt the burden of proof should be shifted to the defendant who claims that he is insane."

Heflin was a leader in establishing a drug czar at the highest level of the federal government, and he was a joint sponsor of the Anti-smuggling Act, which makes it tougher to smuggle drugs into the United States. He was a leader in the passage of legislation making it a federal crime to operate a train, boat, ship, or airplane under the influence of alcohol or drugs, and he helped secure passage of the Child Protection and Obscenity Enforcement Acts.

WORK ON THE ADMINISTRATIVE LAW SYSTEM. In 1987, Heflin introduced legislation to change the administrative law system with an Independent Corps of Administrative Law Judges. In the past, administrative law judges were employed and housed by the agencies they were supposed to oversee, and this represented a clear conflict of interest. "How can a 'judge,' employed by the agency he is serving, be expected to decide cases fairly and impartially?" Heflin asks. The bureaucrats fought the proposal for independence in federal administrative law, and they managed to prevent its passage.

In 1988, Congress passed the Permanent Federal Court Study Act, which Heflin originally introduced in 1980. It established a federal court study committee to plan for the long range needs of the judiciary. It brought about raises of jurisdictional authority in federal diversity cases from $10,000 to $25,000, reauthorized the State Justice Institute, created pilot programs for voluntary court-annexed arbitration, and reformed jury selection. In a letter to Senator Heflin, Chief Justice Rehnquist called the bill "probably the most significant measure affecting the operation and administration of the federal judiciary to be considered by Congress in over a decade. It will significantly enhance the effectiveness of the federal judiciary as a whole."

1986 DEMOCRATIC FIASCO IN ALABAMA. An election for governor and for the Senate seat occupied by Jeremiah Denton was held in Alabama in 1986. Republicans were making steady progress in the state. "The realization by Alabama voters that it really didn't make Confederate veterans rise from their graves to vote Republican meant that Republicans would almost certainly be the majority party in time," Heflin noted. Voters proved him correct by electing Guy Hunt governor. This was due to a fiasco in the Democratic primary where party big-wigs reversed results of the primary and claimed that Republican crossover votes had determined the outcome. Hunt was the first Republican since Reconstruction to win the governor's seat.

Democratic Congressman Richard Shelby announced in January 1985 that he would be a Senate candidate the next year. Shelby hit hard on the theme that incumbent Jeremiah Denton was isolated from

Alabama voters, that he stayed in Washington and didn't communicate with the people. Denton substantiated the charge and sealed his own doom with a disastrous blunder. Thinking a TV interview was over and the cameras off, he said, "I can't spend my time going down there and kissing babies' butts." This was captured on TV and shown repeatedly around the state.

Heflin went to bat for Shelby.

> When I ran in 1984, Jeremiah Denton got fairly active in support of Albert Lee Smith. Most Senators and Congressmen stay out of each other's races for reelection regardless of their party because they are friends and work together for the good of the state. It's sort of an unwritten gentleman's agreement. Two years later, he came to me when he was running for reelection and said, "I hope you're not going to take any part in this election." I answered, "Well now, Jeremiah, I'm not going to do any more against you than you did for Albert Lee Smith." Shelby won by about 6,000 votes, so it was very close.

STEVE RABY REPLACES MIKE HOUSE. Mike House resigned from Heflin's staff in November 1986 to join a Washington law firm. This created an important vacancy, and Heflin began at once getting in touch with Alabama contacts to fill it. One thing he did was to contact the various universities.

Steve Raby recalls, "In late 1983 I was in graduate school at Auburn when, out of the clear blue, the faculty informed me that Judge Heflin's office had called and said they had a vacancy and were going to interview people. Auburn was going to present one person and had chosen me. I got a call from Heflin one day asking me to join him for breakfast at a hotel in Birmingham. A few days after the interview, he called and said, 'I've been thinking about it, and if you'd like to come to work for me, I'd appreciate having you.' I did some campaign work with him in the fall of 1983, and in January 1984, I went to Washington and joined his staff.

"When I first went to work, I was a legislative assistant and was responsible for his work on the Senate agriculture committee, public works, and some of the appropriations. I was 25 years old at the time. For whatever reason, I was quickly involved in Heflin's reelection campaign in 1984. The Judge, my predecessor Mike House, and the state director, Bill Gardiner, recognized that I had some political instinct in rural areas. After the campaign, I continued in the legislative assistant position but would spend more and more time back in the state doing political work. The positions I had were executive secretary, administrative assistant, and finally chief of staff."

Steve Raby grew up in Harvest, Alabama, which is in Madison County close to Huntsville. "I grew up on a cotton farm and thought I was going to be a farmer," he says. "For the life of me I don't know what has happened, but I didn't get there." He did his undergraduate work in agriculture economics at Auburn, worked for the Federal Reserve Bank in Atlanta, and returned to Auburn for graduate work in economics. Raby received his graduate diploma in the Spring of 1984 after he was on the Heflin staff.[23]

19

Strong for Space, Defense, and Research

As he continued into his second term, Heflin was recognized as a Senate leader in agriculture and in matters of the judiciary. Also, he had made his mark as a champion of equal rights for all Americans. Howell was actively involved in social programs such as Social Security and Medicare, and he gave strong support to the war against crime and drugs. As he later explained, support for family values was always intermingled with his other activities.

Other areas of fundamental concern were defense and the space program. Heflin felt strongly that it was essential for the United States to have a defense second to none in the world and for the armed forces to be equipped with the very best weapons. Further, he recognized that the space program was critical in maintaining international leadership in the twenty-first century. He was the first senator to call for building a manned space station. In a display of insight many members of Congress lack, Senator Heflin understood that research and science are essential in keeping this country in the lead in knowledge production and utilization and are keys in the emerging international economy.

When he began his first term, Heflin had two of the three committee assignments he wanted, Judiciary and Commerce. He had also wanted Agriculture, but Donald Stewart, who arrived in the Senate two months earlier than Heflin, took Agriculture. When Stewart was defeated two years later, Heflin went on the Agriculture committee.

In 1987, he had to relinquish one seat because of a new Senate rule that junior members could serve on only two major committees. He could not drop Agriculture because it dealt with his state's largest industry. He would not drop Judiciary because that was his specialty area, the place he could make his greatest contribution to the Senate and the country.[1] He chose to leave the Commerce committee and its science subcommittee, the assignments most directly related to funding of the space program. Afterwards, he stayed abreast of space issues and helped maintain funding for the National Aeronautics and Space Administration (NASA) and the space station.

DEFENSE. Central to Howell Heflin's attitudes toward defense was a deep distrust of the Soviet Union and a conviction that the United States must maintain absolute military superiority. He insisted that any treaty have iron-clad verification procedures and not depend on trusting the Russians to abide by treaty provisions.

He wrote in his column in September 1981, "I have urged the Senate to reconsider the Anti-Ballistic Missile Treaty with the Soviet Union when the pact comes up for renewal in 1982. When the treaty went into effect in 1972, the U.S. held a clear technological advantage over the Soviets in this area, and by not developing this area of strength, we have allowed the Soviets eight free years to catch up. The United States has been engaged in a costly arms race — a losing one — for the past decade despite so-called arms agreements."[2]

Heflin opposed a nuclear freeze treaty with the Soviets. In March 1983, the House passed a resolution directing the U.S. to engage the Soviets in talks aimed at a mutual and verifiable halt in the nuclear arms race, and the Senate was considering the resolution. Heflin said that, while he was open to ideas and would consider the resolution carefully, he did not favor it initially because of the difficulty of verification.[3]

In his enthusiasm for military preparedness, Heflin played a game which the *Birmingham Post-Herald* labeled "The Pentagon Bluff." "It didn't take the military long to learn the game played by the nation's sleazier mayors," the paper stated editorially. "You know the game: Taxes rise to the point where citizens rebel and demand budget cuts. 'All right,' the mayor threatens, 'if you won't provide the money, I'll have to fire policemen, firemen and teachers and eliminate high school football.' ... The Pentagon now is behaving like the city hall fakers. It warns that if President Reagan cuts a total of $30 billion from the fiscal 1983 and 1984 defense budgets, our military power will disappear and we'll all have to learn to speak Russian."[4]

Later, after the Soviet Union fell, Heflin acknowledged that they were probably not as big a threat as most people in the country had been led to believe. He was not crying "wolf" in his statements in the 1980s, however. He knew the history of the Soviet Union well, starting with their failure to live up to agreements at the end of World War II, and he knew that they believed they could win the Cold War and dominate the world.

Heflin felt, as have most members of Congress, that the country should rally behind the President in times of danger, whatever the background causes. "Generally," he says, "I have been proud of the Senate for rallying behind the American President whenever he has determined the necessity of using our armed forces. I have been consistent in embracing the philosophy of supporting the Commander-in-Chief, regardless of the party or what I might have felt personally could have been done differently or better."

Heflin worked hard and with considerable success to see that federal defense money came into Alabama. At the end of 1984, the state was receiving some $1.1 billion a year, an amount half that produced by the largest segment of the state's economy, agriculture. The five military installations in the state were Fort Rucker, the Army helicopter school in Ozark; the Anniston Army Depot and Fort McClellan in Anniston; and Maxwell AFB, site of the Air University, and Gunter AFB in Montgomery. In addition, Redstone Arsenal and the Marshall Space Flight Center were in Huntsville, and Heflin strongly supported both installations.[5]

THE AWACS SALE BATTLE. Heflin was among fifty senators who cosponsored a resolution to stop Reagan's proposed sale of AWACS

(Airborne Warning and Control System) planes and jet fighter gear to Saudi Arabia.[6] The AWACS is a radar-equipped all-weather surveillance and communications plane which gives great advantage in air warfare.

    The AWACS is a story in itself. It was a hotly contested thing. We had Winton "Red" Blount, who had Blount Construction in Montgomery and the contract to build the University of Riyadh in Saudi Arabia. The Saudis put the pressure on him to get my vote. Two planeloads of business people from all over Alabama were brought to Washington, and they had Admiral Moorer and John West from South Carolina who had been Ambassador to Saudi Arabia. I met with all of them, and they really put the pressure on me to support them.

    At the same time, the Jewish people in the state were opposing it. It was a difficult situation, and I, in my deliberate judge-like manner, took a good while to make up my mind. What made up my mind was that we were not only selling the AWACS but we were selling a missile that was fired from fighter planes. It was called the AIM-9L. In fact, 1,177 AIM-9L heat-seeking air-to-air missiles were included in the sale package.

    I was flown down to Alabama to do something for the Air Force. Two fighter pilots were picked up on the way back, and they got to talking to me and found out I was a senator. They said, "For God's sake, vote against that AWACS sale." I asked, "Why are y'all so vehemently opposed to it?" They explained. The proposed sale came right after the fall of the Shah of Iran, and there wasn't any question that Russian agents had been all over Iran and got every weapon we had sold to the Iranians. As a result, the Soviets copied our weapons.

    The pilots said, "The Russians don't have anything like our AIM-9L missile that's being sold along with the AWACS. This is a sophisticated heat-seeking missile. You can fire it at an enemy plane head-on, twenty-five miles away, and it seeks out its target, changes directions, and comes up behind the enemy plane and destroys it. If the Russians get a hold of that and we get into a war with them, fighter pilots are goners." They really convinced me.

They continued, "If you turned it over to the Saudi Arabians, you wouldn't be absolutely sure they would keep it." After the Ayatollah Khomeni took over in Iran, there was a lot of talk about the Shi'ites and a fundamentalist revolution all over the Middle East. Most of the workers in the oil fields of Saudi Arabia are Shi'ite, and a fear in our foreign policy is that Muslim fundamentalists will take control. The Shi'ites are the ones who believe you get to heaven if you get killed on the battlefield.

I went back to Washington and did some investigation and talked to a number of defense leaders. The reason I voted against the AWACS sale wasn't the AWACS itself but that missile. Well, I made all those business people like Red Blount mad, but the Jewish people liked it. The Jewish population in Alabama at the time was only about 9,000, but they were always very loyal to me after that.

Heflin remained opposed through the long battle even though President Reagan personally tried to convince him otherwise. In October 1981, the Senate voted 52-48 in favor of the sale.[7] When Heflin came back from a visit with the President, he was asked, "Did they twist your arm?" He answered, "Yes, now both arms need a transplant."

OTHER PROGRAM SUPPORT. In 1981, Heflin was in favor of building a new strategic bomber to replace the B-52s, and he made several speeches on the subject. The B-1 bomber was intended for this role, but President Carter had scrapped the program. The Senate approved a defense appropriations bill which included funds for the plane.[8] "I went out and saw the B-2," he says. "It was the stealth bomber, and we supported it. They are very expensive, and I'm not sure we will build a large number."

He consistently supported Marine Corps initiatives. One was the V-22, an advanced, tilt-rotor aircraft which could be landed like a helicopter but flown like an airplane. It had greater range and capacity than a helicopter. (This aircraft, commonly known as the Osprey, would be involved in a number of fatal accidents in the late 1990s and early 2000s and would become the subject of intense public debate.) A second initiative was the LHD, a next generation amphibious assault ship, to deliver marines to shore. The LHD is large and has the ability to move in very close to the shore. Senator Heflin knew about this type of vessel from personal experience. He helped articulate to his colleagues why the design was important.[9]

Heflin helped deliver a victory to President Reagan in May 1983 when he joined eleven other Democrats in approving $625 million for further testing of the MX missile.[10] The MX was controversial because it was associated with nuclear warfare and, too, if the missile came too close to Russian airspace, they might mistake the testing for the real thing and retaliate.

THE STRATEGIC DEFENSE INITIATIVE. Heflin supported President Reagan's Strategic Defense Initiative (SDI), earning the President's gratitude for bucking the Democratic party on this matter. In fact, he supported the idea before President Reagan announced it publicly.

> Joe Moquin and another scientist in Huntsville, Bill Davis, who worked with him on SDI got me interested, and I also became interested in laser technology. They educated me. Others in Huntsville who helped educate me were Charles Granger and Jyles Machen. I talked to Reagan and spent some time with him before he announced his Strategic Defense Initiative. The Huntsville people were with Teledyne Brown Engineering and were doing a lot of work on SDI, and, of course that was business for them. It's also business for Alabama and Huntsville. Independently, I got convinced that it was the best thing.

Heflin was more interested in a ground-based approach rather that the far-out "Star Wars," satellite-based system which caught the public imagination, however. He believed in a deliberate, evolutionary development. He felt that the process of weapons development involves learning from a series of mistakes.[11]

Some of the SDI people wanted purely space-based weapons, but

Senator Heflin thought that would be a violation of the ABM treaty with the Soviets, which only allows ground-based missiles. He believed that our development of space-based weapons would cause a problem relative to enforcement and would hamper the peaceful progress we were making at that time with the Russians.[12]

SDI faced tough opposition from its inception. In June 1984, Heflin worked in the Senate to help keep $800 million for SDI from being cut from the budget. Vice President Bush had to break the tie in the Senate. Heflin was credited with persuading five or six Democratic senators, and he reported that the Security Council and the President credited him with swaying the critical votes.[13] Heflin reported that Reagan phoned him and said, "Bless you, bless you." He remembers that Senate Majority Leader Howard Baker told him, "You saved it."

Senators Heflin and Shelby helped save the day for SDI again in 1987. An amendment to cut SDI spending to $3.7 billion, an $800 million cut, was defeated in September. Both Heflin and Shelby spoke before the vote, and Vice President Bush had to break a tie.[14] Funding for SDI was still some $3.5 billion in the FY 1990 budget.[15]

NICARAGUA AND PANAMA. In March 1988, 3,200 U.S. troops were sent into Honduras in reaction to a decision by the Nicaraguan Sandinista government to send its forces across the Honduran border in pursuit of Contra rebels. The Honduran government had requested help. This move created the possibility of direct combat between U.S. forces and the Sandinistas. Heflin and Shelby voiced support.[16]

At the same time, the U.S. was having trouble with Panamanian President Manuel Noriega, so Heflin proposed a trade embargo against Panama and a review of the Panama Canal Treaty. Noriega allegedly had established closer ties with Cuba and the Soviet Union, had sold high-technology equipment to Cuba, and had provided arms to the Sandinistas in Nicaragua and leftist guerrillas in El Salvador. He was also said to be involved in the drug traffic.[17]

Elections were to be held in Panama in 1989, and Noriega created a fuss about taking over the Panama Canal eleven years prior to the date established in the 1979 treaty. Bush sent an extra 2,000 troops to add to the 10,000 already in the Canal Zone. Heflin and Shelby both backed him.[18] It was widely reported in the United States that Noriega was virtually a dictator, and the elections were a sham. Heflin urged Bush to "encourage" the formation of a commando strike force of Latin American soldiers to remove Noriega from Panama.[19]

In December 1989, Bush sent troops into Panama in an effort to depose Noriega and bring him to the U.S. to face drug charges. Heflin praised the action. Noriega had declared the pervious weekend that Panama was in a state of war with the United States, and his soldiers shot and killed an unarmed American serviceman, seriously wounded another, and brutally beat a third and his wife.[20]

The invasion began about midnight on December 20, and it proceeded with very little opposition. Noriega fled to a Catholic church and stayed several days trying to find some escape. The U.S. used voice psychology and loud music to keep him awake so he couldn't sleep. Realizing that the end had come, he surrendered and was arrested on January 5, 1990.

THE SPACE PROGRAM. Senator Heflin had a special interest in the National Aeronautics and Space Administration because of the Marshall Space Flight Center and the Army Missile Command at Redstone Arsenal in Huntsville. As early as 1979, Heflin was trying to get more missions for the Marshall Space Flight Center.[21] After a behind-the-scenes fight, the Senate Science Committee voted in May 1980 to authorize a Solar Electric Propulsion System to be managed at Marshall.[22]

Heflin believes that a permanent presence in space is the next logical step in human advancement.

> Many have complained that the space program is too expensive and yields too little for the investment. But the space program provides a far greater return than its cost. Studies conducted in the early 1970s indicated that the space program brought in $7 to $15 for each dollar spent. Satellites have redefined the way we communicate, and they have

reshaped our economy. The knowledge and technology we gain has proved nearly unlimited. There are unexpected benefits, including what we are learning about our own planet, advances in medical research, and the international diplomacy we will develop with the space station.

Research in space has certain advantages not found on earth. The growth of crystals and a process called electrophoresis, which separates a cell down to the smallest intricate part, can take place far better in space than in the gravity of earth. Several kinds of metals will combine only under the conditions found in space. We are gaining valuable knowledge, and it is very important that the United States maintain world leadership in space.

Heflin believes that the space program should be controlled by civilians and should remain independent of the military services. This way it can avoid service rivalries and be in better position for international cooperation. He notes that the military space budget has grown larger than NASA's, and he considers this an undesirable trend. "It was necessary," he says, "to oppose intrusions such as military control of the heavy lift launch vehicle, which was proposed after the shuttle disaster, and to work as hard as possible each year to see that NASA received the money it needed." In 1982, he helped secure authorizations for NASA's missions to Jupiter and to Haley's comet. Both missions were tremendously successful.

Heflin says that over the years, he was probably more of a friend of the space program than anybody in the Senate except John Glenn. "I suppose John Glenn and myself were the two major proponents of the space program. He didn't serve on Commerce, and I gave it up. After I left the Commerce committee, they allowed me to go back to the subcommittee and participate in hearings and ask questions for several years, because there weren't too many of them that understood what was going on."

Marine Corps Lieutenant Colonel Debra Bieley, who was a Congressional Fellow in Heflin's office, says the Senator "recognized that investment in the space program carried with it spin-off technologies which would ultimately result in improving the standard of living across the spectrum. When he talked about the space program, that's what he envisioned. Not just racing the Russians to the moon, and not just bringing jobs home to Huntsville, but advancing the quality of life and our own ability to manipulate our own environment on earth."[23]

THE SPACE STATION. "I am proudest of being the first Senator to call for the development of a space station," Heflin says. He talked a lot about the space station in 1983 and tried to persuade Reagan to support the idea. The President was almost persuaded but didn't include funds in his budget. Heflin kept working, and in his 1984 State-of-the-Union address, the President announced plans for the space station, for which the Marshall Space Flight Center was to play a major coordination role.[24] Money for space station design at Marshall was included in the budget authorization bill. The bill also provided money for the Hubble space telescope, which was designed and built at Marshall. Thereafter, Reagan strongly supported the space station.

Marshall was to do roughly forty percent of the work on space station design and construction. It would also have responsibility for developing the station's living and working quarters, and it would provide technical direction for the propulsion system, handle adaptation aspects of the international module, and develop and construct the environmental and pressure systems. In the battle to get more space station responsibilities for Marshall, Heflin was in battle part of the time with John Glenn, who was trying to do the same thing for NASA's Lewis Research Center in Cleveland, Ohio.[25]

Uncertainty over what the space station would be used for assured that the appropriations bills would face tough fights in Congress every year. NASA faced a potential loss of 70 percent of its $767 million space station budget for 1988,[26] but the Senate Appropriations Committee restored most of the money. Heflin called it the "first step in regaining preeminence in space research and exploration."[27] He added, "If I were a betting man, I'd say that we've got a 95 percent chance of having a completed space station during the 1990s."

On Dec 1, 1987, Congressional officials announced that the Boeing Company in Huntsville was chosen to serve as the prime contractor for the space station work package. This was a project worth upwards of $2 billion, and it ultimately brought more than 6,000 jobs to Alabama.[28] Commentator Bob Ingram wrote "There is no doubt that Sen. Heflin played a key role in NASA's decision to give the contract to Boeing."[29]

In August 1988, Congressional conferees working on the 1989 budget settled on $900 million in funding for the space station. It was a critical year for the station, and Heflin called the appropriation outstanding, more than supporters had anticipated they would get.[30]

Heflin recalls that, when Michael Dukakis was nominated as Democratic candidate for president, he first came out against the space station. "We spent a lot of time talking to him. We got him to come to Huntsville, and he reversed his position on it. He didn't get elected, so it didn't make much difference."

The next year, after Bush became President, he endorsed the space station as the "first and necessary step for sustained manned exploration" of space.[31] The House voted in July 1989 to cut $395 million from the $2.05 billion NASA requested for the space station for fiscal year 1990. NASA said that if the Senate did the same thing, it could mean the end of the program because the cut would require compromising safety. The Senate Appropriations Committee increased the appropriation to $1.85 billion.[32]

Heflin was selected as a member of the President's delegation to the Farnborough International Aeronautical and Space Exposition in Farnborough, England, in the fall of 1988. This was an exposition of aviation, aeronautics, and space technology attended by representatives from both the West and the Soviet bloc.

> They have the Farnborough Air Show in England every two years. Basically, the big companies like Boeing, McDonald-Douglas, and Airbus exhibit and show all sorts of futuristic stuff. The Russians showed off their MIGs, and we showed our fighter planes, but their

MIGs were generally considered superior to what we had. We wouldn't show anything that was secret or classified, of course. They would have contests with rolls and all sorts of maneuvers, and you'd see commercial and military planes and displays in avionics and other areas that technology and science were developing. It was interesting, and it was a good idea; it helped people to become knowledgeable.

This trip was after Elizabeth Taylor and John Warner split up. I was always telling jokes, and Warner kept insisting that I get up and tell some. I thought everybody was tired of listening because the speeches just went on and on. Anyway, Warner kept insisting. Finally I got up and said, "Well, I'm going to be like what Elizabeth Taylor told John when they first got married." They all perked up, and I said, "What she told all her husbands was, 'I'm not going to keep you long.'" And it broke up the house. John didn't ask me to speak anymore after that. But he's a great friend. I enjoy him. He's a great fellow.

THE SPACE SHUTTLE. In 1979, Heflin worked to ensure that the Commerce Committee approve a $185 million supplemental authorization for Marshall to continue development of the space shuttle, and he continued to support the shuttle throughout his career. The first space shuttle flight was in May 1981. Heflin stated in his weekly column that "Our space program has an enormous positive impact on our economy, on our national sense of pride and our national defense posture." "Two Auburn astronauts were on the fourth launch of the shuttle, which landed on the Fourth of July in 1982," Heflin recalls. "One of them was Ken Mattingly, who was on his second launch. He said he couldn't sleep the night before his first launch, and he got up and went outside close to the shuttle. Lo and behold, he found an electrician out there checking all of the circuits he had installed. Mattingly went up to him and asked, 'What in the world are you doing out here at two o'clock in the morning?' He answered, 'I wanted to make a last minute check. It's not going to fail because of me.' The other astronaut from Auburn was Hank Hartsfield."

The shuttle program gained efficiency and speed during the next few years. From two flights in 1981, the first year the shuttle flew, the number of flights was gradually increased until a total of nine were flown in 1985. NASA officials, with confidence growing, talked about one launch per month.

The program suffered a great setback on January 28, 1986, when the Challenger exploded 73 seconds after launch, killing all seven crew members. Among those on board was Christa McAuliffe, a teacher chosen for the flight after a nation-wide search. McAuliffe was to be the first civilian in space. The Challenger disaster caused great consternation nationally, and it resulted in serious problems in continuing the shuttle's development at Marshall. The military claimed it could do better and began to increase its intervention in space. Its space budget grew to two-thirds the total U.S. space budget, which Heflin found very disturbing. The space station suffered cuts, and launch of the Hubble space telescope was delayed until 1988.

After the Challenger disaster, many congressmen turned on Marshall and on Thiokol, builder of the solid rocket motor which failed during flight. Some believed the two organizations should be held responsible and individuals should be singled out as guilty parties. The investigation was directed more at who was responsible than what went wrong and how to fix it. This was a real concern to the management at Marshall and to Heflin because the most successful launch vehicle development center in the world had been tainted, and it could have a long-lasting, detrimental effect on Marshall's and NASA's future. Senator Heflin worked behind the scenes to see that the investigation was fair. The final report did not indict Marshall nor any individual, but it did recommend some important changes for NASA.[33]

The investigation showed that O-rings in a joint connecting sections of the shuttle's right solid rocket had failed and allowed flames to burn through the wall of the liquid hydrogen fuel tank. Triggering this failure was a launch during the coldest weather in the shuttle's history. The temperature of the solid rocket section which failed was 28 degrees at launch time.

Morale was terrible at Marshall, because some of the finger pointing was at the space activity there. It went on for months. I finally went to Marshall and made a speech in which I went into detail about all of their accomplishments and fully supported Marshall's position on the explosion. Later, it was pretty well established that the fault was more with the contractor who built it than the Marshall people. Sharing the blame was the Johnson Space people in Houston who insisted on a launch in the cold weather even after some warnings had occurred. I was the first to support Marshall, and they deeply appreciated it.

Bob Dole was coming to Alabama when he was running for president in 1988. I told him, "When you go down to Huntsville, you can make some points by praising Marshall. You don't have to say anything about the Challenger, but just say about the history of Marshall Space Flight Center." He came down and made a speech, and it boosted the morale. Even if he was running as a Republican, you can be friendly with him and give him a pointer every once in a while.

According to Steve Raby, Senator Denton had set up a rally-type event in the Shoals area for Dole in 1986, and it became evident it was going to be a flop. Heflin, not wanting to have his friend embarrassed, told his staff to fix it even though Dole was a Republican, and they rounded up several hundred people. "That's just the kind of fellow Heflin is," Raby says.[34]

In the first flight since the Challenger disaster, the space shuttle Discovery was successfully launched on September 30, 1988, two-and-one-half years later, with the new boosters. All went well, and again, the number of flights per year gradually increased. During the 1990s, NASA has averaged seven flights each year, with more than 60 flown since Challenger.

YELLOW CREEK. After the Challenger accident, a very thorough evaluation of solid rocket motor design problems was conducted.

They found problems which the weather caused plus a lot of other

defects, and they came up with plans to change the motor. Then they felt like the redesigned motor wouldn't be good enough for a while. But NASA wanted a new motor, which they called the Advanced Solid Rocket Motor (ASRM). Studies showed that, with new technologies, the U.S. could build a much better solid rocket motor, a more efficient and safer motor with more payload capability. Congress declared that NASA should have a government-owned, contractor-operated facility in developing ASRM so that if the contractor failed to perform as required, NASA could replace them.

We found they were talking about building a plant somewhere, and we had this site called Yellow Creek four miles from the Alabama line in Mississippi. TVA had started a nuclear power plant and had it about thirty percent complete, but after Three Mile Island and Chernobyl, TVA changed its mind and decided not to go forward. An isolated place was needed for the new advanced solid rocket motor, and we thought Yellow Creek fit the bill. For months before any announcement was made, we worked with officials behind the scenes to try to get them to build the ASRM at Yellow Creek.

The company which had redesigned the old O-rings didn't want it at first. Lo and behold, suddenly they were going to build an ASRM plant out from Montgomery, Alabama, if they could get the bid. I think it was some sort of an effort to try to divert attention from the advanced solid rocket motor that was going to be made. They never had all the land under option near Montgomery, but I caught a lot of cain because I had supported the site in Mississippi. They wrote editorials in the *Montgomery Advertiser* that I was Mississippi's third senator and all of that.

I finally had to take sort of a neutral stand in regard to the site location, but that neutral stand didn't work. The *Montgomery Advertiser* continued to harass me, and all of the "politicos" around Montgomery were highly critical. My neutral stand caused people back home to get mad at me, so I was caught in between. It ended up the company that was advocating the Montgomery site never entered a bid for the ASRM contract. In retrospect, I suspect that talk of the Montgomery site was a scheme to divide the Alabama delegation. In Congress the issue was hotly contested. Morton-Thiokol, who had developed the Revised Solid Rocket Motor (RSRM) was able to generate support against the ASRM, saying that it was not needed and would be a waste of money.

We won the battle for the new ASRM in the Senate, but the House couldn't pass it. NASA finally withdrew plans for an advance solid rocket motor, and the plant was never built. A short time later, NASA and Thiokol announced plans for a premier nozzle center at Yellow Creek. The nozzle center would be operated by Thiokol, and there was a big announcement made at Iuka, Mississippi, near the Yellow Creek site by Thiokol and NASA. However, sixteen months later, Thiokol said it was not going forward with the building of a nozzle center.

To me, there was a lot of mystery about all of this, and it had the appearance of shenanigans from beginning to end. I caught a lot of cain from people in the Montgomery area and particularly from the *Montgomery Advertiser*. There were predictions that when I ran again I would never carry Montgomery County. Well, at the next election, I carried it.

Looking back over the years at what happened at the Yellow Creek site, I felt that it was an example of governmental ineptitude and wasteful spending. TVA rescinded a nuclear plan that was thirty percent completed at that site. A billion dollars or more was wasted on the advanced solid rocket motor at that site since Lockheed had been successful in getting the contract and had already built the plant when Congress killed the ASRM. The premier nozzle center never materialized after a lot of money was wasted on it. This saga of the Yellow Creek site ought to go down as an example of inefficiency and disastrous results which can come from governmental bureaucracy and special interest interference.

SUPPORT OF RESEARCH AND SCIENCE. Senator Heflin has understood for years that advanced research and the generation of knowledge are essential to the country's future, and in his view, research funding should be a top federal priority. He helped to pass the University Research Capacity Restoration Act in 1984. He worked hard to get research dollars for universities in his home state and helped develop several research centers.

He wrote in his newspaper column that "The ability of the United States to maintain a competitive edge in science and technology is crucial to the future of our country. Basic research is the fuel for new industry and new jobs. Its importance cannot be underestimated. It is the foundation on which the development of new ideas, products, and procedures is built. We depend on our preeminence in science to enable us to advance technology and maintain our economic and national security."[35]

NASA official Ray Askew commented that Heflin wasn't just after dollars. "Others in Congress would just ask, 'What do you want me to do,' but with Senator Heflin it was a little different. It was, 'Why do we really need to be doing this? And what does it mean to the nation? What does it mean to education for the government to have an SDI science and technology program in universities? What does it mean in the case of our commercial development center?'"[36]

Heflin's bill, the University Research Capacity Restoration Act, became law in 1984. The new law was designed to increase support for the National Institutes of Health, the National Science Foundation, NASA, and the Defense, Energy, and Agriculture Departments by combining university and private industrial research efforts, with the long-range goal of transferring findings to the private sector.

He cosponsored the National Space Grant College Act in the fall of 1986. This legislation established a National Space Grant College and Fellowship Program within NASA. The program provided a framework to conduct space related research.[37] In 1989, NASA selected several Alabama universities to comprise a consortium for the new program. Included were the University of Alabama at Huntsville, UAB, Alabama A&M, the University of Alabama main campus at Tuscaloosa, and Auburn.

SPACE AND OTHER RESEARCH AT AUBURN. In the early 1980s, Auburn University was trying to move to larger, multi-disciplinary and systems oriented research efforts. Senator Heflin assisted the university in its quest and not only influenced the work at Auburn but how the work translated to the state and the region. James Marion, dean of the College of Agriculture, says Heflin had the vision that international problems are also domestic problems.[38]

The Space Power Institute at Auburn was founded in 1985 with a grant from the SDI. Since that time, the Institute's budget has grown to some $10 million a year.

Heflin announced in September 1986 that Auburn had been awarded a $9.9 million contract with the Naval Surface Weapons Laboratory for work in a related area. The contract established the Center for Advanced Technology and provided for research in materials, microelectronics, and space simulation.[39] Dr. Frank Rose, Director of the Space Power Institute at Auburn University, was Auburn's primary researcher in this area.

In July 1987, Heflin helped Auburn get a five-year, $5 million NASA contract for the creation of the Center for Commercial Development for Space Power.[40] The center does research on the generation, storage, and distribution of electrical power in space, all of which depend on advanced electronics. Until that time, power requirements of U.S. space ventures had been low, but future space projects were expected to involve much higher power demands. Auburn worked with industry partners in this project. Chrysler Corporation now puts in its vehicles a new engine controller developed through the work. "When you buy your new Jeep Grand Cherokee," says Ray Askew of NASA, "it's got an Auburn engine controller in it."[41]

At Heflin's encouragement in April 1988, NASA selected Auburn as the pilot program school for the State of Alabama for a new joint NASA/university program. The JOVE (joint venture) Initiative was designed to stimulate science, mathematics and engineering education in the country. Alabama was one of six states in which NASA conducted pilot programs.[42]

Auburn was involved with a number of universities in the United Kingdom in space activities. Congress and the administration felt that American universities needed to be involved with friends in Europe and Asia, particularly those in the United Kingdom. Senator Heflin was a principal figure in setting up this program. Auburn had two significant levels of activity. It served as SDI liaison to the United Kingdom, and it cooperated with British universities in space power research.[43]

MEDICAL RESEARCH. Heflin was intensely involved in medical research, one of the most important areas of which is the fight against cancer. "During the mid-1980's," he recalls, "I had to author several amendments to various spending bills to assure that important cancer research was adequately conducted. Funding for cancer research has been an annual battle."

Heflin says that the Comprehensive Cancer Core Center at UAB is one of the true research flagships in the nation and has been listed among the three top U.S. centers for cancer research. Research crucial to the effort to conquer cancer is also being done at the University of South Alabama (USA) in Mobile, and Southern Research Institute in Birmingham.

"The Marshall Space Flight Center and UAB made a major contribution to cancer research by jointly managing a program for protein crystal growth experiments on the space shuttle," Heflin relates. "For years, UAB has been a world leader in the growth of crystals to understand proteins better. These crystals can be grown many times larger in space than on earth, giving researchers samples large enough for accurate atomic characterization."

Crystal growth research is of basic importance because many diseases attack the body by attacking a protein, and learning how to fight a particular disease requires an understanding of the particular protein involved and how the disease attacks it. This requires that disease be understood at a molecular level.[44]

Senator Heflin was instrumental in bringing UAB and Marshall together in this important area. Heflin was also successful getting funds to establish grants for sickle cell centers at UAB and the University of South Alabama.

    Dr. Larry DeLucas and Dr. Charles Bugg at UAB were involved in the crystal growth. Their idea was to grow bigger protein molecules which you could separate and then be able to determine various things about them. From that, cancer research and all sorts of medical research could occur. At the same time, NASA was involved in doing similar studies at the Marshall Space Flight Center, but NASA was doing it at microgravity or no gravity in space. Neither one of them knew about the other's activities. I got them together and suggested that they do things jointly. UAB and NASA have had a very successful joint effort. It was just a matter of somebody having knowledge of what each was doing. As a result they have grown crystals under UAB's direction on the shuttles, and they plan to grow them on the space station on a permanent basis. The long-range goal is to grow cells big enough so you can identify and work with them and then use the electrophoresis process to separate the molecules down to their smallest integral parts. If you do this, you may be able to make new discoveries.

    Although sickle cell anemia occurs primarily in people of African heritage, with one of 400 African-Americans affected, it also occurs in persons with a Mediterranean origin as well as from other countries. Biomedical research in this and other areas is also being conducted at Alabama A&M University and in the Tuskegee University Veterinary Medicine program.

ENVIRONMENTAL INSTITUTE FOR WASTE MANAGEMENT STUDIES. In February 1984, Heflin and Denton were part of a press conference which announced that the University of Alabama would be the home of the Environmental Institute for Waste Management Studies, a national institute to study the disposal of hazardous wastes. Money to set up the Institute came from Waste Management, Inc., of Oak Brook, Ill, which operated the toxic-waste dump at Emelle, Alabama.[45] Heflin was responsible for federal legislation which required double-lined containers at

Emelle. This is the strictest requirement of any land fill in the country.[46]

THE 1988 ELECTIONS. Nineteen eighty-eight was a presidential election year, and Heflin endorsed Senator Albert Gore as the Democratic candidate. He called Gore the only Democrat among those running who could carry the South.[47] Other Democratic candidates were Missouri Representative Richard Gephardt, Massachusetts Governor Michael Dukakis, Jesse Jackson, and Senator Paul Simon of Illionois. Republicans candidates included George Bush, Bob Dole, Pat Robertson, and Jack Kemp. In the Alabama Democratic primary in Alabama on March 8, Gore was first and Jackson second for the Democrats, while Bush was first and Dole second for the Republicans.

Colorado Senator Gary Hart, an attractive, intelligent young man with progressive ideas, had been a strong contender in the Democratic race. His presidential ambitions crashed when the news media discovered his "liberated" lifestyle. An enterprising reporter found that a pretty young lady, Donna Rice, had spent the night in the Hart residence when Hart's wife was out of town. Hart and Rice claimed it was all innocent and denied having sex with each other. However, it soon came to light that the two of them went to Bimini together on a yacht appropriately named *Monkey Business*.

As the primary season ended and the Democratic convention drew near, it became evident that Michael Dukakis was the leader and Gore didn't have a chance. Dukakis, a pro-choice liberal, had been successful as governor, but his intellectualism made him suspicious to a large segment of voters. He came across as thoughtful but not a man of great passion and immediate action. The Republicans succeeded in portraying him as very liberal, and they played the race card blatantly by generating a phony issue concerning a black man, Willie Horton, who committed a crime after being released from a Massachusetts prison.

During a visit to Birmingham, Dukakis was speaking to an audience at the Sixth Avenue Baptist Church. A woman ran down the aisle shouting, "Abortion is murder. How dare you come into a Baptist Church?" Secret Service agents hustled her out a side door. Someone in the back brought a burst of laughter with the remark, "Some people will do anything to get on TV."

Heflin, Shelby, and Congressman Tom Bevill finally endorsed Dukakis, and Heflin cracked, "It wouldn't make any difference if Attila the Hun was on the ticket. The Republicans in Alabama would classify him as being a Kennedyite."[48]

In November, Bush won a solid victory, but Democrats won control of the Senate. This meant that Democrats would be committee chairpersons. Heflin moved up a notch in seniority in the Agriculture committee and in general gained more power. He resumed chairmanship of the Ethics Committee and of subcommittees within the Judiciary Committee.

After a rule waiver allowed Heflin to take a third major committee seat, he was appointed to the Senate Energy and Natural Resources Committee. The appointment was condemned by environmentalists, who thought Heflin would not be concerned enough about global warming, but it was praised by the energy industry.[49]

Just after the election, on December 4, 1987, Howell Heflin became a grandfather for the first time. Wilson Carmichael Heflin was born to Tom, Jr. and his wife, Cornelia.

20

Iran-Contra, Bork, and the Spotlight

TWO DRAMATIC EVENTS in 1987, the Iran-Contra affair and the fight over the nomination of Robert Bork as Associate Justice on the Supreme Court, thrust Howell Heflin into the national spotlight. His involvement put him regularly on virtually every major TV news program in the United States and on a number of programs overseas.

Heflin was already becoming nationally known. His hulking frame, Southern drawl, and slow deliberate gait made him a perfect image of the stereotypic Southern politician, caricatured as Senator Foghorn Leghorn in movie cartoons and Senator Jack S. Phogbound in the comic strip *Li'l Abner*. He also knew how to keep reporters intrigued by refusing to reveal how he intended to vote and answering their queries with humorous one-liners.

On the day the Iran-Contra report came out, Heflin spoke to a crowded press conference in the Senate TV gallery, gave an interview to BBC that was carried live in Great Britain, and was on both the CBS and ABC evening news shows. He was interviewed via satellite for a live segment on *Dateline*, an Australian TV program similar to NBC's *Today*. According to Marie Cerletty, a producer in Washington for Independent Television News of London, the British liked Heflin's Southern accent and the questions he asked people involved in the arms-sale scandal. He appeared on ABC's "This week with David Brinkley," along with

Attorney General Edwin Meese and Senator Dennis DeConcini. The topic was the Justice Department under Meese.[1] This was one of several appearances on the program.

THE IRAN-CONTRA AFFAIR. The Iran-Contra affair had its roots in the Iran-Iraq War, which lasted from 1980 to 1988, and in a leftist movement in Nicaragua. U.S. policy in the war was to ensure that neither side could win, and achieving this was precarious since Iraq seemed much the stronger of the two. Iran desperately needed weapons. At the same time, the administration was seeking to obtain the release of Americans held hostage in Lebanon. In a secret deal, Iran promised to help with hostage release in return for weapons. This violated the Arms Export Control Act which required that Congress be notified prior to arms sales to foreign countries.

In Central America, the Sandinist National Liberation Front, headed by Daniel Ortega, began an armed rebellion in Nicaragua in the late 1970s and took over the country in 1979. Relations with the U.S. were strained from the start, and in 1981, the U.S. withdrew aid to the country and began supporting an anti-Sandinista group known as the "Contras." The following year, the Nicaraguan government signed an aid pact with the Soviet Union, increasing American fears of another communist government in the western hemisphere. The Contras, with U.S. support, launched a major offensive in 1984. American involvement was very controversial, and in 1985, the House passed the Boland Amendment which rejected Reagan's request for military aid to the Contras and specifically forbade such aid for two more years.

On October 5, 1986, Nicaraguan government soldiers shot down an American cargo plane that was carrying military supplies to Contra forces. One crew member survived and stated he was employed by the CIA. In November, a Lebanese publication reported that the U.S. had been secretly selling arms to Iran. Later that month, Attorney General Meese announced that the Justice Department had discovered proceeds from the Iran arms sales had been diverted to the Contras and the Contra and Iran operations were connected. National Security Advisor Admiral

John Poindexter, and his deputy, Marine Lieutenant Colonel Oliver North, resigned immediately. President Reagan said he had no knowledge of the arrangement.[2]

Heflin had his own explanation.

> The Shi'ites controlled the government in Iran. Public opinion in the U.S. was more on the side of Iraq during the Iran-Iraq War because Iran was considered a greater enemy of the United States, and we were fearful of a Shi'ite uprising. Throughout most Arab nations, the general sentiment was anti-Shi'ite. When it came out that we were selling arms to Iran, there was a big hullaboo. As I recall, 90 percent of the American people opposed arms sales to Iran.
>
> About the same time, the country was split over who the U.S. should support in Nicaragua, the Contras or the Sandinistas. Probably 55 or 60 percent thought it should be the Contras. Just as the publicity was breaking, Ed Meese discovered a document revealing details of the enterprise. It was CIA Director William Casey's idea to sell the arms and use the proceeds to help finance the Contras. This raised the question of whether it violated the Boland Amendment.
>
> I've never seen anything specific, but I've had a gut reaction that the decision was made to do something to counter criticism of our support of Iran, to reveal what had been going on and pit it against the Contra situation. The Contras would take the spotlight off of the arms sales to Iran, and it would generate a situation with 50-50 or 60-40 opposition instead of 90 percent. I always suspected that the disclosure document which caused Poindexter and North to resign wasn't accidentally found, but I can't prove it.

Since the reports potentially implicated Reagan administration officials in illegal activities, Meese sought the appointment of an Independent Counsel to investigate possible criminal wrongdoing. Lawrence E. Walsh was appointed as counsel in December 1986. Later that month, Congress decided to form a Watergate-style committee to investigate the affair.[3]

A Select Committee was set up with sixteen House members and sixteen from the Senate. Howell Heflin was a member. Senate Majority Leader, Democrat Robert Byrd of West Virginia, said, "We want fair, tough investigators who are not out to get anyone or to protect anyone."[4] Daniel K. Inouye, Democrat of Hawaii, was named committee chairman for the Senate.

> I thought it was ironic that, when Oliver North was taking his oath to tell the truth, there was Inouye, who lost his right arm in World War II, giving it to him. He had to give the oath by raising his left arm. Then Oliver North took the Fifth. I think people forget he took the Fifth, and he testified under a grant of immunity. I didn't want to grant him immunity. About three of us opposed immunity.
>
> Inouye appointed George Mitchell and me to recommend who should be the Senate counsel. We interviewed a lot of lawyers, and we finally decided on Arthur Lineman from New York. He was a good counsel. The House counsel had long hair and looked like a hippie. With all that long hair and with Oliver North in his uniform and medals, it sent a message to the Republicans and many other Americans of the difference between them.
>
> The Democrats did some sharing with the Republicans trying to make it more non-partisan or bi-partisan. When the impeachment of President Clinton came, in the beginning there was a lot of talk about Henry Hyde being so impartial and fair-minded — heck, he was on that Iran-Contra committee. I don't remember him asking a question; all he'd do was make speeches. He was always defending Reagan and defending North, whatever the issue was. You talk about someone who had a fixed mind, he was it. Anyway, they were claiming before and during the first part of the impeachment hearings that he was this fair-minded individual.

At the end of 1986, both the Select Committee and the Independent Counsel investigations were under way. In addition, a three-person commission headed by former Senator John Tower, which was appointed in December to investigate the National Security Council, turned its attention to Iran-Contra.

As the investigation proceeded, Heflin said that a disquieting undercurrent of evasion in much of the testimony was troubling, that the legal obstacles were formidable, and that his committee might never get to the bottom of the affair. National security was an issue because the CIA was involved, and many details of their operations had to remain secret. Heflin added that the investigators represented two different branches of government and could arrive at different conclusions on the best way to proceed, including the granting of immunity to witnesses to compel their testimony.[5]

The investigators wanted to question CIA Director Casey, but, as Heflin notes,

> Casey could be real slippery. I think he was the master mind. Most everybody did. They thought he figured out the enterprise and how it would operate, and I think he was giving North orders. This is my assumption. Casey had a brain tumor and died in the middle of the investigation, so nobody ever got to really question him. The lawyers never did interview him.
>
> Casey was a great mumbler. At some point, an issue came up in the Intelligence Committee about having a naval blockade around Nicaragua. Goldwater said, "You never told us anything about that." Casey said, "Yes, I did." They read the record, and it appeared he'd mumbled out something he didn't want anybody to hear. So it was in the record. Some of the most effective Congressmen weren't very articulate; they were mumblers. The official records reflected their mumbled language.
>
> You get in the large House chamber and it's hard to hear; it's even hard in the Senate. I found out I could keep up with what was going on and understand the debate better if I watched it on television in my office. Some of the senators had drone voices and would go on and on. It was difficult to understand what Monyihan said, and Hollings was awfully hard to understand because of his own special variety of Southern accent.

As the size and seriousness of the Iran-Contra affair became evident, media interest exploded. Behind it all loomed the question of how much President Reagan knew, what activities he had approved, and whether he had violated the Boland Amendment by supplying aid to the Contras, failing to inform Congress of the sale of arms to a foreign country, and failing to give Congress timely notification of covert activities.

"I don't know if Reagan knew about it the whole time," Heflin says. "It's hard to say. He was a great delegator. He gave so many people the authority to just go ahead and take action. Bud McFarlane said that he talked with Reagan and that Reagan knew. But I'm not sure. After talking a lot with Reagan, I think he really had some problems with memory. He may have had some Alzheimers when he was in office. I wouldn't express an opinion for certain on it. I thought some of it got a little rough on him, probably rougher than he deserved."

In a February 1987 speech to the Jewish Community Relation Council of New York, where he received the Henry M. Jackson Senate Leadership Award, Heflin castigated unnamed officials in the Reagan Administration for trying to pass the buck and blame Israel for the scandal. He assured his audience that the special relationship between the U.S. and Israel was strong and durable.[6] Heflin recalls that, during the speech, he said, "A moderate Iranian is one without bullets."

The Tower Commission issued a report in March 1987 which was tough on the administration. In an article titled "Can He Recover?" *Time* magazine said the report gave the picture of an inattentive, out-of-touch President and out-of-control operatives in and around the White House. It called Reagan a President in deep trouble.[7]

In a thirteen-minute nationally televised speech March 4, President Reagan acknowledged for the first time that his administration had swapped arms for hostages, and he said this had been a mistake. He admitted he earlier said that arms had not been traded for hostages. He said, "My heart and my best intentions still tell me that is true, but the facts and the evidence tell me it is not."[8] The speech was credited with saving his presidency.[9]

Former national security adviser Robert C. McFarlane testified to the committee for four days, and Heflin called it a bravura display which made it difficult to tell where truth and responsibility lay. McFarlane repeatedly declared that he bore the brunt of responsibility for the mistakes of the affair.[10] He testified that he had conferred with Reagan about a bribe-and-ransom program to win release of the American hostages in Lebanon, and he added that Reagan had approved the program in writing.

Admiral Poindexter testified in July that the Reagan administration decided to sell arms secretly to Iran beginning in 1985 without consulting the chairman of the Joint Chiefs of Staff, the nation's top military officer. He also testified that Reagan consulted Secretary of Defense Casper Weinberger before deciding to go ahead with the sales.[11]

OLIVER NORTH. Investigators found a huge file of computer messages which were exchanged among members of the National Security Council staff, much of it between Lt. Colonel Oliver North and Admiral Poindexter. North, a graduate of the Naval Academy and a Vietnam veteran, turned out to be a key figure in the affair. He had handled many details, including collecting and distributing money. He had knowingly violated the law and was in danger of prosecution. In July 1987, he finally agreed to appear before the Congressional committee.

North was very feisty in his testimony, and he became something of a national hero. People didn't seem to mind that he had broken the law. A large number, particularly in the South, called Congressional offices to support him. Heflin commented in a television interview that, although he admired North's courage, he worried about the danger posed by an "unbridled individual" breaking the law. A barber shop operator in Anniston commented, "Senator Heflin ought to know better than that. All these Democratic Congressmen just set out on this thing to embarrass President Reagan, and these hearings are backfiring on them."[12]

Many people considered North the scapegoat who was to absorb political heat from the affair. North reported that when the affair started to unravel, CIA Director Casey said someone had to stand up and take the hit, "and I shared that belief." After hearing Meese at a press conference, his mind changed from protecting superiors to protecting himself. He said he removed personal notebooks from his office that day and took them home to use as a potential defense.[13]

Heflin questioned North on July 13 and seemed worried about political fallout in Alabama. He did not tear into North in the manner of a prosecutor, as many expected. The *Huntsville Times* editorialized, "Heflin, a folksy type who is above all else careful to not offend constituents, sort of waltzed around North with questions that hardly challenged the newly anointed hero. The senator's performance led a letter writer to declare that Heflin 'did not make sense' and that his style 'evoked the smell of new-mown hay as well as other pasture products.'"[14]

Heflin bristles when reminded of this editorial.

> I was trying to act like a judge more than a prosecutor. I was trying to establish with North what the operation cost. He first said it cost $1 million a month to keep the Contras going. We brought out some facts, and he changed it to $5 million a month.
>
> We didn't want to just come out and say it, but he knew we were investigating the strong possibility that the Contras were involved in a drug deal. They were financing some of their activities through drug money. Of course, we didn't have any proof, but there was a lot of suspicion. I was examining North trying to establish some facts that Linman wanted in regards to costs. I don't think it came over to the public what I was doing. You know, editorials and columnists are going to give you the devil anyway, particularly if they are of a different political persuasion. They have a predisposition to do that.

FAWN HALL. Fawn Hall, the comely, 27-year-old former secretary of North was scheduled to testify in May after she was granted limited immunity. She had said previously that she helped North shred documents shortly before he resigned from the National Security Council. She was expected to testify that she hid documents in her underclothes in order to remove them from the White House. Speaking to reporters in his office, Heflin said, "I suppose she will testify that she stuffed documents in her brassiere and other clothes as she left. I think that's been in the papers, hasn't it? She had a pretty good capacity to carry documents."[15] When several reporters told him they had not heard that account, he said, "I thought I'd seen this. Hasn't this been in the papers?"

Fawn Hall blasted back, "I was shocked to hear what Senator Heflin said about me smuggling documents out in my bra. It is untrue. It is outrageous that he would say that, and it is certainly sexist."[16] The incident received a good amount of media attention.

> It never did come out, but when I had the press interview, I had been told about her some time beforehand. Lineman's staff had interviewed each of the witnesses or had talked to their lawyers. She knew basically what she was going to say. Our lawyers said that she carried out documents in her brassiere and other underclothes. When I was being interviewed, they asked me what she was going to testify, and I said it. I thought it had already appeared in print when the reporters asked me. Then I was afraid maybe I had violated some rule of the committee. Later, I checked and I hadn't. I might have been a little flippant when I was asked about it and shouldn't have been. But anyway, when she came before the committee, my wife gave me instructions, "Don't you get into that stuff." I just stayed away from it. Anyway, she admitted she carried the documents hidden in her undergarments.
>
> A lot of the media thought I chickened out. I could have said I didn't invent the idea that she carried the documents out in her brassiere. When it came up in the hearings, I didn't chicken out, I was just following my wife's orders.

A few months after the Hall incident, Heflin was to speak before the Alabama League of Municipalities convention. In introducing him, Tuskegee Mayor Johnny Ford said he wasn't going to say anything about underwear. "Neither am I," Heflin retorted.[17]

CONCLUSION OF THE INVESTIGATION. In late July 1987, many Committee members said it was clear that President Reagan was fed deliberately falsified intelligence reports that led him to support U.S. arms sales to Iran.[18] Member Lee Hamilton, Democrat of Indiana, said the hearings showed confusion in the White House and a lack of crisp and clear presidential decisions, unclear lines of authority and accountability, excessive secrecy that cut from decisions the very people best equipped to make them, and over-reliance on private citizens and foreigners to carry out U.S. foreign Policy.[19] The Congressional Committee report, published November 18, 1987, said that President Reagan was derelict in carrying out his constitutional duties.

The Independent Counsel's investigation continued several years, and his report was published in 1993 after both Reagan and Bush had left the White House. Among other things, the report stated that the Iran operations were carried out with the knowledge of President Reagan, Vice President Bush, Secretary of State George P. Shultz, Secretary of Defense Casper W. Weinberger, and others. It also said that senior administration officials engaged in a concerted effort to deceive Congress and the public about their knowledge of and support for the operations. "In an important sense, this strategy succeeded," the report concluded. "Independent Counsel discovered much of the best evidence of the cover-up in the final year of active investigation, too late for most prosecutions."[20]

"The Independent Counsel had a pretty tough row to hoe because they had granted North and the others immunity," Heflin notes. "Then the White House would not turn over documents, claiming they were classified or had executive privilege. The Independent Counsel was never able to collect enough information to get a court decision as to whether they were classified or not."

In the end, fourteen persons were charged with criminal offenses. Eleven were convicted, but two of the convictions were overturned on appeal. Two persons were pardoned before trial, and one case was dismissed when the Bush Administration would not declassify information necessary for trial. In March 1988, McFarlane had pleaded guilty to criminal charges of withholding information from Congress on secret aid to the Contras. In 1989, he was fined $20,000 and given two year's probation. On December 24, 1992, a few days before he left office, President Bush pardoned Casper W. Weinberger, Robert C. McFarlane, and four others who were charged.

Oliver North was convicted in May 1989 of accepting an illegal gratuity, aiding and abetting in the obstruction of a Congressional inquiry, and destruction of documents. He was sentenced to a three-year suspended prison term, two years probation, $150,000 in fines, and 1,200 hours community service. A three-judge appeals panel vacated North's conviction, and charges against him were dismissed in September 1991 on the grounds that witnesses were tainted by his nationally televised testimony. Also, he had been given immunity.

THE BORK HEARINGS. In 1987, Associate Justice Lewis F. Powell, who was 79, announced his retirement from the Supreme Court. To replace him, President Reagan nominated Robert H. Bork, a staunchly conservative appeals court judge who was serving on the D. C. Circuit Court of Appeals. The appointment was crucial because Powell was the swing vote between liberals and conservatives on many important decisions, and appointment of a conservative could swing the court. The nomination created a battle royale between liberals and conservatives, Democrats and Republicans.

Control of the judiciary was central to this battle. President Nixon succeeded in the six years he was president in making the federal courts more conservative, and President Ford attempted to continue the trend. Ronald Reagan was in office eight years, and by happenstance, a large number of Supreme Court justices and lower court judges reached retirement age during his term. Reagan appointed three Supreme Court justices, and he elevated another, William Rehnquist, to chief justice. His three appointees joined two other conservative justices in giving the court a conservative majority. Reagan appointed 41 percent of the judges on the federal appeals courts and 39 percent of those on federal district courts, and he appointed a majority of the judges on circuit courts.[21]

There is no question that the federal judiciary was turned significantly in a conservative direction during the Reagan years.

Robert Bork was born in Pittsburgh, Pennsylvania. He received his undergraduate and law degrees at the University of Chicago and was for a time a partner in a law firm. Later he taught constitutional law at Yale Law School.

During the Nixon administration, Bork served as Solicitor General, the lawyer who represents the United States government before the Supreme Court. He played a minor role in the Watergate scandal in 1973. The existence of secret tape recordings of Nixon's conversations in the White House had been discovered, and Watergate Special Prosecutor Archibald Cox insisted that Nixon turn over the tapes. Nixon resisted.

In an episode the night of October 20, 1973, which became known as the "Saturday Night Massacre," Nixon's Chief of Staff, Alexander Haig, ordered Attorney General Elliot Richardson to dismiss Cox. Richardson refused and resigned. Deputy Attorney General William Ruckelshaus was then asked to fire Cox, but he also refused and resigned. Bork, the next in line of the attorneys general, then fired Cox.[22]

When Bork was nominated, Reagan had eighteen months before the end of his term to get a conservative nominee confirmed by the Senate, and he set the stage for controversy by selecting a candidate favored by the far-right.

"Bork had been everything in his political and social outlook," Heflin notes. "He started out as a socialist and had gone to Communist party meetings. Then he changed his philosophy and became conservative. He claimed this was the evolving of his mind as he went through life. He evolved from one extreme to the other, and I really had some questions as to his stability. If he had evolved that much, there's no telling to where he could continue evolving. He was the 'evolving' nominee."

In recent statements and writings, Bork criticized the constitutionality of a number of Supreme Court decisions involving individual rights. He argued for a restrictive interpretation of the Fourteenth Amendment with regard to sex and had written statements which cast doubt on his commitment to equal rights for all citizens. Bork had argued that the right to individual privacy was not guaranteed either explicitly or implicitly by the Constitution, and he criticized court decisions which struck down laws because they impinged on privacy. He had also written that the First Amendment applied only to political speech. There was an overwhelming consensus in the legal and political communities that Robert Bork would shift the balance and overturn a number of Supreme Court precedents on very fundamental civil rights issues.[23]

The Mobile *Inner City News* editorialized, "President Reagan must be kidding. He nominates another arch conservative for the life-long position of U.S. Supreme Court Justice. Then he has the gall to say, 'I hope that we can keep politics out of the confirmation process.' . . . The opinions of the nominee, Robert H. Bork, are more than conservative reflections. They seek to take us back to a time when the rights of African Americans, other racial and ethnic groups, and women were of no worth."[24]

Former President Jimmy Carter called Bork "an obnoxious, extreme-right radical." He added that he would support Heflin for the Supreme Court.[25] Heflin added, "Carter suggested my appointment to the Court during a speech in Tuscaloosa. After Bork was turned down, I was told there was a short list of five at the White House with my name on it. Orin Hatch was on it, and Anthony Kennedy was on it, along with two other folks."

The Bork hearings began September 15, 1987, and they immediately thrust Heflin back into the national spotlight. The Judiciary Committee had eight Democrats and six Republicans. The votes of eleven members were split along party lines and were predictable. The battle focused on three centrist senators, Heflin, Democrat Dennis DeConcini of Arizona, and Republican Arlen Specter of Pennsylvania.

Heflin said he usually felt that the President is entitled to have his nominees, but he noted that in this case Reagan set the stage for an all-out battle between the Senate's liberals and its "far-right" conservatives. "It'll be the 'kamikazes' against the Alamo."[26]

Heflin said he would use the hearings to find out whether Bork was a conservative within the mainstream of American judicial thought or a radical extremist with an agenda for turning back the clock on certain decisions of the Supreme Court. He said he would not decide how to vote until the proper time, again withholding his conclusions until the last possible moment in a behavior pattern which was becoming familiar.[27]

By early September, Heflin was spending several hours a day reviewing position papers on Bork, opinions Bork had written since Reagan appointed him to the U.S. Circuit Court of Appeals, and other Bork writings.[28] After reading the record, he commented, "The guy's a flake."

The judiciary committee hearings on the Bork nomination were intensely partisan and full of tension. Bork was questioned intensively about his stands on abortion, on women's rights, on precedent in Supreme Court rulings, and on freedom of speech. He denied he was a racist or opposed equality for women.[29] Heflin raised the abortion issue, and Bork refused to say how he would vote.[30]

He was accused of altering some of his views simply to obtain confirmation. In response to questions from Heflin, he said he had been consistent as a lawyer, as solicitor general, and as a judge. Heflin responded, "Well, there are those that raise the issue that you began changing your position on certain issues only at a time when a carrot was being dangled before your eyes, when you knew that you'd have to face questioning on your behavior as solicitor general and again when you came up for the U.S. Court of Appeals." Heflin said he wished he was a psychiatrist so he could figure out what Bork would do on the Supreme Court.[31]

Heflin was the first panel member to question Bork on his personal life when he asked why the candidate wore a red beard. This momentarily broke the tension of the hearings. Bork responded that he grew the beard on a canal boat cruise in Europe because the bathroom was too small to shave in, and after a week, "my children had become fascinated with what was then the beginnings of a red beard. They asked me to let it grow, so I did."

Predictably, Heflin was criticized for the question. It wasn't relevant the critics said, and it reflected the Senator's red-neck background and constituency. Howell defends himself. "When I asked the question about his beard, everybody was curious but nobody would ask him. I tried to word it some way or another so it wouldn't embarrass him. 'Well, I've been noticing you and there has been a lot of curiosity about your beard. Do you mind telling us about it?' There was nothing wrong with it. I said I wanted that cleared up because there were a lot of bearded voters out there, and we even had some in Alabama." Heflin added, "Why, my man, Raby, in my office even has a beard." "That just about embarrassed my mother to death." Raby remembers.[32]

Mike House recalls that the business community in Alabama decided this was going to be their *cause celebre*. "They start calling Heflin and saying, 'you've got to be for Bork.' I don't think it was Bork as much as their own egos. Their attitude was, 'By God, we want him to be for Bork.'"[33] At the end of September, Heflin's office said that mail had initially been overwhelming for Bork, but as the hearings progressed it had become almost even.[34] Near the end of the hearings, The *Atlanta Journal and Constitution* published results of a twelve-state poll which showed that 51 percent of Southerners opposed Bork, and only 31 percent were for him.[35]

"I must have received 65-75,000 pieces of mail," Heflin recalls, "and the phones just rang off the wall. They were mostly orchestrated. When he was first nominated, the right-wing groups started putting it out. It was something. All of a sudden we received stacks and stacks of telegrams that had the same message. We had about fifteen different spellings of Bork in those telegrams when the liberal women's groups started their campaign. Altogether, this was the greatest example of orchestration I ever saw."

Heflin regularly discussed the proceedings with his Democratic colleagues. "After a while in the Bork situation, you could see how the hearing was going. We had in the Senate what we called the 'Inner-Sanctum,' a dining room for senators only. There was the regular Senate dining room where you'd carry your guests, but there's this room off to the side where only senators could go to eat. There were actually two rooms. One had a table for Republicans, and in the back were the

Democrats. They wouldn't allow staff or anybody else in there. During all the Bork hearings, I would go in the Inner-Sanctum and get with the Democrats. They'd want to know what was going on, and I'd report to them. As I heard him more and more, I started to lean against him, and I am reasonably sure I influenced some in the Inner-Sanctum."

As the hearings drew to a close in October, Senator DeConcini announced he would vote against confirmation, and this was the seventh negative vote on the fourteen-person committee. This assured that the committee would not approve Bork, but left it undecided whether it would tie and give no recommendation or recommend against confirmation. Despite a twenty-minute White House meeting in which President Reagan was "quite vigorous in his arm twisting," Heflin remained undecided.[36]

Reporters saw that the committee was divided evenly and that Senator Heflin would cast the deciding vote. He became the center of attention, with reporters following him around trying to get some indication of how he was leaning. Heflin played it close to the vest, making the most of his hour in the limelight and answering with humorous remarks which gave no hint.

On October 7, 1987, Heflin voted against confirmation at the nationally televised committee vote. The actual vote was nine to five against confirmation, with Republican Senator Arlen Specter joining in the "no" vote.[37] Heflin also voted against Bork in the full Senate where the nomination was defeated.

The full Senate voted, Heflin explains, because it was a Supreme Court appointment, and "the committee felt that the full Senate ought to decide. They voted to report it to the full Senate but with a negative recommendation. The committee was not obliged to report back to the Senate. If nominees didn't get a majority, then they were killed at the committee. A lot of times the leadership didn't want the nomination debated before the full Senate.

The bottom line in his decision, Heflin said, was that he did not know how Bork would treat essential, fundamental rights in his rulings.

With me it was close on Bork. I tried to get the full facts and listen to all the arguments, but you've got to vote one way or another. In the House, they don't always vote, but in the Senate you're going to have to vote one way or another. I finally decided that, regardless of whether or not I agree with *Roe v. Wade*, I do believe in the right to privacy, and unlike Judge Bork, I do see it in the Constitution.

There is no right of privacy specifically mentioned in the Constitution. Some members of the Supreme Court have said that the right of privacy is contained within the word "liberty," that liberty is a comprehensive word and among its several component parts is privacy. You can base the right to be left alone from the government on liberty, and so on. That makes sense to me, and I think it's important. In other opinions, they said it is a basic right that is implied. The right of privacy is the right on which *Roe v. Wade* was based.

Robert Novak and Robert Evans wrote in their column on October 20, 1987, that the rejection of Bork by the Senate triggered the 500-point drop in the Dow-Jones average on what became known as "Black Monday." "When Senator Howell Heflin of Alabama announced his opposition on October 6, signaling the markets that conservative Southerners were deserting Reagan, the Dow Jones fell almost 50 points in an hour."[38] A week later, Randy Quarles of the *Huntsville Times* joked, "The columnists may be on to something. A careful examination of the facts reveals that every fluctuation in the stock market indeed does coincide with some action or non-action on Heflin's part."[39]

Reagan next nominated Douglas H. Ginsburg, a federal appeals court judge from Washington. It turned out that Ginsburg had used marijuana in the 1960s and 1970s when he was at Harvard as a law professor, and he asked that his name be withdrawn.

The third person nominated for the position was Anthony Kennedy, a federal appeals court judge from California. In January 1988, Kennedy was unanimously approved by the Judiciary Committee. He was confirmed by the Senate and was sworn in on February 18.

Since leaving the bench, Robert Bork has assumed the role of conservative scholar. A senior fellow at the American Enterprise Institute, he recently wrote a best-selling book, *Slouching Toward Gomorrah*, which is considered on the fringe even by many on the right. According to one reviewer, the book "burns with contempt for the court and its current members, whose rulings, he proposes, should be subject to reversal by a simple majority in Congress."[40]

Ten years after the hearings, the *New York Times* commented, "Among the Bork opponents, it is an article of faith that there is a deeper meaning to the story, that the effect of successfully depicting Bork as 'out of the mainstream' was to define the mainstream itself in a way that ratified the modern course of constitutional law, unenumerated rights and all."[41]

REHNQUIST AND SCALIA. President Reagan nominated Associate Justice William H. Rehnquist to be chief justice when Warren E. Burger retired in 1986. Rehnquist had originally been named to the Court by President Nixon. Liberals complained that Rehnquist was too conservative, but he was approved, with Heflin among those who voted for him. "Every stream has a right bank and a left bank," Heflin said, and he observed that Rehnquist's views were "always close to the right boundary of the stream. But they are within the mainstream of modern judicial thought."[42]

The elevation of Rehnquist created a vacancy on the Court, and Reagan nominated Antonin Scalia, a judge on United States Court of Appeals for the District of Columbia Circuit and a strong conservative. Scalia went through the hearings with little trouble and was sworn in on September 26, 1986.

> Scalia and Rehnquist were nominated back to back, with no intervening time. The liberals decided they were going after Rehnquist instead of Scalia. They spent all their time rehashing the confirmation Rehnquist had gone through when he was nominated as an associate justice. They went back to his activities in Arizona when he had been a Republican and a big political operator. I think they made a mistake. Everybody knew who Rehnquist was. He had a conservative record and

was going to be conservative. When Scalia was questioned, he just said, "I'm not going to answer that; it might come up before the court." They let him off because they were tired.

All the Italians in the Senate were introducing Scalia. Senator D'Amato said, "This is ah the great-is-est a day for the Italian Americans in the his-i-tory of the country. Mama sends her love to you, Antonio." Then here comes Domenici who's Italian, "It's the great-is-est ah day for the Italian Americans." And then DeConcini and two or three others who were Italian. It was surprising how many Irishmen were half Italian. It came my time, and I told them, "I want to welcome you to the hearing on behalf of the 4,329 Italian Americans in Alabama, and I would be remiss if I didn't tell you that my great-grandfather married a widow who had been previously married to an Italian American."

OTHER NOMINEES. Heflin was also involved in other nomination processes. In 1990, President Bush nominated David H. Souter to be an associate justice. In the twenty-two years since he left private law practice, Souter had not given a speech, written a law review article or taken a position on the correctness of the Supreme Court's precedents on abortion or any other issue. Heflin called him the "stealth nominee" because nobody knew anything about him or his background. However, with Heflin's vote, Souter was confirmed by the Senate and was sworn into office on October 9, 1990.

Early in 1989, President Bush nominated John Tower, former senator from Texas, to be Secretary of Defense. Tower was accused of drinking and philandering.[43] Heflin would not commit himself on Tower even after President Bush met privately with him in the White House to urge confirmation.[44] Asked about Tower's alleged "womanizing," Heflin said that maybe other people were "manizing" because two people are required for sexual liaisons.[45]

Heflin spent a lot of time reading all the FBI reports on Tower, and noted that he had never personally witnessed any misconduct. Heflin remarked, "I asked my wife — you know the Senate wives meet and have been known to gossip on occasion — 'Did you ever hear anything about his excessive drinking or being drunk?' She said, 'No, I haven't heard anything about that.'"

In a speech to the Senate, Heflin indicated he was willing to give Tower a chance, "Giving one a chance to prove himself or herself is one of the great redeeming values of the American way of life." But even with Heflin's support, Tower was rejected, and it was Bush's first major defeat.[46]

In 1989, President Bush nominated William C. Lucas to head the Civil Rights Division of the Justice Department, and civil rights groups claimed that the nominee lacked the experience needed for the job. Lucas had a law degree but had never argued a case in court. He was born in Harlem, had worked for the FBI and the Justice Department, was sheriff and chief executive of Wayne County, Michigan. When asked during the hearings about his view on recent Supreme Court rulings, he drew a gasp when he answered, "I'm new to the law."[47]

Heflin was the swing vote in the Judiciary Committee, and held up a vote on the nomination so that he could study new information. A few days later Heflin voted no, and his was the deciding vote. Heflin said, "I do not believe I can state strongly enough my belief in the substantive and symbolic importance of nominating blacks to these positions. However, when I weighed the evidence, I found that Mr. Lucas simply was not qualified to head the Civil Rights Division. The head of the Division has more responsibility perhaps than any other single individual for ensuring the security of our civil rights. The individual who assumes this role should be well qualified to deal with the intricacies of the law."

JEFFERSON SESSIONS. An interesting confirmation hearing for Senator Heflin was that of Jefferson Sessions, a U.S. Attorney from Mobile, Alabama, who was nominated by President Reagan to become a federal district judge in Alabama. On June 5, 1986, the Senate Judiciary Committee voted 8-6 against recommending him. He had what one newspaper called "a record splotched with racist remarks, slurs on respected social-activist groups and the questionable prosecution of civil rights workers who later were acquitted." All of this showed a gross insensitivity to racial matters, it was argued, and this alone disqualified him.[48]

> Admiral Denton, who was a Senator then, was Sessions's big sponsor, and he was big on giving testimony. Denton interrupted the schedule to put on a man who was going to be out of Washington for a while. The witness was J. Gerald Herbert, Senior Trial Attorney, Civil Rights Division in the United States Department of Justice and had worked with Sessions on numerous cases during the past five years.

Steve Raby recalls that the witness really killed Sessions. "It was not so much what the witness said but what transpired. Senator Denton was reading these questions and asked, 'In the sense that you believe he would do what he says, do you believe he could be a fair and impartial judge?' Senator Denton never looked up because he was supposed to get 'yes' or 'no' and go forward. But there was no answer. Denton looked up, and the man was still sitting there. Silence gathered everyone's attention. I don't remember if Senator Denton actually said something else to the witness or just waited. Finally Mr. Herbert replied, 'I would hope he could; I do not know.' Now, this was a Justice Department lawyer who had worked with the U.S. Attorney in Mobile on civil rights vote fraud cases."[49]

The hearing continued with Senator Joseph Biden's question:

"Let me be more specific. It is a tough question to ask you. Based on the comments that Mr. Sessions has made to you, in jest or to challenge or in seriousness, whatever the context or the collection of contexts, if you left the Justice Department and were handling a case for the NAACP, a voting rights case, and it came before Judge Sessions, would you not at least raise the question with co-counsel and/or your client that you should make a motion to recuse Judge Sessions on that case?"

Mr. Herbert answered, "I would certainly raise the issue, absolutely." [50]

Senator Heflin's position can be summed up in a June 7, 1986, editorial written by Richard J. Hughes for the *Philadelphia Inquirer*:

Sen. Howell Heflin (D., Ala.) cast the critical vote Thursday leading the Senate Judiciary Committee to kill the nomination of Jefferson B. Sessions III for a federal judgeship. It is the first time any of President Reagan's district court nominees has been rejected.

Mr. Sessions' record of racial insensitivity persuaded all seven other Democrats on Judiciary, as well as Republicans Charles Mathais of Maryland and Arlen Specter of Pennsylvania, that he was unfit to be given lifetime federal judicial authority. But it was a much harder choice for Sen. Heflin because Mr. Sessions is an Alabamian, and the judgeship was in Alabama. Quite obviously Sen. Heflin stood to offend far more voters than he gained by opposing the Sessions nomination - but that's what he did.

"I regret that I cannot vote for confirmation," said Sen. Heflin, a former chief justice of the Alabama Supreme Court, when his turn came, "but my duty to uphold the Constitution and my duty to the justice system is greater than any duty to any individual."

That took courage. He didn't waver either—unlike Sen. Specter, who first voted against Mr. Session, but then voted to send his nomination to the full Senate anyhow to give him one more shot at confirmation. Sen. Heflin opposed that ploy too, and because he did, the nomination died on a tie 9-9 vote.

Sen. Heflin did his duty. Let everyone who would presume to serve in elective office reflect on the gravity of his words and emulate his courageous example of what public service is all about.

When the vote came up, I said I was in doubt because this was a lifetime appointment. If his appointment were for a four-year or a six-year term, I probably would have voted for Sessions. But since it was lifetime and I had so many questions I had not resolved in my mind, I voted no. The *Mobile Register* had a scathing editorial and called me a traitor and a Benedict Arnold.

Actually, throughout the hearings the newspaper did something I had never seen before. They went on an advocacy roll where they ran

"write or phone Senator Heflin" in boxes all over the paper. I thought it was unusual for a newspaper to tell its readers to write, call, or telegraph some senator on a specific issue. Maybe it was all right. I sort of thought they lost their perspective a bit.

Afterward Jeff Sessions was elected attorney general of Alabama. He hired Richard Allen, who was my finest law clerk when I was on the Supreme Court, to be his chief deputy. Sessions was a law school classmate of Richard. Richard straightened out a lot of our differences. Since Jeff has been in the Senate, he has been exceptionally nice to me.

Senator Dennis DeConcini, Democrat of Arizona, commented on the Senate floor on the June 6, 1986, *Register* editorial. Noting that the paper had used the words "traitor" and "Benedict Arnold," DeConcini called it a "vicious personal and thoroughly unwarranted attack on one of the fairest men in the United States Senate."[51]

ON THE JUDICIAL TEMPERAMENT. Heflin's judicial temperament, his insistence on getting all of the facts and weighing them carefully before he made a decision, disappointed people who wanted a more partisan, aggressive approach. They could not understand that he was going to make up his own mind and not follow a predefined position.

The *Washington Post* commented, "Senator Howell T. Heflin, D-Ala, has entrenched himself as one of Washington's larger mysteries. Again and again, circumstances have handed this folksy hulk of a Southerner — affectionately dubbed Mount Heflin — a chance to play the role of a bold statesman on judicial matters. Again and again, he has demurred, or tried to."[53]

In discussing his demeanor, Heflin says, "I always tried to keep an open mind until the end of hearings, because I believe hearings are meaningless if senators do not examine the facts impartially. I consistently articulated the view that we, as senators, needed to act as judges in the confirmation process."

Ralph Neas, former executive director of the Leadership Conference on Civil Rights, says, "One of the things that many of us like most about Senator Heflin is his deliberative nature, and he's called the Judge, not just because he was a Supreme Court Judge in Alabama, but because that really is his temperament. He is a very thoughtful, methodical thinker, and weighs all the pros and the cons."[54]

Heflin notes that the voters didn't seem to mind his deliberative manner. "I was often criticized as being indecisive because I withheld my decision until the end of committee consideration. I got reelected by a 61 percent margin later, so maybe the people didn't fall out with me altogether when that came up."

21

Bane of Environmentalists

SENATOR HEFLIN was consistently on the progressive side in social issues, and this gained admiration even from those who disagreed with him. In the area of environmental concerns, however, his logic and explanations weren't clear-cut, and he created ill feelings which persist to this day. He was slow to grasp the motivations of environmentalists and the subtleties of their movement and concerns.

Heflin defended himself against environmentalists' criticisms by explaining that he had to weigh consideration for the environment with economic concerns and the need to create jobs, and he often referred to environmentalists as extremists, people ready to take jobs from workers in carrying out cockeyed schemes. As he admits today, he was very conservative on matters of the environment when he arrived in the Senate.

THE SIPSEY WILDERNESS FIGHT. Irritation with Heflin grew to major proportions through the 1980s during the fight to expand the Sipsey Wilderness in the Bankhead National Forest in northern Alabama. This controversy dragged on six years and generated much controversy.

The first Sipsey Wilderness bill was introduced to Congress in April 1971 by Senators Jim Allen and John Sparkman. Representatives Bob Jones and Tom Bevill introduced a similar bill in the House. As a result, in 1975, a wilderness with 12,726 acres was created and was Alabama's first federally designated wilderness area.

Representative Ronnie Flippo introduced a bill to enlarge the Sipsey in 1981. He was supported by Lawrence County residents who would be most affected, and his bill had the endorsement of Governor Fob James.[1] The House approved the bill in July. Either Senators Heflin or Denton had to introduce similar legislation in the Senate. They hesitated.

In a related action, Representative Bill Nichols in May 1982 introduced a bill which would designate another area of the state, 6,700 acres along the ridge of the Talladega Mountains south of Cheaha State Park, as "wilderness." This would protect the land and set up the Odum Scout Trail. Heflin and Denton announced they would support Nichols' bill when it came up in the Senate.[2]

The House passed legislation which included both the Sipsey and Cheaha areas in August, and the White House announced its opposition. The bill was controversial because it removed land from commercial development. Denton wanted the Sipsey taken out of the wilderness bill because, he said, he needed more time to study it.[3] In November, Heflin said he supported the Sipsey Wilderness, but was uncertain how big it should be.[4]

As hearings got under way, Heflin told the Senate Committee on Energy and Natural Resources that he was a "wilderness fan but not a wilderness fanatic," and he asked the Committee to consider the economic impact of the proposed legislation. He said, "We cannot afford to lose a single wage earner through the enactment of any piece of legislation."[5] The Committee approved the Cheaha early in December but delayed action on the Sipsey. The Cheaha bill was passed in December, and President Reagan signed it the next month.

In April 1983, Flippo again introduced legislation to enlarge the Sipsey, this time with the endorsement of Governor Fob James, the Alabama Department of Conservation and Natural Resources, the state's major newspapers, Chambers of Commerce, tourism agencies, and a host of other elected officials.[6] Heflin said little until August, when he announced he was seeking a compromise. He felt the acreage in the bill was too large. "The projections are that by the year 2000 there is going to be a serious shortage of lumber in Alabama," he said. "It's not that big a deal with most folks in Alabama. Primarily the most ardent Sipsey supporters are elitists who want to backpack or be bird watchers."[7]

Heflin received a lot of flack for the last remark. State Representative Roger Dutton, who supported the bill, said that his grandfather was buried in the area that would be included. "Being an elitist," Dutton said sarcastically, "he drove a garbage truck in Moulton most of his life."[8]

Heflin and Denton pigeonholed the bill, and it did not come up for Senate action in the 1983 Congressional session. It could be taken up the next session in 1984 since it was the same Congress. Heflin was roundly criticized by papers across the state, including the *Birmingham News*, which called Flippo's bill "a beneficial piece of legislation."[9]

In April 1984, the Forest Service proposed designating twenty-eight miles of the west branch of the Sipsey River as part of the National Wild and Scenic Rivers System. Heflin said he was optimistic the proposal would lead to a compromise in the fight. No further action was taken in the 98th Congress, so again, Flippo's bill died.[10]

In January 1985, after a new Congress was seated, proponents of the Sipsey offered to compromise and cut the size of the area to be added to the wilderness from 28,000 acres to 17,972 acres.[11] Three months later, the Forest Service issued a report that had been requested by Denton, which recommended expanding the Sipsey by 9,793 acres.[12]

Finally, in December 1985, all sides agreed to a four-part compromise, which would:

1) Add 10,900 acres to the Sipsey Wilderness.

2) Designate the West Fork of the Sipsey River and its major tributaries, about 9,500 acres, as part of the National Wild and Scenic River System.

3) Designate as "semi-primitive" approximately 15,000 acres of land adjoining the Sipsey Wilderness. This action would restrict timber cutting and mandate management of the forest.

4) Create a wilderness out of 8,460-acre Dugger Mountain in the Talladega National Forest in East Alabama.[13]

Heflin prepared and distributed a draft bill in April 1986. It included 10,000 acres, 900 less than the December compromise. Heflin's plan allowed cars, trucks and other motorized vehicles on all existing roads in the area, authorized the Department of Agriculture to build a dam as part of the "Wild and Scenic River" system, ordered the Department of Agriculture to build a paved road from a public highway to the new lake, and established a "National Recreation Area" around the Sipsey Wilderness Area and the lake.[14] The following August, Heflin introduced his bill to the Senate.

Before introducing legislation in the House, Flippo worked with Heflin and Denton to reach a compromise that could go through both houses of Congress quickly. On September 13, Flippo introduced a bill that added 7,700 acres. He had deliberately waited until Heflin introduced the Senate bill before taking the compromise to the House. A House committee approved Flippo's bill after deleting provisions for a dam and lake, and it was passed by the full House on September 30.

Heflin delayed things by insisting that the legislation contain provisions for fighting the Southern pine beetle in the Sipsey. The 99th Congress adjourned in October without the issue being settled. Heflin came under heavy criticism again for failure of the legislation to pass. He countered by blaming national environmentalists.

In September 1988, Heflin and Flippo reached a compromise that would add 13,260 acres to the Sipsey. It would also preserve 5,085 acres in the West Fork Sipsey River by giving it National Wild and Scenic River designation and add 710 acres to the 6,700-acre Cheaha Wilderness Area in the Talladega National Forest. Identical bills were introduced in the House and Senate.[15] They quickly cleared both the House and Senate and were passed into law.

> I've got problems philosophically with just creating a wilderness. The Forest Service has done a pretty good job of timber management. You can't even build a road through a wilderness.
> One of the issues we had when I first went to the Senate was a wilderness in Alaska. The issue was about setting aside some fifteen

million acres of land. Well, I reckon Alaska has a lot of wasted land that nobody would use. But I felt the Bankhead Forest, where the Sipsey is, was under good management.

I have great admiration for Congressman Ronnie Flippo, and he was pushing it. I felt terrible not being able to support what he was trying to push through. Ronnie is a friend, and he had helped us with the Judicial Article when he was in the legislature. I finally went along as a favor to Flippo. I'm not a wilderness fan. Oh, it's all right to have some of it, but if you've already got something like 20,000 acres, that's enough to wander around in and watch birds.

These newspaper editorial writers, they love the wilderness. They love all the environmental issues, even though they're conservative on everything else. I think it's sort of elitist to show they have an understanding of the ozone or various things like global warming and the effect of it. You have to have some knowledge of science to understand some of these things.

ACID RAIN, COAL, AND COKE. Early in Heflin's Senate career, one of the big issues before Congress was acid rain, which was in Maine, Canada, New Hampshire, and Vermont.

You don't hear much about it now. Supposedly, acid rain came from sulfur dioxide that was released in heavy industrial areas in the Midwest. The prevailing wind would carry it eastward and dump it on the Northeast. Those concerned with the issue had a lot of scientists who established this theory; there was no question that the forests were dying in the Northeast. Scientists on the other side said the dioxide would diffuse in traveling a thousand miles and the death of the forests was due to other causes.

George Mitchell was the Majority Leader of the Senate, and he was a Democrat. He was from Maine, and acid rain was his number one priority. He was going to get the Clean Air Act passed.

Then supporters expanded the proposed legislation to cover all emissions that could affect clean air. First was the issue of steam plants that were operated by fossil fuels, either by coal or by oil. Coal was used almost exclusively in steam plants in Alabama. When the first proposal came out to clean up emissions from these plants, the Southern Company, a utility company, told a group of Southern senators that it would raise electrical rates by forty percent. Well, we worked on that and got some changes in the bill.

Then electrical companies were saying that even these changes would raise electrical rates about fifteen or twenty percent. We finally worked out an acceptable compromise, and the Clean Air Act was passed in April 1990. I think the legislation will eventually affect rates substantially.

Another issue that affected Alabama and the nation as a whole that I was heavily involved in concerned the coke industry. You make coke out of coal, and coke is used in melting steel. Steel making has declined in Alabama, but at that time there was a fairly good steel business. All the foundries used coke. The proposed language in one of the clean air bills would outlaw the manufacture of coke.

The American Coke Institute gave me credit for saving that industry. If you couldn't produce steel, you couldn't produce tanks or ships. You couldn't produce anything in construction. In recent years, they have been developing a system of making steel without coke; however, it is still in the developmental stage. The fight didn't get a lot of publicity even though the coke industry was big in those days. We got an agreeable compromise that was acceptable to the environmentalists, and it saved the industry.

THE CAHABA RIVER. Another environmental battle Heflin was involved in concerned the Cahaba River, which flows through the Birmingham Metropolitan Area and is an important source of drinking water.

There were two issues related to the Cahaba. One was the little fish called the Cahaba Shiner and the other was the flow of the river. All of these developers in northern Shelby County and south Jefferson County had plans. The environmentalists were threatening to put the Cahaba

Shiner on the endangered species list. The developers came to us, and the way they interpreted the effect was, if the Shiner went on the endangered species list, they couldn't develop these areas.

After further study, the Cahaba Shiner was put on the threatened list rather than the endangered species list. It allowed development to take place, and it has been a tremendous development. Sometimes I get in a joking manner and say, "I don't know whether I ought to have helped them or not. They all turned out to be Republicans."

The flow of water in the Cahaba is a concern and has to be considered in any development. At times, certain sections of the river would almost dry up as it came into Jefferson and Shelby County. We got the Corps of Engineers to work on this problem. Concern about the flow of water is still a major problem as large-scale development continues in the area.

THE KEMP-RIDLEY TURTLE. Attempting to protect five endangered species of sea turtles in 1988, Congress passed a bill which placed restrictions on Gulf shrimpers. It required them to carry something called "turtle-excluder dividers" (TEDs) in their nets. TEDs allow turtles to escape from the nets. This would cause shrimpers to lose large amounts of shrimp through the turtle escape holes. Since shrimping is a major industry along the Alabama Gulf Coast, Heflin was concerned. In March, he placed a hold on the bill.

In a scathing editorial on June 30, 1988, the *Anniston Star*, a generally liberal newspaper in a conservative state, called Heflin the "shrimp senator" and said his mind set was playing havoc with conservation. The piece continued:

> This is not his first bout with turtle phobia.
>
> Heflin formerly tried to block the flattened musk turtle from the threatened species list for fear protecting it would devastate the mining industry of northern Alabama. The miners themselves report no problems. Now the senator is trying to protect an industry in South Alabama needlessly. And he is holding the whole environment hostage.

It is said that the gods first drive crazy whom they would destroy. The shrimp idol that sits above the little world of Howell Heflin has filled his mind with fears and anxieties that set the senator too far apart from common reality.

This is not the first time Heflin has tried to do the political thing for one narrow constituency and ended up looking hopelessly aberrant. But it is the first time the consequences were so dire for national policy and for the good name of Alabama.[16]

"I see that the *Anniston Star* wrote something about the Flattened Musk Turtle," Heflin says. "There never was much publicity about it, but the Flattened Musk Turtle was actually a big issue for the coal mines, in spite of what the *Star* said. The Flattened Musk Turtle was proposed for listing as an endangered species. The coal people ended up getting some scientists who supported their position that it wasn't endangered. They convinced the concerned agency of the Department of the Interior that it wasn't endangered. According to what the coal miners said, it would have closed every coal mine in the state if it had been placed on the endangered list. It was an environmental issue that sort of went away after the scientists made their report."

The bill on the Kemp-Ridley Sea Turtle passed, though Heflin was successful in postponing implementation of TED use until May 1, 1988, in off-shore waters and May 1, 1990, in in-shore waters. He then asked the Secretary of Commerce to delay the May 1 implementation because he wanted the National Academy of Sciences to determine if the Kemp-Ridley Turtle was really endangered.[17]

Heflin rationalized his stand by explaining he was trying to keep the price of shrimp within the reach of average Americans. He argued that the natural breeding ground of the turtles was along the Yucatan Peninsula, and that was the place of greatest danger. He claimed the TEDs were ineffective and costly.[18]

In his column the last week in June 1988, Heflin said he had reached an agreement with sponsors of the Endangered Species Act to add an amendment mandating a new study by an independent panel to determine if the turtle was really an endangered species. The amendment postponed implementation of TED regulations for twenty-two months for inshore waters and ten months for offshore waters.[19]

By the middle of July, two federal courts had ruled the TED regulations were valid, and a federal appeals court ruled that the devices would be required beginning September 1. Heflin, under heavy attack, then reached a compromise that shrimpers would not have to carry the devices until the following May. This would give the shrimpers more time and allow more study.[20] Heflin removed his "hold," and the legislation was passed by the Senate on July 28, 1988, by a margin of 93-2.

In May 1990, the National Academy of Sciences issued a report on the study which Heflin had requested. The report said that shrimpers killed four times more turtles than previously thought and that the TEDs, although imperfect, were the best means available to protect the sea turtles. After reviewing the report, Heflin urged greater flexibility "to ensure that neither the turtles nor the shrimpers become extinct."[21]

Howell says the Kemp-Ridley Turtle has become endangered because of what happens with their eggs. "The turtles come ashore at a certain place in Mexico and lay their eggs. Well, the Mexicans think that it helps their sexual prowess to eat those eggs, that it's an aphrodisiac. That's why there is a shortage and why they are endangered. The thing they have to do is establish hatcheries, and there's one now started in the United States as a result of the attention given this turtle."

HIKING TRAIL IN THE TALLADEGA NATIONAL FOREST. Heflin did something environmentalists liked in July 1990 when he proposed an amendment to the 1990 Farm Bill which would increase the size of the Talladega National Forest. The proposed change to the legislation was to extend a hiking trail in Alabama, bringing it closer to the popular Appalachian Trail which runs from Georgia to Maine. The amendment was passed by the Senate Agriculture Committee.[22] Environmentalists, suspicious by now, expressed the opinion that Heflin's actions were political since it was an election year. The *Tuscaloosa News* commented editorially, "If politicking nudged the Appalachian Trail along a few miles, so be it. We'll take that result and run with it, right up to the Georgia state line."[23]

The administration opposed the proposal, and Heflin charged that the "Republican administration isn't as serious about improving our environment as it claims to be." The expansion would have cost $500,000, and this did not seem excessive since the 1990 budget proposal included $206 million for Forest Service acquisitions in other states.[24] The 1990 Farm Bill added 1,700 acres to the Talladega National Forest. This was less than the 4,000 acres originally sought, but it was a start.

LITTLE RIVER CANYON. In 1991, Democratic Representative Tom Bevill introduced legislation to bring some 14,000 acres in northeast Alabama under federal protection as the Little River Canyon National Preserve. The House passed the bill in April. The preserve would contain DeSoto State Park lands, including Little River Canyon.[25] Heflin said he would make no stand on the bill until Shelby did, since Shelby was a member of the Senate Energy and Natural Resources Committee.[26] Shelby proved reluctant to get behind the bill, and Heflin continued to be non- committal.[27]

As usual, the editorial writers were for Little River Canyon, and they chided Heflin and Shelby for being slow to support the measure. In August, both Shelby and Heflin announced that they would back Little River Canyon, and the bill was approved by the Senate Energy and Natural Resources Committee the third week in September.

A few days before the November 1992 general election, President Bush signed the bill into law, creating Little River Canyon National Preserve. It was Alabama's first national park dedicated solely to a national area. Little River Canyon was dedicated on April 9, 1995.[28]

EMELLE. "When the Clean Water Act came up," Heflin says, "we had this problem about Emelle, down in Sumter County, where they were storing extra hazardous PCBs. I got what is known as the Alabama Amendment passed. It required that, if extra hazardous materials are stored there, it has to have double liners, either plastic or metal. It has to have rocks in between two liners of either plastic or metal to keep it from getting in the streams and the water supply. We are the only state with this provision."

A GRADUAL EVOLUTION IN THOUGHT. In 1981, the League of Conservation Voters gave Heflin a rating of 20 out of a possible 100 on environmental votes. Scores indicated the percent of legislation on which the individual supported the League's position. That year he received $2,000 in campaign contributions from companies which were anti-environmental, according to Environmental Action, a non-profit research and education organization founded in 1970 by the organizers of Earth Day. In August 1981, he cosponsored the Hayakawa Anti-Wilderness Bill, which would end the extension of wilderness areas in the United States.[29]

In an interview in June 1988, Heflin called environmentalists "extremist" and maintained that his role was to balance environmental protection with industry and jobs. A coalition of thirty-one environmental groups, including the National Audubon Society and the Sierra Club, made it known that they were against him.[30]

In a new rating of Congressmen a few months later, the League of Conservation Voters gave Heflin a 10 out of a possible 100. Senator Shelby scored 20, and next lowest among the Alabama delegation were Republicans Bill Dickinson and H. L. "Sonny" Callahan, with 13 and 19 respectively.[31]

The Sierra Club said in April 1990 that Heflin was deceptive in writing in his column that he had supported the environment.[32] Heflin's press secretary, Tom McMahon responded, "Sen. Heflin did not put that article in his newsletter to say to everybody, 'Hey, I'm the greatest environmentalist this state has ever had.' It is just our response to the people of the state of Alabama." McMahon said that most people get up in the morning and go to work and that environmental issues are among the least of their worries.[33] In September, Environmental Action named

Heflin to its 1990 "dirty dozen" list, the twelve congressmen running for reelection they'd like to see defeated.[34]

Heflin seemed to have broadened his view when, in April 1988, he wrote in his column about the need to protect the ozone layer. He reported that the Senate recently ratified an international treaty limiting production of chemicals that destroy the ozone.

> Despite its limited quantity, the ozone is extremely important to the life processes on the earth. The earth's ozone layer acts as a filter, shielding this planet's surface from some of the ultraviolet rays expended from the sun. This is very important because ultraviolet radiation causes skin cancer and cataracts, suppresses the human immune system, damages crops and aquatic organisms, contributes to the formation of smog, and accelerates the deterioration of outdoor construction materials.[35]

In a column four years later, he showed still more evolution in thought and a greater appreciation of long-range concerns in environmental matters. He wrote, "The 'disposable' society of the early 1980s has long since been replaced by a realization that, as caretakers of this planet, we must make the environment a primary concern. With this goal, I worked this year to ensure that Alabama's wildlife areas will be preserved and protected." He listed several things, such as the Talladega National Forest, land acquisition at two national wildlife refuges in South Alabama, designation of eight Central Alabama counties as a Resource Conservation and Development Area, and continued funding for Auburn's Water Management Research program.[36] Skeptics, of course, interpreted this as changing his tune as the environmentalists got more and more on his case.

An important question in all of this is the extent to which the people of Alabama agreed with Heflin's stands on the environment. This brings to mind the always-cogent question: on a key issue, should a representative of the people vote according to the views of the group he represents, or should he do what he thinks is right? Apparently Heflin was at ease with the issue because he could do both. The environmentalists embrace their issue with great passion and assure us that the continued ability of earth to support life depends on heeding their warnings and following their advice. Even today, they really don't have much political clout, though increases in lung disorders, the plight of many of the creatures on this earth, and the threat of global warming are bringing more attention to the issue.

CURRENT ENVIRONMENTAL ATTITUDES. Senator Heflin evolved in his thinking, but he still feels a balanced approach is needed in dealing with environmental matters.

> The problem is that you get zealots in the bureaucracy. They really are sold, and they're going to do everything for their cause. They want notches on their guns. A lot of times, they over-react to charges, and then you have to have studies by some disinterested group, like we had on the Kemp-Ridley Turtle and the TEDs.
>
> We preached to the shrimpers that they had to win through science, but they never would hire scientists. Right now, the environmentalists have been going on for a good while about the Alabama sturgeon. The waterways' users hired scientists who can distinguish one type of sturgeon from the other. The issue is whether the Alabama sturgeon is a separate species or a member of a plentiful sturgeon family. Continued studies have failed to give definitive answers on this matter.
>
> They finally found an Alabama sturgeon. They couldn't find one for three or four years, and they thought they were gone, that they were not indigenous to Alabama, but they finally found one. They put it in a pool of water, and a turtle ate it. It was the only one for a while, but I understand they have recently found some that the environmentalists claim are "Alabama sturgeon."

ISSUES HE SUPPORTED. Heflin has supported many environmental issues, despite what his opponents may say. But environmental concerns for Heflin must always be balanced against potential jobs lost or gained.

There are some environmental issues I strongly supported. On the other hand, I have to admit that when I grew up, people thought of jobs when they saw smoke stacks. When they didn't see any smoke coming out of the smoke stacks, they knew there weren't any jobs. That was in the Depression days, and it was pretty well ingrained into me.

I lived here in Birmingham and went to school at Southern. You'd get up some mornings in those days in the 40s after the dew had fallen. Good Lord, the soot that you'd collect on an automobile was thick. You'd have to wash the windshield off in the morning to be able to drive. You could smell it. You never saw such soot that was collected here, and we breathed all of that stuff. Then they came along with various programs over the years, and they have pretty good air quality controls now in the Birmingham area. I support that, of course. It just makes sense. Of course, there are not many steel mills any more.

I was a strong supporter of a program called "Mission Planet Earth." It is the environmental program that got Al Gore interested in the space program in a much more intensified way. It basically involves looking down from space in a shuttle or space station and monitoring the earth, — the cloud covers, the ozone area, and other important factors.

ON BECOMING MORE PROGRESSIVE. Asked whether in his view there actually was an evolution in his thinking on environmental matters during his Senate career, Heflin answered:

Well, I reckon that's true with some things. When I was on the state Supreme Court I was pretty progressive, and politically I had always been a Democrat and supported the national ticket. But when I went to the Senate, Reagan came in, and there was a pretty good conservative movement. I ran on issues I believed in, like doing something about the deficit and the Constitutional amendment to require a balanced budget.

On civil rights issues, I was progressive all the time and stayed that way. When I went to the Senate, we still had Talmadge and Stennis. Eastland had just left. A lot of Southern senators were still pretty conservative on these issues. I believe I was a factor in moving the Southerners to change their attitudes.

Generally the premise that I became more progressive on environmental issues is well founded. I may be more progressive, but I still don't like the wilderness movement. I think you ought to have wildernesses, but I don't want to turn a large portion of the country over to non-productive activities. In the future we are going to need land and forests for essential needs.

THE NATIONAL ENVIRONMENTAL AND FERTILIZER RESEARCH CENTERS. Heflin tells of another fight he waged throughout his Senate career that had environmental implications.

The TVA up in my home area had a national fertilizer research center because the language of the TVA Act gave them directions to develop fertilizers for farmers. At one time, TVA owned some 70 percent of all patents on fertilizers that had been developed in the last 50 years. When Reagan came in, Republicans were looking for ways to cut the budget, and they said, "Well, this can be done by private enterprise." I had a constant battle to keep the appropriations. I remember going to the Chief of Staff then, who was Jim Baker and pleading with him. We were pretty well able to keep it going, but every year it would always be an issue.

Because of that, TVA decided they'd better change their emphasis to the environment. They became the National Environmental Research Center. When Bush came in, we started having battles over that. We'd have battles within TVA because they would have just so much money that was discretionary, and the Environmental Research Center was in competition with economical and community development and other activities.

We kept up the fight until the new chairman of TVA, Craven Crowell, said that he didn't want any more non-power appropriated funds given to the TVA. Chairman Crowell later changed his position. Of course, the TVA has always been unpopular with the privately owned investor-type utilities. TVA is now in a situation where there will be no appropriated funds. It will have to rely strictly on its power revenues, thus ending regional development. I fought to keep the fertilizer and the environmental activities going during my time in the Senate.

In the last few years, the National Environmental Research Center has started developing contract work, mostly with other governmental agencies. So they will probably continue to exist on contracts, but that's specific research. They are still doing a lot of general research. The Center is developing constructed wetlands. It is doing research pertaining to the ozone and is involved in water management. Now, for example, if some army post has to be cleaned up from shells, artillery, and other chemical wastes, the Center gets a contract to help in the cleanup. It comes up with methods to clean up that one post, and at the same time does general cleanup research. I believe restricting it entirely to contract work is a big mistake, but that's probably what is going to continue.

THE BATTLE FOR CHATTAHOOCHEE RIVER WATER. Heflin was involved in an ongoing fight over water in the Chattahoochee River, which separates Alabama and Georgia for some 150 miles. Atlanta keeps wanting to take the water, and people in Alabama say this would hurt them.

The Atlanta Regional Commission in 1989 proposed to divert water from Georgia reservoirs that fed the Chattahoochee, and the Army Corps of Engineers, after completing a study, recommended that 397 million gallons of water from three north Georgia lakes be diverted daily. William Sumption, executive director of the Tri-Rivers Waterway Development Association, said the Corps report didn't study the growth desires of anyone but Atlanta.[37]

In August 1990, Heflin helped get Senate approval of a controversial water resources bill which limited the authority of the Army Corps of

Engineers to reallocate water in federal hydroelectric projects without specific authorization from Congress.[38]

> We sort of slipped that by the Georgia group. That was back when use of water was so controversial. It still is, and it's going to be a big issue. But we passed it, saying that the Corps couldn't change the present allocations without coming to Congress and getting approval. When the bill got over to the House, the provision was killed.
>
> This fight continues. Atlanta is growing rapidly and desperately needs more water, but other interests along the Chattahoochee have succeeded to this point in assuring sufficient flow in the river to meet their needs. The Chattahoochee River affects Georgia and Alabama downstream. It affects transportation and barges and recreation and Lake Eufaula. They think if they divert all that water, it would dry up Lake Eufaula.

22

Senior Senator

GEORGE BUSH'S FIRST YEAR in office, 1989, was a time of momentous events. The Soviet Union, the other superpower in the 45-year Cold War struggle for world dominance, showed signs of severe strain. The world political scene had been dominated half a century by the struggle, with countries lined up on one side or the other and everybody facing the frightening specter of mutual atomic destruction if fighting between the two superpowers broke out.

Mikhail Gorbachev had become Soviet leader on March 11, 1985, and it was soon clear he was not like his predecessors. He was an idealist who promoted glasnost (openness), and he wanted perestroika (change) in his country. He wanted to teach the people about democracy, and he wanted to improve their lives.

Under glasnost, people were more free to express themselves, and a political crisis began developing in Communist East Germany. It reached such proportions by the fall of 1989 that the existence of the government was threatened. East Germans could travel to Communist Czechoslovakia, and they began pouring across the Czech border to West Germany. In October and early November more than 50,000 fled their homeland via this route. Responding to the pressure, the East German government announced that travel restrictions for its citizens had been lifted and that they could travel and emigrate freely.[1]

The Berlin Wall, the stark symbol of repression which was built in 1961 to prevent East Germans from traveling to the West, fell in 1989 with great symbolic force. The Cold War was drawing to a close, with the United States the only one real superpower remaining. Atomic war on a worldwide scale would no longer threaten, but the world situation would become much more complex as local and regional hostilities, which had been held in abeyance during the great life-and-death struggle, came to the fore.

Heflin notes that several factors contributed to the Soviet fall.

> They never really developed their infrastructure, like highways and other transportation systems. I think one reason they neglected their infrastructure was the amount they were having to spend on their military to keep up with us. So in a sense, their own policy contributed greatly to their fall. People don't realize how important infrastructure was in their collapse.
>
> I believe that the Warsaw Pact was weakening as Poland changed. This was before the Berlin Wall fell. The Solidarity movement of Poland had an effect on the Warsaw Pact. Then the Soviet's involvement in Afghanistan and Chechnya weakened them.
>
> Our intelligence was probably wrong on the desire and ability of the Soviet Union to go into a war. We failed to consider all the casualties they had in World War II. They had something like thirty million people killed. I think that before any Russian leader other than a crazy man would have entered a war with the United States, he would have thought a long time about those casualties. You know, almost every family lost somebody. I don't think they had the appetite for it. I think they used the military also to keep unemployment down.

The second momentous event in 1989 was the Tiananmen Square Massacre in China. The trouble began on April 15, following the death of deposed Communist Party reformer Hu Yaobang. This prompted tens of thousands of students to gather in several cities to protest government corruption and to demand democratic reforms. Martial law was declared on May 20 as the government moved to suppress the disturbance.

One of the largest demonstrations was at Tiananmen Square, which is in the center of China's capital, Beijing, and has been the location of student demonstrations throughout the twentieth century. Mao Zedong had proclaimed the establishment of the People's Republic of China in Tiananmen Square on October 1, 1949.

The demonstrators at Tiananmen were joined by workers, intellectuals, and civil servants, until over a million people filled the square. On June 3, the powder keg exploded as military units from distant provinces were called in to move against the crowds. On the nights of June 3 and 4, troops and tanks killed thousands in quelling what the government called a "counter-revolutionary rebellion." Thousands of people were arrested.

This use of military suppression demonstrated that, while the Soviet Union might be changing and the Cold War ending, the Communist government of China remained firmly in place. In a world moving toward freedom and democracy, it was a dramatic ruthless demonstration of dictatorship in one of the largest and most powerful countries.

THE 1990 ELECTION. Howell Heflin, was 68, in good health, and a national figure when he faced another election in 1990. He announced he would run in December 1988. A month earlier, Republican William Jelks Cabiness, III, of Mountain Brook, a wealthy Birmingham suburb, had announced that he would challenge Heflin. The grandson of former Governor William Jelks, Cabiness had served in the Alabama House of Representatives and the state Senate, and he was chairman of the 1988 Alabama delegation to the Republican National Convention in New Orleans.[2] Cabiness, 50, was president of Precision Grinding and had earned a reputation of being all business.

Republicans worried about Cabiness's ability to communicate with the regular Alabamians—the farmers, blue collar workers, and middle-class voters with whom Howell Heflin had such rapport.[3] Sensing this early in the campaign, Heflin called him, "my Grey Poupon Republican opponent."

The Grey Poupon ad featured a rich stuffy man in a limousine pronouncing the name of the mustard in ritzy tones. The line went over so well, I added to it and embellished it, and it finally came out, "my Gucci clothed, Jacuzzi-soaking, Mercedes-driving, Perrier-drinking, polo-playing, debutante-dancing, high society ritzy-rich Republican who has a summer home in Kennebunkport, but who eats broccoli."

That nearly drove his supporters wild. All the big newspapers, like the *Birmingham News* where Victor Hanson was publisher, were friendly with Cabiness. The *Montgomery Advertiser* and a bunch of newspapers editorialized for him, what a great state senator he'd been and how he would help the state in Washington. They wrote editorials that I ought not to be using all of that Grey Poupon language, and all that did was publicize it more. I never did use any TV commercials to publicize this, though I probably should have. Everybody was trying to quote it. Using a hoity-toity voice, I called him my "Grey Poo-pon opponent" to working audiences.

Cabiness had a close relationship with George Bush. He has a summer home in Kennebunkport which is close to Bush's house. I got along with Bush fine, but the Republicans were pushing to win. I think Bush had some reluctance at first to get involved, but he was convinced by the Republicans that Cabiness had a chance and would be well financed with the Birmingham business community.

Bush came to Alabama four times all together to raise money for Cabiness. My friend Vic Gold told me that he told Bush, "Mr. President, there isn't any way you gonna beat Heflin with Cabiness." Bush answered, "Well, I like Heflin, but all of the Republican Committee members think they've got a great chance to win, and he's going to be well financed." The soft money is not disclosed; at least newspapers never publish it. So, with the Republican soft money, he spent as much as I did, probably more.

Heflin's only opponent in the June 5 primary was Margaret (Mrs. Frank Ross) Stewart, who had also run in the 1984 election. She was the widow of a former president of Troy State University. Mrs. Stewart made the bizarre suggestion that Heflin was the antichrist of Biblical prophecy. "I am a Bible student," she said, "and there is some indication he is fulfilling the prophecy set out in Revelation." She pointed out that the Bible says the antichrist would be marked by the number 666 and that each of the three names, Howell Thomas Heflin, had six letters.[4] "I asked her if she had counted the number of letters in the name, Ronald Wilson Reagan," Heflin says. In the primary, Heflin received 81 percent of the vote.

Cabiness had a hard time finding issues because of Heflin's conservative voting record, and he tried to play the environment in a big way. In response, Heflin devoted a page of his newsletter to his environmental record. Sierra Club chairman Mike Dalen said, "Smelling a strong challenge for his congressional seat, Alabama Senator Howell Heflin suddenly has jumped onto the environmental bandwagon. His voting record over the past decade, however, reveals Heflin a polluter in green clothing."[5] Both the League of Conservation Voters and the Alabama Chapter of the Sierra Club endorsed Heflin's opponent. Cabiness's environmental strategy proved badly flawed because the large majority of Alabama voters agreed with Heflin.

> I was catching the devil from the Cahaba River Society. During the campaign, I tried to make amends with them and went down with a group to look at the Cahaba River. Well, he was down there, too, so they had both of us there. There was a lot of pro-environment. I didn't stay long. I said, "I believe I'm in the camp of the enemy."
>
> All the environmental groups came out for Cabiness. Cabiness's record on the environment in the state House and Senate wasn't very good. In fact, it was pretty bad. The Republican media experts brought in a handler and consultant for every Republican candidate, and this fellow Eddie Maye came, directed the campaign, and made the TV ads. They made a bunch of TV commercials on the environment, and we

found out one of them was fake. They piled a lot of debris and barrels to make a river scene look horrible, and one of my TV ads accused them of falsifying their ads. It showed a much cleaner river scene to verify our charges.

As might be expected, Cabiness supporters injected the race issue. Cabiness announced he was forming a "grass-roots coalition" against a civil rights bill he said would force hiring quotas. "He (Heflin) and they call it the Civil Rights Bill of 1990; I call it the 'Ted Kennedy quota bill.'" Heflin responded that the bill included language barring it from imposing quotas.[6]

Heflin didn't start campaigning seriously until after Labor Day. In an article that month, *Birmingham News* writer Elaine Witt called Heflin one of Alabama's most popular elected officials. It was David and Goliath, she said. "Without working up too much of a sweat, Heflin has maintained a comfortable margin in the polls by establishing what some have called a 'moderate-conservative' voting record." Democratic Party official Al LaPierre noted that Heflin had an organization in all 67 counties.[7]

Cabiness's attacks on Heflin became heavier as the campaign progressed. Heflin was his usual jovial self, poking a lot of fun and keeping things lighter, and he said, "Basically, I'm a Democrat conservative and he's a Republican conservative. The difference between them is that Democrats care about people."[8]

Heflin called the campaign the worst he had been in with regard to "sleazy, negative" ads by his opponent,[9] and writer Ted Bryant said 1990 would go down "as a time when the practice of civilized politics in Alabama was mugged, stomped on, kicked, bloodied and finally tumbled to the mat like Buster Douglas."[10] In the November 6 general election, Heflin received 61 percent of the vote to 39 percent for Cabiness.

Heflin says he never got mad at Cabiness and maintains he is a very decent man, but, Heflin adds, he let his Republican handlers get out of hand.

WINNING THROUGH ORGANIZATION. Steve Raby explains that Heflin won elections through organization and continuous activity. "Judge Heflin didn't campaign just the campaign year. He campaigned all the time from 1970 through 1997. He was always prepared in a campaign, and he felt that his own political work and campaigning work was part of his responsibility as a senator. We worked every week and every day. It's just his philosophy that you campaign every day. When the election comes you won't have a problem.

"As AA, I was one of the designated fundraisers, and one of the persons who could legitimately handle the funds on the staff, and I was very much involved in the campaign. I was on the finance side, the strategic counsel side, and the polling side. Bill Gardiner, whom we called 'Big Daddy,' was manager, and he did things like making sure that every county had the needed staffing. Gardiner had been mayor of Tuscumbia. He and the Judge went so far back that Heflin had been his campaign manager. Bill had great political instincts about the people out there.

"We had four offices, and we divided the state based on them. In each county, we had a coordinator, a finance chairman, and usually a youth chairman and some other positions. Where possible, we would have a young Democrat designated. Depending on the county, we would have Farmers for Heflin. In Huntsville, we worked on the aerospace side. We would try to always make sure some of the coordinators or finance people were lawyers. In practically every county, we had at least one elected official who would be the key but who would not necessarily want to be the county coordinator.

"The organization and organizing were continuous. Judge Heflin visited those people in every county every year. We would use these people to set up our town meetings and county meetings. The staff would use the town meetings to get a crowd together and raise money, though Judge Heflin always had a message that he wanted to bring home, and he wanted a question/answer period. We never would just run into a meeting and let him talk twenty minutes and say, 'We're late. We've got to go.' We would try to have enough staff there for different issues. Judge would just point to somebody, 'You need to see my man or my woman, Jan, or whatever.' He genuinely and legitimately knew those people. He would remember them and remember their family because he had such a sense of history. He always told some kind of story that tied to some of his family or some event. It was just a joy to watch him. He had those meetings to hear what the people were saying.

"Bob Morrissette was the Mobile office director and was kin to everybody down there. Tom Coker was director in Montgomery at first, and then it was Sam McClurkin. Tim Brown, who is in Montgomery now, was there the longest. He was responsible for a large area around Montgomery and the Wiregrass. Stan Vines was director in the Birmingham office. He was primarily responsible for Jefferson County and parts of Blount County. The state office was in Tuscumbia, and working with Big Daddy there was Jan Johnson, who was the field person. Huntsville was handled out of the Tuscumbia office. That being my home, I would take care of a lot of that.

"I worked with Bill Gardiner and he in turn worked with the regional office people to set up meetings. Every week was different. A Senate recess was different. I would basically relay to Big Daddy the things we needed to do that week, and, depending on what part of the state we needed to be in, they would set it up. I was the Washington office liaison with Gardiner. It could be generated from the other way, too. Big Daddy might call me and say, "When's the next recess coming up? What are you doing in September? I've got this guy that's done such and such for us. I've asked him to do whatever. You've got to make Heflin go over there and do such and such."[11]

THE KEATING FIVE. In November 1989, five senators were accused of wrongdoing in a case which was part of the national Savings and Loan crisis. Four were Democrats — Alan Cranston of California, Dennis DeConcini of Arizona, John Glenn of Ohio, and Donald Riegle of Michigan — and the fifth was Republican John McCain of Arizona. They were accused of attempting to influence bank investigators who were examining the collapsing Lincoln Savings and Loan of Irvine,

California, in 1987. Lincoln's chairman was Charles H. Keating, Jr., of Phoenix, Arizona, who had contributed to each of the senators' campaigns. The group became known as the "Keating Five."

This situation grew out of the much larger savings and loan (S&L) scandal which reached major proportions in the mid-1980s. In the 1970s, S&Ls were in a competitive disadvantage relative to banks and other financial institutions, and pressures were brought to soften regulations and allow them to broaden the scope of their investments. When this legislation occurred, a boom in real estate contributed to overbuilding and falling prices. At the same time regulations were being softened, the staff of the Home Loan Bank Board, the regulating authority, was significantly reduced, so there was less supervision. S&L assets increased by 56 percent between 1982 and 1985. Forty Texas S&Ls tripled in size, with many of them growing by 100 percent each year. S&Ls in California followed a similar pattern.

Trouble was brewing. The easing of regulations led to massive defections of state-chartered S&Ls to the federal system. To counter this trend, California passed the Nolan Bill, which allowed California-chartered S&Ls to invest 100 percent of deposits in any venture. Similar plans were adopted in Texas and Florida. By 1983, a Bank Board report estimated that nine percent of all S&Ls were actually insolvent when evaluated by stringent accounting standards.

In March 1984, Empire Savings of Mesquite, Texas, failed, costing taxpayers some $300 million. Investigation showed that "Land flips" and other criminal activities were a pattern at the bank. The situation began to snowball. Failures in Ohio and Maryland helped kill state deposit insurance funds, and in August 1985, only $4.6 billion remained in the Federal Savings and Loan Insurance Corporation (FSLIC) insurance fund. The Government Accounting Office estimated the loss to the insurance fund to be around $20 billion, and it declared the fund insolvent by at least $3.8 billion.

Edwin Gray's term as chairman of the Home Loan Bank Board ended in June 1987. Before his departure, he was summoned to the office of Senator Dennis DeConcini. McCain, Cranston, Glenn, and Riegle were also present. Gray was questioned about the appropriateness of Bank Board investigations into Lincoln Savings and Loan, owned by Charles Keating. Regulators had recommended a government takeover of Lincoln Savings in 1987, but because of interference, the seizure was delayed two years.

Keating's parent company, American Continental Company, went bankrupt in April 1989 at the same time that Lincoln Savings was seized by regulators. The cost to taxpayers to cover insured deposits exceeded $2 billion, and Keating was sentenced to a long prison term for fraud. His was the most prominent case in the savings and loan scandal.

Howell Heflin was chairman of the Senate Ethics Committee when the Keating Five scandal broke in 1989. He had remained on the committee, either as chairman or as ranking minority member, since his initial appointment.[12] On December 23, the committee announced it would formally investigate, and once again, Heflin was at center stage.

Hearings on the Keating Five moved slowly. Special counsel Robert Bennett, who would later be President Clinton's personal attorney in several investigations, submitted a 350-page report to the committee on September 10, and closed-door sessions began the third week in October. Republican Senators pressed to move things faster, and they pleaded for the committee to render its judgment before Congress adjourned.

Republicans demanded the dropping of charges against McCain and Glenn on the ground that they were less involved with Keating than the other three senators. The media saw this as an effort to reduce the Keating Five to the Keating Three (all Democrats) so it could be an issue in the upcoming elections. Heflin answered on the floor by stating he couldn't reveal information from closed sessions but that he had read a *Common Cause* press release which said that each senator being investigated had received substantial benefits from Keating and that the measures the senators took to influence regulatory activity were improper. "It is not my purpose to say that the *Common Cause* statement is correct," Heflin added, "but to say it should be given careful consideration."[13] The Ethics Committee ignored Republican critics and scheduled a post-election hearing for November 15.

On the first day of the hearings, Heflin told the five, "Many of our fellow citizens believe that your services were bought by Charles Keating, that you were bribed, that you sold your office, that you traded your honor and your good names for contributions and other benefits."[14]

Bank Board chairman Gray testified that Senator DeConcini, flanked by the others, had opened the 1987 meeting by referring to Keating as "our friend from Lincoln Savings." He called it an intimidating session and said he considered it improper.[15] William K. Black, a senior career regulator, testified that the five caused enforcement delays of "probably the worst institution in America" and inflated the cost of the eventual federal bailout. "Five U.S. Senators are a heck of a lot bigger than this boy," he added. "I felt that Charles Keating had clearly set up the session to be intimidating."[16] Keating refused to testify under the Fifth Amendment.

On February 28, the Committee issued verbal rebukes only to DeConcini, Glenn, McCain, and Riegle. The Committee found that because of the jobs Keating's companies provided in each of the accused senators' states, there was a legitimate reason for involvement on behalf of Keating, even if the extent of the involvement was questionable judgment. But the Committee decided this was an insufficient sanction for Cranston. It said that Cranston engaged in an impermissible pattern of conduct in which fund-raising and official activities were substantially linked.[17] It later recommended that Cranston be reprimanded, and the Senate issued the reprimand. Cranston had already decided he would not seek reelection in 1992. This ended the Keating Five investigation, and the Committee was widely criticized for its leniency.

"During the hearings, it was discovered that Cranston had prostate cancer," Heflin points out. "Warren Rudman and I took a deposition from his doctor over the phone. Cranston lived longer than everybody thought he would. The cancer, plus the fact he had announced that he was not going to run again, influenced the way the Committee handled it."

McCain's involvement with Keating went back to when McCain was in the House. It was significant because Keating, his associates, and friends contributed $56,000 for McCain's two House races and $54,000 for his 1986 Senate race. They also provided transportation to the Bahamas for McCain and his wife on several occasions, and on at least one occasion for his child and her babysitter. Keating also provided transportation to McCain's wife for trips to Los Angeles and the Grand Canyon.

Under the ethics rules of the House and the Senate, such trips had to be disclosed on semi-annual ethics disclosure forms. McCain's problem was that he failed to disclose these trips for a number of years, until he was elected to the Senate, even though there was considerable publicity in the Arizona media concerning Keating and his activities at the time the relevant ethics disclosure forms were filed by McCain. Several years later, McCain reimbursed Keating's company for the airfare, contending he thought the transportation costs had previously been paid.

A question of jurisdiction was raised. The Committee felt it didn't have jurisdiction to be involved in a determination of House ethics rules violations.

Presenting the committee's case against Cranston on the Senate floor was Heflin's last duty as Ethics Committee chairman. Later he decided to retire from the Ethics Committee. In his resignation speech, he estimated that he had issued well over a thousand advisory opinions, but he said the Cranston case was by far the toughest matter he had to deal with and he was ready to give up the Ethics responsibilities.[18] Majority Leader George Mitchell announced he was granting Heflin's request to leave the Committee.[19]

Later investigation revealed that more than a dozen members of Congress were involved with Charles Keating.

> There was evidence of Executive branch participation in the Keating affair, though you couldn't prove anything. I don't think Reagan had anything to do with it because he usually didn't get involved at that level. They have a liaison in the White House who deals with savings and loan banks and their regulating agencies. They let it be known if the administration has an interest. Keating didn't just rely on senators. He

was one of these people who contributed heavily to presidential races and to both parties.

Contacting regulatory agencies for constituents is not unusual. You have all sorts of business people who get into trouble with the regulatory agencies, and you meet with them. A lot of times there's a misunderstanding, so you'd ask the director or the assistant director to come in, and you say that you'd appreciate if he'd listen to this man from Alabama who's got a problem. Sometimes you'd sit in on it, and sometimes you wouldn't. The question with the Keating Five was whether undue pressure was used. Then there was an issue of whether Keating's campaign contributions had any connection with the activity of a particular senator. He contributed to a great number of people.

In January 1993, after he left the Ethics Committee, Heflin said it was time for the Senate to rewrite its code of ethics and spell out more clearly what was acceptable conduct and what was not.

Earlier we attempted to rewrite the code, and it turned out some members' ideas were different from mine. Our advisory group did a lot of work, but they wanted to regulate filibusters and went a little overboard. I said, "My Lord, you think we'd ever get something like that passed? That's one of our cherished traditions." We tried to rewrite the code then, but we couldn't get very far.

THE CLARENCE THOMAS HEARINGS. Early in 1991, President Bush nominated Clarence Thomas to replace Thurgood Marshall as an associate justice on the Supreme Court. Thomas, grandson of a black Georgia sharecropper, grew up in Savannah, which was racially segregated in his youth. He had overcome segregation and poverty, and this gave him a strong belief in self-help. He attended Holy Cross University and graduated from Yale University Law School. Thomas had been chairman of the Equal Employment Opportunity Commission during the 1980s and was named to the U.S. Court of Appeals in Washington in February 1990.

Thomas was a conservative, and liberals immediately mounted a fight against him, stirring a controversy which threatened to reach the intensity of the Bork hearings. Blacks were split. Democratic members of the Congressional Black Caucus voted unanimously to oppose Thomas, but the Urban League and the NAACP declared their neutrality or postponed a decision.[20] Later, the NAACP announced that it opposed the nomination.

As usual, Heflin received national attention as one of the swing votes, and as usual, he didn't commit himself. After meeting with Thomas and studying the record, he said that some of Thomas's writings raised questions. They were "replete with a legal notion called 'natural rights,'" supposed universal moral principles that are implied but not specifically set out in the Constitution. Heflin called this "a minefield of ambiguous and potentially explosive approaches that fell out of the legal mainstream decades ago."[21]

> Basically, I didn't think Thomas was qualified. In his writings, he had criticized Oliver Wendell Holmes. Then when the hearings came, he thought Holmes was the greatest justice that ever was, so we thought he had a little touch of "confirmation conversion." In my first speech, which was fairly early in the debate on Clarence Thomas, I made a statement that he was going to be confirmed, but I felt that I ought to go ahead and read all the old background information on him. That was before any of us knew anything about Anita Hill.

The hearings began in September 1991. Thomas admitted to a dalliance with marijuana in college and denied that his onetime admiration of Nation of Islam leader Louis Farrakhan indicated he was anti-Semitic. He had expressed distaste for affirmative action programs and criticized *Brown v. Board of Education*. Ironically, he had benefitted from affirmative action in being admitted to Yale Law School.[22]

Heflin announced on September 26 that he would oppose the nomination because Thomas failed during the hearings to remove doubts about his qualities as a jurist.[23] A day later, the Judiciary Committee deadlocked with a 7-7 vote. All six Republicans and one Democrat (DeConcini) voted for Thomas. The other seven Democrats voted against him. This meant the nomination would go to the full Senate with no recommendation. No Supreme Court nominee had ever won Senate confirmation without the committee's endorsement.[24]

Shortly after the floor debate opened, a flap developed when Anita Hill, a black 37-year-old law professor at the University of Oklahoma, alleged that Thomas was guilty of sexual harassment in his relationship with her.[25] The Senate decided to delay the final vote until Hill's allegations could be investigated.

"When Anita Hill came along, a lot of people had a lot of questions," Heflin says. "There was a growing demand to have further hearings, and the Republicans and Thomas agreed to a second round. Thomas testified that the second round of hearings was a high-tech lynching, though he had agreed to the second round of hearings. Every Democrat and every Republican questioned him."

Since the charges involved sex, the media went into one of its periodic frenzies, and the session was carried live by ABC, NBC, CBS, CNN, PBS, and C-SPAN. In addition to Hill, other witnesses included Angela Wright, a former Thomas aide at EEOC, Susan J. Joerchner, administrative law judge for the California Workers Compensation Appeals Board, and Joel Paul, American University Law Professor.[26]

Hill said Thomas pressured her for dates, boasted of his own sexual prowess, and gave the unmistakable impression he was seeking sex. She said the incidents occurred between 1981 and 1983 when she worked for him at two government agencies, and she added she had feared for her career as a lawyer if she quit or lodged a formal complaint.[27]

Heflin was the first questioner in the televised session.

> I got criticized when I first started and asked him only a few questions. I was going to ask about his former media representative who had left his office and become a newspaper reporter in a city in one of the Carolinas. Her deposition had been taken, and she testified he had sexually harassed her on several occasions when she was employed

by him. He claimed he hadn't been told about the deposition of this woman. I started asking him about it, and he said, "I don't know. I haven't read any of that." I decided it would be unfair to him to be asked about this witness' claims until after he heard her testify from the witness chair.

I realized that the language he supposedly used in the alleged sexual harassment of Anita Hill was about as vile as you would ever hear. Here we were on a Friday night, with every television network in the world showing the thing and probably 80 or 100 million people watching. I said to myself, "Am I going to repeat all that vile profane language? He has to be asked if he made such statements, and he'll end up denying it like he's denied everything else. I'm going to leave that to the Republicans, because I don't want to be heard all over the world asking questions about such language."

I had finished a certain amount of my time, and I said, "I'm going to reserve the balance of my time for later." The Republicans went through every bit of the vile profane language, and he denied it. Then I came back and went into some of the other things. One of the biggest criticisms of the whole hearings was that vile, terrible language, and many people talked about children hearing it. Later, it was decided that if another occasion arose where such language was involved, the Senate would go into Executive Session which would not be televised.

On October 16, the Senate voted 52-48 to confirm Thomas. It was the closest confirmation vote for a Supreme Court Justice in Senate history. Heflin voted against Thomas, and Shelby voted for him. Democrats voted 11-46 against and Republicans 41-2 for.[28]

Helfin afterward commented on the outcome.

I had reservations based on the contradictory nature of Thomas's statements on his fundamental view of the Constitution. I was deeply concerned that he would become an advocate with an activist Supreme Court which would strike down many of the gains made in individual rights. I believe that modern constitutional jurisprudence has moved to the point that individual rights are just as important as property rights, perhaps even more so.

Mark Young, former Heflin staff member, relates, "I was on the Senate floor when Senator Heflin made his speech and announced he would vote against Thomas's confirmation. Later, as we walked to the subway, I told him how proud I was of his decision — that he stuck to his convictions. Senator Heflin replied, 'Mark, I know a little about Constitutional Law, and that man doesn't know a thing.'"[29]

A poll in October 1992 showed that Heflin's approval rating had dropped sharply among Alabama voters after the Clarence Thomas hearings.[30]

OTHER NOMINATIONS. As a senior Senator, Heflin again found himself involved in other nomination processes.

In June 1993, President Clinton nominated Ruth Bader Ginsburg to replace Associate Justice Byron White in June 1993. Ginsburg was a strong advocate of women's rights. A dean at Harvard Law School had proposed her to Justice Felix Frankfurter of the Supreme Court as a law clerk. Justice Frankfurter said that, while the candidate was impressive, he wasn't ready to hire a woman. From 1973 to 1976 she argued six women's rights cases before the Supreme Court and won five.

When he spoke at the beginning of her confirmation hearing, Heflin credited Ginsburg with bringing a new atmosphere of good will to the confirmation hearings. "I believe we will see a process remarkably free of acrimony and partisan bickering. What a change of atmosphere from that of the recent past. Congeniality prevails over confrontation; back-slapping has replaced back stabbing; inquiry is the motivation rather than injury."[31] Ginsburg was approved. She was sworn in on October 10, 1993, as the second female Supreme Court Justice.

Clinton nominated Federal Appeals Judge Stephen G. Breyer to the Supreme Court in May 1994 to fill the vacated seat of Harry A. Blackmun. He had an impressive background, which indicated he was well suited to the job. Breyer was easily confirmed.

In April 1991, President Bush nominated Kenneth L. Ryskamp of Florida to the Eleventh Circuit Court of Appeals. Opposition, which developed quickly, included more than fifty local and national groups and represented Jews, Blacks, Hispanics, women, senior citizens, and unions. They cited his "insensitivity" in his rulings as a federal judge. Heflin was a swing vote, and Ryskamp's defeat gave Bush his first defeat in 77 judicial nominees.

Edward Carnes of Alabama was then nominated to fill the Eleventh Circuit Court vacancy. Carnes was approved early by the Senate Judiciary Committee, but his nomination also became controversial. "It was primarily the Southern Christian Leadership Council that opposed him," Heflin recalls. "Carnes had handled a great number of capital punishment cases, and this organization led the fight against him because of his capital punishment stand.

The final vote was delayed for several months to allow a full debate. Heflin and Shelby were credited with getting Carnes approved.[32]

A CHANGE OF ADMINISTRATION. Two years into Heflin's third Senate term, Democrat Bill Clinton was elected President, ending twelve years of Republican occupation of the office. Bush had seemed unbeatable just a few months prior to the 1992 election, with approval ratings that soared to 80 percent after the Gulf War. The war was in reaction to the invasion of Kuwait by Iraq in August 1990. Large volumes of oil were at stake in the volatile Middle East, and President Bush immediately dispatched troops to Saudi Arabia. A U.S. military buildup, known as "Operation Desert Shield," was undertaken. A number of other countries joined the U.S. in sending forces.

Heflin notes that the War Powers Act was a big issue when Bush was getting ready to seek Congressional approval of the operation.

> The War Powers Act was designed to give Congress more knowledge and participation in undeclared wars. All the Presidents before him, whether Democrats or Republicans, felt it was interference with the executive rights of the presidency. I told Bush I thought his

resolution seeking approval ought to be drafted in some of the language of the War Powers Act without making him take any position on the Act, which I knew he opposed. He could take language from the Act, and this would make it more palatable for some of the senators. He said, "Boyden Gray's been talking about that, and y'all get together." I spoke with Gray, his White House counsel, and he drafted the resolution in that manner. It passed on a close vote, something like 52-48.

Massive air strikes began in mid-January 1991, and the invasion began at the end of February in an operation known as "Desert Storm." For several months Iraqi leader Saddam Hussein had bragged that his army could defeat anyone who tried to invade. He said it would be the "mother of all battles." The war lasted three days, with very low casualties on the Allied side.

The Iraqis were totally defeated, and the invading forces could easily have occupied the country and set up a new government. When fighting halted, the British First Armored Division was forty miles from Bagdad, and the Iraqis didn't even know they were there. The U.S. and its partners decided to leave Hussein in power. To many, this was a serious strategic mistake. "On the matter of the troops going to Baghdad, the question was the future balance between Iran and Iraq," Heflin says. "Also, the United Nation's resolution didn't authorize this move; it just authorized removing the Iraqis from Kuwait."

Bush gave a widely hailed victory speech to Congress on March 7 and reached the height of his popularity. The war also made a hero of General Colin Powell, chairman of the Joint Chiefs of Staff, who became a hot political property, a black who could add strength to a presidential ticket. The field commander, General H. Norman Schwarzkopf, popularly called "Stormin Norman," also emerged as a hero.

> Colin Powell's wife is from Birmingham. Alma's father was a high school principal during some of the violent days of the civil rights movement in Birmingham. As to why he didn't run, I think her background probably influenced him a lot in deciding. I think she

figured he would have been a target.

Right after the war, we visited Saudi Arabia and Kuwait, and we went up into Iraq. We visited with General Schwarzkopf. Everybody was talking about the fact that air war had proven itself to be effective, but Iraqi terrain was wide open spaces, just desert with no place for troops to hide. Air warfare in a jungle country like in Vietnam didn't work as well. Our military had to resort to defoliation bombs and agent orange. It still didn't work effectively. Some people would say that Kosovo proves air war can do it all, but again our Air Force had selected targets. I'm sure that I wouldn't want to rely strictly in air power alone, especially in a guerilla situation.

By the end of 1991, the collapse of the Soviet Union was complete. This set a new dynamic for international relations and affected foreign policy aspects of the 1992 presidential election. A recession which began in the fall of 1991 would also effect the election.

THE 1992 ELECTIONS. Heflin announced in May 1992 that he was endorsing young Arkansas Governor Bill Clinton as the Democratic nominee for president. Clinton captured needed delegates in the primaries and received the party's official nod at its National Convention in July. He selected Tennessee Senator Albert Gore, Jr. as his running mate.

President Bush waged a weak campaign, and Clinton won by a substantial margin. He was an attractive young man who was popular nationally, but he had already shown a penchant for arousing strong passions in those who opposed him. Questions of womanizing were raised in the election, and arch enemies, such as Little Rock attorney Cliff Jackson and *The American Spectator,* were hard at work trying to destroy Clinton politically.

I went into about eight states altogether campaigning for Clinton. I was up in Tennessee. Governor Ned McWherter, who's quite a character, invited me out to the mansion, and we had a fine dinner. He's a widower, and the lady who ran his kitchen brought out some cakes and pies and desserts. He said, "Bring me my regular dessert." She brought him out a glass of buttermilk and some cornbread, and he crumbled it up and put it in with the buttermilk. I said, "That's what I want for dessert."

MORE SPACE AND DEFENSE. The space station had met strong opposition every year, and Heflin and others had to fight hard to maintain funding. President Bush was a strong supporter, but new danger came at the beginning of the Clinton Administration. By the time of Clinton's election, the name "Space Station Freedom" had been chosen for the project. In 1993, Clinton began a program of downsizing the government, and his original budget recommended cancellation of the space station. Heflin and others conducted a long fight to save it.

> The space station is an interesting story. There had always been a pretty good fight on the station. Senator Bumpers of Arkansas always fought to kill it, and he may have gotten to Clinton. Well, Gore was vice president, and he supported the station. I was urging him to get Clinton's support. We had a recess in February 1993, and about that time, we found out Clinton's budget left it out
>
> I was supposed to come back to Alabama and make a bunch of speeches and hold town meetings. I canceled all of the schedule and stayed in Washington to try to save the space station. I was working primarily with Gore. Gore would still go to the Senate gym, and I figured out the times he'd be there. I would arrange to be at the gym and talk to him about the space station and urge him on. Previously, I was talking to Bob Hager and Chris Hanson of Boeing, and Amy Bonderant, attorney representing McDonald Douglas about how to get the space station back in the new administration's proposed budget. They gave me ideas, and I'd pass them on to Gore. Anyway, Clinton ended up putting it in his budget. About the time I left the Senate, the Boeing people presented me with a cartoon labeled "political strategy at its finest." The cartoon has Gore on the massage table and I have his clothes and am saying, "I'm not going to give your clothes back until

you get Clinton to put the space station back in the budget."

When the House voted on the space station, I went over and did a lot of politicking among the House members, which rarely you do.

On June 24, the House almost killed the space station with a vote of 216-215. This was the closest House vote during the history of the fight.[33]

Democratic Senator Barbara Mikulski of Maryland, chairperson of the Senate subcommittee which decided space station funding, had been a lukewarm supporter. Heflin organized a fundraiser in Huntsville to aid in her reelection bid in 1992. "She had Goddard Space Center in Maryland," Heflin says. "So she wasn't opposed to the space station; she had just never been very active. We had been trying to get her to visit Marshall, and she finally came." Mikulski was given an excellent education on the space station as well as the royal treatment in Huntsville, and she said after the visit that she was absolutely committed to saving the station.[34]

On September 22, 1993, the Senate voted to provide the full $2.1 billion Clinton requested for the space station the following year. Opposition was led by Democratic Senators James Sasser of Tennessee and Dale Bumpers of Arkansas. The vote was 59-40, indicating that the program had sufficient momentum to withstand any future attempts to stop it.[35]

SDI. In February 1991, Heflin said the administration's refocused SDI program probably wouldn't win support because of its continued reliance on space-based weapons. Heflin had been generally supportive of SDI but from his earliest Senate days had fought to focus on ground-based rather than space-based weapons. He said the new program "envisions an application of space weapons which is even more questionable than in the original program."[36]

The following July, the Senate Armed Services Committee approved a $4.6 billion SDI plan that concentrated on development of ground-based interceptors. This was good news for Huntsville, where the heart of the research and development would be.[37] Similar appropriations continued during Heflin's remaining years in the Senate. The Senate passed a Cohen Amendment which called for deployment of a strategic missile system which Heflin helped initiate.

Late in 1992, the Army chose Lockheed to build a new ground-based theater missile defense system, and Lockheed indicated it would locate its assembly plant at Courtland, a few miles from Huntsville. The missile would be the THAAD, the Theater High Altitude Area Defense system.[38]

Ground was broken for the Courtland plant in April 1993, and it began missile production in July 1994. The first THAAD was unveiled in March 1996, and a successful test was conducted in 1999.

23

His Finest Hour

ONE OF THE MOST touching and telling moments in Senator Heflin's Senate career came in 1993 during a vote on granting an extension to the United Daughters of the Confederacy (UDC) for a special patent for their insignia, which included the first national flag of the Confederacy.

The Senate Judiciary Committee voted unanimously to extend the patent the previous year and was expected to approve again. However, Democrat Carol Moseley-Braun of Illinois, the only black senator at the time, argued against the extension. She told the Judicial Committee that she did not oppose the group's freedom to use whatever symbol they chose, but she questioned the need for Congress to give a Confederate symbol special treatment when an extension could be obtained through the Patent Office in the normal manner. The Senate Judiciary Committee responded 12-3 to reject the patent application. Heflin was absent when the vote was taken.

The issue resurfaced on July 22 when Senator Jesse Helms, in a surprise move, attached the insignia patent bill as an amendment to other legislation. When a motion to table the Helms amendment failed 52-48, Moseley-Braun took the floor. She said, "Those of us whose ancestors fought on a different side in the Civil War or who were held as human chattel under the Confederate flag are duty bound to honor our ancestors by asking whether such recognition by the U.S. Senate is appropriate."

Heflin was in his office at the time, but he and staff members saw what was happening on the closed-circuit TV.

> The first time it came up, I went to the floor and voted with Helms. Then I went back to the office, and I was feeling emotional about it. I talked with several staff members, including Winston Lett, Steve Raby, and my black legislative assistant, Mansel Long, and they urged me to vote against the Helms amendment. Several members of my family belong to the UDC, and if I voted against the Helms amendment, it would irritate them and be a big political issue in Alabama. This time, the insignia was more symbolic, for in the face of controversy it would put the stamp of approval of the Senate on it, and it would be a slap in the face of the blacks.
>
> So I said, "I'll vote against it." I went on the floor and let Carol Moseley-Braun know I was going to support her. She said, "The Senator from Alabama has a question he would like to put. I yield for that purpose, without losing my right to the floor."

Senator Heflin then delivered these remarks:

> Mr. President. I rise with a conflict that is deeply rooted in many aspects of controversy. First, the conflict arises for the love of my Southland. I feel today, however, that we also have a conflict in modern America.
>
> I come from a family background that is deeply rooted in the Confederacy. My great-grandfather on my mother's side was one of the signers of the Ordinance of Secession by which the State of Alabama seceded from the Union. My grandfather on my father's side was a surgeon in the Confederate Army.
>
> I have many connections through my family with the Daughters of the Confederacy organization and the Children of the Confederacy, and I have a deep feeling, relative to my family's background, that what they did at the time they thought was right.
>
> History, as we look back, always can give perspectives on what

existed at the particular time. But I revere my family, and I respect those who thought whatever they were doing was right at that particular time in our Nation's history.

But we live today in a different world. We live in a nation that every day is trying to heal the scars of racism that have occurred in the past. We are trying to heal problems of racism in the world in which we live today. Perhaps racism is one of the great scars and one of the most serious illnesses that we still suffer today.

The United Daughters of the Confederacy has done a lot of good work. Its support for soldiers in arms in times of war and national conflict, and its support for the sale of war bonds, and its charitable donations to orphans, and the countless hours donated to veterans in our national veterans hospitals, are certainly admirable.

I do not believe the organization today really has racism at its heart or in its activity. But the Senator from Illinois, Senator Carol Moseley-Braun, is a descendent of those that suffered the ills of slavery. I have a legislative director whose great, great-grandfather was a slave. I said to my legislative director, "Well, if I vote with Senator Moseley-Braun, my mother, grandmother, and other ancestors will turn over in their graves." He said, "Well, likewise, my ancestors will turn over in their graves if you vote against the amendment." But I strongly feel that if they were alive today, they would stand for what is right and honorable, and they would agree with me that it is time to move forward in our Nation's history.

We live in a world today where symbols mean a great deal. They are important to this Nation and to its people. This matter is indeed an issue of symbolism that has been so eloquently raised by the junior Senator from Illinois.

In my State, we have a new Governor, and he has just begun his term of office by banning the Confederate battle flag from flying over the State capitol dome. Instead, he has ordered that it will be duly recognized by flying it from the first White House of the Confederacy, which is near the capitol grounds. The flying of the Confederate flag was and is offensive to a large segment of the people in Alabama, both black and white. I think that he moved in a proper manner to see that the flying of the Confederate battle flag at the top of the capitol dome be stopped.

I think we do live in a world of symbolisms. Many distinctions can be made, however, between the granting of the extension to the design pattern sought by the United Daughters of the Confederacy and flying the Confederate battle flag atop the State capitol dome. But the whole matter boils down to what Senator Moseley-Braun contends — that it is an issue of symbolism. We must get racism behind us, and we must move forward.

Therefore, I will support a reconsideration of this motion, and I do it with conflict. Nevertheless, we must realize that we live in America of today. We live in a world in which we are so proud of the fact that we have made so much progress in removing the ills of racism, and we must realize that we must move forward to eradicate all of the racism that still exists. We live in a country which we believe that all men and women — as stated in the Declaration of Independence — are created equal and are endowed by our Creator with the right of life, liberty, and the pursuit of happiness.

I feel that, today, this is a symbolic step. If we move forward to put the stamp of approval of the U.S. Senate and the Congress on a symbol that is offensive to a large segment of Americans, I think we will not be moving in the right direction, and it is a wrong approach to the ideals for which this country must stand.[1]

An emotion-charged debate on racism and the Confederacy followed, and the Senate voted 76-24 to reconsider the Helms amendment. Then it killed the amendment 75-25. Heflin's speech was credited with being the deciding factor in the debate. Fellow Alabama Senator Richard Shelby joined in voting against the UDC request.

Senator Moseley-Braun later said of Heflin, "His integrity, his intelligence, his commitment and faith in the Constitution of these United States, faith in what the American dream has always stood for and can be in the future, has led Judge Heflin in a direction that I think is without peer and without parallel in this body. He has been a force for good, he has been a force for right."

Senator Paul Simon, Democrat of Illinois, told Heflin he was "very, very proud today to be your colleague. It took courage to do what you have done." Senator Donald Riegle of Michigan, said he could not recall another moment in his twenty-seven years in Congress when he had been moved more by a speech from a colleague. He said Heflin and Moseley-Braun "put this country together across the lines of racism and region and history."

There was a loud outcry in Alabama, and Heflin received a blasting from a number of the state's most influential newspapers. *The Gadsden Times* wrote that he had "turned his back on his Confederate forefathers." The Montgomery chapter of the Sons of Confederate Veterans gave Heflin their "Scalawag of the Year" award for his UDC stand. Heflin's press secretary retorted that maybe the Senator would get a carpetbag.[2]

The Decatur Daily took another view when it editorialized that Heflin "was eloquent when his usually rambling speech was honed to sharpness and his words pierced thick hides. . . . Moderate Alabamians must hail the senator's lead in defeating the measure. He took the high moral ground and denounced the racial symbolism of the Confederate flag. . . . The Confederate flag is offensive to millions of Americans because it was under that banner that blacks were enslaved. Its only status should be historical."[3]

Heflin's stand, one of the finest moments of his busy and productive life, helped to move the nation and his home state forward in the quest for equality.

CONTINUED SUPPORT OF CIVIL RIGHTS. Heflin was involved in the Civil Rights Restoration Bill of 1988, widely known as the "Grove City" Bill, which brought on a big fight with the Reagan administration. With Grove City, Congress sought to restore rights guaranteed under several laws which Supreme Court decisions had restricted. Debate on the 1988 bill was more acrimonious than usual because opponents worked to get the bill involved in the abortion issue. This created a divisive climate, and it got the religious community involved.[4]

"Grove City" took its name from a 1984 Supreme Court decision, *Grove City College v. Bell*, which altered the interpretation of Title IX of the Education Amendments of 1972. The court found this law, which prohibited sex discrimination in federally funded institutions, applied only to the particular activity directly receiving funds. This meant that other programs were not bound by the anti-discrimination language, and it greatly weakened enforcement of anti-discrimination laws. The bill sought to restore the institution-wide application of federal anti-discrimination laws. The Supreme Court ruling was especially significant because of the potential impact on the Civil Rights Act, the Age Discrimination Act, and the Rehabilitation Act, all of which used similar language. It clearly limited the government's ability to fight discrimination.

When the act came up for a vote, Heflin joined Shelby in voting for it, after bucking the Democrats by supporting an amendment which put some limits on abortion. It passed 75-15. Reagan vetoed the bill, and the veto was overridden. Heflin was said to be very effective in helping to get the bill passed and the veto overridden by explaining the legislation in a way that it could be broadly supported.[5]

The bill, Heflin said, "sends a clear signal that discrimination is illegal and will be prohibited. It closed a major loophole in our civil rights laws and preserved two decades of hard-won civil rights for all Americans. I had tremendous political pressure on me to oppose it. My vote for the override was referred to as 'another nail in my coffin.' I received over 6,000 calls and letters from constituents who criticized me for supporting the bill."

THE CLINTON ADMINISTRATION. Bill Clinton was inaugurated President in January 1993, and the 103rd Congress was seated. The country was coming out of a recession, and Clinton was young, charismatic, and full of ideas. There was talk of "a new beginning" and of new hope.

Almost immediately Clinton stirred up a hornet's nest when he announced he would sign an executive order which lifted the ban on lesbians, gay men, and bisexuals in the military. Few things stir conservative passions more than gay rights. The far-right accused Clinton of vile motives and was ready to start impeachment proceedings right then except that their godfather, retired Senator Barry Goldwater, made a public announcement supporting the President.

Actually, the new policy wasn't much of a change. It held that recruits would not be asked about their sexual orientation during enlistment, and no investigations would be initiated solely because of allegations that a service member was gay. Open practice of homosexuality was still prohibited, however, and investigations could be initiated at the discretion of a unit commander if he had "credible information" that a member had engaged in or had a propensity to engage in prohibited conduct.

Heflin was strongly opposed to the move. Steve Raby recalls that Clinton took it on himself to come to the Capitol building to meet with the Democratic Senators who normally have a weekly caucus at lunch. "It's unprecedented to invite the President and for the President to attend. When we found out that was happening, we all got a little excited.

"Twelve-thirty rolls around, the time the caucus normally starts, and the Judge was still in the office. I said, 'Judge, you need to get to the caucus lunch with the President.' 'Oh, all right.' Twelve-forty-five rolled around. 'Judge, you need to get on over there.' Well, he messed around again, and it was after one o'clock. I said, 'Judge, let's go over some things, and I'll walk with you to the caucus as you go over there.' He waited a little while longer and walked in over there.

"When he walked into the caucus room, the President was facing the Senators so he could see all of them, and the Judge sat so he was even with the President. The President couldn't see him eye-to-eye unless he deliberately looked. As soon as the President finished speaking, Heflin bolted for the door. The President sort of hopped over a chair, and, said 'Judge, Judge, I need to talk to you a minute.' 'All right, Mr. President.' The President grabbed him and said, 'I need you to think about this issue.' 'No, Mr. President, you don't need me to think about this issue.' Clinton finally said, 'Judge, just listen. I just need you to pray over this one. Just pray over it.' Judge Heflin pushed the President back and said, 'I have prayed over it, and I read my Bible, and I'm not with you on this one.' I think the President was a little struck at such a response from a senator."[6]

Heflin was among the supporters of a line-item veto bill, which came up in January 1993. This issue had appeared a number of times before and had never been passed. Heflin had always been a supporter of it when it was written in constitutionally permissible language. Clinton strongly supported it, and so did a number of Republicans. In February 1995, the House passed the bill and the Senate followed. The legislation became law on April 9, 1996, but it was not used until the following year because of an agreement between presidential candidates Clinton and Dole. Clinton exercised the veto a few times in 1997. The law was declared unconstitutional by the Supreme Court in 1998 on the ground that, by allowing the President to intrude in legislative matters, it violated the separation of powers which is at the heart of the U.S. political system.

CLINTON'S HEALTH CARE INITIATIVE. The Clinton administration started in 1993 to work on a comprehensive health care plan, with First Lady Hillary Clinton spearheading the effort. Heavy opposition by the health-care industry and the right-wing soon appeared. Heflin noted he was concerned about costs and inflation, and freshmen Republican Congressman Spencer Bachus of Birmingham said, "The National Health Board will serve as a Politburo for health care, determining what each American receives in care and deciding what each American contributes in taxes."[7]

The plan created health alliances, huge insurance-purchasing pools. It provided a choice from a variety of health plans offered by insurers, doctors, and hospitals; guaranteed quality care at the lowest price possible; provided health-care benefits for everyone, including individuals, families and small business employees; and it called for payment of 80 percent of employee premiums by employers.[8]

Heflin said he supported general principles of the plan, but he stressed that months of tedious negotiations lay ahead. A key, he said, was the administration's willingness to compromise.[9] In his column on October 6, he outlined a number of problems with the current system and pointed out that the greatest need was cost control. Health care costs, which were rising fifteen to twenty percent a year, were far outpacing the rate of inflation. "This is the first time that this vital issue has had such an elevated forum of discussion," he wrote. "We must seize the opportunity to pull together and get to work."

The plan ultimately failed and never came up for a vote. In explaining why, Heflin says that the First Lady and her staff did not engage in the legislative process.

> They worked and worked on the health care plan. They had considered this and that, and they had compromised a lot from the original proposal. But when it got to consideration by Congress, there weren't any compromisers. They met with all sorts of health and hospital special interest groups. The groups would agree to some degree, and the First Lady and her staff thought they were getting their support. But they didn't deal with individual Congressmen, and that's where they made their mistake.
>
> If they had gone through the legislative process and then developed the needed compromises in Congress, the outcome might have been different. But she wanted to get it all prepared as a package and then introduce it. You have to sit down with your Congressional opponents and say, "What are your problems with it?" A group of senators might then list ten things. You agree, "All right, we'll make changes to accommodate your first seven objections. Then will you support it?" Most of the time a compromise can be worked out.

BALANCING THE FEDERAL BUDGET. One of Clinton's campaign promises had been to cut the size of the government and reduce the federal budget, and he began the attempt immediately. The budget deficit had been out of control through most of the twelve years of the Reagan and

Bush presidencies, with the national debt quadrupling from $1 trillion to more than $4 trillion. A standard Republican campaign tactic was to complain about "free spending" Democrats and promise to cut the budget. Clinton grabbed the center on this issue and was beating the opposition at its own game, further increasing their irritation with him.

Heflin was for Clinton's economic plan, the Omnibus Budget Reconciliation Act of 1993, because, "It is the very best hope we have now or in the near future of finally getting a handle on our massive budget debt and yearly deficits."[10] A bitter fight ensued. In the final vote in August, the House passed the President's budget 218-216. The Senate vote was 50-50, and Vice President Gore had to break the tie.

> It was a tough situation. This was the vote that increased taxes, but it also reduced the deficit. There was big pressure from Wall Street to do something about the deficit. The public was aroused and wanted action to reduce the deficit, but a lot of people were against the tax raise. I got a lot of phone calls and a lot of pressure from business people in Alabama opposing it.
>
> In my opinion, that bill really set the stage for the prosperous growth that we've had since then and the elimination of the annual deficit. It was one of those bills I believe the historians will give a lot of credit to Clinton for, and they will recognize his leadership on deficit reduction.

The administration's success in balancing the budget diminished the argument for a balanced-budget amendment, the proposal Heflin had introduced at the beginning of each new Congress. Clinton staged a preemptive strike in February 1994 by announcing that such an amendment would cost Alabama $3 billion to $3.5 billion a year in higher taxes or benefit cuts, and he called the proposed amendment a "gimmick" which could harm the economy.[11]

"The amendment has never been passed," Heflin says, "but the fight for it did spotlight the issue and resulted in deficit reduction. Our efforts over the years to bring about some control over deficit spending were productive even though we did not get the amendment."

ANTI-CRIME LEGISLATION. In another early action in September 1993, Clinton announced a comprehensive anti-crime initiative. He pointed out that the first duty of any government is to keep its citizens safe, and that far too many Americans lived in fear of crime. A key provision was to expand police presence in cities and towns by putting 100,000 more police on the streets. Heflin strongly supported the initiative.[12] It passed and has worked well.

The Brady Handgun Control Bill, which requires a five-day waiting period for the purchase of a handgun, was passed in November 1993. This measure was named after James S. Brady, President Reagan's former press secretary, who was shot in the head and permanently disabled during the 1983 attempt to assassinate the President. The measure had fierce opposition from both Republicans and Democrats, including Alabama Senators Heflin and Shelby. The bill was approved by the Senate the day after the anti-crime bill passed.[13]

Heflin recalls supporting a bill that outlawed foreign weapons like the AK-47.

> I caught a lot of hell from supporting that vote. The gun lobby ran against Congressman Bud Cramer who had voted for the bill. They nearly beat him. The AK-47 ban was a big issue in all races in Alabama.
>
> When I originally ran, the National Rifle Association endorsed Flowers, and they proved they were pretty powerful. We thought we were going to win without a run-off, and I think they kept us from doing it. They opposed controls on the AK-47. Why in the world do they want to oppose such a ban? The NRA has a lot of sportsmen and others who believe that the Second Amendment gives them the right to bear arms, and their right to bear arms shall not be infringed. They felt that the AK-47 ban was an infringement on their right to bear arms. I made a speech on the floor on the AK-47 matter, and Clinton liked it. I said I didn't know of any hunters who have shot any quail down in Alabama using an AK-47.

Public attitudes on gun control seem to be changing, but whether more action will be taken depends on what happens in the future and whether there are more incidences like Littleton. Reaction to guns may continue to build, just as it did with tobacco. In the end, it was the ingenuity of the lawyers who realized they would not be very successful in suits against tobacco companies for individuals, because the individual had the choice of whether or not to smoke. Most smokers knew it was going to harm them. So lawyers convinced the state attorneys general to sue on the basis of reimbursing Medicaid and Medicare since they couldn't use effectively the defense of individual choice.

THE ISRAELI-PALESTINE TREATY. One of Clinton's early triumphs was the signing of a peace treaty between Palestinians and Israelis on September 14, 1993. Yasser Arafat, chairman of the Palestine Liberation Organization (PLO), and Yitzhak Rabin, Prime Minister of Israel, signed the treaty which pledged peace and acknowledged the right of both Israelis and Palestinians to exist in the Middle East. Former Presidents Carter and Bush were present, and Heflin was among the congressmen who attended.[14]

THE 1994 TAX PACKAGE. Heflin applauded Clinton's new tax package at the end of 1994, saying it should be called "the middle class, family values tax cut plan."[15] Speaking to a Democratic meeting in Birmingham, Heflin pointed out that the economy was better in Alabama twenty-two months after Clinton became President. Some 4,200 new manufacturing jobs were created, compared with 600 lost in the previous four years; the unemployment rate dropped from 7.2 percent to 5.2 percent; business failures had dropped 10 percent; home sales had increased 10 percent; and bank lending had grown to $2.8 billion a year which was more than two-and-a-half times greater than the $1 billion a year during the previous four years.[16]

GATT AND NAFTA. Early in his presidency, Clinton had a big fight on his hands trying to win approval for the North American Free Trade

Agreement (NAFTA) Treaty, most of the work on which had been done under Bush. The treaty was signed in August 1992 before the election, and it was coming up for Senate approval. NAFTA involved the U.S., Mexico, and Canada, and it would eliminate tariffs and create the world's largest trading bloc. It was very controversial. Heflin had said, "I most certainly plan to vote against the agreement . . . and will join like-minded senators in the fight to see that it is defeated." Both Heflin and Shelby said the agreement would hurt Alabama farmers and factory workers.[17] The fear was that manufacturers would move jobs to Mexico, where wages were lower and regulations not as stringent.

The legislation Clinton sent to Congress in November 1993 to implement NAFTA contained a requirement that all peanuts and peanut products imported into the U.S. meet the same quality and sanitation standards as those grown domestically. Heflin said, "They have given us almost 100 percent of what we asked." He said he still opposed the treaty.[18] The Senate approved NAFTA in November 1993 with a majority of Republicans voting in favor.[19]

Another treaty involving trade, the General Agreement on Tariffs and Trade (GATT), came up later in 1994. This was an international trade agreement which dated back to 1948. GATT included 123 nations which accounted for four-fifths of all world trade. It had been expanded several times through the years, and the change under consideration resulted from negotiations which began under President Bush.

The new agreement expanded coverage in several areas, including agricultural trade, and it cut tariffs in developed nations by an average of 38 percent over five years. The major change in the agreement was creation of the World Trade Organization (WTO), which had the power to enforce trade rules over the objections of individual members. Previously, each member was free to choose which provisions it would accept. Unlike the United Nations, the U.S. would have no veto in the WTO. This created widespread concern.

Heflin indicated in January that he might support GATT, but he said he would demand assurances similar to those included in NAFTA that required imported peanuts to meet the same quality standards as those produced in the U.S.[20] In November he said he would vote against GATT because he felt it would result in a net loss for American workers.[21] GATT was approved by the Senate in December with Heflin and Shelby voting against.

    I opposed both GATT and NAFTA largely because of the agricultural and textile situations. At the time, we had well over 100,000 jobs in the state that were involved in the manufacture of textiles and wearing apparel. I went down to Reynoso, Mexico, and looked at the "Maquiladora" program. This program, which was established by Mexico in 1963, allows U.S. companies to come into Mexico, build plants, and ship their products back into the United States without any tariffs. The U.S. companies couldn't ship to Mexico without tariffs, so there was still a barrier, with Mexicans protecting their own products.

    American plants were all up and down the border. In fact, there were then more than 5,000 Maquiladora plants. There would usually be an American city in Texas right across the border, and there would be a Mexican city. All the executives would live in America and go across the border. They were paying workers anything from the minimum wage, which was 59 cents an hour, to about $2.00 an hour.

    NAFTA meant you would have accelerated closings and movement. All of our wearing apparel and textile business is slowly moving there or offshore. You almost can't buy anything now in men's and women's apparel unless it's made in some foreign country. We're under the treaty allowing their farm products to come in, and there's a lot of problems with that.

    On the other hand, we've sold a lot of high tech and other things under GATT. But every year our trade deficit increases. The biggest deficits are with Mexico, Canada, and Japan. The Canadians sell us a lot more than we sell them, and the Mexicans are doing the same and increasing their sales in the U.S. yearly. The only thing the statistics show is that we're selling stuff in Mexico. The stuff we're selling them is raw materials.

    I think that, with regard to NAFTA, we'll finally hear that big sucking sound that Perot talked about. We've already lost a lot of wearing apparel business, and are going to lose more and more. Free trade is good as long as it's fair trade. In the long run, with internationalization, there must probably be free trade. But certain countries, particularly those with such low wages and such a disparity between wages here and there, need sort of a quasi-free trade program for a time. There's no question that, in Europe and the United States and to some degree in some of the Pacific Rim countries, the free trade policy and the GATT program are good.

The peanut farmers particularly were opposed to NAFTA because it would allow Mexican peanuts or other foreign peanuts to come through Mexico into this country, and the GATT program is similar. It is basically designed to remove all barriers and have free trade. The old farm bill set a certain quota of foreign peanuts, cotton, sugar and other things to come in, and it's being phased out.

SHELBY TURNS REPUBLICAN. Senator Shelby and President Clinton found themselves at cross purposes early in the Clinton presidency. It began when Shelby criticized the Clinton economic plan after a meeting with Vice President Gore. Shelby walked out and, according to Steve Raby, said to the TV camera right in front of the door, "As far as I'm concerned with Al Gore, the tax man cometh." "This was right after a behind-the-scenes meeting to deal with the problem. Gore is not easy to get riled," Raby observes, "but this time he was furious."[22]

Thomas Oliphant of the *Boston Globe* said that Shelby went out of his way to stick a knife in the President and deliberately insulted Gore.[23] Soon afterward it was announced that 90 space station management jobs would be transferred from Marshall to Johnson. In response, Shelby said his vote was "not for sale, even to the White House,"[24] and he continued to oppose Clinton's initiatives.

Shelby's stance won him no friends in the White House, and the ire of the executive mansion was shown when the Alabama football team visited in March 1993, two months after they beat Miami in the Sugar

Bowl for the national championship. Heflin received fifteen tickets to the event, and Shelby got one.

In November 1994, Shelby announced he had joined the Republican party. He said, "I've tried hard to work with the Democratic Party, the party I grew up with in the South." He added that Democrats were now the party of "no hope, but all dependency." Heflin was asked if he would also switch, and he answered firmly that he would not.

Heflin blames the trouble between Clinton and Shelby on Clinton's "young Turks" in the White House.

> They decided to take away jobs from Huntsville because Shelby had criticized Clinton's economic plan. Clinton called me one Saturday morning, and I went over to the Oval Office. I took my AA, Steve Raby, with me. The President was very casually dressed, and he talked about a number of matters. He finally got around to what he had called me over for. He asked, "How can I make up with Shelby?" I told him, "Well, these young Turks you got around you in the White House, they create problems. What answer could Shelby have given other than 'his vote was not for sale' when it was publicized about the job loss at Huntsville?"
>
> I told Clinton, "The way you get back on good terms with Shelby is through his wife. She is a professor out at Georgetown, and you are a graduate of Georgetown. What you ought to do is have a dinner and invite the president of Georgetown, the Shelbys, and some other prominent Georgetown alumni or professors that are friends of hers. Pay more attention to both of them in the future. You will find he will support you when you are right, but he is not going to support you all the time, for he is a conservative just like I am on most matters. Also, have someone on your staff educate your young Turks."
>
> Then Vince Foster committed suicide. Vince lived just three or four doors from Shelby. Clinton went over to Foster's house and was expressing his sympathy. Somebody told him that Shelby lived just up the street, and he just walked up there and knocked on the door. He sat down in the kitchen and talked with Shelby and his wife for about an

hour. I think maybe he thought that was the way of making amends, but it didn't work. Shelby's wife is smart. She's also a great campaigner for she really helped Shelby get elected.

Anyway, these young Turks over-reacted when they threatened to take a NASA project away from Huntsville. I asked Clinton, "When you were Governor of Arkansas, did you ever take bridge projects or road projects away from legislators who opposed you?" He answered, "I never did." I said, "Well, your young Turks are threatening to do something similar in Alabama." In the end they did not do it, and the jobs stayed in Alabama.

Many Democrats like Clinton get young staff who are not acquainted with practical politics. They're young liberals who have just come out of college, and they're gung-ho and going to save the world. They have no political moxey whatsoever. Some of those Clinton had around him caused more problems than he ever knew. Some of them don't have much personality, and many turned out not to have any loyalty. The same can be said about the Republican young Turks who are radically right-wing.

Shelby and I both were conservative. The Republicans worked on me a lot. Dole talked to me several times, and Strom Thurmond talked to me almost monthly about switching parties and becoming Republican. I kept telling them, "I'm not interested. I'm a Democrat. I was born a Democrat. I was raised a Democrat. I was nurtured on Democratic food, and I'm going to die a Democrat." I said all that on television after Shelby switched."

WHITEWATER AND SCANDAL. Almost from the moment Bill Clinton took office as President, he was under attack by the far-right for alleged moral lapses and illegal dealings. He and the First Lady faced persistent questions stemming from their role in the Whitewater Development Corporation, a failed real estate venture that involved 42 lots among the Whitewater River in northern Arkansas. Federal investigators were probing the dealings of the Madison Guaranty Savings and Loan, a failed Arkansas thrift. Madison's owner, James B. McDougal, was a partner with Bill and Hillary Clinton in the Whitewater venture. One question was whether federally insured deposits from Madison were illegally diverted to Clinton's gubernatorial campaign.

Republicans pushed hard for an independent counsel to investigate Clinton's role in the Whitewater affair. Attorney General Janet Reno replied that the Justice Department was conducting its own probe, and Heflin defended her, saying she had to have credible evidence of a violation before she could appoint an independent counsel.[25] Finally, Kenneth Starr was appointed special prosecutor to investigate Whitewater in August 1994. In a vote of 98-0, the Senate joined the House in voting to hold congressional hearings.

Over time, the Whitewater investigations grew beyond the allegations related to the Clinton's financial and legal dealings in Arkansas. Allegations included the firing of White House travel office clerks, Mrs. Clinton's billing records connected with legal work for McDougal's savings and loan, the suicide of White House counsel Vince Foster, and other matters. The Clintons came through all these allegations with their credibility shaken but not destroyed.

Then the matter of President Clinton's sexual misconduct surfaced, first with Paula Jones and then the Monica Lewinsky affair. Kenneth Starr became tenacious in his investigation, and other allegations followed. Senate hearings were conducted, and the President was impeached. He made an official apology for his actions to the American public.

As a final chapter, Clinton settled the Paula Jones case. On January 19, 2001, he issued a statement about the Monia Lewinsky investigation, which brought an end to the proceedings. He accepted a five-year suspension of his law license, agreed to pay a $25,000 fine to cover counsel fees, and acknowledged a violation of an Arkansas rule of professional conduct because of his testimony in the Paula Jones case deposition.

On October 1999, Starr officially relinquished control of his five year investigation of Clinton. Robert Ray became his successor. In September 20, 2000, CNN report, Ray said that there was insufficient evidence that either President Clinton or the First Lady had engaged in criminal wrongdoing. Thus the Whitewater era came to an end.

THE 1995 BUDGET FIGHT. A bitter fight on the new budget started early in 1995, with the Republican majority in Congress determined to have its way. Skirmishing between parties went along at high pitch through the summer and fall months, with considerable press attention and very little negotiation with the White House. The Republican leadership clearly thought it could force the administration to do what it wanted.

In May, the Senate and House passed a Republican plan to cut $958 billion in spending by 2002. The savings would come from Medicare, Medicaid, and other benefits, and 181 agencies and programs would be eliminated. Heflin voted against the budget because of the harsh effects he thought it would have on senior citizens, students, the poor, farmers, veterans and average American workers. The plan passed and put Congress on a collision course with the President.[26]

In a guest editorial, Heflin said the Republican budget-cutting plan was like the story of a lamb deceived by a wolf in sheep's clothing. While using popular terms like "balanced" and "tax cuts," he said, "the law would attack the most vulnerable elements of society. The Republican plan cuts future economic growth and asks hard working lower and middle income Americans to bear the brunt. These are the wrong choices for our economy and our society. While I fully support a balanced budget, I cannot vote to sacrifice the principles of equality and fairness."[27]

By November, the budget battle had grown to major proportions. The old budget had expired, and continuing resolutions were needed to allow spending and keep the government operating. The House, under Speaker Newt Gingrich, kept including elements of the Republican budget plan in the temporary spending and borrowing bills, and Clinton kept vetoing them. The danger of a government shut down was growing, and Gingrich and the Republicans believed that Clinton would cave in rather than have this happen.[28]

Heflin urged his colleagues on both sides of the aisle to reach a compromise. "It is a matter of trying to be reasonable in getting together," he said. His judicial experiences in the settlement of lawsuits, he warned, showed that lengthy pauses in negotiations can lead to re-entrenchment of ideas and an end of the give-and-take necessary in compromise and diplomacy. "Part of the problem," he added, "is the very real difference between the government styles of the leadership in the Senate and the freshman-heavy House. Many in the House are hard-nosed and extreme. I don't think there is any question that the majority in the Senate, including Republicans, see the House as very extreme. Gingrich was unable to control them to some degree."[29]

By mid-November, the government started laying off workers, and it soon shutdown all "non-essential" offices and operations. The game of chicken between Clinton and the Republicans continued with neither side budging. By the turn of the new year, it was becoming apparent the American people believed the Republicans bore most of the fault in the situation and that Gingrich and his colleagues were hurting themselves enormously by continuing the fight. In the early months of 1996, Republicans surrendered and indicated they were ready to compromise. Negotiations started, and a budget bill was finally passed on April 26. The new bill cut federal spending $20 billion below 1995 levels.[30]

The 1995-96 budget fight proved to be a colossal strategic blunder by Gingrich and his followers. They had Clinton on the ropes after the 1994 elections, with low approval ratings and declining prospects for reelection. When the budget battle ended, the situation had reversed, with Clinton's approval rating at 60 percent and that of Congress at new lows. Clinton's prospects for the 1996 election looked much brighter.

THE GREAT UNDERWEAR FLAP AND OTHER TALES. Heflin witticisms and yarns, with the joke sometimes on himself and sometimes pointedly on others, were legendary during his years in Washington. Once a yarn was spread about an electric hand dryer in the men's room at the Atlanta Airport Crown Room. Some jokester was said to have placed above the device a sign reading, "Press here for a message from Howell Heflin." Heflin retorted, "After you press the button, at least the hot air runs out in about a minute. I wish the same were true of the Medicare-cutting, Crown Room-lounging, Grey Poupon Republican budget architects in Washington."

He also liked to tell these stories:

> There's a good story we told about Sister Emma Ledbetter. She was hot about the evils of alcohol and demon rum. She was teaching the Sunday School lesson, and she was giving demon rum hell. She says, "You'll never go to heaven drinking whiskey. If you let wine touch your lips, you're going straight to hell." A fellow in the Sunday School class says, "Now, Sister Ledbetter, says right here in the Bible that Jesus turned water into wine." She says, "I'd thought a lot more of him if he hadn't done it!"

> I've never been fond of snakes, and I woke up one night in Bougainville [during World War II] with a snake wrapped around my leg. I grabbed hold of it and threw it outside the foxhole. It was dark, and I don't know what type snake it was. It didn't bite me. Many years later I went down to Opp, Alabama, just before they were going to have their rattlesnake roundup. They wanted to wrap this rattlesnake around my neck and take promotional pictures for the roundup. They claimed several other people in public life had done it. I said, "Not me. You can hold him over there and put three people between us."

And one of the most celebrated Heflin incidents took place on July 20, 1994. He was in the Senate cafeteria at lunch with reporters when he felt the need to wipe his face. Reaching for what he thought was his handkerchief, he pulled a pair of his wife's underwear out of his back pocket and was clearly embarrassed. The incident was widely reported, and two major gossip columnists in Washington featured the story.[31]

> I caught immortal hell from that for a long time. What happened was, we had our bedroom, and there was an extra bedroom with twin beds. I'd go in the extra bedroom at night and change into my pajamas

and take things out of my pocket, and I'd routinely put my handkerchief down on one of the twin beds. Then I'd go on to bed. My wife would undress in that room later and come into our bedroom. She'd leave her white panties on the same twin bed. They were about the size of my handkerchief, and one morning I just picked them up and put them in my pocket by mistake.

I got all sorts of little bitty panties through the mail, and then I got bandannas, these red handkerchiefs that the cowboys use, which had been made into panties. I told the media, "From now on, I'm going to use colored handkerchiefs." Some paper said, "If he hadn't been so big and fat and ugly, he never would have lived that down."

THE NORTH ATLANTIC ASSEMBLY. In April 1993, Heflin was chosen chairman of the Senate Delegation to the North Atlantic Assembly, the legislative arm of NATO. One reason he was selected was his knowledge of constitutional law. Heflin said he would try to foster closer ties with Eastern Europe and would discuss NATO's future military status.[32]

Later in September, he led a delegation of senators to England and Scotland to meet with members of Parliament. The war in Bosnia and the future of NATO were among the topics discussed. A month later, Heflin traveled to Denmark for a weekend NATO meeting which focused on events in Somalia and on Russia's fledgling moves toward democracy.

The last week in May 1994, Heflin went to Oslo, Norway, for a North Atlantic Assembly meeting. He served as host chairman when the Assembly met in Washington the following November. At this meeting, the assembly approved a plan, coauthored by Heflin, to provide guidelines for admission of new members, including former Warsaw Pact nations. The other author was Republican Representative Douglas Bereuter of Nebraska.

"The heads of state would make the decision on NATO membership," Heflin says, "but the country wanting to be a member still has to join the North Atlantic Assembly. As a result of the Heflin-Bereuter Resolution, these petitioning countries started looking at adoption of extradition treaties and other essential treaties that many had not signed. The resolution had its impact."

SPACE ALIEN. In May 1994, Heflin was among a dozen senators "exposed" as space aliens by the *Weekly World News* tabloid. He told the media, "I always thought my parents were heaven-sent." Senator Gramm, who was among the twelve, said, "It's all true. We are space aliens. I'm amazed that it's taken you so long to find out." Predictably, Heflin's office got calls from worried citizens asking if the story were true.[33]

HEALTH PROBLEMS DEVELOP. In May 1993, Heflin, who was then 71, began experiencing chest pains. He went to the National Naval Medical Center at Bethesda, Maryland, for a angioplasty to clear a clogged artery in his heart. Chest pains returned a week later, and he decided to have further tests in Birmingham.[34] At UAB, a stent, a stainless steel device designed to support a blood vessel, was implanted in a branch of his right coronary artery, which was in danger of collapsing.[35]

UAB received approval from the Food and Drug Administration to use stents on June 2, two weeks after Heflin's operation. Heflin said he didn't think publicity about his case led to the approval. "I'll do a lot for Alabama," he cracked, "but I don't want to go through that experience again just to help a dear constituent."[36]

Heflin dropped twenty pounds and was told to give up cigars. He said he had to listen for an hour to a diet specialist explain what he could and couldn't eat. "After she left, I said bring in the psychiatrist, I'm in a state of depression." He said he would have to slow down a little, for he had maintained a grueling schedule for years.

On August 5, 1994, he experienced chest pains again and went to Bethesda Naval Hospital for tests. He then flew to Birmingham, and a pacemaker was installed. He was back in Washington after two days, and his Birmingham cardiologist said his long-term prognosis was excellent. In September, he said in an interview with *The Huntsville Times* that he planned to run again, that he had felt great since the pacemaker was installed.[37]

24

At the End, a Man Respected

Since the late 1960s, the country had been moving to the right politically. The stage was set for this by the civil rights revolution and unrest associated with the Vietnam War. Two architects of the move, intellectually and ideologically, were George Wallace and Barry Goldwater, though they did their work in very different ways.

Barry Goldwater spoke openly against civil rights laws and was a military hawk in the 1964 presidential election, but his resounding defeat by Lyndon Johnson cast doubt on the political viability of his ideas. Wallace picked up many of Goldwater's thoughts, added his own brand of vitriolic, rabble-rousing populism, and revealed the depths of anti-government feeling, particularly among blue-collar and middle-income voters. He demonstrated the power of these ideas when he won eighteen percent of the vote in the 1968 presidential election, the most of any third party candidate in more than 100 years.

The right-wing movement was gaining strength through the first six years of Nixon's term. Then it was interrupted by Watergate and its repercussions, two of which were the Ford and Carter presidencies. Conservatism regained its momentum with the election of Reagan and then was strengthened through his appointments to the Supreme Court.

A powerful force was added when Christian conservatives began working in a disciplined way to gain power in the Republican party and to shape the party's agenda. Anthony Lewis commented in the *New York*

Times on new restrictions on abortion, including an intended Constitutional amendment to outlaw it, concern with sexual matters, and legislation to limit U.S. aid for population control efforts around the world. He noted that criminal law was a possible area for punitive moralism.[1]

The Birmingham News reported in November 1996 that politics was showing up in pulpits in Alabama, with some ministers urging people to vote for particular candidates. Carl Grafton, political science professor at Auburn University, remarked that he saw no correlation between ethical soundness in government and religious practices. "Some of the biggest crooks in Alabama political history have been good churchgoers," he noted. "What self-respecting crook would declare himself to be an agnostic or atheist?"[2]

The move to the right reached a critical new stage in the 1994 elections when Republicans captured the U.S. House of Representatives and the Senate. The 1994 freshmen class of House members contained a number of far-right ideologues who were burdened with fixed ideas and positions and were unwilling to negotiate and compromise. Representative Terry Everett of Alabama—a conservative Republican—commented on the invective showing up on the House and Senate floors, "I find it difficult at times to hide my disgust at the language members use to describe other members."[3]

THE DECISION TO RETIRE. In March of 1995, Heflin was on a list of possible retirees identified by the Senate Democratic campaign chief, Bob Kerry. Heflin said, "I'm going through a series of medical examinations. I want to be sure about my health before I make a decision to run again."[4]

Steve Raby recalls what happened next. "When Bill Gardiner died, I think it made Heflin recognize another campaign might be difficult. Several months after that, I had these computer printouts, and I was taking Fob James's vote county-by-county and assuming that James or whoever would get the same vote in that county. Could we win another one? [Heflin] studied this stuff over a weekend, and then he just threw it down and said, 'I know we can win one more, and it probably won't be as pretty as the other ones. I know that, but I'm not worried about that election. I'm worried about the six years after it. If I'm fortunate enough to be alive and I'm in office, Tuscumbia won't be home. My buddies are down there right now, and I can go to lunch with them. That old house, that's Elizabeth Ann's. I don't care about that, but I want to go home.'"[5]

On March 30, Senator Heflin announced that he would not seek reelection. This was more than a year in advance of the next election, and it gave those interested in replacing him plenty of time to think things through and get organized. Jockeying to run for his seat was soon underway.

Heflin appeared on the Phil Donahue show on December 12, 1995, with fellow retirees, Senators Paul Simon of Illinois and James Exon of Nebraska and Representative Pat Schroeder of Colorado. Heflin said he was going home to baby-sit his grandchildren. "I might fool with a law practice again, I may go fishing, I may even watch the Donahue show."[6]

NASA AND DEFENSE MATTERS. There were still attempts to cut the space station during Heflin's final Senate years. Great progress had been made in the program, and a number of countries were cooperating in building and maintaining the station. Cuts now made no sense.

In September 1995, the Senate rejected 64-35 an amendment by Arkansas Senator Dale Bumpers to cut $1.8 billion from NASA's budget and prohibit the agency from spending any more on the space station. In arguing against the amendment, Heflin said, "Research in medicine, materials and processes, engineering and technology will have immediate, practical application and will create jobs and economic opportunities today and in the decade to come."[7] He knew personally how true that was.

The previous October, in a speech not long after his recovery from heart surgery, he said he owed his life to the space program. The angioplasty, his pacemaker, and the stent all had roots to space-based or related research. "I stand as a living example of the spinoff from the space program."[8]

The Republican Congress passed budget proposals early in 1995 that would have severely cut NASA, and Clinton vetoed them. House Republicans announced that they would close the Marshall Space Flight Center by 1998, along with other NASA facilities in Maryland and Virginia. Heflin and others worked furiously behind the scenes, and by December this threat had been eliminated.

In 1996, Senator Heflin's last year in the Senate, NASA and the space station enjoyed a banner year. Congress approved a NASA budget of $14.37 billion which included $2.1 billion for Space Station Freedom, now international in scope.

A fight had started in the 1980s over closing Fort McClellan near Anniston, Alabama. Early in 1990, the base was on a list of closings released by Secretary of Defense Richard Cheney. The Defense Department argued that budget constraints and the changing nature of the Soviet threat forced troop cuts, and fewer training facilities were needed. Senators Heflin and Shelby joined Representative Glen Browder of Anniston and the rest of the Alabama delegation in strongly opposing the closing.

The next year, Fort McClellan was again on the closing list, and the Alabama delegation fought intensely. A federal commission visited the base at the end of June and voted to keep it open. What the commission did officially was to remove McClellan from the closure list it presented to President Bush. Bush could accept the recommendations or not. McClellan's status as the Army's sole chemical warfare training site probably saved it on this occasion. The 1990 Gulf War, which involved the threat of chemical weapons, had heightened awareness.

Fort McClellan was on the closure list again in 1995, and within a short time it became clear it would not escape, the efforts of Heflin and other members of the Alabama delegation not withstanding.[9] Clinton signed the closure bill, and the fight ended.

> When the base closure commission voted, it was a tie. The chairman, Allen Dixon, practiced law in Illinois across the river from Missouri, the state that would receive the units removed from a closed Fort McClellan. He really got the McClellan closing through. In my

judgment, he did some unfair maneuvering. We'd won the issue three times before.

Chemical warfare is, along with the proliferation of biological weapons and terrorism, an increasing threat to American security. Even though Fort McClellan is being closed, I still hold the conviction that the U.S. must continue vital chemical warfare defensive training, and it must keep the live agent training at the same facility.

The Army announced in June of 1995 that more than 2,500 jobs would go to Redstone Arsenal in Huntsville. A New Aviation and Missile Command was to be formed. General William Gilbert T. Tuttle, Jr., commander of the Army Material Command, had commissioned a study of the various bases under him, and he recommended consolidating them all and moving a combined operation to Redstone Arsenal. "Later, others didn't want to lose their bases and politics raised its head," Heflin says. "Another general came along with some question about it, and they didn't do it. The 2,500 jobs we got at Redstone was following General Tuttle's consolidation concept at Redstone. One of these days, Redstone may end up with much more."

Despite the closing of Fort McClellan, Alabama gained more than $1.3 billion in defense spending in fiscal 1996 as a result of a new effort to build a national missile defense system. Projects benefiting in Alabama included the THADD missile, the Army's Anti-Satellite Program (ASAT), new electronic test equipment produced in Huntsville, bodies of 60 new Blackhawk helicopters to be made in Tallassee, and the Hellfire and Javelin missiles built by Lockheed-Martin in Troy.

THE 1996 ELECTION. In May 1996, Senate Majority Leader Robert Dole resigned to seek the Republican nomination for president. Dole could have run without resigning. Heflin, a close Senate friend, said he believed Dole felt it had become impossible to compromise with radical Republican House members. "I think he did not want to be a part of an ineffective Congress while running for president."[10]

Heflin's seat would be up for grabs in the election, and a scramble began for each party's nomination. Seven Republicans and four Democrats entered the primaries. Among Republicans was Jefferson Sessions, state attorney general and former U.S. attorney in Mobile, whose bid for a federal judgeship Heflin had helped to derail in 1986. Democratic hopefuls included Representative Glen Browder (a Ph.D. in political science), and Roger Bedford, a leader in the state Senate and brother-in-law of former Alabama and New York Jets star Richard Todd.

Sessions and Bedford won run-offs after their respective primaries and opposed each other in the November 5 general election, conducted amidst general voter apathy.[11] During the campaign, columnist Bob Ingram related the following story about state politics. "Once in a rural Alabama county, a long-time probate judge, the unquestioned political boss of his county, was challenged by an young upstart. The judge had made vote-stealing an art form. To everybody's surprise, the judge barely won. The next day, when he was asked about the election, he said, 'Had I known it was gonna be that close, it wouldn't a been that close.'"[12]

Alabamians were asked in a poll which mattered to them most in picking a presidential candidate, issue or personal characteristics. Sixty percent responded "issues" and only twenty-four percent "personal characteristics," showing that conservative Alabamians, like most Americans, care more about issues than the character of the candidates.[13] This preference by the people was to drive pundits and right-wingers close to madness in the impeachment investigation and trial two years later. The poll of Alabama voters also revealed the perception that government doesn't respond to the average citizen but to particular interests.

Clinton made a reelection speech at Birmingham-Southern College on October 26, and Heflin introduced him with the widely quoted remarks, "Throughout the campaign the radical far-right pachyderms have been raising their snouts and trumpeting their mud-slinging politics of desperation and thundering sounds of doom, as well as spraying their venom of unsubstantiated charges, concocted libel, and vicious slander. But in the last few days we are beginning to hear from a large segment of the herd the groans of anticipated defeat."

After the speech, a correspondent from the *London Times* came up to

Heflin and said, "You stole the show with that speech." National Public Radio carried part of Heflin's remarks the next day.

Republicans scored big in Alabama in the 1996 general elections. Dole captured the state, and so did Sessions. Alabama Republicans now held the Governor's chair, both U.S. Senate seats, five of seven House seats, most Court of Criminal Appeals positions, the presidency of the Public Service Commission, and many more offices. It was the first time since the Goldwater sweep in 1964 that the GOP had a majority of the state's U.S. House delegation.[14]

Heflin believes the Democrats could have won Alabama in 1996 if they had turned out their voters on election day. He noted that 40,000 people attended Clinton's speech in Birmingham, but only 3,000 came out to hear Dole in Montgomery the same day. "It scared the Republicans to death that they were going to lose Alabama, and they poured the money in to get the vote out. When Clinton came here, the Democratic party officials had written off Alabama. All the newspapers were Republican and were for Bush. But we had a real chance if the national party had given us some get-out-the-vote money," Heflin said.

In a fine irony, newly elected Senator Sessions found himself on the Senate Judiciary Committee. This was the same committee which ten years before had rejected his nomination to the U.S. district judgeship in Mobile, and the same committee on which Heflin had cast the deciding vote against him.[15]

FINAL BUSINESS. In December 1994, Clinton fired U.S. Surgeon General Dr. Joycelyn Elders following a conservative outcry after she stated in a moment of unguarded public candor that children should be taught about masturbation. Clinton nominated Henry Foster, a black physician, as her successor. Foster grew up in Alabama and was for eight years an obstetrician-gynecologist in Tuskegee. In 1973 he moved to Nashville. The right-wing was soon on Foster because he had once performed abortions, and there were allegations that he was connected with the Tuskegee Syphilis Study, the tragic federal study in which hundreds of black men with syphilis were left untreated for four decades so that the progression of the disease could be studied. Shelby said the nomination should be withdrawn. Heflin did not take a position, saying he would wait for the confirmation hearing to decide if Foster was qualified.[16]

The fight went on several months, and the Senate Labor and Human Resources Committee finally approved the nomination 9-7. The Senate refused to vote on confirmation. Republicans staged a filibuster to keep it from coming up, and the attempt to end the filibuster failed 57-43. Heflin made a speech on Foster's behalf and was among those voting to end debate.[17] The outcome was called a victory for Christian conservatives and the National Right to Life Committee. Republican Senator Arlen Specter of Pennsylvania said his party was cowering before the Christian right and turning mainstream Americans away in droves.[18]

At the beginning of his third term, Heflin had cosponsored a comprehensive judicial act with three major parts: 1) The Civil Justice Reform Act, which required selected U.S. courts to implement expense and delay reduction plans; 2) the Federal Judgeships Act, which created 74 new U.S. district judges and 11 new U.S. circuit judges; and, 3) the Federal Courts Study Committee Implementation Act, which dealt with such things as television violence, computer software rental, judicial discipline, and the rights of visual artists. The latter incorporated procedures for disciplining federal judges and establishing a National Commission on Judicial Discipline. The Federal Courts Administration Act of 1992 contained four Heflin-sponsored bills and a provision he cosponsored which created a new civil cause of action in federal court for victims of international terrorism.

Through the years, Heflin was the moving force behind passage of the Omnibus Victims Protection Act of 1982, the bill establishing the State Justice Institute in 1984, the Justice Assistance Act and the Permanent Federal Court Study Act in 1984, the Judicial Improvements and Access to Justice Act of 1989, the Civil Justice Reform Act of 1990, and the Bankruptcy Reform Act of 1994.

In 1995, the Alabama state legislature voted to mark the Trail of Tears as a historical reminder of the suffering of American Indians during their exodus from the Southeast in the 1830s. The Removal Act of 1830 had resulted in the forced relocation of about 17,000 Creeks and members of other tribes, and about 4,000 died on the march west. Heflin supported the measure.[19]

Heflin announced in September 1995 that he would use his leftover campaign money, a little over $1 million, for scholarships to help needy Alabama students attend Alabama universities.[20]

ACCOLADES AND THE RETURN HOME. In his eighteen years in the Senate, Heflin was a crucial vote in an uncanny number of important issues. An editorial in the conservative *Mobile Register*, which had often criticized him, noted that integrity marked Heflin's service, and twice his peers had made him the keeper of the Senate's standards as the Ethics Committee chairmen. It continued,

> Born with a famous name and a keen mind, Howell Heflin enjoyed a head start on the politicians of his generation. He could think quicker and talk faster than most of them. Just as important, he avoided the racial baggage that separated the old-style politicians from the new. Such qualities put him at the top of his class as Alabama's senior U.S. senator.
>
> Mr. Heflin's humor lost some of its warmth and bite when translated through the youthful medium of television. (His) prominent role during the televised Clarence Thomas hearings underscored his distance in style and generation from the Senate's sound-bite masters. Yet Mr. Heflin towered over most of them with his impeccable knowledge of the law.[21]

Joe Azbell of the *Montgomery Independent* wrote that Heflin had been a great senator in every way. "We have kept our military bases and gained," he noted. "We have seen a man of dignity. He is known nationally by probably more people than anyone since Senator John Sparkman, who was Democratic Party vice presidential candidate. Heflin is loved and hated. He fights for what is right."[22] The Cumberland School of Law gave him its Lifetime Achievement Award.[23]

Heflin was lauded by members of the Alabama Farmers Federation at a luncheon in Washington on March 19. Outgoing national affairs director Dick Fifield called Heflin "one of the greatest senators that ever lived" and lauded him for standing up for farmers "during those difficult years when people were trying to kill farm bills." "You have looked out after us down through the years," said peanut farmer James Mobley.[24]

He was recognized in June at the North Alabama Annual Conference of the United Methodist Church for his life-long contribution to the United States, Alabama, and the United Methodist Church. In accepting the award, Heflin said he looked forward to becoming active in his home church and added that "By God's guidance, we can solve our problems."[25]

Auburn hosted an appreciation dinner on September 20. Former Representative Glen Browder described Heflin as "a complete workhorse for our state interests." Pete Turnham, a long-time state senator, called Heflin "a national treasure."[26]

He received NASA's Distinguished Service Medal in November 1996. NASA Administrator Dan Goldin noted that Heflin was the first senator to propose the space station and that very few people were given the award.[27] In response to a remark during that event about Elizabeth Ann, Heflin said, "It just proves you can go to Washington and stay married to the same woman."[28]

Dr. William Stewart, chairman of the political Science department at the University of Alabama, stated, "I think Howell Heflin is the most outstanding Alabama Senator in this century." Other Alabama senators in the twentieth century included Lister Hill, John Sparkman, Hugo Black, William Bankhead, Tom Heflin, and Oscar W. Underwood, so Stewart's remark was quite a compliment.[29]

Just before Heflin retired, Dr. Mary Frances Berry, chairperson of the U.S. Commission on Civil Rights, and a former chancellor of the University of Colorado, said, "I have known Senator Heflin since he came to the Senate of the United States, and he has been a champion on issues of justice and equality for his entire career. He will be very much missed."[30]

Senator Heflin received a large number of other awards during his career. His awards and special recognitions are listed in Appendix A.

President Clinton said that Heflin's "solid belief in right and wrong and his sense of humor have helped the nation confront some of our toughest issues head-on, while his efforts in areas of education and race relations have changed the course of the country."[31]

Tuesday, October 2, 1996, was a day of tributes for retiring members of the Senate. In speaking of Heflin, Senator Trent Lott of Mississippi said, "Some people say he talks a little funny. I never noticed it. I think he has no accent whatsoever, but I do get a little chuckle out of the fact sometimes that people come over and say, 'Interpret that for me.' Whatever he's saying, it is worth listening to."[32]

Lott may have heard of the March visit between President Clinton and the University of North Alabama football team, which had won three consecutive national championships in NCAA Division II. UNA was the first school in any division to achieve this feat. The UNA defense was called the "Purple Swarm," and in introducing the champions, Heflin pronounced "Swarm" as "Swaam," in a way which rhymed with bomb. The media was perplexed, and he repeated himself several times, with little success. Finally, he spelled it out, "Swaam — s-w-a-r-m."[33]

Senator Larry Pressler of South Dakota said the Senate would miss the homespun ditties of Heflin. He recalled, "As the Senate deliberated whether or not to designate the rose as America's flower, Heflin recited a poem: 'Roses are red. Violets are blue. Why must I choose between the two?'"[34]

Senator Bennett Johnston of Louisiana said, "I am inclined to think that Howell Heflin is the last of the great Southern senators who reflect these old-time values and style and warmth."[35] Senator James Exon of Nebraska called him, "A true workhorse and not a show horse of the Senate." Republican Senator Kay Bailey Hutchison from Texas commented that "Senator Heflin has the deep respect of people from both sides of the aisle."

Senator Ted Kennedy reflected, "On issues ranging from civil rights to controversial judicial nominations to constitutional law, Senator

Heflin consistently displays an uncanny ability to bring people together and to find common ground without regard to party politics. Sen. Heflin was called 'The Judge' by myself and the rest of my Senate colleagues. This was a nickname given out of enormous respect for his steady demeanor, his judicious temperament, and his extraordinary grasp of the law and its consequences. Every major court reform measure passed in the last 18 years bears his mark. Without Sen. Heflin's deep understanding of these and many other issues, the Senate would not have acted in the best interests of the American people."[36]

Robert Dole said, "He has become known, in the words of the Almanac of American Politics, as a careful lawyer who picks at the rules of law with the delicate touch of a watch repairman."

Ted Stevens, Republican of Alaska, stated, "I know of no state that has sent a better representative to the Senate in the time I have been here than Alabama when they sent Howell Heflin."[37]

One might suspect that all these accolades and many others not repeated here were typical for a retiring Senator from his colleagues. But they were not. Steve Raby said it was unusual for so many senators to come to the floor. "What normally happens is that someone will say, 'Mr. President, there is unanimous consent that I be allowed the statement be recorded as read,' and they don't spend much time. This went on six or eight hours. It shut down a full day and a half of the Senate. They usually do it during the morning business.[38]

BACK HOME. Heflin's Senate career ended the first week of October 1996, the day the 104th Congress adjourned. He remained in office officially until January 3 when the next Congress was seated, but there was no further legislative business after October. Heflin cast his last Senate vote on October 3.

In closing the office, Heflin's staff cataloged 962 mementos and more than 700 boxes of letters, photographs, videotapes, news clippings and bills. Most of this archival material was given to the Library of the University of Alabama Law School.

On returning home to Tuscumbia, Heflin said only two things were certain—he was going on vacation and he wouldn't be under foot at home from nine to five. "The main thing my wife tells me is she wants me out of the house at 9:00, and I can come back about 5:00. So I'm going to have to have a place to hang out." He expected the hanging-out place would be his son Tom's law office in Tuscumbia.

25

Candidate of the Alfalfa Club

AS MUCH AS ANY single event, a banquet speech delivered in jest in 1989 depicted the wit for which Howell Heflin was widely known. Heflin's speech was given at the annual dinner of the Alfalfa Club in Washington, and in it he accepted the nomination for president on the Alfalfa ticket.

The Alfalfa Club, formed in 1913, has a limited membership and includes people from all walks of American life. The *New York Times* describes an Alfalfa Club dinner as a "largely white male power elite having lobster, champagne and filet mignon," and it notes that the event is always attended by the President, the Vice President, and the First Lady. In the audience is "a dazzling array of Washington luminaries, Cabinet members, jurists, ambassadors, lobbyists, presidential contenders and leading CEOs dressed in black tie. Several members of Congress also attend."[1] When Heflin made his speech, the Club had 225 members, twelve of whom were senators. Heflin had become a member in 1986.

Members can bring two guests a year to the dinner, and Heflin had invited on various occasions his Shoals buddies, Ed Mauldin, Bert Haltom, Sherry Winford, and Joe Ware. All were highly impressed. Ed Mauldin recalls that he and his wife, Mildred, stayed in the Capitol Hilton, and he says "I have never seen so many four-star generals, so many people who were former Secretary of State and Secretary of Defense and such, TV celebrities, a number of senators, and some House members. Elizabeth Taylor was there with her husband, John Warner."

Bert Haltom remembers, "The party starts at 5:30, and it lasts till 11:00. The booze was flowing. I knew damn well I'd get drunk if I wasn't careful, so I held up on the drinks. Clinton and his wife attended along with all the cabinet members and their wives. They came in, of course, to the usual fanfare, and while dinner was going on, they were sitting at a higher level than the rest of us.

"While we were all eating, Heflin sneaked all over the floor seeing who he wanted to introduce us to. His first choice was the President and his wife, and while the dinner was in progress, he took me and Tom Christopher, the former dean of our law school, up there. It is an imposition while somebody's eating to do that, but the President didn't give any evidence of being offended at all. I met General Colin Powell and his son.

"It impressed the hell out of me because I'd never seen such celebrities like that. There was not a single business executive in the country who was top-notch in my judgment who was not an invited guest or a member. I can't even remember what I ate, I was so excited about it."

The United States Marine Band provided music at the 1989 meeting where Howell made his acceptance speech, and among those present were Anthony Acland, the British Ambassador to the United States; Howard Baker; former Attorney General Griffin Bell; Lloyd M. Bentsen, who had just been defeated in a run for vice president; Secretary of the Treasury Nicholas F. Brady; financier Warren E. Buffett; banker David Rockefellow; former Chief Justice Warren E. Burger; President George Bush; Admiral William J. Crowe, Jr., Chairman of the Joint Chiefs of Staff; Secretary of Housing and Urban Development Jack Kemp; Alan Greenspan; Henry Kissinger; Vice President Dan Quayle; General Colin Powell; and Elliot Richardson.

Heflin's nomination for president by the Alfalfa Club was a good-natured joke, of course, cooked up by Sam Nunn and some of the other members. It was a way to let Heflin display his famous humor and provide entertainment for the evening. His "acceptance" speech is included in the Appendix.

26

The Qualities of an Effective Senator

THE FOUNDING FATHERS, in their wisdom and their knowledge of human nature, set up a system of checks and balances in the government of the United States. They made the legislature the most powerful branch of government, and for good measure, they divided it into two parts which check each other. The House of Representatives is a body of relative youngsters who often represent a homogeneous constituency, full of vigor and new ideas, and often carried away with issues of the moment. The Senate, in contrast, is the place for deliberation; for a concern with history, tradition, and stability; and for a national view and the ability to see and act on the big picture. In short, the Senate is a place for statesmen.

Howell Heflin was ideal for his role as senator. Among the characteristics which made Heflin an effective Senator were great mental capacity with ability to comprehend the whole, patience, and a strong work ethic which showed itself in strenuous preparation to handle the tasks at hand. Heflin studied issues in depth and, as his colleagues soon learned, he was always prepared for discussion and debate. He showed great perseverance and almost always managed to achieve success with an issue, even when the odds were against him. He was known for his ability to work with people, to take a bipartisan approach, and to make the compromises necessary to reach a fair and workable solution.

Howell Heflin also demonstrated wisdom. After his retirement was announced, Senator Bennett Johnston of Louisiana said, "As I began to contemplate his service here, I wondered what was the single word that best epitomized Senator Heflin's service. The word that came to mind first was 'wisdom.' Wisdom is a rare thing. Our Creator has been very generous with Senator Heflin in endowing him with a large amount of wisdom and a large amount of ability. He has acquired both the skill and the knowledge to be, indeed, one of the wisest members of this body."[1]

INTEGRITY. Howell Heflin is a man of honesty and integrity, and this has been one of his great strengths as a politician, both in Washington and at home. The people of Alabama knew he was honest, and they valued this characteristic highly, proving several times that honesty and integrity were more important to them than unpopular stands he took on civil rights and such matters as Bork and Iran-Contra.

Senator Heflin looked over an early outline of this book and said to me, the author, "You need to add some warts. And there are plenty." Taking him at his word, I searched for warts, but they were difficult to find. When they were found, they were on the order of his slowness in understanding the implications of the women's and the environmental movements.

In all of the research and interviewing for this book, I had an unique experience. Not once was Senator Heflin's honesty or integrity questioned, whether it pertained to his personal life or his professional life. This was true even though interviewees were probed for criticism. I felt like the author of the following editorial, which was written during his campaign for chief justice:

> Try as we did, we couldn't find a single criticism, flaw or weakness (in Heflin). From lawyers and non-lawyers alike, from Democrats and Republicans, came the same extravagant praise. After a time, it got downright monotonous.
>
> It was an unsettling experience. Although we first knew Heflin more than 20 years ago at the University of Alabama and recognized his potential even then, surely in his 22 years of practice and public service

he has offended somebody or done something we could offer by way of showing that he is, after all, flawed like the rest of us.

Finally, after vigorous cross-examination, we did get one lawyer to admit a minor grievance. When Heflin was President of the state bar, the man said, "He may have driven some lawyers a little too hard in some of the committees."[2]

Steve Raby speaks of one thing which might be considered by some a sizable wart. "Situations like Iran Contra, the Bork hearings, Anita Hill, and Justice Thomas's hearings were not good for Heflin in terms of political perception because of his insistence of being a judge all the time. Heflin's love for the Judiciary Committee created the only political problems we had. If it were not for that, we would not have had any.

"Before a hearing of the magnitude of Iran-Contra, you're months and months taking depositions. The day of the hearing, committee members knew what each witness was going to say and what their answers would be. Good staff would prepare their senators so they gave the appearance of trapping the witness as they questioned. Judge Heflin would sit through a lot of these depositions, and the rest he would read and highlight with his pencil. He wanted to find answers. Depending upon the hearing, questioners had maybe five or seven minutes. He didn't want to weave a web for four minutes because he may not get all of his questions answered. So he would just jump on them. There was no flow to the questions he asked because he wouldn't work though all of this stuff getting to it. For television, it looked unorganized.

"You'd talk to him about it. 'Judge, look pretty, wear your blue suit and your blue shirt, you know your colors look bad. Here's the questions. You need to read them tonight to get ready for tomorrow,' and he'd say, 'Aw, I'm not worried about what people think.' It would have been so much easier for him just to get a general overview the week before the hearings started. He literally would know more about it than the general counsel. It looked just awful on television, and he didn't care. He would say, 'Y'all leave me alone. I'm not a hair sprayed senator, I'm not a blow-dried senator. Y'all leave me alone on that stuff.'"

Another possible wart, Raby recalls, was Heflin's tendency to come across as a little rude at times. "He would just get abrupt in the middle of working, and if you didn't know him, you could be offended by it. That's really not much of a wart, is it?

"He was seen as waffling, but I can assure you he never was waffling. I know from watching his mental process he was never waffling. He would never make up his mind until he felt he had enough information to make up his mind. And once he made up his mind, I've never seen a person who could be so mentally at ease. No regrets, no hindsight."[3]

On the matter of integrity, Raby tells of an incident during a campaign. "In 1984, Bill Gardiner had spent time with me talking about federal races. 'You can't take cash for them. We're not going to do it, and anybody that does it is fired.' We had this nice campaign event set up at a little restaurant on the river, and one of our county coordinators walked up and shook the Judge's hand. He said, 'Judge, we're glad to have you here. We're going to have a good crowd.' You could tell it was one these funky handshakes. Heflin pulled away, and I just happened to be standing right there. There was a wad of money, and Heflin put it in his pocket. My first thought was, 'By God, we've just gone through all this stuff and they told me such and such.' It was just tremendous disappointment to see that.

"He gave the rah-rah speech, and after the meeting, he was standing on the front porch of this place. The coordinator said, 'Judge, I'll see you.' Heflin answered, 'Naw, naw, I want to talk to you a minute.' The guy tried to leave two or three times, and Heflin said to Tim and me, 'Don't let him leave. I need to talk to him.' When everybody left, he grabbed this fellow around his neck and pulled him up close. He reached in his pocket and stuck that money down that man's coat pocket. 'I appreciate this. This was such a good job. You're just one of my best coordinators.' Nobody saw it as far as he knew. It just stuck with me that this man had such integrity. He wasn't aware of anybody looking, and he did that. He's for real. He's for real."[4]

Heflin's integrity comes in part from his religious background. He does not wear his religion on his sleeve, so to speak, but strong religious beliefs have influenced him deeply throughout his life. He has been a leading layman in the United Methodist Church. He taught the men's Bible class in his church in Tuscumbia for fifteen years, he is currently on the administrative board of the First United Methodist Church of Tuscumbia, and he has been involved in his church in many other ways.

It is not widely known that Senator Heflin and Senator Ted Stevens, a Republican from Alaska, cochaired a weekly Senate prayer breakfast for a number of years. Senator Mark Hatfield of Oregon said it was "one place where we leave our masks, our labels — moderate, liberal, conservative, our party identification — at the door. Probably there is no other part of the Senate institution in which people feel so comfortable in being themselves."[5] Senator Kay Bailey Hutchison of Texas added that the prayer breakfasts were a very important time for senators to come together on a bipartisan basis and talk about "things that are bringing us together" and about "doing what is right rather than what is expedient, rather than something of a partisan nature."[6]

THE MASTERFUL POLITICIAN. Senator Heflin was a politician of consummate skill. He was smart and persistent, and he knew how to handle himself on the Senate floor. Many people have commented on Heflin's keen intellect. L. O. Bishop, a farmer and leader in the Alabama Farm Federation, has known Heflin since high school and worked with him professionally. "As I watched through the years," Bishop says, "I realized what great mental capacity Senator Heflin had. He wasn't a farmer, but when he was exposed to the farm programs and regulations, he comprehended them very quickly. I've had many people who dealt with him, including staff people and lobbyists, marvel at how quickly he could comprehend what was involved in a farm program."[7]

Robert Springer, a Clinton appointee to the Farm Service Agency, comments, "I have worked with a lot of state and national legislators, and I'll tell you unequivocally that there's not anybody from an intelligence standpoint, a quickness standpoint, a cognitive standpoint, you'll ever work with who is any better than Senator Heflin. You would begin to explain, and before you could get through he was already ahead of you.

He could stand up to the mike and answer questions, he could defend himself."[8]

Heflin is always one step ahead of the other side according to Mike House. "He's always done his homework. He's an incredibly smart man, but you wouldn't call Howell Heflin a genius. He's just smart. When other people are watching TV, Howell Heflin's figuring out how to do something. Nobody could work the Senate floor better than Howell Heflin. When he was on an issue, he would work that issue day in and day out. He knew where every vote was. He's like a chess master; he's thinking ten steps down the road. Most people, including the new breed of Senator, don't have the patience, the time, or the ability to think like that."[9]

Heflin believed in forming strong advocacy groups and working with his friends for different causes. He also did favors for other Senate members and then collected on those debts when he needed help. He had lists of senators he had supported on one issue or another over the years. As a vote on an issue approached, out would come the lists.

Former staff member Fred Clark says that, in his knowledge, Heflin never lost an issue totally because, even in compromise, he was a superb negotiator. "After negotiating all the way through in the Senate, the winner most of the time is the one who is standing at the end. Senator Heflin was always standing in the end. He was always the one who stayed the late hours. When there were conferences between the House and Senate, he was the last Senator to leave because he knew the very end was when the final compromise would be made."[10]

Heflin's great tenacity also made him effective. Charles E. Grainger, vice president of administration for Teledyne Brown Engineering in Huntsville, says, "I have never been around an officeholder who was more tenacious. In a body where processes are tied to the committee system, he regularly offered successful amendments and carried the day on issues such as NASA and defense even though he was not a member of the committee of jurisdiction."[11]

Steve Raby notes that Heflin was never one to accept legislative defeat without trying to find an alternative,[12] and former staff member Fred

Clark says, "One of the main lessons I learned from Senator Heflin was never to accept defeat. Make the people on the other side of the issue show you they can beat you. When they have shown you that they can beat you in terms of votes, then compromise. In compromising, still win."[13]

Heflin could also be stern when the situation demanded it. Former staff member Mark Young recalls, "One time J. R. Thompson, head of the Marshall Space Flight Center, came in. Marshall had just killed a program called OMB, a NASA program, without telling us. When you're a politician, a lack of information is your worst enemy. We wouldn't have let them kill OMB, and Heflin just hated being blindsided. Thompson came into the office, sat down and said, 'Now Senator, let me start.' Heflin struck the table with his hand and said, 'No, I'll start, and I'll finish.' You can bet that while J. R. Thompson was at Marshall, nothing else happened without him talking to us first."[14]

Young also relates an incident which shows Heflin's practical side. "Once the *Wall Street Journal* wrote an editorial about SDI stating that Senators Heflin, Kennedy, and others of that ilk never supported the Patriot program and other missile defense programs because they're not in their states. It was untrue because Heflin had always supported the Patriot program. So I said, 'Senator Heflin, we have got to write a response to this. We have got to point out that they are totally lying.' Senator Heflin said, 'Mark, never get into letter writing wars with people who buy ink by the barrel.'"[15]

WINNING BY WORKING. One of the keys to Howell Heflin's success was plain hard work. He won many an issue by working harder and being better prepared than the opposition. While others entertained themselves with social events and relaxed on weekends with golf or some similar activity, Heflin worked. During his entire Senate career, he either worked on weekends or went home to Alabama to take care of business there.[16]

Former staff member Fred Clark, now president of the Alabama Rural Electric Association, says of Heflin, "He built a reputation as someone who did not get into an issue that he was not prepared for. His colleagues in the Senate many times would refuse to debate him because they knew that he knew more about the issue than they did. Every issue that he was involved with, he knew he was going to win because he was going to be prepared, and he had done the work to build a successful coalition."[17]

One incident illustrates the attention Heflin would give an issue. A bill introduced by Senator Kennedy in the Judiciary Committee would overturn a Supreme Court decision on a civil rights issue. Kennedy's staff pressed from the beginning to determine where Heflin stood. Heflin met with and listened to both sides but would only say, "We'll study it," when pressed on what he was going to do. On the day of the vote, Heflin still had not indicated what he would do. When he spoke, he noted he had heard the arguments of senators, staff members, and lobbyists on both sides of the issue. He still could not make up his mind, so he went to the source of the debate, the Supreme Court decision. After studying the opinion, he was convinced that the Court was correct, and he would oppose the pending legislation.

Marine Lieutenant Colonel Debra Beily, who served a year as a Heflin Congressional Fellow, recalls how Heflin's sharp mind and work habits served him well. "When he had a meeting with an individual on an issue, his best weapon was his keen mind and the research he had done. No one would ever try to buffalo Senator Heflin either on the technical aspects of a program or the state of play on the Hill. He could always argue the technical aspects with the best of them."[18]

Steve Raby says that Heflin was always thinking ahead. "I remember our first farm bill in '85. The process started in January, and the bill was finally signed in December, so it was almost a full year's work. The committee finally reached an agreement. Staff were hugging their senators and shaking hands, and senators were congratulating each other. I felt all good about it. Judge Heflin turned around and grabbed my lapel and wanted me to step outside. I thought, 'Oh this is wonderful. He's going to congratulate me on being here only one year and doing such a fine job,' because we had accomplished everything we wanted to, or practically everything we wanted to. As we walked out, he grabbed my lapel again and said, 'Now this is what we do in the morning.' While everybody else was patting themselves on the back, he was planning for the next step."[19]

A CAPACITY FOR FRIENDLY DISAGREEMENT. As widely noted, Howell Heflin approached his job in the manner of a judge when he was studying issues, and he believed people could disagree with him and still be his friend. He spoke many times about how distasteful he found the increased partisanship in Washington in recent years and how harmful he believes it is to the country for those on one side of an issue to demonize their opponents and try to claim their own point of view is holy.

Heflin's moderation was another key to his success.

> We foster democratic principles throughout the world and have seen democracy make great strides in many non-democratic countries. Yet our own democracy faces its greatest threat from within. Elected officials, media personalities, elements of political parties, and other organizations strive to pit one group of Americans against another. We must set a new course in Congress and across the land — a course of moderation, tolerance, responsibility, and compassion. We need to return to the traditional value of being just plain neighborly.[20]
>
> Government has worked best when it has operated from the center of the spectrum. Only when we have strayed too far to the left or right have we fallen so out of favor with the citizenry. In such a complex, diverse and large country as ours, extreme rigid views on either side can only perpetuate alienation from and dissatisfaction with government.[21]
>
> There should be a ladies' and gentlemen's agreement making it a taboo to demonize your political opponents. Far too much of today's debate consists of trying to promote one's position through the character assassination of an opponent. Even in circumstances where this tactic succeeds, the victory is inherently hollow and will not stand the test of time.[22]

Former Alabama Supreme Court Justice Sam Beatty said of Heflin, "Few persons reach the pinnacle of complete accommodation with both the nobler purposes of life and the art of the practical. Howell Heflin is one of these. The rest of us are his beneficiaries."[23]

SOUTHERN HUMOR. Senator Heflin's quick wit and Southern humor are legendary, and they served him well in several respects. He was always able to lower tension and ease a difficult situation by making a quip or telling a story at just the right time. His humor also helped him greatly in keeping his ties with the home folks and maintaining popularity among the electorate. Mark Russell, the piano-playing political humorist, remarked, "When you talk about humor and politics in Alabama, you eventually reach the subject of Howell Heflin." With Heflin, Russell said, the mood in Washington took an upswing. "Here is a scholar who could speak the genuine (gen-yoo-wine) Southern language of Cornpone on a par with . . . Sam Ervin."[24]

Howell Heflin is much more than just humorous, however. He is, in fact, a very complex man. As noted, he is exceptionally bright and a very hard worker. He is ambitious and driven to accomplish his goals, and he infused his staff with this intensity and demanded much of them. He wants to be in total control when business is being conducted to be sure everything is as it should be. These characteristics are in sharp contrast to the easy-going, Foghorn Leghorn image he often projects.

Yet, the easy-going image is true to an extent. When he relaxes and is away from his desk and the tasks at hand, he is naturally funny. He is very witty in casual conversation and makes a meal or other social event a pleasant experience. When he associated with the people of his state, they felt he was one of them and not part of that wealthy, uppity "goochie-poochie" crowd.

In the Senate, Heflin's natural humor was used to great effect on many occasions. Former staff member Fred Clark comments that, "Senator Heflin was known as someone who could go into a committee meeting of fifteen senators in heated partisan debate, lighten the debate, say some kind words, say some things that brought people back down to earth, and achieve that compromise."[25]

L. O. Bishop tells of eating with Heflin once in Washington. "A group of us took the Senator out to eat. We were in one of those places which had fellows, with no expression on their face, standing against the wall to get what you needed before you knew you needed it. Senator Heflin and I would talk a lot about Freedom Hills and Coon Dog Cemetery and illegal whiskey operations. While we were telling these stories, my wife noticed that the young men who were waiting on us would have to leave and let somebody else take their place so they could hear and laugh about Senator Heflin's stories."[26]

Raby tells another story that demonstrated Heflin's wit. "It was at some point after his first health problems. We were in Washington, and the state medical association came up. There were usually between 400 and 500 people in attendance. On Sunday evening, Judge Heflin was speaking to this group. He has a tendency to lean on the podium. The PA wiring system was under the podium, wrapped up like a spring. As he had pushed the podium out, this thing sort of came out and wrapped around his feet. When he finished speaking, he turned to walk off with it wrapped around him, and he fell off the stage. These doctors came running over there and started pulling on him to get him up. I didn't know what it had done to his heart. I tried to get everybody out of the way, and I held my hand out to help him get up. He pulled himself up and dusted off. Everybody was so silent, ooing and aahing and everything. He stepped back up on the stage, grabbed the microphone, and said, 'Is there a lawyer in the house?'"[27]

One story which got considerable play among writers involved Ted Kennedy. Kennedy, who strongly opposed off-shore drilling as a danger to the environment, was having a little vacation on a yacht. A *Boston Globe* reporter took pictures from a helicopter showing the Massachusetts Senator in a compromising position with a young lady. The story was circulated that, the next time Heflin saw Kennedy in the Senate cloakroom, he said, "Well, Teddy, I see you have changed your position on off-shore drilling." Heflin claims this was a rumor spread by Republicans and he never said it, but it has all the earmarks of one of his witticisms.

REMEMBERING THE HOME FOLKS. Howell Heflin never forgot that he represented the people of Alabama nor that he himself was an Alabamian. He returned home very often on weekends to stay in touch with the folks. During his eighteen years in the Senate, he held more than 1,000 town meetings throughout Alabama to talk with and listen to farmers, businessmen, and other citizens. Except for the period when he had serious health problems, he visited every one of Alabama's sixty-seven counties each year he was a senator. He impressed people with his ability to listen, and many of his positions in the Senate were developed through discussions with the home folks. He was especially popular among those in rural areas who knew he was waging the good fight for them in Washington.

Heflin's bond with the common people of his state was real and not a political ploy. Fred Clark, president of the Alabama Rural Electric Association and a former staff member said, "Senator Heflin has demonstrated a great love for the people of rural Alabama. The rural vote in Alabama has been a strong Heflin vote, and this was due to the people's belief in and support of his leadership. I have known Senator Heflin as a great leader, a great debater, and a great winner — a winner being a legislator successful in achieving things that are positive and helpful to the people he represents."[28]

Heflin reintroduced the town meeting tradition to Alabama. State Senator Ed Horton, who was a member of the Judicial Commission in the 1970s and worked with Heflin closely in later years, explains what a town meeting was like. "These were meetings to talk with farmers and university economists and so forth," he says. "It was so interesting the way he would listen as much to an older fellow in overalls as he would to a Ph.D. economist from a university or research organization. It was a combination of a learning experience for him and a political effort for reelection. He could articulate the issues so that people could understand them. He talked softly; he conveyed sincerity; and he made you feel as though you were important to him. He was always at ease; he was always knowledgeable; and he never had to worry about covering up because he didn't know about an issue."[29]

In recalling his experiences in town meetings, Heflin says, "They'd ask you all sorts of things. They would want to know, 'How much do you eat?' 'cause I was so big. Then they'd ask you, 'How much money do you make?' One time somebody asked me 'where is your body guard?' One time at a place, one fellow came in with big stick, and I thought he was going to hit me or something. He was, you know, violently opposed to this and that and everything. Finally he gave me the stick and said, 'Go take it to Washington, and give a whuppin' to Ronald Reagan.'"

Senator Heflin also liked to meet with high school students, and he had more than five hundred appearances in high schools during his Senate career. He says he got the idea for high school meetings from John Sparkman. "I was a boy at Colbert County High in Leighton. Sparkman came to speak to us, and I always remembered it."[30] Heflin enjoyed meeting the students and considered it a learning experience for them. He wanted to help them become better citizens.

Of course those appearances could take unexpected turns. Heflin was once appearing before a group of high school students when the the discussion turned to sexual behavior. He had taken a strong stand for abstinence and then a student asked, "Did you ever have premarital sex?" Relating this story later, the Senator said, with a glint in his eye, "I carefully evaded the question."

Howell Heflin's record reveals traits of statesmanship of the highest order. Harry Truman, Barry Goldwater, and Howell Heflin all exemplify the qualities we value most highly in our public servants — unquestioned integrity, productivity, straight talk, and dedication to the fundamental values of our country.

27

Views of the Country and the Presidency

During his eighteen years in the Senate, Howell Heflin was in an unique position as a Washington insider to observe the domestic and foreign affairs of the United States. In supporting research and development, the space program and Space Station Freedom, civil rights, and in serving as U.S. Representative to the North Atlantic Assembly, Heflin proved himself unusually insightful in understanding how present actions affect the future. Heflin's insightfulness has not diminished. Even though he is in full retirement from the Senate, he has not retired from the Washington scene. His contact with the Democratic Party, political cronies and friends, and his penchant for keeping up with the news allows him to stay informed and close to the inside track. When some domestic or international crisis looms, journalists still make their telephone calls to or knock on the door of the former Senator.

Potential Problems. Asked to comment on the challenges and opportunities the country faces in the new century, Heflin quickly enumerates. Domestically, he feels that one of our greatest needs is to improve the education system. Other primary needs involve health, Social Security, and energy:

> You are now hearing about energy needs, and it will be a growing

problem with the depletion of oil reserves, increased needs for electricity, and the need for alternative sources. Transportation needs and inflation are also matters we must face. Continuing trade deficits may finally be a major problem. We must realize there is an interaction between our trade policy and our concern for farmers, jobs, environment, and human rights.

Internationally, Heflin expresses concern about the free market economy, the survival of democracy, the consequences of unchecked population growth, the environment, and biological warfare conducted by terrorists and smaller countries. Also, he feels there is the possible rebirth of Marxism and authoritative rule in some countries, as well as the erosion of human rights. Looming over the international scene is China and its growing power and influence. Heflin says all of these are important, but most significant are "maintaining international leadership, the presidency, education, diversity and the race problem, the people's faith in their democratic system, difficulties associated with world population growth, and the growing threat of terrorism."

THE PRESIDENCY. Senator Heflin served under four U.S. presidents during a period of change, unrest, turmoil, and cultural transition from the nation's past history. His Senate tenure witnessed the dissolution of the Soviet Union, the reunification of Germany, the rapid advance of the Information Age with a closely-integrated international economy, an assault on American's civil rights gains, huge deficit spending, and advancing technology in all fields including medical science. He believes that maintaining international leadership and managing domestic affairs requires strong, capable presidents, and he respects the enormous responsibility that falls on the office.

> In my opinion, the four Presidents I served with — Carter, Reagan, Bush, and Clinton — were all good Presidents and were all successful in different ways. Who will historians pick as the most outstanding President among those with whom I served? After I retired, I once

earned my way across the Atlantic giving talks on the *Queen Elizabeth II*; I sang for my supper, so to speak. During those talks, I mentioned a number of criteria I believe historians will use as they evaluate presidents. Among the most important are:

A. The President's vision for America and the steps he implemented to advance the country toward that vision, with such examples as the avoidance of World War III and the reduction of many of our societal ills.

B. The success with which the President handled crises. To judge this, we need to look at these factors: 1) The severity and magnitude of each crisis he faced; 2) Final outcome and the effectiveness with which he handled each crisis; 3) Risks that the President recognized and took; and, 4) Whether he did what he felt was right for the country in spite of personal and political risks.

I am a Democrat who strongly supported Al Gore in the 2000 election, but I have tried to be objective using the above criteria in making my observations. If I had to make a choice right now as to the most effective of the four, I would select George [Herbert Walker] Bush. Let's look at Carter, Reagan, and Clinton briefly, and then I will defend my choice of Bush.

Carter was a very religious individual motivated by what he thought was best for the country. He had compassion, and he approached things in moderation. Carter aspired to make government competent, compassionate, and responsive to the needs of the American people. But times were difficult, with rising energy costs, inflation, high interest rates, and foreign tension.

Domestically, Carter reduced deficit spending with his zero-plus budget policy and faced the energy crisis with considerable success. In foreign policy, he achieved the Camp David Accords, which laid the groundwork for peace in the Middle East, settled the Panama Canal issue, and faced the Iran crisis. Eventually we'll have to return to his program of alternative energy sources because our conventional sources will be diminished by greater demand.

His demand for increased military preparedness with a call for all nations to increase by 3 percent their military budgets was the beginning of the Allies build-up to meet the Warsaw Pact nations' threat. His research program on "smart weapons" was a major factor in the subsequent Persian Gulf War victory.

The Iran situation doomed him politically. It stemmed from our military buildup there and support for the Shah. The Shah fell, a Shi'ite/fundamentalist revolution occurred, American hostages were captured and held, and a rescue attempt failed.

Tip O'Neil, who was once Speaker of the House, served under seven presidents beginning with Eisenhower and ending with Reagan. After he retired, O'Neil commented that Carter was the smartest of the presidents under whom he served. But Carter's effectiveness was compromised, O'Neil said, because of failure to delegate as he should have and his insistence on personally studying each issue in great detail.

Carter was a better President than I think he's been given credit for. Max Cleland, now a U. S. Senator and a member of his cabinet, gave him as a farewell gift a plaque engraved with an inspirational Thomas Jefferson quote, "I have the consolation to reflect that during the period of my administration not a drop of blood of a single citizen was shed by the sword of war." Carter has certainly been our most active former president.

Ronald Reagan was very personable. I had the rare pleasure of going to some story-swapping sessions at the White House when Nancy was out of town, and it gave me a chance to know him better than I would have otherwise. Reagan was "The Great Communicator" and was a popular president. He was proud of his country and stood tall with his head high. He made Americans feel good about themselves, and this was very important because mental depression from Vietnam and Watergate still lingered. Reagan did the country a great favor by restoring pride in America, patriotism, and faith in our institutions.

Following Carter's first attempts to bolster the armed forces in more than a decade, Reagan greatly accelerated the military buildup, and this contributed substantially to the fall of the Soviet Union.

The largest tax cuts in history occurred under Reagan, with the maximum rate falling from 70 percent to 28 percent in two years. People threw caution aside and indulged themselves, using credit as they never had before. Inflation and interest rates remained high. Of course, this led to the largest budget deficits in history and to a quadrupling of the national debt.

Reagan often gave the appearance of not quite being sure what was going on. I think Reagan was smarter than many people have given him credit for. I think he knew a great deal about overall policy, but Reagan was the ultimate delegator. It got him into great trouble, especially in the Iran-Contra affair. He was the opposite of Carter in this respect. Reagan didn't want to be bothered because he was a big-picture booster. He let staff handle details and sometimes make decisions that should have been his own.

Generally, Reagan cut non-defense programs and increased defense programs substantially, and this was very helpful in breaking down the Soviet Union. But, at the same time, he lowered taxes, and the deficit went sky-rocketing. The 1986 tax cut was portrayed as being revenue neutral, but it didn't turn out that way. We lost a lot of money, and military spending was substantially more than he had cut in non-defense spending.

William F. Buckley, Jr. wrote in the March/April 1997 *Policy Review* that "Reagan's designation of the Soviet Union as an evil empire froze the blood of international diplomacy, but agitated the moral imagination and did more to advance U.S. national objectives than a year's Pentagon spending." Buckley makes a point.

I think there are three things for which Reagan will be remembered. I think he will be remembered for laying the groundwork for the decline of the Soviet bloc. He'll be known for the biggest tax cut in history, and he'll be known for the greatest deficit in history.

Bill Clinton is probably the best charmer of any of them, especially on a one-to-one basis. There is no doubt he grew in the duties of his office. He started out making unpopular decisions like gays-in-the-military, but his outstanding intellect soon captured national economy and global issues.

As Clinton ended his tenure, the country was enjoying the longest period of economic prosperity in its history. He came to grips with deficit spending and, along with Congress, took steps that produced a balanced budget which will generate large surpluses in the future. I think Clinton's economic programs, particularly his deficit reduction packages, are substantially responsible for the prosperity today.

Under Clinton, there has been substantial reduction in crime. Without question we have advanced in the civil rights and women's rights areas. The controversial NAFTA and GATT trade agreements were ratified. Pushing his programs in education with tax deduction and credits was another achievement. Clinton's most obvious domestic failure was not getting the universal health care bill passed.

On the international scene, Clinton displayed extraordinary leadership in Bosnia, Haiti, Northern Ireland, the Middle East, and Kosovo. He did a remarkable job in getting and keeping unanimity among the NATO members, and he justly points to the fact that very few Americans became casualties in military actions. He got China and Russia not to veto the Bosnia and Kosovo resolutions in the Security Council. Clinton maintained arms-length friendly relations with Russia, supported their attempt to move toward a more democratic country and, generally, his policy towards China improved economic relations between the countries.

There will always be the question of his character. He will go down in history as only the second president to be impeached. He was subjected to scurrilous attacks by people who hated him from the time he became president and from persistent attempts to destroy him, by whatever means. The impeachment hearings and trial produced much rancor and mean-spiritedness, and it took great amounts of time which Congress and the President could have used productively in other ways. Whether it was justified and Clinton deserved what happened can only be answered by historians. Some of his pardons at the end of his tenure were unpardonable. How historians will relate his private life to his overall record will be viewed with a great deal of objectivity as well as historians' subjective evaluations.

George Bush came to office with more government experience than practically anybody else in our history, with his congressional, vice presidency, CIA, UN, and China experiences. This background helped him in meeting the challenges he faced. He is a very decent individual, and he had a lot of courage. His downfall, unfortunately, was his efforts to control deficit spending. He had the courage to support a tax increase, which led to his defeat.

Early in his presidency, Bush was faced with the fall of the Soviet Union and all of the resulting problems and dealings with Gorbachev and Yeltsin. There was great unrest in Russia and the other Soviet republics. Bush handled the situation exceptionally well. His CIA experience was very helpful, particularly in evaluating the Russian army, the KGB, and the Russian peoples' feelings toward a change from a communistic way of life.

He had been in China as the equivalent of an ambassador, and this helped him because China was conscious of what was going on in the Soviet Union. The Chinese feared the downfall of a communist regime that was similar to their own, and they had to be handled with kid gloves. Throughout, Bush had to gain the support of our European allies as well as former Warsaw Pact nations.

The unification of Germany was adroitly handled. There was fear among other countries that Germany would rise again as a super power in Europe. The surrounding nations still have strong feelings toward Germany today as a result of the two World Wars and other historic instances of attempted German expansion.

Bush did a remarkable job in the Desert Shield and Desert Storm operations, particularly in getting approval of the United Nations (UN). There was a question of whether military strength should be used or whether we should rely on sanctions. He succeeded in getting UN authorization for military action in spite of the possibility of

Security Council vetos. He achieved Congressional approval in a very close vote (52-48) in the Senate. Bush kept Israel from retaliating against the SCUD missile attacks during the war. It would have created considerable danger if Israel had retaliated because of the animosity against Israel from its Arab neighbors.

On the domestic scene, Bush took a number of risks knowing his actions would be unpopular and could possibly defeat him in his bid for reelection, particularly in light of his campaign rhetoric about "Read my lips." He took such action anyway because he considered it right for the country. It takes courage for any politician to vote for a tax increase. He hasn't been given enough credit for actions taken to improve the country's economy. Among the important steps was the reappointment of Alan Greenspan when Greenspan had indicated that he would follow a tight monetary policy which Bush did not consider to be helpful. Bush turned things around. He increased the taxes and got us moving toward deficit reduction.

Bush also stands high on the character issue. Richard Vigilante wrote with regard to Bush, "We need strength of character more than policy papers. We need someone who cares about making the right choice even when the country may not credit him for it because the choices are complicated and obscure and difficult to explain in a sound bite. We need someone who expects virtue to be its own reward, a man who cares more about doing just right the tasks history hands him."[1] This is an excellent statement about a fine man. My selection of George Bush as the most outstanding of the four presidents under whom I served is, I think, well founded. I believe historians will give him high marks.

ULTIMATELY, Each President contributed with different ideas and actions. There's a continuity of policy that emanates from all of them, starting with Carter. Each advocated research and development in most science, health, and military issues. Bush advanced many of Reagan's policies. Clinton continued much of what Bush was doing with foreign policy. All of them contributed to the movement of the U.S. toward a leadership position in spreading democracy.

Each did his part in preventing World War III and trying to maintain peace around the globe. In my opinion, the presidency is solid and has been handled well enough; of course, there are problems and differences of opinion. There is much to be accomplished. But I think there is a good working balance with Congress on the majority of issues. Further, I think the federal system is strong and is doing well. It is functioning well for its citizens, and our democracy is working well. Our government right now is probably the strongest government in history.

A FINAL ASSESSMENT. The problems America faces in the new century are immense, as tough choices and difficult decisions lie ahead. Heflin admits the problems won't go away; there will continue to be growing pains and challenges in the nature of social problems, world threats, and ideological divides. He points out that we have weathered all of the storms we faced in the past, and by boarding up against the storms of the future, we will become stronger and better able to meet and adapt to changing demands and conditions. He summarizes his feelings when he says, "I remain positive. I have faith, and I believe our best years lie ahead."

28

An Affirmation of America

Howell and Elizabeth Ann Heflin live in their quiet neighborhood in Tuscumbia, in the same house they have owned for forty some-odd years. It is a large comfortable two-story Dutch Colonial house close to the center of town. Heflin drives around Tuscumbia in a 1986 Pontiac, acting and appearing old hat in a way that "shows us what made him a political success."[1]

The Heflins live a comfortable life, but they do not live a quiet life. Howell remains in great demand as a speaker and guest of honor, people approach him with requests as though he were still senator, and he represents a few clients with governmental business in Washington. He has a large office in a building occupied by his son's law firm.

Howell was 80 years old on June 19, 2001, and he has health problems. He continues to struggle with his weight, his heart troubles continue, and he suffers from diabetes. He has to rest periodically to recover his strength. However, he works out in a gym about three times per week.

Despite these problems, he remains active. Bad health will have a battle getting the best of a man of his will and determination. Besides, as everyone who has retired from a satisfying, responsible job knows, changing roles in this way is very difficult. The daily contact with colleagues, the power to direct and change things, the daily routine full of busy tasks, the accolades — all are sorely missed.

Writer Peter St. Onge says that Heflin,

> is a lot like many retired guys from these parts, bragging on his grandchildren, complaining about his medicine, hitching his pants up past plausible heights.
> "I'm really enjoying it here," he (Heflin) says.
> Did anyone doubt he would?
> He is an oddity in Washington politics — a powerful man who wanted to come home, a small-town boy who never let it leave him. Today, Bob Dole spends most nights at the Watergate Hotel, not in Kansas. So many others hang on for lobbying and lawyer work, never quite getting the smoky back rooms out of their fabric.[2]

Mr. St. Onge has it almost right. Heflin remains basically a small-town boy, in tune with the people of his state and community, but he doesn't quite have the smoky back rooms out of his fabric. In spite of being well-off financially, he still has the urge to be active, working, needed, and on the Washington scene from time to time. He doesn't miss an Alfalfa Club dinner if he can help it.

He has the satisfaction of knowing he is held in high esteem, both in his home state and nationally. The State Justice Institute, the federally funded state courts organization devoted to improving the administration of justice which Senator Heflin helped found, gives an annual Howell Heflin Award. In February 1998, the new Heflin Complex was dedicated at Redstone Arsenal. The two-building complex will house 1,100 people who are developing technology for the Army's missile and aviation systems. A portrait of Heflin, by Huntsville artist Cynthia Parsons, hangs in the lobby.

On May 21, 2001, the Howell and Elizabeth Ann Heflin Center for Human Genetics at the University of Alabama at Birmingham was dedicated. The center will be devoted largely to molecular biology research, and the research conducted in it will aid in the discovery of new and life-changing treatments in the areas of arthritis, diabetes, and cancer.[3]

The School of Law at the University of Alabama has honored him by displaying memorabilia from his years on the court and in the Senate in a specially designated room. A lectureship is also named in Heflin's honor.

The first Howell Heflin Statesmanship Awards were given in April 1999 at the Howell Heflin Statesmanship Awards Dinner, held at the Von Braun Center in Huntsville. The awards are sponsored by the Alabama Constitutional Village Association and are based on contributions in business, technology, government, education, and the arts and humanities. Each award winner was given a bronze medallion bearing Heflin's likeness.[4] Elected officials and the heads of major companies from around the state help to host the event. Governor Don Siegelman was honorary chairman.[5]

Howell Heflin holds fourteen honorary degrees, several from his home state, and a Howell Heflin Award is given annually by the Alabama Unified Justice System to the individual who contributes the most to the improvement of the administration of justice. He is a life member of the Board of Trustees of Birmingham-Southern College. Southern has a chair named the Howell Heflin Professor of Political Science and Government and a seminar room named in his honor.

In the Shoals area, the University of North Alabama, where he served on the faculty for several years, displays memorabilia in its historic Wesleyan Hall. The Tuscumbia Public Library also houses a Howell Heflin conference room with a display of memorabilia, and a new federal building in Tuscumbia will bear his name.

A one-day symposium was held on February 11, 1999, to review progress in reforming Alabama's judicial system. It was the twenty-fifth anniversary of the passage of the Judicial Article and was jointly sponsored by The Supreme Court of Alabama and Cumberland School of Law at Samford University. More than anything else, it gave the top people in Alabama's legal establishment the chance to express their esteem for Howell Heflin.

Among the speakers was Sandra Radcliff Daffron, executive director of the American Judicature Society, which had helped conduct the

Citizens' Conferences. Ms. Daffron said that the Alabama judicial system was still the national leader, and she expressed the belief that the unusual success of judicial reform in Alabama was related in considerable part to the extensive involvement of citizens in the effort. This, of course, was Heflin's idea.

Heflin was the banquet speaker and was his usual engaging self, managing to be humorous and to bring incisive analyses in the same speech. When Alabama Chief Justice Perry O. Hooper gave the introduction, he called Heflin "the father of the judicial system in Alabama."

The following resolution, adopted by the Judicial Conference of the Eleventh Circuit Court of Appeals in May 1997, is a sure indication of the wide esteem with which Howell Heflin is held:

> *Whereas*, Howell Heflin served the United States of America and the state of Alabama with patriotism and skill as a soldier, attorney, judge, United States Senator and statesman;
>
> *Whereas*, Howell Heflin, as Chief Justice of the Alabama Supreme Court, reformed the 'Judicial Article' of the Alabama State Constitution, modernizing Alabama's system of justice;
>
> *Whereas*, Judge Heflin served as a member, chairman, and ranking member of the United State Senate Judiciary Committee's subcommittee overseeing the courts and judicial administration and in that capacity brought to the Senate an understanding that efficient judicial administration is a necessary component of justice;
>
> *Whereas*, Judge Heflin introduced and shepherded to passage the bill that divided the United States Court of Appeals for the Eleventh Circuit.
>
> *Whereas*, Judge Heflin sponsored both the 'Civil Justice Reform Act' requiring implementation of expense and delay reduction plans, and the 'Federal Judgeship Act of 1990' which created eighty-five federal judgeships;
>
> *Whereas*, Judge Heflin effected passage of the 'Federal Courts Administration Act' containing several bills which instituted the Federal Courts Study Committee and made improvements to the Judicial

Survivors Annuities System as well as the 'Bankruptcy Reform Act of 1994,' bringing about substantive change and improvements in the Bankruptcy Court;

Whereas, Judge Heflin sponsored the 'Omnibus Victims Protection Act of 1982,' which provided protection and assistance to victims and witnesses in Federal cases. Now Therefore,

Be it Resolved that the Judicial Conference of the Eleventh Circuit pays tribute to the remarkable life and legal career of Howell Heflin and his many accomplishments, and express to him its everlasting appreciation, heartfelt thanks, and sincere affection.

THE POLITICIAN'S GREATEST ASSET. One of Howell Heflin's greatest accomplishments was persuading Elizabeth Ann to be his wife. She is a warm, gracious, beautiful woman who has been an important asset to him and who has contributed significantly to his successes.

Howell and Elizabeth Ann are approaching their 50th wedding anniversary, and they are deeply devoted to each other. Ed Mauldin, one of the Senator's best friends, says, "Heflin has always loved his wife, and she loves him. He always puts her first. They've had an enjoyable marriage. They had two children, but the little girl died at childbirth. Tom, their son, was a good boy, and he's a lawyer and doing real well."

Tom married Cornelia Morgan Hood of Florence on July 28, 1984, at Trinity Episcopal Church in Florence, and Howell served as his son's best man.[6] Tom and Cornelia have two children.

Howell and Elizabeth Ann are fun to be around. From old work habits, he has the urge to be in control and can be a little inflexible in interviews. When Elizabeth Ann is present, she keeps him loose, and their repartee can be downright funny.

Elizabeth Ann never made any bones about her initial opposition to Howell's entering politics. "Before we married, I really didn't know he had political aspirations," she says. "I didn't think he would actually go into politics, not if I could help it. That's being brutally honest."

Howell counters, "You say that."

"That's what he keeps saying," Elizabeth Ann responds. "He thinks

I'm just using those words but don't mean them."

"That's a good line."

"Noooooooo. After twenty-one years, I thought I had talked him out of running for anything, and that's when he ran for chief justice. I was not a very good campaigner at that point. I went out and campaigned after it was a done deal. After he announced."

Heflin has commented that Elizabeth Ann could have stopped his political career if she had disliked it so much. She responds that once he had committed to a political course, she would never have opposed what he felt led to do.

Elizabeth Ann maintained her own interests while living in Washington. "Howell has his own idea about things, and I understood that," she says. "I just went ahead and did what I wanted to.

"Some things the papers write would make you mad, and then you'd remember as Howell always says, 'The newspapers have more ink than you do. Why complain?' Things can incense you, and you want to go out there and fight. But you know you're not going to do it, and it's not going to help if you do. But beware of somebody that doesn't give Howell credit for all of his intelligence, etc., and just thinks he's folksy. Beware."

When the Senate had a recess, Howell would often have speaking or other commitments in Alabama and would have to fly quickly to a particular location. Elizabeth Ann would drive back, usually alone. Until Honey died, she had the dog to ride with her. "I drove back and forth for eighteen years," she recalls.

She made it a strict practice never to say anything in public in opposition to a position Howell had taken. When asked how she managed not to say things that would get him in trouble, she answered, "My main aim in life is to keep my foot out of his mouth. If I can manage that, I will be doing fine. Never, never when he was in office, as far as I know, did I publicly oppose whatever Howell had said or whatever he believed. I thought it was wrong to make a statement opposing his idea or his statement. I might not always agree with him, but I wasn't about to say I didn't.

"It's tough being in the attention of the press all of the time. I expect it with him, but not with me. It's just part of public life, I guess. You either fight it or just forget it and don't worry about it. I can walk down the street perfectly well and not have people stopping me everywhere. But if Howell's with me, we won't get two feet without people stopping him. That's been true for a long time. I laugh and say it just takes a while to get where we are going. Howell is not going through a room without shaking every hand in it. You'd think he was running tomorrow.

"I had no influence, really, on his decision to retire," she confided. "He said he was thinking about it, and I said, 'Good idea.'"

Howell adds, "You said, 'I'm ready to go home. I've been ready to go home since I came here.'"

A REMARKABLE LIFE. Howell Heflin has had a remarkable life and has been very successful in four different endeavors:

1. As a Marine Corps officer,
2. As a Trial Lawyer,
3. As Chief Justice of Alabama,
4. As United States Senator.

A World War II Marine, he served in Guadalcanal, won the Silver Star during the invasion of Bougainville, and was seriously wounded on Guam.

He was an outstanding trial lawyer and was named a fellow of the American College of Trial Lawyers, the International Academy of Trial Lawyers, and of the International Society of Barristers. As Chief Justice of the Alabama Supreme Court, he directed total reform of the state's judicial system. In recognition of this effort, he received the Award of Merit of the American Judges Association, was selected the country's most outstanding appellate judge by the Association of Trial Lawyers, and was elected chairman of the National Conference of Chief Justices.

In his eighteen-year Senate career he was an expert in agriculture, defense, space, and judiciary matters, and he served as a United States representative to the North Atlantic Treaty Organization Assembly. In every election save one, a primary with several opponents, he won more than 60 percent of the vote.

An Alabama progressive in the Hugo Black tradition, Howell Heflin resists labels like "conservative" and "liberal," preferring instead to say he is motivated by compassionate moderation. Many longtime friends and colleagues consider him an "old-fashioned populist," that is, a politician who identifies with and represents directly the interests of the common people. Of party leanings, he says, "Instead of being so concerned with policies that are left and right, government should be concerned with the principles of right and wrong, which come from approaching issues in measured, moderate, and compassionate tones."[7]

Heflin believes deeply in the fundamental principles of American democracy, which he has studied extensively. He is a strong advocate of the doctrine of separation of powers, with three distinct and equal branches of government. He was recognized as an authority on the Constitution and on constitutional law when he was chief justice and in the Senate.

He says he supports a moderately conservative Supreme Court, "but," he continues, "I oppose a right-wing court which would embrace a regressive philosophy, which would attempt to rewrite or strike laws written to overcome years of racism in America."

Dr. Joe Reed, Chairman of the Alabama Democratic Conference, says of Heflin, "I never saw him as a flaming liberal. I saw him as an extremely honest man. He was a Southerner. He knew the land. He knew the circumstances. He knew the problems that blacks experienced. I think in his own way, he would try to right every wrong that he possibly could without calling a press conference, without getting on a stump — just doing it. I think he firmly believed in the Fatherhood of God and the Brotherhood of Man. I saw him acting this way throughout his career, not out of sheer politics, but out of a commitment, out of convictions. Is this fair? Is this right? Is this wrong? He took these considerations into account more than any person I've run across in my long political career."[8]

FULFILLING THE AMERICA DREAM. So what is the basis for our statement that Howell Heflin's life represents an affirmation of America? Let us elaborate. Fundamental to the American system are the concepts of freedom and of equal opportunity. The ideal, outlined in our most precious documents, holds that whatever a person's background, he can in a climate of freedom go as far as his talents, desire, willingness to work, and integrity will take him, and he can always be assured of equal protection under the law.

The goals set forth by the founding fathers are subsumed in the term, "The American Dream." High School students in Allentown, New Jersey, recently provided thoughtful insight into what comprises that dream. Ms. Cindy Natter's 11th Grade American Literature class, participating in "Exploring the American Dream," a project utilizing the resources of the American Memory Collections of the Library of Congress, wrote a series of touching and meaningful personal interpretations. To quote a few:

> When I turn eighteen, I want to be firefighter. As a firefighter I'll have the chance to help people whose homes are burning. I'll save them and then deep down I'll know that I've succeeded, for I will be following my dream to help people. I will do whatever it takes, but most of all I will never give up. I will reach as far as I can and do whatever it takes to make this possible. —Jamie Francis

> In my world, I wish that we could appreciate each other and each others' color. Racism has a big effect on this world, and if we would get to know people for their soul and personality, and not for their color, then the world would be a better place. In my country, I dream that we would give everyone a chance: rich, poor, ugly, beautiful. We are all warm-hearted people, and we are all equal no matter what we look like. I also dream that I can change people's minds about the different types of people we have around the world. I know if I can change one person's mind, it will make a difference. —Vivianne Martins

> In my mind, peace among all people symbolizes the real dream — life, liberty, and the pursuit of happiness. When will we stop judging

others by the outside, and look deeper? Everything we do must start somewhere, why not have it start in your own town? —Desiree' Painchaud

I dream of becoming a cosmetologist and owning my own salon. I also dream of having a nice, loving family with three kids and a husband. Being a cosmetologist will make people happy one person at a time. I will make people feel less stressed-out and feel good about themselves. To make my dreams come true, I am going to keep trying and never give up. I just have to keep reaching for my goals until I succeed. —Cristy Torrey

I dream that I will make a difference in children's lives. My dreams are not to acquire money or material possessions, but to help make the lives of those around me better. My dream fits into America's future in a big way. Since I plan on helping kids, I will be helping the future. I believe that our country doesn't focus on children and their abilities enough. Kids are the best dreamers and they don't discriminate. Children have a lot to say, and what they have to say many times means more than the phony stuff adults make up. This is why my dream is to help kids in need. My dream, the "American Dream," is all about hope. I want to give other people hope. —Christine Vignali

Ms. Natter and her class discovered that the American Dream is a paradox, that it doesn't fit neatly inside a box but means different things to different people. To these young people, however, it is clear that a common thread is idealism and a desire to help others, whatever outcome they want for themselves, and they remind us that caring for each other is an essential part of America.[9]

Howell Heflin demonstrated something else that is essential, that democracy requires all of us to work together. He was not an ideologist, and he did not see those who disagreed with him as evil. His manner was to be friends with everybody on both sides of the aisle. He says, "When you disagree on matters, you get together and work it out. You find the middle ground that everybody can accept. Compromise is not an evil act or a sign of weakness. It is, rather, part of the fine art of politics in a system which is by, for, and of the people." The danger of polarized bipartisanship is that it allows no way to find a middle ground and no way to resolve differences.

Democracy works best when everyone, of whatever persuasion, realizes that all are after the same things fundamentally — a country based on the ideas stated in the Declaration of Independence and in the Constitution. Disagreements are about how to achieve these things. We can disagree strongly, fight hard for our own views, and still be friends and recognize the honesty and sincerity of the opposition.

Howell Heflin has demonstrated the American Dream through his life. Though his father never made much money, Howell grew up in privileged circumstances in that love and caring prevailed in his home, higher education was valued highly, and he was encouraged to excel. Also, he came from a family with a well-known name. He was privileged in many respects, but this detracts in no way from his accomplishments nor makes him less an affirmation of America. Like the rest of us, he made plenty of mistakes and lost many battles, but he never let that stop him. He has made the most of his opportunities.

Further, as the students in Allentown High School remind us, an essential aspect of the American Dream is to respect all people, be positive and idealistic, and be caring and helpful in relationships with others. These qualities have been central in Howell Heflin's life.

Howell Heflin is a person who exemplifies the finest American values and who has made a great success of his life, personally, in private law practice, and in public service. The man gives us a model, the way that we the people can each secure to ourselves the blessings of liberty.

Appendix

This speech was delivered by Heflin as his "acceptance" of the nomination of the Alfalfa Party for the Presidency in 1989 (see Chapter 25).

Mr. President, Mr. Vice President, Mr. Chief Justice, Delegates to this convention:

I accept your nomination.

But before I start addressing this upcoming campaign, let me thank Senator Nunn for his warm and kind introduction. It was much better than one I received in Alabama when the audience was told, "We'll now hear the latest dope from Washington." Thank the Lord there are no dopes among the Alfalfaians, but the other two parties are full of them.

Let me tell you about one of those dopes. He is a government official with an advanced case of Potomac swamp fever who has done all the things that he shouldn't — drinking, carousing, visiting poker games. One night he returned to his home towards the wee hours of dawn. His nerves were so unsteady that he couldn't put the key into the front door lock, making a lot of noise until finally his wife slung open the door. He splattered into the inside — fell on the floor. He was looking up at his wife when she said, "What have you got to say for yourself?" He replied, "I don't have an opening statement, but I will respond to questions from the floor."

If the Alfalfa Party is to be successful, we must return to the founding principles which gave the original Alfalfa movement its birth. There have been too many metro presidents and urbanized cabinet members. This nation has become too citified. The ideals of earth grubbers and cowpokes must be reestablished on Pennsylvania Avenue. America must respond to the messages of the soil. The Alfalfa Party should espouse the values of the plow and the saddle. My campaign will bring forth a new breeze of Alfalfa history and tradition.

Let me first tell you about my national Alfalfa Party Campaign Committee Chairman. He is a tough, no-holds-barred politician. He is William Hawkins of Corn, Oklahoma, better known as "Beltless Bill" Hawkins. He doesn't wear a belt — only suspenders. He is a gallus philosopher. Ole Beltless Bill will rare back and philosophize on any and all subjects.

He once ran for sheriff, and a Republican beat him. He never forgave his opponent. Later in life the Lord came to him in a dream and told him he must remove the hatred of his old opponent from his heart. "I'm going to grant you one wish, but I'm going to double that wish for your old Republican enemy. If you want a new house, he gets two new houses. If you want a new car, he gets two new cars. Now what is your wish?" Old Bill replied, "Strike me blind in one eye." Tough, wise, tenacious — Old Beltless Bill will give the pachyderms and jennies firesome hell in the upcoming campaign. He will make Lee Atwater holler, "Calf rope."

In fact, most of the members of my cabinet will be kin to old Beltless Bill Hawkins. This family, that now lives in numerous rural sections of America, originated in Vina, Alabama, a country town of 68 people. My Ambassador to the United Nations lives there and goes by the name of "Sockless Sam" Hawkins. He wears no socks.

A group of nuns was traveling through the countryside near Vina, when their Buick automobile gave out of gas. The robed nuns were frustrated since it was very hot. Soon, one observed a filling station around the curve about 200 yards away. They walked to the filling station and inquired of the owner if they could borrow a gasoline can. A search was made for the gasoline can, but none could be found. The only container that could be found to carry the gasoline back to the automobile was an old bedpan. So they filled the bedpan full of gasoline and took it back to the Buick automobile and were in the process of pouring the gasoline from the bedpan into the tank when down the road driving his 1975 Ford automobile comes Sockless Sam Hawkins. He sees what's going on, comes to a stop and says, "I want to watch this. If that car cranks and runs, I'm a trad'n cars and switch'n churches."

With his ability to observe and his responding flexibility, he will make a great Ambassador to the United Nations.

Now Sockless Sam has a son who never wears a necktie and is known as "Tieless Tom" Hawkins. He was sweet on a young lady who lived across the south 40 and came to his father and told old Sockless Sam he was going to get married. Sam replied, "That's mighty fine. But where are you going to live?" Young Tom said, "Well, I thought I'd bring her here to the house." Sockless Sam said, "Well, son, you know we are awfully crowded here in the house. There is just no room." Tieless Tom replied, "Well, Paw, I've got to do something. I'm going to get married on Saturday night."

Sockless Sam said, "Well, maybe we can fix up a bedroom down in the barn in the hayloft." They did and the wedding night was spent there. The next morning Old Sam goes down to the barn and looks up to the hayloft, and there he sees Tieless Tom grinning like a Cheshire cat. Tom says, "Paw, you know my squirrel rifle that I'm so proud of. I want you to have that. Paw, you know my prize photograph that has me in my high school football uniform standing beside Bear Bryant. I want you to have that. Paw, if you go back into my old bedroom that I shared with two of my brothers, you will find underneath that bed a loose plank, and if you pick it up you will find a fruit jar under it. It's got $11.63 in it. It's my savings. I want you to have that."

Sockless Sam looked at him and said, "Now son, here you've got yourself married. You've got responsibilities. You can't be giving away your worldly goods." And Old Tieless Tom looked down and said, "Paw, you just don't understand. I ain't never coming down from up here."

Well, young Tieless Tom has got his values straight. He is a true Alfalfian. I would like to appoint him to be head of my Congressional Liaison Office if I can get him to come down from the hayloft.

Now Beltless Bill, Sockless Sam, and Tieless Tom Hawkins have a cousin who lives in Horse Creek, Colorado, by the name of "Hairless Harry" Hawkins. He is completely baldheaded. Old Hairless Harry is a shade-tree veterinarian.

There were two old maids whose cattle operation was fast deteriorating and bringing financial stress on them. It became apparent that their bull had lost his prowess. They had had some of the best university veterinarians examine the bull and treat him, but to no avail. Finally, they heard about Old Hairless Harry. He came to examine the bull. After using a stethoscope, he pulled a corn cob out of his little black bag and began to rub the bull between the horns. He took another rougher corn cob and rubbed the bull until blood came. Then he took a third rougher corn cob and rubbed until all of the hair came off. All of a sudden, the bull began to snort and paw the earth, and he jumped the fence and began to carry out his bully duties. That night the two old maids were discussing the event and Agatha said to Samantha, "I believe our cattle operation has been saved, and we will be secure in our old age." Then Samantha said, "Agatha, I learned something else today." "What's that?" Agatha replied, "I learned why there are so many baldheaded men like Ole Hairless Harry."

Ole Doc Hairless Harry Hawkins will make a superb National Science Advisor.

One of the most important positions left to be filled in my cabinet is Secretary of State, and I have decided on another Hawkins. He is from Oaktown, Indiana. He never wears a coat and is known as "Coatless Charlie" Hawkins. Shortly after he reached the age of 60, his wife died. After about six months, Coatless Charlie married a spry 26 year old filly. About a year after they were married, she caught him running around with a 58-year-old woman. His young wife confronted him and asked, "What does this 58-year-old hussy have that I haven't got?" Coatless Charlie answered, "Patience." This convinced me that Coatless Charlie has the patience of a George Schulz and sufficient adventurous spirit to make a great Secretary of State. However, my first executive order will require him to wear a coat.

Recently I was asked what my position is on new taxes. "Well," I said, "I'm a lip reader." That conversation gave me an idea for two White House positions. I am going to have an official Lip Reader and an official Lip Zipper. The addition of these positions reflects the growing importance of lips to the American people. There are so many varieties of lips going around today that a President must be advised to keep up with them all. There are quivering lips, puckered lips, whistle lips, closed lips, motor lips, and kissing lips. We used to have bird lips, but now those have become Quayle lips. But to a President perhaps the most important type of lips can be slipped lips. I remember an Edgar A. Guest poem that sums up the attitude my cabinet will take toward slipped lips. It goes like this:

> If you your lips would keep from slips,
> Five things observe with care:
> Of whom you speak, to whom you speak,
> And who and when and where.

One of the most important decisions of this campaign will be my selection of a running mate. I am in nearly the same position that George Bush was before the Republican Convention in 1988. I am behind 15 or 20 points in the polls. The gender gap is even wider. I must select a Vice Presidential nominee who will help me get the female vote. I had narrowed the selection down to two — Arnold Schwarzenegger and Senator John Warner. We need a nominee who is athletic, muscular, and agile, but handsome, dapper, urbane, and sophisticated. Either Arnold or John would be a great magnet for the female vote. I was leaning toward John Warner since he was unmarried, but my final decision came as a result of a conversation with a Catholic priest. After discussing numerous Alfalfian issues, the priest asked me if I knew John Warner. I told him I did and that he was a close, personal friend. The priest replied, "I want to meet him," and he asked other questions about him. I finally asked the priest, "Why this great interest in John Warner? You are not from Virginia." He said, "Well you see, I live just across the District line in Maryland, but his name comes up frequently in confessions." John Warner will make a great Vice President as well as guarantee the ticket victory.

I believe that you can get a flavor of my campaign from my remarks thus far. But, frankly, as we enter this campaign our emphasis ought to be about our great country. We must proclaim that for all Americans to enjoy our freedoms we must be strong as a nation. The strength of our nation is dependent upon patriotism and upon the willingness of our countrymen to defend our freedoms. During the War of 1812 Francis Scott Key wrote our national anthem, "The Star Spangled Banner," amidst the crash of shells in the heat of battle. He ended its first stanza with a question:

> Oh! Say, does that Star-Spangled Banner yet wave
> O'er the land of the free and the home of the brave?

As we consider the history of our great nation, it comes through loud and clear that if America is to continue to be the land of the free, it must also be the home of the brave. So at this Alfalfa Party convention, regardless of our Republican or Democrat backgrounds, let us never forget that above all else we are Americans — and Americans strong and free. Let me paraphrase the final words of the fourth stanza of our national anthem as an expression of hope for the future of our beloved country:

> Blest with vict'ry and peace, may this Heav'n-rescued land
> Praise the Pow'r that hath made and preserved us a nation.
> Defend it we must — may our cause always be just,
> And this be our motto, "In God is our trust."
> And may the Star-Spangled Banner continue to wave
> O'er the land of the free and the home of the brave.

Notes

Chapter 1
[1] Ingram, Bob. Editorial on WSFA-TV, Montgomery, March 27, 1982.
[2] "Chief Justice Heflin: He's Rocking some Boats, Stepping on Some Toes... In the name of Justice." *Alabama News Magazine*. Vol. 39, No. 1, January 1973. p. 8.
[3] Greenhaw, Wayne. "A Super Tuesday Circuit Ride." *Alabama Magazine*. Vol. 52, No. 3. May/June 1988. p. 19.
[4] Haynes, Lynn. "Editorial." *Daily Home*. Talladega, Alabama. October 16, 1987.
[5] Remini, Robert V. *Andrew Jackson: Volume Three, The Course of American Democracy, 1833-1845*. Baltimore: Johns Hopkins University Press, 1984. pp. 16-25.
[6] Yarbrough, Marie. "Former U.S. Senator Reflects on Work with Past Presidents." *The Crimson White*. (University of Alabama). March 28, 1998. p. 1.
[7] Wellstone, Paul. "Tribute to Howell Heflin." *Congressional Record*. March 29, 1995.

Chapter 2
[1] "Heflin Family." Biographical File. Alabama Department of Archives and History, Montgomery.
[2] Barnett, Frank Willis. "Louina, Randolph County, An Important Center in the Early Days." *The Birmingham News*. July 18, 1911.
[3] Barnett, Frank Willis. *The Birmingham News*. July 15, 1923.
[4] Barnett, 1911. *Loc. Cit.*
[5] Clarke, W. E. "For My Children." November 13, 1895.
[6] Tanner, Ralph Melvis. "James Thomas Heflin: United States Senator, 1920-1931." Doctoral Dissertation. University of Alabama, Department of History, 1967. p. 5.
[7] Tanner. *Op. Cit.* p. 8.
[8] Tanner. *Op. Cit.* p. 9.
[9] Heflin, Howell. *Congressional Record*, Senate. May 8, 1986. p. S5687.
[10] Political Advertisement. *The Guntersville Advertiser and Democrat*. April 25, 1934.
[11] Tanner. *Op. Cit.* p. 93.
[12] Congressional Record, House. 67th Congress. 1922. p. 10145.
[13] Tanner. *Op. Cit.* p. 31.
[14] Tanner. *Op. Cit.* P. 124.
[15] *The Birmingham News*. "Democrats Bar Heflin, Locke 27-21." December 16, 1929.
[16] Hayman, John. *Bitter Harvest: Richmond Flowers and the Civil Rights Revolution*. Montgomery AL: Black Belt Press, 1996. p. 49.
[17] Mencken, Henry L. "What's Going On in The World." *American Mercury*. Vol. 28. January, 1933. pp. 4-6.
[18] Greenhaw, Wayne. "A Super Tuesday Circuit Ride," Alabama Magazine, Vol. 52, No. 3. May/June 1988. P. 15.
[19] Tanner. Op. Cit. p. 6
[20] *The Roanoke Leader*. 1905.
[21] Spencer, Thomas. "150-Year Old 'Time Capsule' Heflin's Ancestral Home." *The Anniston Star*. January 6, 1995. p. 6A.

Chapter 3
[1] Wordsworth, William. "The Rainbow." *In A Treasury of the World's Best Loved Poems*. New York: Avenel Books, 1961. p. 47.

Chapter 5
[1] "History of the College." 1997-1999 Catalog. Birmingham, AL: Birmingham-Southern College, 1997. p. 11.
[2] *The Birmingham News*. July 21, 1942.

Chapter 6.
[1] Barker, A. J. *Pearl Harbor*. New York: Ballantine Books, Inc., 1969. p. 13.
[2] Churchill, Winston S. *Memoirs of the Second World War*. London: Houghton Mifflin Company. 1959. p. 509.
[3] Manchester, William. *American Caesar*. Boston: Little, Brown and Company. 1978. p. 292.
[4] Carbaugh, Harvey C. Statement recorded June 18, 1993.

Chapter 7
[1] "The GI Bill: The Law that Changed America." PBS Online. October 22, 1997; "Remembering the GI Bulge." Syracuse University Archives Exhibit. May-August, 1997.
[2] Greenhaw, Wayne. "A Super Tuesday Circuit Ride." *Alabama Magazine*. Vol. 52, No. 3. May/June 1988. p. 16.
[3] *The Birmingham Post-Herald*. March 14, 1948.
[4] Greenhaw. *Loc. Cit.* p. 17.
[5] Greenhaw. *Loc. Cit.* p. 16.

Chapter 8
[1] The Alabama Legionnaire. July 1949.

Chapter 9
[1] Hayman, John. *Bitter Harvest: Richmond Flowers and the Civil Rights Revolution*. Montgomery, AL: Black Belt Press, 1996. p. 93.
[2] Greenhaw, Wayne. "A Super Tuesday Circuit Ride." *Alabama Magazine*. Vol. 52, No. 3. May/June 1988. p. 17.
[3] Horton, Ed. Alabama State Senator. Statement recorded December 12, 1996.

Chapter 10
[1] Rogers, William Warren, Robert David Ward, Leah Rawls Atkins, and Wayne Flynt. *Alabama: The History of a Deep South State*. Tuscaloosa, AL: The University of Alabama Press, 1994. p. 579.
[2] Johnson, Gerald W. "Report on Judicial Reform in Alabama." 1989. p. 33.
[3] Heflin, Howell T. "Scope and Function of New Commit-

tees." *The Alabama Lawyer.* Vol.26, No.4. October 1965. pp. 359-360.
[4]*Ibid.* p. 327.
[5]Heflin, Howell T. "President's Address." Alabama Bar Association, July 23, 1966. *The Alabama Lawyer.* Vol. 27, No. 4. October 1966. p. 333.
[6]Hayman, John. *Bitter Harvest: Richmond Flowers and the Civil Rights Revolution.* Montgomery AL: Black Belt Press, 1996. pp. 286-289.
[7]*The Birmingham Post-Herald.* September 30, 1969.

CHAPTER 11

[1]Cole, Charles D. "Judicial Reform in Alabama: A Reflection." *The Alabama Lawyer.* Vol. 60, No. 3. May 1999. p. 186.
[2]Tarr, G. Alan, and Mary Cornelia Aldis Porter. *State Supreme Courts in State and Nation.* New Haven: Yale University Press, 1988. pp. 69-70.
[3]*Ibid.* pp. 82-85.
[4]Cole. *Loc. Cit.* p. 187.
[5]Tarr. *Loc. Cit.* p. 87.
[6]Shores, Janie L. "The Alabama Experience Over the Past Five Years." *New York State Bar Journal.* Vol. 49, No. 2. February 1977. p. 99.
[7]Tarr. *Loc. Cit.* pp. 74-75.
[8]Tarr. *Loc. Cit.* p. 81.
[9]Tarr. *Loc. Cit.* p. 85.
[10]Cole. *Loc. Cit.* p. 187.
[11]Cole. *Ibid.*
[12]Nazary. *Loc. Cit.* p. 18.
[13]Maddox, Hugh. "Reflections on the 25th Anniversary of the Judicial Article." *The Alabama Lawyer.* Vol. 60, No. 3. May 1999. p. 182.
[14]Nazary. *Ibid.*
[15]Reed, Joe. Chairman of the Alabama Democratic Conference. Statement recorded November 12, 1996.
[16]Cole. *Loc. Cit.* p. 189.
[17]Martin, Robert A. "Alabama Courts -- Six Years of Change." *The Alabama Lawyer.* Vol. 38, No. 1, January 1977. p 11.
[18]Shores. *Loc. Cit.* p. 419.
[19]Martin. *Loc. Cit.* p. 12.
[20]Heflin, Howell T., "State of the Judiciary." The Alabama Lawyer. Vol. 33, No. 4. October 1972. pp. 371-378.
[21]Martin. *Loc. Cit.* p. 13.
[22]Martin. *Ibid.*
[23]Martin. *Loc. Cit.* p. 12.
[24]Jones, Elaine R. Director-Counsel of the NAACP Legal Defense Fund. Statement recorded December 6, 1996.
[25]House, Mike. Former Heflin Chief of Staff. Statement recorded December 20, 1996.
[26]House. *Ibid.*
[27]Martin. *Loc. Cit.* p. 13.

CHAPTER 12

[1]McMillan, Malcolm Cook. "Constitutional Development in Alabama, 1798-1901: A Study in Politics, the Negro, and Sectionalism." Chapel Hill: North Carolina Press. 1955. p. 232.
[2]Martin, Robert. "Alabama Courts -- Six Years of Change." *The Alabama Lawyer.* Vol. 38, No. 1. January 1977. p 14.
[3]Tarr, G. Alan, and Mary Cornelia Aldis Porter. *State Supreme Courts in State and Nation.* New Haven: Yale University Press, 1988. p. 95
[4]Johnson, Gerald W. and Robert S. Montjoy. "Report on Judicial Reform." Prepared for the Administrative Office of Courts, State of Alabama. Auburn University. 1989. p. 14.
[5]House, Mike. From interview conducted by Gerald W. Johnson on May 8, 1981.
[6]*Ibid.*
[7]Martin, Robert. *Loc. Cit.* p 15.
[8]*Ibid.* p. 197.
[9]House, Mike. Former Heflin Chief of Staff. Statement recorded December 20, 1996.
[10]*Ibid.*
[11]*Ibid.*
[12]Cole, Charles D. "Judicial Reform in Alabama: A Reflection." *The Alabama Lawyer.* Vol. 60, No. 3. May 1999. p. 191.
[13]House, Mike. Former Heflin Chief of Staff. Statement recorded December 20, 1996.
[14]Martin. *Loc. Cit.* p. 18.
[15]*Ibid.*
[16]Martin. *Loc. Cit.* pp. 17-18.
[17]House, Mike. From interview conducted by Gerald W. Johnson on May 8, 1981.
[18]Cole. *Loc. Cit.* pp. 188-193.
[19]Tarr. *Loc. Cit.* p. 95
[20]House. From interview conducted by Gerald W. Johnson on May 8, 1981.
[21]Martin, Robert. "It Was About Power and Judicial Independence." *The Alabama Lawyer.* Vol. 60, No. 3. May 1999. p 196.

CHAPTER 13

[1]Cole, Charles D. "Judicial Reform in Alabama: A Reflection." *The Alabama Lawyer.* Vol. 60, No. 3. May 1999. p. 192.
[2]*Ibid.* p. 193.
[3]House, Mike. From interview conducted by Gerald W. Johnson on May 8, 1981.
[4]Shores, Janie L. "A Tribute to Howell Thomas Heflin and His Achievements as Chief Justice of the Alabama Supreme Court." *Alabama Law Review.* Vol. 49, No. 2. Winter 1997. pp. 421- 422.
[5]Martin, Robert. "It Was About Power and Judicial Independence." *The Alabama Lawyer.* Vol. 60, No. 3. May 1999. p. 199.
[6]House. *Loc. Cit.*
[7]Roberson, Peggy. *The Birmingham News.* September 22, 1974.
[8]Nazary, Jeri. "Majority of the Court." *Alabama Alumni Magazine.* Vol. 74, No. 5. August- September 1994. p. 19.
[9]*Ibid.*
[10]Shores. *Loc. Cit.* p. 418.
[11]Tarr, G. Alan, and Mary Cornelia Aldis Porter. *State Supreme Courts in State and Nation.* New Haven: Yale University Press. 1988. 283 pp.
[12]*Ibid.* p. 97.
[13]*Ibid.* p. 122.
[14]*The Mobile Register.* February 29, 1976.
[15]Reveley, W. Taylor, III. Dean, School of Law, William and Mary College. Personal letter to author with copies of Heflin/

Spong correspondence. February 24, 1999.

Chapter 14

[1] The Clayton Record. October 27, 1977.
[2] House, Mike. Personal correspondence with author. August 10, 1999.
[3] House. *Ibid.*
[4] House. *Ibid.*
[5] *Facts on File.* 1978. p. 362.
[6] *The Birmingham News.* February 17, 1998.
[7] Reed, Joe. Chairman of the Alabama Democratic Conference. Statement recorded November 12, 1996.
[8] House. *Loc. Cit.*
[9] Friedman, Richard. "Donald Stewart's Political Quest One of Big State Stories." *The Birmingham News.* October 22, 1978. p. 10-A.
[10] Wassner, Rich. *Athens News-Courier.* January 12, 1979.

Chapter 15

[1] *The Birmingham News.* January 15, 1979. p. 2.
[2] Scarritt, Tom. *The Birmingham News.* March 27, 1980.
[3] *The Birmingham Post-Herald.* May 29, 1979.
[4] Raby, Steve. Interview conducted September 17, 1999.
[5] *The Montgomery Advertiser.* October 31, 1979.
[6] Kantor, Seith. *The Atlanta Journal and Constitution.* November 22, 1979. p. 8A.
[7] *Ibid.*
[8] Morring, Frank, Jr. *The Birmingham Post-Herald.* November 19, 1979.
[9] *The Onlooker.* November 26, 1979.
[10] Benson, Miles. *The Huntsville Times.* February 5, 1980. p. 1.
[11] Adams, Jim. *The Mobile Register.* February 6, 1980.
[12] Morring, Frank, Jr. The Birmingham Post-Herald. May 4, 1981.
[13] Opelika-Auburn News. August 25, 1981.
[14] *The Birmingham Post-Herald.* September 11, 1981.
[15] Gold, Victor. "Southern Style." *Capitol Hill.* April 1994. p. 44.
[16] Scarritt, Tom. *The Birmingham News.* March 4, 1982.
[17] Ehrenhalt, Alan. *The Anniston Star.* Quoting Congressional Quarterly. April 1, 1982.
[18] Hayes, Drew. *The Decatur Daily.* February 12, 1980.
[19] Roberson, Peggy. The Alabama Journal. February 3, 1982.
[20] Scarritt, Tom. *The Birmingham News.* September 10, 1980.
[21] Coburn, Peter. *The Mobile Register.* November 5, 1981.
[22] *The Florence Times.* September 15, 1981. p. 1.
[23] *Richmond News-Leader.* Richmond, Virginia. October 13, 1980.
[24] Heflin, Howell. Weekly Column. July 10, 1980.
[25] Roberson, Peggy. *The Alabama Journal.* March 19, 1980.
[26] Allen, Richard. Alabama Chief Deputy Attorney General and former Heflin Staff Member. Statement written in 1996.
[27] *Southern State.* Ozark, Alabama. May 30, 1979.
[28] Roberson, Peggy. *The Alabama Journal.* November 24, 1979.
[29] *The Florence Times.* December 28, 1979.

Chapter 16

[1] Roberson, Peggy. *The Montgomery Advertiser.* December 5, 1981.
[2] Coburn, Peter. *The Huntsville Times.* September 27, 1981.
[3] *The Huntsville Times.* April 16, 1984.
[4] Fifield, Richard. Formerly of the Alabama Farmers Federation. From a written statement recorded November 12, 1996.
[5] Fick, Bob. *The Anniston Star.* September 19, 1981.
[6] Raby, Steve. Former Chief of Staff for Senator Heflin. Statement recorded in December 1996.
[7] Scarritt, Tom. *The Birmingham Post-Herald.* September 17, 1981.
[8] Raby. *Loc. Cit.*
[9] Fifield. *Loc. Cit.*
[10] Springer, Robert. Farm Service Agency. Statement recorded November 13, 1996.
[11] *The Dothan Eagle.* November 27, 1979.
[12] Horton, Ed. Alabama State Senator. Statement recorded December 12, 1996.
[13] *The Montgomery Advertiser.* July 15, 1984.
[14] Clark, Fred. President, Alabama Rural Electric Association. Statement recorded November 17, 1996.
[15] *Ibid.*
[16] *Ibid.*
[17] O'Shea, Brian. *The Huntsville Times.* December 14, 1982.
[18] *The Huntsville Times.* January 6, 1983.
[19] Scarritt, Tom. *The Birmingham News.* August 2, 1983.
[20] Quarles, Randy. *The Huntsville Times.* May 16, 1984; Pater, J. L. *The Florence Times.* May 23, 1984.
[21] *The Dothan Eagle.* August 7, 1986.
[22] *The Huntsville Times.* September 11, 1986.
[23] *The Decatur Daily.* March 10, 1985.
[24] Fifield. *Loc Cit.*
[25] Fifield. *Loc Cit.*
[26] Kocker, Ray. *The Montgomery Advertiser.* December 19, 1985.
[27] *The Southern Star.* Ozark, Alabama. December 16, 1987.
[28] Moreno, Mylene. The Anniston Star. May 19, 1989.
[29] *The Decatur Daily.* May 19, 1989.
[30] Davis, Debra. *The Montgomery Advertiser.* February 2, 1989.
[31] *The Decatur Daily.* April 25, 1989.
[32] Davis, Debra. *The Montgomery Advertiser.* February 15, 1990.
[33] Heflin, Howell. Weekly Column. July 28, 1990.
[34] *Andalusia Star-News.* April 3, 1990.
[35] Thompson News Service. May 4, 1994.
[36] Kennedy, James H. *The Birmingham News.* March 5, 1995.
[37] Hardy, Jeff. *The Mobile Register.* March 14, 1995.
[38] *The Birmingham News.* September 9, 1995.
[39] Pace, David. T*he Mobile Press.* September 24, 1995.
[40] Heflin, Howell. Weekly Col-

umn. February 21, 1996.
[41]Brumas, Michael. *The Birmingham News.* March 4, 1996.
[42]Marion, James E. Dean, College of Agriculture, Auburn University. Statement recorded November 14, 1996.
[43]*Ibid.*
[44]Frobish, Lowell. Former Director of the Alabama Agriculture Experiment Station, Auburn University. Statement recorded November 18, 1996.
[45]*Ibid.*

CHAPTER 17

[1]Reed, Joe. Chairman of the Alabama Democratic Conference. Statement recorded November 12, 1996.
[2]Neas, Ralph G. Former Executive Director of the Leadership Conference on Civil Rights. Statement recorded December 5, 1996.
[3]*The Alabama Journal.* October 17, 1984.
[4]*The Anniston Star.* June 23, 1982.
[5]Scarritt, Tom. *The Birmingham News.* June 23, 1982.
[6]*Enterprise Ledger.* January 13, 1982.
[7]Scarritt, Tom. *The Birmingham News.* January 23, 1983.
[8]House, Mike. Former Heflin Chief of Staff. Statement recorded December 20, 1996.
[9]*The Montgomery Advertiser.* October 9, 1980.
[10]Ibid.
[11]*The Mobile Press.* November 6, 1980.
[12]Raby, Steve. Former Heflin Chief of Staff. Statement recorded in December 1996.
[13]Heflin, Howell. Weekly column. May 17, 1984.
[14]Scarritt, Tom. *The Birmingham News.* November 4, 1980.
[15]*The Montgomery Advertiser.* February 5, 1982.
[16]Quinn, Diana. *The Florence Time*s. March 7, 1982.
[17]*The Alabama Journal.* March 10, 1982.
[18]Neas. *Loc. Cit.*
[19]Shanahan, Mike. Associated Press. April 27, 1982.
[20]Roberson, Peggy. *The Montgomery Advertiser.* May 3, 1982.
[21]Berry, Mary Francis, Chairperson of the U. S. Commission on Civil Rights. Statement recorded October 25, 1996.
[22]Sanders, Steve. *The Birmingham Post-Herald.* June 16, 1982.
[23]Roberson, Peggy. *The Alabama Journal.* June 19, 1982.
[24]Neas. *Loc. Cit.*
[25]*The Mobile Register.* May 6, 1982.
[26]*Talladega Daily Home.* June 22, 1982.
[27]Berry. *Loc. Cit.*
[28]Pate, J. L. *The Florence Times.* October 20, 1983.
[29]House. *Loc. Cit.*
[30]*The Birmingham News.* May 6, 1983.
[31]Quinn, Diana. *The Florence Times.* November 17, 1981.
[32]Scarritt, Tom. *The Birmingham News.* September 26, 1982.
[33]*The Birmingham Post-Herald.* March 22, 1984.
[34]Neas, Ralph G. Former Executive Director of the Leadership Conference on Civil Rights. Statement recorded December 12, 1996.

CHAPTER 18

[1]*The Mobile Press.* June 5, 1983.
[2]McCracken, Gayle. *The Birmingham Post-Herald.* July 27, 1982.
[3]Barton, Olivia. *The Birmingham News.* January 28, 1985.
[4]Quarles, Randy. *The Huntsville Times.* February 18, 1983.
[5]*The Birmingham News.* June 16, 1983.
[6]Quarles, Randy. *The Huntsville Times.* June 26, 1983.
[7]McCracken, Gayle. *The Birmingham Post-Herald.* February 14, 1984.
[8]*The Huntsville Times.* August 22, 1984.
[9]Bunch, William. *The Birmingham News.* September 5, 1984.
[10]*The Mobile County Press.* August 2, 1984.
[11]*The Tuscaloosa News.* September 5, 1984.
[12]Burch, William. *The Birmingham News.* September 20, 1984.
[13]Herring, Amy. *The Montgomery Advertiser.* September 28, 1984.
[14]Zumwalt, Norman. *The Florence Times.* October 22, 1984.
[15]Martin, Ann Marie. *The Huntsville Times.* November 14, 1984.
[16]*The Huntsville Times.* October 21, 1982.
[17]Quarles, Randy. *The Huntsville Times.* November 7, 1982.
[18]*The Huntsville Times.* November 23, 1982.
[19]*The Mobile Press.* March 24, 1983.
[20]Bolton, Bo. *Demopolis Times.* April 3, 1983.
[21]Watkins, Ed. "Lock is Renamed in Honor of Heflin." The Tuscaloosa News. March 28, 1997. p. B1
[22]Heflin, Howell. Weekly Column. December 3, 1986.
[23]Raby, Steve. Interview conducted August 4, 1999.

CHAPTER 19

[1]Fowler, Mark. Former Heflin staff member. Statement recorded November 18, 1996.
[2]Heflin, Howell. Weekly Column. September 12, 1981.
[3]Simendinger, Alexis. *The Anniston Star.* March 9, 1983.
[4]*The Birmingham Post-Herald.* September 9, 1981.
[5]Sheppard, Scott. *The Birmingham News.* December 17, 1984.
[6]*The Huntsville Times.* September 18, 1981.
[7]Scarritt, Tom. *The Birmingham News.* October 28, 1981.
[8]*Sylacauga News.* July 1, 1981.
[9]Biely, Debra. Lieutenant Colonel, U. S. Marine Corps. Former Heflin Congressional Fellow. Statement recorded December 16, 1996.
[10]*The Birmingham Post-Herald.* May 26, 1983.
[11]McCorkel, Bill. Redstone Arsenal. Statement recorded on November 13, 1996.
[12]Machen, Jyles. NASA. Former Heflin Congressional Fellow. Statement recorded on November 15, 1996.
[13]Quarles, Randy. *The Huntsville*

Times. June 15, 1984.
[14] McNeil, Robert B. *The Anniston Star.* September 23, 1987.
[15] Davis, Brett. *The Huntsville Times.* September 29, 1989.
[16] *The Birmingham News.* March 18, 1988.
[17] Heflin, Howell. Weekly Column. March 24, 1988.
[18] *The Florence Times.* May 12, 1989.
[19] *The Tuscaloosa News.* May 19, 1989.
[20] Rutherford, Ken. *The Decatur Daily.* December 20, 1989.
[21] Dooling, Dave. *The Huntsville Times.* January 9, 1980. p. 1.
[22] Coburn, Peter. *The Huntsville Times.* May 8, 1980.
[23] Biely, Debra. Lieutenant Colonel, U. S. Marine Corps. Former Heflin Congressional Fellow. Statement recorded December 16, 1996.
[24] Beard, Danny. *The Huntsville News.* January 10, 1984.
[25] Quarles, Randy. *The Huntsville Times.* May 13, 1984.
[26] *The Birmingham News.* December 14, 1987.
[27] Heflin, Howell. Weekly Column. October 15, 1987.
[28] *The Alabama Journal.* December 1, 1987.
[29] Alexander City Outlook. December 9, 1987.
[30] Brumas, Michael. *The Birmingham Post-Herald.* August 4, 1988.
[31] *The Mobile Register.* July 21, 1989.
[32] Davis, Brett. *The Huntsville Times.* September 14, 1989.
[33] Lee, Jack. Former Director of the Marshall Space Flight Center. Statement recorded November 15, 1996.
[34] Raby, Steve. Interview conducted September 17, 1999.
[35] Heflin, Howell. Weekly Column. August 5, 1983.
[36] Askew, Ray. NASA. Statement recorded in December 1996.
[37] Heflin, Howell. Weekly Column. November 24, 1986.
[38] Marion, James E. Dean, College of Agriculture, Auburn University. Statement recorded

November 14, 1996.
[39] Robinson, Carol. *The Birmingham News.* September 19, 1986.
[40] *The Anniston Star.* July 29, 1987.
[41] Askew, Ray. NASA. Statement recorded in December 1996.
[42] Heflin, Howell. Weekly Column. April 13, 1988.
[43] Askew. *Loc. Cit.*
[44] Askew. *Loc. Cit.*
[45] Quarles, Randy. *The Huntsville Times.* February 9, 1984.
[46] Raby, Steve. Interview conducted September 17, 1999.
[47] *The Birmingham News.* February 23, 1988.
[48] Binkley, John. *The Birmingham News.* August 13, 1988.
[49] McNeil, Robert B. *The Montgomery Advertiser.* December 8, 1988.

CHAPTER 20

[1] *The Huntsville Times.* August 2, 1987.
[2] *The Montgomery Advertiser.* November 26, 1986.
[3] Haas, Clif. *The Huntsville Times.* December 3, 1986.
[4] McNeil, Robert. *The Florence Times.* December 25, 1986.
[5] *The Birmingham News.* July 8, 1987.
[6] Ruby, Walter. Jewish World. February 13-19, 1987.
[7] "Can He Recover?" Time. March 9, 1987. p. 21.
[8] Roberts, Steven V. "Reagan Concedes 'Mistake' in Arms-for-Hostage Policy; Takes Blame, Vows Changes." *The New York Times.* March 5, 1987. p. 1.
[9] *The Birmingham News.* March 5, 1987.
[10] AP Story. *The Birmingham News.* May 15, 1987.
[11] *The Alabama Journal.* July 21, 1987.
[12] *The New York Times* News Service. July 12, 1987.
[13] *The Decatur Daily.* July 10, 1987.
[14] Hollis, Guy. "Editorial." *The Huntsville Times.* July 26, 1987.
[15] Clemenson, Brad. *The Huntsville Times.* May 15, 1987.

[16] Pace, David. Associated Press. May 7, 1987.
[17] *The Dothan Eagle.* May 17, 1987.
[18] Gay, Lance, and Walter Friedenberg. *The Birmingham Post-Herald.* July 25, 1987.
[19] *The Birmingham News.* August 3, 1987.
[20] Gonslaves, Bob. "Summary of the Report of the Independent Counsel." Iran-Contra Investigation. 1993.
[21] Lewis, Jesse J., and John Hayman. *Empowerment of a Race: The Revitalization of Black Institutions.* Montgomery, AL: Black Belt Press, 1999. p. 37
[22] *The Anniston Star.* July 3, 1987.
[23] Neas, Ralph G. Former Executive Director of the Leadership Conference on Civil Rights. Statement recorded December 5, 1996.
[24] "Editorial" Inner City News. Mobile, Alabama. July 18, 1987.
[25] Kennedy, James H. *The Birmingham News.* September 22, 1987.
[26] McNeil, Robert B. *The Anniston Star.* July 3, 1987.
[27] McNeil, Robert B. *The Gadsden Times.* September 15, 1987.
[28] Herring, Amy. *The Montgomery Advertiser.* September 12, 1987.
[29] *The Alabama Journal.* September 17, 1987.
[30] Brumas, Michael. *The Birmingham News.* September 17, 1987.
[31] *The Decatur Daily.* September 17, 1987.
[32] Raby, Steve. Interview conducted September 17, 1999.
[33] House, Mike. Former Heflin Chief of Staff. Statement recorded December 20, 1996.
[34] Hamilton, Bob. *The Birmingham Post-Herald.* September 30, 1987.
[35] Kahler, Kathryn. *The Birmingham News.* October 1, 1987.
[36] *The Decatur Daily.* October 2, 1987.
[37] Brenner, Ellot. Crimson White. University of Alabama. October 7, 1987.

[38] Evans, Robert and Robert Novak. *The Mobile Register*. October 20, 1987.
[39] Quarles, Randy. *The Huntsville Times*. October 25, 1987.
[40] Greenhouse, Linda. *The New York Times*. October 5, 1997. p. 2.
[41] *Ibid*.
[42] McNeil, Robert B. *The Anniston Star*. September 18, 1986.
[43] Williams, Cresandra. *The Tuscaloosa News*. February 18, 1989.
[44] Brumas, Michael. *The Birmingham News*. February 28, 1989.
[45] Clemenson, Brad. *Mobile Press-Register*. March 2, 1989.
[46] Cassata, Donna. *The Montgomery Advertiser*. March 10, 1989.
[47] Robinson, Mike. . July 23, 1989.
[48] From the Cleveland Plain Dealer, June 7, 1986. *Congressional Record — Senate*. June 25, 1986. p. 15408.
[49] Raby, Steve. Interview conducted August 4, 1999.
[50] Transcript of Proceedings: United States Senate Committee on the Judiciary Confirmation Hearings. Washington, D.C. May 6, 1986. pp. 121-135.
[51] DeConcini, Dennis. *Congressional Record — Senate*. June 10, 1986. p. 13086.
[52] Russakoff, Dale. *Washington Post*. August 6, 1989.
[53] Neas, Ralph G. Former Executive Director of the Leadership Conference on Civil Rights. Statement recorded December 5, 1996.
[54] The Mobile Press-Register. July 30, 1989.

Chapter 21

[1] *The Birmingham News*. March 20, 1982. p. 3A.
[2] *The Anniston Star*. May 21, 1982.
[3] *The Decatur Daily*. September 9, 1982.
[4] Quarles, Randy. *The Huntsville Times*. November 16, 1982.
[5] Gardner, Tom. *The Montgomery Advertiser*. December 2, 1982.
[6] Hayman, Clara Ruth. *Protecting Alabama: A History of the Alabama Environmental Council*. Birmingham, AL: Alabama Environmental Council, April 1997. p. 19.
[7] Pate, J. L. *The Decatur Daily*. August 6, 1983.
[8] *The Decatur Daily*. August 16, 1983.
[9] *The Birmingham News*. November 20, 1983.
[10] Ratliff, Freida. The Decatur Daily. April 6, 1984.
[11] *The Florence Times*. February 5, 1985.
[12] *The Birmingham News*. April 11, 1985.
[13] Mullan, Shelia. *The Anniston Star*. December 17, 1985.
[14] *The Anniston Star*. May 2, 1986.
[15] Brumas, Michael. *The Birmingham News*. September 29, 1988.
[16] *The Anniston Star*. June 30, 1988.
[17] Brumas, Michael. *The Birmingham News*. April 27, 1988.
[18] *The Florence Times*. June 18, 1988.
[19] Heflin, Howell. Weekly Column. June 27, 1988.
[20] *The Birmingham News*. July 13, 1988.
[21] Hargrove, Thomas. *The Birmingham Post-Herald*. May 18, 1990.
22 Heflin, Howell. Weekly Column. July 11, 1990.
[23] *The Tuscaloosa News*. July 11, 1990.
[24] Brumas, Michael. *The Birmingham News*. July 20, 1990.
[25] *The Anniston Star*. April 8, 1992.
[26] *The Birmingham News*. April 29, 1992.
[27] *The Birmingham News*. July 8, 1992.
[28] Hayman. *Loc. Cit.* p. 46.
[29] *The Mobile Register*. August 20, 1981.
[30] Brumas, Michael. *The Birmingham News*. June 19, 1988.
[31] Brumas, Michael. *The Birmingham News*. October 7, 1988.
[32] Clemenson, Brad. *The Mobile Press*. April 20, 1990.
[33] Kipp, Stephen. *The Birmingham Post-Herald*. April 24, 1990.
[34] *The Anniston Star*. September 6, 1990.
[35] Heflin, Howell. Weekly Column. April 21, 1988.
[36] Heflin, Howell. Weekly Column. October 29, 1982.
[37] Connell, Brian. *The Dothan Eagle*. September 2, 1990.
[38] *The Gadsden Times*. August 3, 1990.

Chapter 22

[1] McCartney, Robert J. "East Germany Opens Berlin Wall and Borders." *The Washington Post*. November 10, 1989.
[2] *Talladega Daily Home*. November 18, 1988.
[3] Gordon, Tom. *The Birmingham News*. May 14, 1989.
[4] Kipp, Stephen. *The Birmingham Post-Herald*. April 24, 1990.
[5] Lewis, Pat. *The Montgomery Advertiser*. May 20, 1990.
[6] Witt, Elaine. *The Birmingham Post-Herald*. September 6, 1990.
[7] Witt, Elaine. **The Birmingham News**. September 15, 1990.
[8] Sloan, Paul. *The Anniston Star*. October 17, 1990.
[9] Colquitt, Ron and Guy Busby. *The Mobile Press*. October 31, 1990.
[10] *The Birmingham Post-Herald*. November 3, 1990.
[11] Raby, Steve. Interview conducted August 4, 1999.
[12] *The Tuscaloosa News*. November 12, 1989.
[13] *The Anniston Star*. October 23, 1990.
[14] Welch, William M. *The Mobile Press*. November 28, 1990.
[15] *The Columbus Ledger-Enquirer*. December 6, 1990.
[16] Abramson, Jill. *The Wall Street Journal*. February 28, 1991.
[17] *Congressional Record*. 102nd Congress Report 102-103. Report submitted by Howell Heflin from the Select Committee on Ethics. November 1991. pp. 18-19.
[18] Brumas, Michael. *The Birmingham News*. December 15, 1991.
[19] *The Mobile Press*. May 23, 1991.

[20] McNeil, Bob. *The Tuscaloosa News.* July 28, 1991.
[21] Page, Clarence. *The Birmingham News.* July 11. 1991.
[22] McGonigle, Steve. *Dallas Morning News.* September 9, 1991.
[23] *The Tuscaloosa News.* September 26, 1991.
[24] Rowley, James. *The Dothan Eagle.* September 28, 1991.
[25] *The Birmingham Post-Herald.* October 2, 1991.
[26] *The Anniston Star.* October 11, 1991.
[27] Berke, Richard L. *The New York Times.* October 12, 1991.
[28] Pace, David. *The Huntsville Times.* October 16, 1991.
[29] Young, Mark. Former Heflin Staff Member. Statement recorded November 15, 1996.
[30] Tanber, George J. *The Anniston Star.* October 8, 1992.
[31] *The Dothan Eagle.* July 21, 1993.
[32] Brumas, Michael and Stan Bailey. *The Birmingham News.* September 10,1992.
[33] *The Mobile Press.* June 24, 1993.
[34] Anderson, John. *The Huntsville Times.* July 2, 1991.
[35] Rosenthal, Harry F. *The Montgomery Advertiser.* September 22, 1993.
[36] Pace, David. *The Huntsville Times.* February 7, 1991.
[37] Hargrove, Thomas. *The Birmingham Post-Herald.* July 18, 1991.
[38] McNeil, Robert B. *The Florence Times.* September 5, 1992.

CHAPTER 23

[1] *Congressional Record — Senate.* July 22, 1993. pp. 16687-16688.
[2] *The Birmingham Post-Herald.* April 12, 1994.
[3] *The Decatur Daily.* August 3, 1993.
[4] Berry, Mary Frances. Chairperson of the U. S. Commission on Civil Rights. Statement recorded October 25, 1996.
[5] *The Decatur Daily.* March 31, 1988.
[6] Raby, Steve. Interview conducted August 4, 1999.
[7] Pekkanem, Sarah. *The Florence Times.* September 23, 1993.
[8] Mosley, Beckie. Alexander City Outlook. September 24, 1993.
[9] *The Mobile Register.* September 24, 1993
[10] St. Clair News-Agis. Pell City, Alabama. July 1, 1993.
[11] Pace, David. *The Montgomery Advertiser.* February 15, 1994.
[12] Heflin, Howell. Weekly Column. September 9, 1993.
[13] Margasak, Larry. *The Mobile Register.* November 21, 1993.
[14] Welp, Catherine. *Andalusia Star-News.* September 15, 1993.
[15] Kendrick, Melissa. *Andalusia Star-News.* December 23, 1994.
[16] *West Alabama Gazette.* Millport, Alabama. February 16, 1995.
[17] *The Birmingham Post-Herald.* August 13, 1992.
[18] Pace, David. *The Montgomery Advertiser.* November 5, 1993.
[19] Espo, David. *The Mobile Register.* November 21, 1993.
[20] Pace, David. *The Birmingham News.* January 17, 1994.
[21] Barnett, Jennifer. *The Huntsville News.* November 30, 1994.
[22] Raby, Steve. Interview conducted September 17, 1999.
[23] *The Huntsville Times.* March 4, 1993.
[24] Hardy, Jeff. *The Mobile Register.* March 7, 1993.
[25] Skorneck, Carolyn. *The Birmingham News.* January 8, 1994.
[26] Kennedy, James H. *The Birmingham News.* March 5, 1995.
[27] Hardy, Jeff. *The Mobile Register.* March 14, 1995.
[28] *The Birmingham News.* September 9, 1995.
[29] Pace, David. *The Mobile Press.* September 24, 1995.
[30] Heflin, Howell. Weekly Column. February 21, 1996.
[31] Willens, Patricia. *The Cullman Times.* July 23, 1994.
[32] Pekkanen, Sarah. *The Florence Times.* April 8, 1993.
[33] Pekkanen, Sarah. *The Anniston Star.* May 26, 1994.
[34] *The Decatur Daily.* May 7, 1993.
[35] Staed, John. *The Birmingham Post-Herald.* May 18, 1993.
[36] Pace, David. *The Huntsville Times.* June 8, 1993.
[37] *The Huntsville Times.* September 6, 1994.

CHAPTER 24

[1] Lewis, Anthony. "The Piper and the Tune." *The New York Times.* September 29, 1998.
[2] Brumas, Michael and Michael Sznajderman. *The Birmingham News.* November 4, 1996.
[3] *The Florence Times.* February 4, 1996.
[4] *The Birmingham Post-Herald.* March 24, 1995.
[5] Raby, Steve. Interview conducted August 4, 1999.
[6] Helms, Dave. *The Mobile Register.* December 13, 1995.
[7] *The Decatur Daily.* September 27, 1995.
[8] Peck, John. *The Huntsville Times.* October 28, 1994.
[9] *The Anniston Star.* June 8, 1995.
[10] Brumas, Michael. *The Birmingham News.* May 16, 1996.
[11] Alcorn, John D. *The Montgomery Advertiser.* June 2, 1996.
[12] Ingram, Bob. *The Montgomery Advertiser.* June 4, 1996.
[13] Owens, Gene. *The Mobile Press.* September 15, 1996.
[14] Burger, Frederick. *The Anniston Star.* November 6, 1996.
[15] *The Birmingham News.* December 6, 1996.
[16] Hood, Lilla. *Opelika-Auburn News.* March 1, 1995.
[17] *The Birmingham Post-Herald.* June 22, 1995.
[18] *The Birmingham News.* June 23, 1995.
[19] Abdullah, Halimah. *The Huntsville Times.* June 28, 1996.
[20] *The Florence Times.* September 6, 1995.
[21] *The Mobile Register.* March 30, 1995.
[22] *Montgomery Independent.* April 20, 1995.
[23] *The Birmingham News.* March 16, 1996.
[24] Brumas, Michael. *The Birmingham News.* March 19, 1996.

²⁵ *The Methodist Voice*. Birmingham, AL. June 1996. p. 4.
²⁶ Beyerle, Dana. *The Florence Times*. September 21, 1996.
²⁷ Faulk, Kent. *The Birmingham News*. November 13, 1996.
²⁸ Rutherford, Ken. *The Decatur Daily*. November 17, 1996.
²⁹ Yarbrough, Marie. "Former U.S. Senator Reflects on Work with Past Presidents." *The Crimson White*. (University of Alabama). March 28, 1998.
³⁰ Berry, Mary Frances. Chairperson of the U.S. Civil Rights Commission. Statement recorded October 25, 1996.
³¹ Hargrove, Thomas. *The Birmingham Post-Herald*. March 31, 1995.
³² Redden, Clay. *The Decatur Daily*. October 2, 1996.
³³ The Tuscaloosa News. March 31, 1996.
³⁴ The Selma Times-Journal. September 30, 1996.
³⁵ Hulse, Carl. "The Senator Comes Home." Riverviews. Vol. 3, No. 9. November/December 1996. p. 17.
³⁶ Kennedy, Ted. "'The Judge' Brightened the Senate." Special to *The Tuscaloosa News*. December 26, 1996.
³⁷ Stephens, Ted. United States Senator from Alaska. Congressional Record. March 29, 1995.
³⁸ Raby, Steve. Interview conducted August 4, 1999.

CHAPTER 25
¹ Stanley, Alessandra. "President Makes Absence Felt Among the Powerful." *The New York Times*. February 2, 1998.

CHAPTER 26
¹ Johnston, Bennett. United States Senator from Louisiana. *Congressional Record*. March 29, 1995.
² *The Birmingham News*. March 29, 1970.
³ Raby, Steve. Interview conducted September 17, 1999.
⁴ Raby, Steve. Interview conducted August 4, 1999.
⁵ Hatfield, Mark. United States Senator from Oregon. *Congressional Record*. March 29, 1995.
⁶ Hutchinson, Kay Bailey. United States Senator from Texas. *Congressional Record*. March 29, 1995.
⁷ Bishop, L. O. A Farmer in Northwest Alabama. Statement recorded November 21, 1996.
⁸ Springer, Robert. Farm Service Agency. Statement recorded November 13, 1996.
⁹ House, Mike. Washington Attorney and former Heflin Chief of Staff. Statement recorded December 20, 1996.
¹⁰ Clark, Fred. President, Alabama Rural Electric Association. Statement recorded November 17, 1996.
¹¹ Grainger, Charles E. Vice President of Administration, Teledyne Brown Engineering, Huntsville, Alabama. Written statement prepared in March 1997.
¹² Raby, Steve. Interview conducted August 4, 1999.
¹³ Clark. *Loc. Cit.*
¹⁴ Young, Mark. Former Heflin Staff Member. Statement recorded November 15, 1996.
¹⁵ *Ibid.*
¹⁶ *Ibid.*
¹⁷ Clark. *Loc. Cit.*
¹⁸ Biely, Debra. Lieutenant Colonel, U. S. Marine Corps. Former Heflin Congressional Fellow. Statement recorded December 16, 1996.
¹⁹ Raby, Steve. Interview conducted August 4, 1999.
²⁰ Gordon, Tom. "Heflin: Political Center is Strength." *The Birmingham News*. December 28, 1996. p. 4A.
²¹ *Ibid.*
²² *Ibid.*
²³ Shores, Janie L. "A Tribute to Howell Thomas Heflin and His Achievements as Chief Justice of the Alabama Supreme Court." Alabama Law Review. Vol. 49, No. 2. Winter 1997. p. 430.
²⁴ Owens, Gene. "Political Humorist Mark Russell Reminisces about 'Son of Sam.'" Mobile Register. September 19, 1999.
²⁵ Clark. *Loc. Cit.*
²⁶ Bishop. *Loc. Cit.*
²⁷ Raby, Steve. Interview conducted August 4, 1999.
²⁸ Clark. *Loc. Cit.*
²⁹ Horton, Ed. Alabama State Senator. Statement recorded December 12, 1996.
³⁰ Greenhaw, Wayne. "A Super Tuesday Circuit Ride." Alabama Magazine. Vol. 52, No. 3. May/June 1988. p. 15.

CHAPTER 27
¹ Viglante, Richard. *The New Republic*. August 31, 1992. p. 21.

CHAPTER 28
¹ St. Onge, Peter. "Heflin's Heart Never Left his Hometown. *The Huntsville Times*. October 25, 1998. p. A27.
² *Ibid.*
³ Clark, Leigh Ann. "UAB's Heflin Genetic Center Breaks Ground for Construction." *The Birmingham News*. October 20, 1998.
⁴ Faulk, Kent. "Two Birmingham Residents Among Heflin Honorees." *The Birmingham News*. April 18, 1999. p. 26A.
⁵ *The Birmingham News*. April 12, 1999.
⁶ *Colbert County Reporter*. August 9, 1984.
⁷ Gordon, Tom. "Heflin: Political Center is Strength." *The Birmingham News*. December 28, 1996. p. 1.
⁸ Reed, Joe. Chairman of the Alabama Democratic Conference. Statement recorded November 12, 1996.
⁹ "Exploring the American Dream." America Dreams WebQuest. An Internet-based project that utilizes source documents from the Library of Congress American Memory Collection. Internet address: www.internet-catalyst.org/projects/amproject/toc.html

Index

A

abortion, issue of   19, 392, 411
ABSCAM   229
Acland, Anthony   424
Adair, Charlie   95
Adams, Oscar Jr.   199
Adcock, Hobson   62, 87, 96
Age Discrimination Act   392
Agnew, Spiro   207
Agriculture Subcommittee on Rural Development   247
Aikman, Alex   201
Airborne Warning and Control System   304
Alabama   20
  1901 Constitution   29, 109, 132, 148, 154, 156, 174, 186
  Constitutional Convention of 1875   27
  Secession Convention of 1861   28
  the Black Belt   20, 137, 154
Alabama A&M University   269, 320
Alabama Business and Professional Women   185
Alabama Constitutional Commission   147, 159, 175
Alabama Cooperative Extension Service   253
Alabama Crusade for Children   103
Alabama Democratic Conference   163, 185, 213, 263
Alabama Department of Conservation and Natural Res   348
Alabama Education Association   153, 163, 185
Alabama Ethics Commission   138
Alabama Labor Council   185, 191
Alabama Law Review   198
Alabama Polytechnic Institute. *See* Auburn University
Alabama Poultry and Egg Association   261
Alabama Public Service Commission   136
Alabama Rural Electric Association   431, 436
Alabama State Bar Association   142, 147, 152
Alabama State Chamber of Commerce   185
Alfalfa Club   423–424, 447
Allen, James B.   136, 152, 211, 213, 219, 347
Allen, Maryon   212, 215
Allen, Richard   219, 345
Allentown High School   456
American Association of University Women   185
American Bar Association   152, 267
American College of Trial Lawyers   135, 452
American Federation of Labor   30, 208
American Judicature Society   146, 152
Anderson, Jack   230
Anglo-American Legal Exchange   227
Animal Research Facilities Protection Act   258
Anniston Star   353
Anti-smuggling Act   297
Arafat, Yasser   398
Arant, Douglas   101
Armey, Dick   256
Arms Export Control Act   324
Army's Anti-Satellite Program   414
Askew, Ray   317, 318
Atlanta Journal and Constitution   337
Auburn University   28, 170, 253, 258, 269, 299, 318–319, 411, 419
Avondale Mills   123
Azbell, Joe   418

B

Bachus, Spencer   394
Bailey, Kay   429
Baker, Howard   307, 424
Baker, Jim   361
Baker, John   212
Bamburg, Red   250
Bankhead, John   23, 31
Bankhead, John Jr.   32

Bankhead National Forest   347
Bankhead, William   419
Bankruptcy Reform Act of 1995   296
Battle of Gettysburg   33
Battle of Horseshoe Bend   25
Baxley, Bill   267
Bayh, Birch   273
Beasley, Ingram   169
Beasley, Jere   165, 181, 184
Beatty, Sam   434
Beck, W. M.   117
Bedford, Roger   415
Beecher, Johnny Daniel   170
Beil, Debra   309, 432
Bell, Griffin   203, 266, 424
Bennett, Jeff   96
Bennett, Robert   373
Bentsen, Lloyd M.   424
Bereuter, Douglas   408
Berry, Marion   257
Berry, Mary Frances   274, 275, 419
Betenbaugh, Carlton   219, 220
Bevill, Tom   247, 322, 347, 356
Biden, Joseph   343
Birmingham Humane Society   218
Birmingham News   139, 163, 196, 212, 349, 367, 369, 411
Birmingham Post-Herald   204, 302
Birmingham-Southern College   28, 41, 56, 60–68, 196, 415, 448
Bishop, L. O.   429, 435
Black, Hugo   31, 32, 118, 170, 172, 222, 268, 419, 453
Black Monday   21
Black, William K.   374
Blanton, Dick   62
Blount, Winton   215, 304
Boland Amendment   324
Bolden v. City of Mobile   274
Bonderant, Amy   384
Borden, Charles Wayne   291
Bork, Robert   22, 323, 333–346
Bostick, Fred   49
Boston Globe   401, 435
Boswell Amendment   156
Bourbons   154
Boutwell, Wayne   245
Brady Handgun Control Bill   397
Brady, James S.   397
Brady, Nicholas F.   424
Brewer, Albert   151, 158, 162, 204

Breyer, Stephen G.   380–381
Breznev, Leonid   236
Brinkley, David   323
Browder, Glen   413, 415, 419
Brown, Bill   98
Brown, Tim   371
Brown v. Board of Education   156, 377
Bryant, Herbert   128
Bryant, Ted   369
Buchanan, John   292
Buckley, William F. Jr.   441
Buffett, Warren   424
Bugg, Charles   320
Bumpers, Dale   385, 412
Burger, Warren   202, 223, 227, 340, 424
Bush, Barbara   286, 288
Bush, George   230, 256, 307, 308, 311, 321, 332, 341, 356, 361, 364, 367, 376, 381, 381–383, 383, 396, 398, 399, 424, 438, 439, 442
Byrd, Robert C.   228, 229, 232, 237, 326

C

Cabiness, William Jelks III   366
Callahan, H. L.   357
Camp David Accords   439
Carbaugh, Harvey   81–82
Carmichael, Archie   109, 148, 206
Carmichael, Charles   104, 116, 147, 150, 153
Carmichael, Elizabeth Ann. *See* Heflin, Elizabeth Ann
Carmichael, Jesse Malcolm   109
Carnes, Edward   381
Carter, Jimmy   203, 214, 222, 236, 237, 238, 239, 241, 258, 265, 268, 269, 289, 305, 335, 398, 410, 438, 439–440, 444
Casey, William   325, 327, 329
Cashion, James Robert   49
Cerletty, Marie   323
Challenger disaster   313–314
Chappie James Preventive Health Center   269
Chesterton, C. K.   194
Childers, James Saxon   65
Christopher, Tom   96, 98, 118, 424
Christopher, Warren   203
Churchill, Randolph   286
Churchill, Winston II   286
CIA   227, 324, 327, 329, 442

Citizens' Conference   146, 147, 157, 158–159, 171, 179, 180, 183, 207
Civil Rights Act   392
Civil Rights Movement   121, 132, 136, 161, 224, 262
Civil War   28, 50, 57, 174
Clark, Fred   430, 431, 436
Clarke, Julia Reese   28
Clarke, William Edward   28
Clayton, Graham   235
Clements, Marc Ray   99, 102
Clemon, U. W.   266
Clinton, Bill   197, 203, 256, 257, 265, 286, 326, 373, 380, 381, 383, 392–409, 413, 415, 420, 424, 429, 438, 441–442, 444
Clinton, Hillary   286, 394, 404
Coburn, Paul   135
Coburn, Peter   241, 269
Cochran, Thad   243
Coker, Tom   220, 371
Colbert County High School   52, 53, 54, 55
Cold War   121, 303, 304, 306–307, 323–346
    end of   364–365
Cole, Charles   184, 190
Columbia University   36, 267
Confederacy   24, 50, 262, 388
Congressional Quarterly   264, 273, 275
Conrad, Kent   254
Contras   325, 330
Cook, Camille   95
Corretti, Doug   95
Cox, Archibald   334
Cox, Bob   164
Cramer, Bud   397
Cranston, Alan   371, 374
Crisp, Charlie   43
Croker, Bill   295
Crowe, William J.   424
Crowell, Craven   361
Crump, Gene   208

D

Daffron, Sandra Radcliff   448
Dalen, Mike   368
Davis, Bill   306
Dawkins, Joe   123
de Graffenried, Ryan   95
Decatur Daily   138, 391

DeConcini, Dennis   324, 335, 338, 341, 345, 371, 374–376
DeLucas, Larry   320
Democratic Party   31, 37, 58, 100, 120, 121, 136, 137, 141, 164, 243, 257, 264, 289, 292, 298, 306, 311, 321, 329, 333, 337, 378, 402
Dempsey, Walker   50
Denton, Jeremiah   235, 273, 277, 289, 298, 314, 343, 349
Deshler High School   216
Dickinson, Bill   357
Dill, Tom   62
Dixiecrats   32, 100, 121
Dixon, Allen   413
Doaks, Joe   183
Dole, Elizabeth   289
Dole, Robert   93, 273, 289, 314, 321, 403, 414, 421
Domenici, Pete   294, 341
Dominick, Frank   95
Downing, Casey   181
Dukakis, Michael   311, 321
Durr, Clifford   20
Dushuck, Jane Kimbrough   95
Dutton, Roger   349

E

Eastland, James   224
Edgar, Robert   290
Edwards, Macon   243
Edwards-Lackey Commission   123
Eighteenth Amendment   32
Eisenhower, Dwight D.   121, 136, 440
Elders, Joycelyn   416
Elliott, Carl   141
Ervin, Mae   151
Ervin, Sam   283, 434
Evans, Marcie Fred   65
Evans, Michael   290
Evans, Robert   339
Everett, Terry   411
Evins, Virginia   64
Exon, James   412, 420

F

Fair Employment Practices Board   100
Farley, Chris   21
Farley, Jim   58
Farm Bureau Federation
    Alabama   185, 191, 251, 257, 261,

419, 429
  American   30, 261
Farnborough International Aeronautical and Space E   311
Farrah, Albert   118
Farrah Law Society   118, 162
Farrakhan, Louis   377
Faulkner, Jimmy   136
FBI   226, 228, 229, 342
Federal Trade Commission   239
Feeney Study   223
Feinberg, Kenneth   204
Fennel, Edward   119–120
Fennel, Jim Kirk   105
Fifield, Dick   244, 257, 419
Finch, Peyton   97
Fine, Joe   181
Flippo, Ronnie   182, 192, 216, 239, 348, 350, 351
Florence State Teachers College. *See* University of North Alabama
Florence Study Club   151
Florence Times   134, 181
Flowers, Richmond   99
Flowers, Walter   208, 212, 213
Folsom, Jim   20, 99, 117, 123, 154, 157
Forney, John   209
Forrest, Nathan Bedford   57
Forrestal, James   91
Fort McClellan   235, 303, 413
Fort Rucker   235, 303
Foster, Henry   416
Foster, Luther   269
Fowler, Conrad   67–68, 70, 71, 72–75, 79, 82, 85, 95, 97, 159, 173, 175, 179
Fowler, Wyche   255
Francis, Jamie   454
Frankfurter, Felix   380

G

G.I. Bill   93–102, 96, 111, 121
Gadsden Time   391
Gaines, Ralph   95
Gardiner, Bill   126, 181, 187, 207, 210, 220, 300, 370, 428
  death of   411
Gary, Loren   107, 108
GATT legislation   243, 251, 399, 442
George, Walter   58
Gephardt, Richard   321

Gewin, Walter   134
Gingrich, Newt   405
Ginsburg, Douglas H.   339
Ginsburg, Ruth Bader   380–381
Glass, Groggy   82
Glenn, John   293, 309, 310, 371, 374–376
Godbold, John   225
Gold, Vic   141, 207, 367
Goldin, Dan   419
Goldwater, Barry   138, 140, 143, 278, 289, 393, 410, 416
Gompers, Samuel   30
Gorbachev, Mikhail   364, 443
Gore, Al   208, 360, 383, 384, 396, 402, 439
Gore, Albert Sr.   283, 321
Gore, Tipper   286
Grafton, Carl   411
Granger, Charles   139, 306, 430
Grassley, Charles E.   223
Gray, Boyden   382
Gray, Edwin   372
Gray, Fred   267
Great Depression   48, 52, 57, 251
Green, Roy   95, 97
Greenspan, Alan   424, 444
Grenier, John   141
Guilott, Robert   96
Guin, J. Foy   95
Gulf War   381–383
Gunter Air Force Base   303

H

Hager, Bob   384
Haley, James   195
Hall, Fawn   278, 330
Haltom, Bert   95, 99, 106, 107, 117, 120, 129, 131, 136–138, 162, 164, 208, 215, 268, 423–424
Hamilton, Lee   332
Hanson, Chris   384
Hanson, Victor   367
Hardin, Paul   101
Hardin, Taylor   165
Harding, W. P. G.   30–31
Harding, Warren   30
Hardwick, Guy   137, 139
Hare, Francis   143, 219
Harriman, Averell   286
Harriman, Pamela   285

Harris, John 175
Harrison, Karl 101
Harrison, Leigh 92, 115, 157
Hart, Gary 319
Hart, Peter 203, 207
Harvard University 28–29, 34
Hatch, Orin 271, 292, 333
Hatchett, Joseph 223
Hatfield, Antoinette 282
Hatfield, Mark 427
Hawkins, George 138
Hayakawa Anti-Wilderness Bill 355
Hearin, William 202
Heflin, Ann (niece) 39
Heflin, Charles 22
Heflin, "Cotton Tom" 21, 24, 26–31, 30, 31, 35, 42, 58, 88, 136, 202, 278, 417. *See* Heflin, J. Thomas
Heflin, Dr. Watson 23
Heflin, Dr. Wilson L. 23–24, 24, 26
Heflin, Dr. Wyatt 85
Heflin, Elizabeth Ann 49, 76, 96, 100, 107–112, 130, 159, 162, 204, 215, 268, 275, 280, 410, 417, 445, 449–451
  Meeting Howell Heflin 99–100
  meeting interesting people 283–286
Heflin, Harrington P. 24
Heflin, Howell 17–18
  as attorney 101–118, 112–114, 122, 123–124, 126–129, 132–133, 147–151
  as chairman for the North Atlantic Assembly 406–407
  as Chief Justice of Alabama Supreme Court 162–171, 172–186, 187–202
  as civil rights reformer 260–279, 358, 389–390
  as college teacher 105
  as President of the Alabama State Bar Association 140–145
  as Southern humorist 432–434
  at Birmingham-Southern College 58–66
  awarded Silver Star 80, 89
  beginning a career in politics 200–202
  birth of 22
  civic and church activities 106, 109, 115, 155
  current thoughts on enviroment 357–361
  current views on U.S.A. and its future 436–444
  delivering a speech to the Alfalfa Club 421–422
  during the Great Depression 51
  early childhood 33–44
  endorsing Bill Clinton 381–382, 396
  exposed as a space alien 407
  family history 22–32
  fighting for the space station 382–383
  final years in Congress 410–420
  first job 42–43
  in Congress 215–237, 238–259, 280–298, 299–320, 423
  in retirement 445–455
  in School 45–57
  in U.S. Marine Corps 67–90, 278
  investigating the Iran Contra affair and fighting the Robert Bork nomination 321–344
  investigating the "Keating Five" 371–374
  involved in politics 133–137, 427–429
  marriage of 108–109
  meeting Elizabeth Ann 99–100
  on the fall of the USSR 363
  personal beliefs 19–20, 343, 424–427, 452
  playing high school football 52
  refuting his uncle Cotton Tom 31
  ruling against Environmentalists 345–361
  running for Chief Justice 158–161
  running for Congress again 364–367
  Senate race of 1978 203–214
  standing against the Confederate flag 385–388
Heflin, Howell T. 24
Heflin, James 22
Heflin, Joab 22
Heflin, John 22
Heflin, John T. 24
Heflin, Judge John T. 23
Heflin, Julia 38
Heflin, Kitty (niece) 39
Heflin, LaVicie 24
Heflin, Marvin 25, 33–34, 34–35, 50
  death of 44
  retirement of 45

Heflin, Robert L.   26
Heflin, Robert S.   25, 34
Heflin, Tom (son)   111, 113
Heflin, Walter   26
Heflin, William   24
Heflin, Wilson   36, 40–41
Heflin, Wilson Carmichael   322
Heflin, Wyatt Homer   24–25, 26, 34
Helms, Dot   288
Helms, Jesse   223, 242, 271, 276, 279, 288, 387
Hepburn, William   94
Herbert, J. Gerald   343
Herndon, Bill   192
Herndon, Maud Floyd   56
Herring, William   204
Hill, Anita   377–380
Hill, Benjamin   44, 55
Hill, Bob   182, 192
Hill, Lister   23, 58, 99, 100, 138, 141, 152, 216, 219, 234, 262, 289, 419
Hinckley, John   264, 297
Hobbs, Sam Earle   95, 96
Hobbs, Truman   268
Hocklander, Joe   195
Hollings, Fritz   231
Holmes, Oliver Wendell   377
Hood, Cornelia Morgan   450
Hooper, Perry   195
Hoover, Herbert   58
Horton, Ed   138, 436
House, Mike   170, 179, 181, 183, 188, 191, 194, 204, 205, 213, 219, 266, 277, 299, 337, 430
   as Heflin's campaign manager   207–216
Hubble space telescope   310, 313
Huddleston, George, Jr.   62, 95–97, 97–98, 102
Huddleston, George, Sr.   62
Huddleston, Jane   62
Huddleston, John   62
Huddleston, Mary   62
Huddleston, Nancy   62
Hughes, Richard J.   343
Hunt, Guy   298
Huntsville Times   163, 241, 330, 339, 409
Hussein, Saddam   382
Hyde, Henry   326

I

in law school   94–102
Inge, Herndon   95
Ingram, Bob   311, 415
Inner City News   335
Inouye, Daniel   231, 326
International Academy of Trial Lawyers   135, 452
International Society of Barristers   135, 452
Iran-Contra affair   278, 323–331, 441
Iran-Contra hearings   22
Iran-Iraq War   324, 325

J

Jackson, Cliff   383
Jackson, Jesse   321
James, Chappie   269
James, Fob   204, 216, 348, 411
Jarvis, Anna   29
Jefferies, Bill   65
Jepson, "Cotton Roger"   243, 254
Joerchner, Susan J.   378
Johnson, Cass   56
Johnson, Frank   193, 216, 224, 266
Johnson, Jan   371
Johnson, Lyndon   120, 140, 410
Johnston, Bennett   271, 420, 426
Johnston, Paul   187
Jones, Bob   347
Jones, Elaine   169
Jones, Ernie   88
Jones, Paula   404
Jones, Red   172
Jordan, Mollie   177
Justice Assistance Act   297, 417

K

Kassouf, Paul   62
Kaul, Hugh   123
Keating, Charles H. Jr.   372, 374–376
Keller, Helen   239
Kemp, Jack   321, 424
Kemp-Roth bill   265
Kennedy, Anthony   335, 339
Kennedy, Edward   273
Kennedy, John F.   77, 120, 137, 238
   assassination of   140
Kennedy, Robert   140
Kennedy, Ted   204, 225, 278, 369, 420,

432, 435
Kerry, Bob   411
Kiger, Joe   62
King Hussein   288
King, Martin Luther Jr.   140, 276
Kirbo, Charlie   203
Kirk, Claude   99
Kissinger, Henry   424
Knight, Ben   139
Korean War   121
Ku Klux Klan   117, 136, 139

L

LaPierre, Al   369
Law Enforcement Assistance Administration   169, 178, 190, 192, 202, 225
Laxalt, Carol   287
League of Conservation Voters   357, 368
League of Women Voters   185, 191, 277, 293
Leahy, Patrick   254
Lee, Harper   96
Lett, Winston   388
Lewinsky, Monica   404
Lewis, Anthony   410
Lile, Virginia   86
Lindbergh kidnapping   37
Lineman, Arthur   326, 331
Lipscomb, Oscar   158, 181
Livingston, Ed   160
LoBuglio, Albert   295
Locke, Hugh   87
London Times   415
Long, William Mansel, Jr.   219, 388
Lott, Trent   420
Lucas, William C.   342
Lugar, Richard   244
Lyons, Sage   165, 176

M

MacArthur, Douglas   69
Machen, Jyles   306
Maddox, Hugh   159, 180
Marion, James   318
Marshall Space Flight Center   20, 235
Marshall, Thurgood   376
Martin, James   138, 140, 216
Martin, Robert   182, 185
Martins, Vivianne   454
Masters, John   94
Mathais, Charles   344

Mattingly, Ken   312
Mattingly, Mack   244
Mauldin, Edward   35, 51–52, 52, 53–54, 105, 119–120, 139, 148, 153, 162, 208, 423, 450
Mauldin, Mildred   51, 162
Maxwell Air Force Base   303
Maye, Eddie   368
McAuliffe, Christa   313
McCain, John   371, 374–376
McCall, Winston   143
McClurkin, Sam   371
McDonald, Bill   98
McDonald, Sid   204
McDougal, James B.   403
McFarlane, Bud   328, 332
McGee, H. C.   116
McGrory, Mary   230
McKenzie, Billy   40
McMahon, Tom   357
McWherter, Ned   383
McWilliams, Richebourg Gaillard   65
Meador, Daniel J.   164, 222
Meese, Edwin   324, 330
Merrill, Pelham   157, 180
Mikulski, Barbara   385
Milan, Tim   125
Mitchell, Bill   172
Mitchell, Charles   219
Mitchell, George   234, 287, 326, 351, 375
Mobile Press   269
Mobile Press-Register   204
Mobile Register   199, 274, 344, 418
Mobley, James Earl   244, 419
Mondale, Walter   292
Montgomery Advertiser   315, 367
Montgomery Independent   418
Moore, Bill   95
Moore, Joe   128
Moquin, Joe   306
Morgan, Chuck   141, 208
Morrill Act   269
Morrissette, Bob   98, 371
Moseley, Jack   290
Moseley-Braun, Carol   19, 387, 389
Mother's Day Act   29
Moynihan, Daniel Patrick   233
Munsey, Stanley   134, 200
Myrick, Goodwin   251

INDEX

N

NAACP 156, 270, 343, 377
  Legal Defense Fund 169
Nabers, Dayton 101
NAFTA 251, 399, 442
NASA 221, 302, 308, 311, 313–314, 315–316, 318–319, 320, 403, 412, 419, 431
Nashville Banner 197
National Agricultural Advisory Commission 120
National Conference of Chief Justices 200, 452
National Cotton Council 245
National Institutes of Health 238
National Space Grant College Act 317
NATO 214, 236, 408, 442
Natter, Cindy 454
Naval Academy 65
Neas, Ralph 274, 280, 346
New Deal 20, 32, 57, 152
New York Times 65, 196, 290, 340, 410, 423
Nichols, Bill 123, 247, 348
Nixon, Richard 212, 223, 263, 333, 340, 410
Nolan Bill 372
Noriega, Manuel 307–308
North, Jim 101
North, Oliver 325, 326–346
Norvell, Helen 38
Norvell, Samuel Strudwick 98
Novak, Robert 339

O

O'Bannon, Stewart 181, 187
O'Connor, Sandra Day 227
Oliphant, Thomas 401
Omnibus Budget Reconciliation Act 396
Omnibus Victims Protection Act 417
O'Neal, Emmet 156
O'Neill, Tip 212, 440
Onge, Peter St. 447
OPEC 238, 258
Operation Desert Shield 381
Ortega, Daniel 324

P

Page, J. T. 54
Painchaud, Desiree' 455

Palestine Liberation Organization 398
Panama Canal treaty 237
Parks, Rosa 121, 225
Parsons, Cynthia 447
Patterson, John 95, 99, 123, 136, 160, 161, 163, 175
Paty, Raymond 87, 94
Paul, Eris 139
Paul, Joel 378
People's Republic of China 366
Pepper, Claude 290
Permanent Federal Court Study Act 298, 417
Peters, Annie Mae 113, 134
Peyton, Benjamin 269
Pfeifle, Bill 74
Phelps, Joe 195
Philadelphia Inquirer 343
Pipes, Sam 165
Pittman, Jim 295
Poellnitz, Richard 95
Pohost, Gerald 98
Poindexter, John 325, 329
Poole, Victor 213
Porter, Mary 154, 176, 188, 198
Povost, Gerald 295
Powell, Colin 382, 424
Powell, Lewis 333
Pressler, Larry 420
Pride, Nancy 56
Propst, Robert 268
Pruett, Sam 62
Pruitt, Leonard 119
Pryor, David 231

Q

Quayle, Dan 424
Quayle, Marilyn 286

R

Rabin, Yitzhak 398
Raby, Steve 219, 221, 299, 314, 337, 343, 370, 388, 393, 402, 411, 421, 427, 430
Raines, Howell 65, 290
Ramirez, Bladina Cardenas 275
Ray, A. E. 107
Ray, Robert 404
Reagan, Nancy 287
Reagan, Ronald 226, 232, 236, 238, 241, 247, 248, 251, 253, 258, 263,

264, 265, 267, 269, 271, 273, 285, 287, 290, 292, 295, 301, 303, 304, 308, 322, 326, 330, 332, 336, 340, 358, 359, 366, 373, 389, 393, 395, 435, 437, 439, 439–440
Redden, Drew   93, 94
Redstone Arsenal   233
Reed, Joe   161, 202, 211, 212, 214, 261, 452
Rehabilitation Act   390
Rehnquist, William   296, 331, 338
Reid, Haden   24
Reno, Janet   195, 402
Republican Party   28, 119, 138, 172, 239, 241, 246, 255, 266, 282, 287, 289, 296, 312, 319, 324, 331, 338, 366, 371, 376, 392, 403, 409, 414
Revolutionary War   22, 25
Rice, Donna   319
Richardson, Elliot   332, 422
Richardson, Pat   93
Ricks, Edgar   50
Ride, Sally   275
Riegle, Donald   369, 372–374, 389
Riley, Richard   201
Roanoke Leader   32
Robertson, Pat   319
Robinson, Bert   125
Rochester, Mary Catherine   39
Rockefellow, David   422
Rodino, Peter   210
Roe v. Wade   337
Roosevelt, Franklin D.   18, 30, 55–57, 63
Roosevelt, Theodore   27
Rose, Frank   316
Rosen, Gordon   93
Rosenbaum, Louis   103
Rosser, Charles   103, 105, 127, 129, 147–149, 162, 198
 partnership with Howell Heflin   132–133
Rouse, R. Dennis   257
Ruckelshaus, William   332
Rudman, Warren   372
Rural Partnerships Act   252
Russell, Mark   432
Russell, Richard   41
Ryskamp, Kenneth L.   379

S

Saboteur, Jamie   70
Salt (Strategic Arms Limitation Treaty) II   234
Saltzman, Murray   273
Samford, Jr., Frank   93
Samford University   208
Sandinist National Liberation Front   322
Sandinistas   305, 323
Sasser, James   383
Scalia, Antonin   338
Schlafly, Phyllis   290
Schroeder, Pat   410
Schwarzkopf, H. Norman   380
Selden, Armistead   93, 136
Self, Mitch   206
Selma-to-Montgomery March   138
Senate Judiciary Committee   20
Sessions, Jeff   202, 340, 343, 413
Shanks, Henry   63
Shelby, Richard   296, 305, 320, 354, 377, 390, 397, 399
Shelton, Barrett   136
Shepard, Scott   239
Sheppard, Lemuel   71
Shockley, Bill   69, 88
Shores, Janie   154, 170, 183, 196, 197
Shultz, George P.   330
Sierra Club   355, 366
Simon, Paul   319, 389, 410
Smallwood, Milan   103
Smith, Albert Lee   289–290, 297
Smith, Alfred E.   29–30
Smith, Bob   93
Smith, Erskine   139
Smith, Eunice   290
Smith, Holland M.   75, 116
Smith, Sally Bedell   284
Smith, Suzelle   217
Snodgrass, John   169, 193
Social Security   299
Souter, David   339
Spangler, James   54–55
Sparkman, John   21, 52, 97, 98, 134, 139, 203, 204, 210, 214, 345, 416, 417
Specter, Arlen   240, 333, 336, 342, 415
Spong, Bill   198
Springer, Robert   427
Squier, Bob   206, 208, 212

INDEX

Starr, Kenneth 404
State Supreme Courts in State and Nation 176
Stell, Sarah A. 24, 26
Stennis, John 283, 361
Sterne, Mervin 123
Stevens, Ted 229, 421, 429
Stevenson, Adlai 136, 228
Stewart, Donald 215, 216, 221, 266, 268, 301
Stewart, Margaret 291, 368
Stewart, William 23, 419
Stone, Edward Durell 96
Strategic Defense Initiative 22, 306–307, 317, 385–386, 431
Strudwick, Carter 38, 39
Strudwick, Louise 27, 38–39, 52
   death of 45
Strudwick, Samuel 28, 39
Sullivan, Bill 195
Sumption, William 362

T

Talladega Daily Home 274
Talmadge, Gene 36
Talmadge, Herman 36, 228, 237, 241
Tanner, Ralph M. 31
Tarr, Alan 154, 176, 188, 198
Taylor, Elizabeth 218, 288, 312, 424
Taylor, Tazewell 200
Tease, J. Edward 171, 181, 195
Tennessee River 104
Tennessee Valley Authority 58, 232, 234, 260, 315, 316, 361–362
Tennessee-Tombigbee Waterway Project 231, 232, 293
The Valley Voice 139
Theater High Altitude Area Defense system 386
Thigpen, Martha 98, 101
Thomas, Clarence 21, 376–380
Thompson, Charles W. 29
Thompson, J. R. 431
Thompson, Myron 267
Three Mile Island 259
Thurmond, Strom 100, 263, 268, 273, 403
Tiananmen Square Massacre 365
Time 328
Tiner, "Long Time" 167
Todd, Richard 415

Torbert, C.C. 158, 181, 182, 190, 192, 216, 227
Torrey, Cristy 455
Tower, John 326, 341
Troy State University 368
Truman, Harry 100, 108
Tuscaloosa News 355
Tuscumbia Housing Authority 107–109, 110
Tuskegee
  Syphilis Study 416
  University 267, 269, 320
Tuttle, Albert 224
Tutwiler, Julia Strudwick 28, 38
Tutwiler, Margaret 290

U

U.S. House of Representatives 27
U.S. Marine Corps 67–68
Underwood, Oscar W. 31, 419
United Daughters of the Confederacy 19, 387, 389
United Negro College Fund 270
United States Supreme Court 222
University of Alabama 35, 41, 67, 107, 117, 120, 170, 196, 210, 215, 222, 224, 278, 320
  integration of 140
University of Alabama in Birmingham 26, 319, 409, 447
  University Hospital 26
University of Chicago 36, 334
University of Colorado 419
University of Georgia 219
University of Georgia Augusta Medical College 25
University of North Alabama 107, 448
University of South Alabama 319
University of Texas at Austin 59
University Research Capacity Restoration Act 317
USDA 254
USSR 235, 265, 302, 304, 324
  fall of 364–365
  invasion of Afghanistan 237, 239

V

Vanderbilt University 36, 41
Vanderhoef, Jerry 171, 182, 195
Vann, David 101, 141
Vietnam War 410

Vigilante, Richard 444
Vignali, Christine 455
Vines, Stan 371
Vinson, Nelson 206
Voorhies, Jack 161

W

Wall Street Journal 431
Wallace, Don 243
Wallace, George 95, 100, 122, 135, 136, 138–139, 140, 152, 156, 158, 160, 162, 164, 175, 176, 189, 193, 205, 209, 210–216, 250, 263, 272, 410
Wallace, Jack 165
Wallace, Lurleen 139, 158
Wallop, Malcolm 228
Walsh, Lawrence 325
War Powers Act 381
Ward, Jake 65
Ware, Joe 139, 151, 162, 423
Warner, John 218, 244, 288, 312, 424
Warren, Earl 172
Warsaw Pact 365, 408, 440, 443
Washington Post 346
Watergate 334, 410
Webster, Bill 227
Weekly World News 409
Weeks, Barney 208
Weinberger, Casper 329, 332
Wellstone, Paul 23
West, Charles 62
West, John 304
Whatley, Barney 118
White, Byron 380
Whitewater scandal 403–404
Whitten, Jamie 234
Williams, Harrison A. Jr. 229
Williams, Hobert 208
Wilson, Jane 218
Wilson, Lewis 78, 218
Wilson, Pete 243
Wilson, Ross 244
Wilson, Woodrow 29
Winford, F. S. 208
Winford, Sherry 423
Wisdom, John Minor 224
Witt, Elaine 369
World War I 30, 36, 57
World War II 41, 55, 66, 69–92, 121, 174, 227, 303, 326, 365, 452
Wright, Angela 378
Wright, Charles Allen 157
Wright, Fielding 100
Wright, "Spud" 168

Y

Yale University 267, 376
Yamamoto, Isoroku 69
Yaobang, Hu 365
Yeltsin, Boris 295, 443
Young, Mark 380, 431
Young, Willie 115
Younger, Bill 158

Z

Zimmer, Dick 257